Collect, Combine, and Transform Data Using Power Query in Excel and Power BI

Gil Raviv

COLLECT, COMBINE, AND TRANSFORM DATA USING POWER QUERY IN EXCEL AND POWER BI

Published with the authorization of Microsoft Corporation by:
Pearson Education, Inc.

Copyright © 2019 by Gil Raviv

ISBN-13: 978-1-5093-0795-1
ISBN-10: 1-5093-0795-8

Library of Congress Control Number: 2018954693

01 18

Trademarks

Warning and Disclaimer

Special Sales

For information about buying this title in bulk quantities, or for special sales opportunities (which may include electronic versions; custom cover designs; and content particular to your business, training goals, marketing focus, or branding interests), please contact our corporate sales department at corpsales@pearsoned.com or (800) 382-3419.

For government sales inquiries, please contact governmentsales@pearsoned.com.

For questions about sales outside the U.S., please contact intlcs@pearson.com.

PUBLISHER
Mark Taub

ACQUISITIONS EDITOR
Trina MacDonald

DEVELOPMENT EDITOR
Ellie Bru

MANAGING EDITOR
Sandra Schroeder

SENIOR PROJECT EDITOR
Tonya Simpson

COPY EDITOR
Kitty Wilson

INDEXER
Erika Millen

PROOFREADER
Abigail Manheim

TECHNICAL EDITOR
Justin DeVault

COVER DESIGNER
Twist Creative, Seattle

COMPOSITOR
codemantra

COVER IMAGE
Malosee Dolo/ShutterStock

Contents at a Glance

Contents

Chapter 9   Introduction to the Power Query M Formula Language   205

Chapter 10 **From Pitfalls to Robust Queries** **247**

Figure Credits

Chapter 1, "Introduction to Power Query," Figures 1-1 through 1-9 courtesy of Microsoft Corporation.

Chapter 2, "Basic Data Preparation Challenges," Figures 2-1 through 2-16 courtesy of Microsoft Corporation.

Chapter 3, "Combining Data from Multiple Sources," Figures 3-1 through 3-8 courtesy of Microsoft Corporation.

Chapter 4, "Combining Mismatched Tables," Figures 4-1 through 4-11 courtesy of Microsoft Corporation.

Chapter 5, "Preserving Context," Figures 5-1 through 5-11 courtesy of Microsoft Corporation.

Chapter 6, "Unpivoting Tables," Figures 6-1 through 6-9 courtesy of Microsoft Corporation.

Chapter 7, "Advanced Unpivoting and Pivoting of Tables," Figures 7-1 through 7-5 courtesy of Microsoft Corporation.

Chapter 8, "Addressing Collaboration Challenges," Figures 8-1 through 8-10 courtesy of Microsoft Corporation.

Chapter 9, "Introduction to the Power Query M Formula Language," Figures 9-2 through 9-10 courtesy of Microsoft Corporation.

Chapter 10, "From Pitfalls to Robust Queries," Figures 10-2 through 10-9 courtesy of Microsoft Corporation.

Chapter 11, "Basic Text Analytics," Figures 11-1 through 11-14, Figures 11-16 and 11-17 courtesy of Microsoft Corporation.

Chapter 12, "Advanced Text Analytics: Extracting Meaning," Figures 12-3 through 12-8, Figures 12-10 through 12-14 courtesy of Microsoft Corporation.

Chapter 13, "Social Network Analytics," Figures 13-1 through 13-11 courtesy of Microsoft Corporation.

Chapter 14, "Final Project: Combining It All Together," Figures 14-1 through 14-3 courtesy of Microsoft Corporation.

Foreword

When we set out to build the original Power Query add-in for Excel, we had a simple yet ambitious mission: connecting to and transforming the world's data. Five years later, we've moved beyond the original Excel add-in with native integration into Excel, Power BI, Power Apps, and a growing set of products that need to extract and transform data. But our original mission remains largely unchanged. With the ever-increasing heterogeneity of data, in many ways, our mission feels even more ambitious and challenging than ever. Much of today's computing landscape is centered around data, but data isn't always where or how you need it—we continue to advance Power Query with the goal of bridging that gap between the raw and desired states of data.

Throughout the Power Query journey, the user community has played a critical role in shaping the product through suggestions and feedback. The community has also played a central role in developing valuable educational content. As one of the key drivers of Power Query's native integration into Excel 2016, Gil is well placed to provide valuable insights and tips for a variety of scenarios. Even after his tenure at Microsoft, Gil has remained an active and influential member of the Power Query community. Happy querying!

—*Sid Jayadevan, Engineering Manager for Power Query,*
Microsoft Corporation

For readers not familiar with Power Query, it is an incredibly powerful and extensible engine that is the core of Microsoft BI tools. It enhances self-service business intelligence (BI) with an intuitive and consistent experience for discovering, combining, and refining data across a wide variety of sources. With data preparation typically touted as 80% of any BI solution, having a firm grasp of Power Query should be your first step in any sort of reporting or data discovery initiative. In addition to the core Power Query functionalities, Gil covers more advanced topics, such as how to use Power Query to automate data preparation and cleansing, how to connect to social networks to capture what your customers are saying about your business, how to use services like machine learning to do sentiment analysis, and how to use the M language to make practically any type of raw data a source of insights you glean value from. This book stands out in that it provides additional companion content with completed samples, data sources, and step-by-step tutorials.

Gil is a former member of the Excel team and the Microsoft Data Team. He directly contributed to the features and design of Power Query and has an amazing wealth of knowledge using Power Query and showing how it can make difficult data integration problems easy. That said, despite Power Query's inherently extensible and easy-to-use design, mastering it for enterprise scenarios can still be difficult. Luckily for the reader, as an avid community member, forum contributor, conference presenter, peer mentor, and Power BI MVP, Gil Raviv is a master at taking complex concepts and decomposing them into very easy-to-follow steps, setting the reader up for success and making this book a must have for any BI specialist, data systems owner, or businessperson who wants to get value out of the data around him.

—*Charles Sterling, Senior Program Manager,*
Microsoft Corporation

About the Author

Gil Raviv is a Microsoft MVP and a Power BI blogger at https://DataChant.com. As a Senior Program Manager on the Microsoft Excel Product team, Gil led the design and integration of Power Query as the next-generation Get Data and data-wrangling technology in Excel 2016, and he has been a devoted M practitioner ever since.

With 20 years of software development experience, and four U.S. patents in the fields of social networks, cyber security, and analytics, Gil has held a variety of innovative roles in cyber security and data analytics, and he has delivered a wide range of software products, from advanced threat detection enterprise systems to protection of kids on Facebook.

In his blog, DataChant.com, Gil has been chanting about Power BI and Power Query since he moved to his new home in the Chicago area in early 2016. As a Group Manager in Avanade's Analytics Practice, Gil is helping Fortune 500 clients create modern self-service analytics capability and solutions by leveraging Power BI and Azure.

You can contact Gil at gilra@datachant.com.

Acknowledgments

Writing this book is one of the scariest things I have willingly chosen to do, knowing I was going to journey into an uncharted land where only a few people have gone before and approach an ever-evolving technology that is relatively unfamiliar yet can drastically improve the professional lives of many users. How can I share the knowledge of this technology in a way that will enable you to harness its true essence and empower you to make a real impact on your business?

The writing of this book would not have been possible without the help and inspiration I received from many people.

First, I would like to thank my readers at DataChant.com. Your feedback and support made this endeavor possible. You have taught me the power of sharing.

Thank you to my wife and children, for being stranded at home with me for many days in late 2017 and the colder parts of 2018 to support my work. Thank you for your support. I hope you can also blame the winter in Chicago for staying with me so many weekends.

Special thanks to Trina MacDonald, my senior editor at Pearson. You reached out to me one day with an idea to write a book and have been supporting me all the way in publishing a completely different one. Good luck in your new journey.

Thank you to Justin DeVault, my first Six Sigma Master Black Belt client. As a technical editor, you combined your business savvy and technical prowess to review 14 chapters, 71 exercises, and 211 exercise files to ensure that the book can deliver on its promise. Without your insights, we could not have made it. You were the best person for this job.

To Microsoft Press, Pearson, Loretta Yates and the whole publishing team that contributed to the project, thank you! Thank you, Songlin Qiu, Ellie Bru, and Kitty Wilson for editing and proofreading and Tonya Simpson for orchestrating the production efforts; you have all magically transformed 14 chapters of Word documents into this book.

To my dear friend Yohai Nir, thank you for the rapport and guidance through the initial stages of the book.

Thank you to Luis Cabrera-Cordon, for reviewing Chapter 12. I hope that this chapter will help more business analysts use Microsoft Cognitive Services and gain new insights without the help of developers or data scientists.

To the amazing Program Managers Guy Hunkin, Miguel Llopis, Matt Masson, and Chuck Sterling: Thank you for the ongoing support and technical advice. Your work is truly inspirational.

Sid Jayadevan, Eli Schwarz, Vladik Branevich, and the brilliant people on the Redmond and Israeli development teams: It was a real pleasure working with you to deliver Power Query in Excel 2016.

To Yigal Edery, special thanks for accepting me into the ranks of the Microsoft Excel team and for challenging me to do more. I will never forget the night you pulled me over on the side of the road to share feedback and thank me.

Rob Collie, I wouldn't be here without you. You had welcomed me to PowerPivotPro.com as a guest blogger and a principal consultant, and you helped me make the leap into a brave new world.

Marco Russo, Ken Puls, Chris Webb, Matt Allington, and Reza Rad—My fellow Microsoft MVPs and Power BI bloggers—you are my role models, and I thank you for the inspiration and vast knowledge.

Since I joined the Avanade Analytics team in early 2017, I have learned so much from all of you at Avanade. Special thanks to Neelesh Raheja for your mentorship and leadership. You have truly expanded my horizons in the sea of analytics.

Finally, to my parents. Although I now live 6,208 miles away, I want to thank you. Dad, you had taught me how to crunch numbers and use formulas in Excel many years ago. And, Mom, your artistic talent is influencing my Power BI visuals every day.

—*Gil Raviv*

Introduction

Did you know that there is a data transformation technology inside Microsoft Excel, Power BI, and other products that allows you to work miracles on your data, avoid repetitive manual work, and save up to 80% of your time?

- Every time you copy/paste similar data to your workbook and manually clean it, you are wasting precious time, possibly unaware of the alternative way to do it better and faster.

- Every time you rely on others to get your data in the right shape and condition, you should know that there is an easier way to reshape your data once and enjoy an automation that works for you.

- Every time you need to make quick informed decisions but confront massive data cleansing challenges, know you can now easily address these challenges and gain unprecedented potential to reduce the time to insight.

Are you ready for the change? You are about to replace the maddening frustration of the repetitive manual data cleansing effort with sheer excitement and fun, and throughout this process, you may even improve your data quality and tap in to new insights.

Excel, Power BI, Analysis Services, and PowerApps share a game-changing data connectivity and transformation technology, Power Query, that empowers any person with basic Excel skills to perform and automate data importing, reshaping, and cleansing. With simple UI clicks and a unified user experience across wide variety of data sources and formats, you can resolve any data preparation challenge and become a master data wrangler.

In this book, you will tackle real data challenges and learn how to resolve them with Power Query. With more than 70 challenges and 200 exercise files in the companion content, you will import messy and disjointed tables and work your way through the creation of automated and well-structured datasets that are ready for analysis. Most of the techniques are simple to follow and can be easily reused in your own business context.

Who this book is for

This book was written to empower business users and report authors in Microsoft Excel and Power BI. The book is also relevant for SQL Server or Azure Analysis Services developers who wish to speed up their ETL development. Users who create apps using Microsoft PowerApps can also take advantage of this book to integrate complex datasets into their business logic.

Whether you are in charge of repetitive data preparation tasks in Excel or you develop Power BI reports for your corporation, this book is for you. Analysts, business intelligence specialists, and ETL developers can boost their productivity by learning the techniques in this book. As Power Query technology has become the primary data stack in Excel, and as Power BI adoption has been tremendously accelerating, this book will help you pave the way in your company and make a bigger impact.

The book was written to empower all Power Query users. Whether you are a new, moderate, or advanced user, you will find useful techniques that will help you move to the next level.

Assumptions

Prior knowledge of Excel or Power BI is expected. While any Excel user can benefit from this book, you would gain much more from it if you meet one of the following criteria. (Note that meeting a single criterion is sufficient.)

- You frequently copy and paste data into Excel from the same sources and often need to clean that data

- You build reports in Excel or Power BI that are connected to external sources, and wish to improve them

- You are familiar with PivotTables in Excel

- You are familiar with Power Pivot in Excel and wish to simplify your data models

- You are familiar with Power Query and want to move to the next level

- You develop business applications using PowerApps and need to connect to data sources with messy datasets

- You are a developer in Analysis Services and wish to speed up your ETL development

How this book is organized

The book is organized into 14 chapters that start from generic and simpler data challenges and move on to advanced and specific scenarios to master. It is packed with hands-on exercises and step-by-step solutions that provide the necessary techniques for mastering real-life data preparation challenges and serve as a long-term learning resource, no matter how many new features will be released in Power Query in the future.

In Chapter 1, "Introduction to Power Query," you will be introduced to Power Query and gain the baseline knowledge to start the exercises that follow.

In Chapter 2, "Basic Data Preparation Challenges," you will learn how to tackle relatively basic common data challenges. If you carry out frequent data cleansing tasks at work, you will find this chapter extremely helpful. You will be introduced to the simplest techniques to automate your data cleansing duties, with simple mouse clicks and no software development skills. If you are new to Power Query, you will already start saving time by following the techniques in this chapter.

In Chapter 3, "Combining Data from Multiple Sources," you will learn how to combine disjointed datasets and append multiple tables in the Power Query Editor. You will learn how to append together multiple workbooks from a folder and combine multiple worksheets in a robust manner—so when new worksheets are added, a single refresh of the report will suffice to append the new data into your report.

In Chapter 4, "Combining Mismatched Tables," you will move to the next level and learn how to combine mismatched tables. In real-life scenarios your data is segmented and siloed, and often is not consistent in its format and structure. Learning how to normalize mismatched tables will enable you to gain new insights in strategic business scenarios.

In Chapter 5, "Preserving Context," you will learn how to extract and preserve external context in your tables and combine titles and other meta information, such as filenames and worksheet names, to enrich your appended tables.

In Chapter 6, "Unpivoting Tables," you will learn how to improve your table structure to utilize a better representation of the entities that the data represents. You will learn how the Unpivot transformation is a cornerstone in addressing badly designed tables, and harness the power of Unpivot to restructure your tables for better analysis. You will also learn how to address nested tables and why and how to ignore totals and subtotals from your source data.

In Chapter 7, "Advanced Unpivoting and Pivoting of Tables," you will continue the journey in Unpivot transformations and generalize a solution that will help you unpivot any summarized table, no matter how many levels of hierarchies you might have as rows and columns. Then, you will learn how to apply Pivot to handle multiline records. The techniques you learn in this chapter will enable you to perform a wide range of transformations and reshape overly structured datasets into a powerful and agile analytics platform.

As a report author, you will often share your reports with other authors in your team or company. In Chapter 8, "Addressing Collaboration Challenges," you will learn about basic collaboration challenges and how to resolve them using parameters and templates.

In Chapter 9, "Introduction to the Power Query M Formula Language," you will embark in a deep dive into M, the query language that can be used to customize your queries to achieve more, and reuse your transformation on a larger scale of challenges. In this chapter, you will learn the main building blocks of M—its syntax, operators, types, and a wide variety of built-in functions. If you are not an advanced user, you can skip this chapter and return later in your journey. Mastering M is not a prerequisite to becoming a master data wrangler, but the ability to modify the M formulas when needed can boost your powers significantly.

The user experience of the Power Query Editor in Excel and Power BI is extremely rewarding because it can turn your mundane, yet crucial, data preparation tasks into an automated refresh flow. Unfortunately, as you progress on your journey to master data wrangling, there are common mistakes you might be prone to making in the Power Query Editor, which will lead to the creation of vulnerable queries that will fail to refresh, or lead to incorrect results when the data changes. In Chapter 10, "From Pitfalls to Robust Queries," you will learn the common mistakes, or pitfalls, and how to avoid them by building robust queries that will not fail to refresh and will not lead to incorrect results.

In Chapter 11, "Basic Text Analytics," you will harness Power Query to gain fundamental insights into textual feeds. Many tables in your reports may already contain abundant textual columns that are often ignored in the analysis. You will learn how to apply common transformations to extract meaning from words, detect keywords, ignore common words (also known as stop words), and use Cartesian Product to apply complex text searches.

In Chapter 12, "Advanced Text Analytics: Extracting Meaning," you will progress from basic to advanced text analytics and learn how to apply language translation, sentiment analysis, and key phrase detection using Microsoft Cognitive Services. Using Power Query Web connector and a few basic M functions, you will be able to truly extract meaning from text and harness the power of artificial intelligence, without the help of data scientists or software developers.

In Chapter 13, "Social Network Analytics," you will learn how to analyze social network data and find how easy it is to connect to Facebook and gain insights into social activity and audience engagement on any brand, company, or product on Facebook. This exercise will also enable you to work on unstructured JSON datasets and practice Power Query on public datasets.

Finally, in Chapter 14, "Final Project: Combining It All Together," you will face the final challenge of the book and put all your knowledge to the test applying your new data-wrangling powers on a large-scale challenge. Apply the techniques from this book to combine dozens of worksheets from multiple workbooks, unpivot and pivot the data, and save Wide World Importers from a large-scale cyber-attack!

About the companion content

We have included this companion content to enrich your learning experience. You can download this book's companion content by following these instructions:

1. Register your book by going to www.microsoftpressstore.com and logging in or creating a new account.

2. On the Register a Product page, enter this book's ISBN (9781509307951), and click Submit.

3. Answer the challenge question as proof of book ownership.

4. On the Registered Products tab of your account page, click on the Access Bonus Content link to go to the page where your downloadable content is available.

The companion content includes the following:

- Excel workbooks and CSV files that will be used as messy and badly formatted data sources for all the exercises in the book. No need to install any external database to complete the exercises.

- Solution workbooks and Power BI reports that include the necessary queries to resolve each of the data challenges.

The following table lists the practice files that are required to perform the exercises in this book.

Chapter	File(s)
Chapter 1: Introduction to Power Query	C01E01.xlsx
	C01E01 - Solution.xlsx
	C01E01 - Solution.pbix
Chapter 2: Basic Data Preparation Challenges	C02E01.xlsx
	C02E01 - Solution.xlsx
	C02E02.xlsx
	C02E02 - Solution - Part 1.xlsx
	C02E02 - Solution - Part 2.xlsx
	C02E02 - Solution - Part 3.xlsx
	C02E02 - Solution - Part 1.pbix
	C02E02 - Solution - Part 2.pbix
	C02E02 - Solution - Part 3.pbix
	C02E03 - Solution.xlsx
	C02E03 - Solution - Part 2.xlsx
	C02E03 - Solution.pbix
	C02E03 - Solution - Part 2.pbix
	C02E04.xlsx
	C02E04 - Solution.xlsx
	C02E04 - Solution.pbix
	C02E05.xlsx
	C02E05 - Solution.xlsx
	C02E05 - Solution.pbix
	C02E06.xlsx
	C02E06 - Solution.xlsx
	C02E06 - Solution.pbix

Chapter	File(s)
	C02E07.xlsx
	C02E07 - Solution.xlsx
	C02E07 - Solution.pbix
	C02E08.xlsx
	C02E08 - Solution.xlsx
	C02E08 - Solution.pbix
Chapter 3: Combining Data from Multiple Sources	C03E01 - Accessories.xlsx
	C03E01 - Bikes.xlsx
	C03E01 - Clothing.xlsx
	C03E01 - Components.xlsx
	C03E03 - Products.zip
	C03E03 - Solution.xlsx
	C03E03 - Solution.pbix
	C03E04 - Year per Worksheet.xlsx
	C03E04 - Solution 01.xlsx
	C03E04 - Solution 02.xlsx
	C03E04 - Solution 01.pbix
	C03E04 - Solution 02.pbix
Chapter 4: Combining Mismatched Tables	C04E01 - Accessories.xlsx
	C04E01 - Bikes.xlsx
	C04E02 - Products.zip
	C04E02 - Solution.xlsx
	C04E02 - Solution.pbix
	C04E03 - Products.zip
	C04E03 - Solution.xlsx
	C04E03 - Solution.pbix
	C04E04 - Products.zip
	C04E04 - Conversion Table.xlsx
	C04E04 - Solution - Transpose.xlsx
	C04E04 - Solution - Transpose.pbix
	C04E05 - Solution - Unpivot.xlsx
	C04E05 - Solution - Unpivot.pbix
	C04E06 - Solution - Transpose Headers.xlsx
	C04E06 - Solution - Transpose Headers.pbix
	C04E07 - Solution - M.xlsx
	C04E07 - Solution - M.pbix
Chapter 5: Preserving Context	C05E01 - Accessories.xlsx
	C05E01 - Bikes & Accessories.xlsx
	C05E01 - Bikes.xlsx
	C05E01 - Solution.xlsx
	C05E01 - Solution 2.xlsx
	C05E01 - Solution.pbix
	C05E01 - Solution 2.pbix

Chapter	File(s)
	C05E02 - Bikes.xlsx
	C05E02 - Solution.xlsx
	C05E02 - Solution.pbix
	C05E03 - Products.zip
	C05E03 - Solution.xlsx
	C05E03 - Solution.pbix
	C05E04 - Products.xlsx
	C05E04 - Solution.xlsx
	C05E04 - Solution.pbix
	C05E05 - Products.xlsx
	C05E05 - Solution.xlsx
	C05E05 - Solution.pbix
	C05E06 - Products.xlsx
	C05E06 - Jump Start.xlsx
	C05E06 - Jump Start.pbix
	C05E06 - Solution.xlsx
	C05E06 - Solution.pbix
Chapter 6: Unpivoting Tables	C06E01.xlsx
	C06E02.xlsx
	C06E03.xlsx
	C06E03 - Wrong Solution.pbix
	C06E03 - Solution.xlsx
	C06E03 - Solution.pbix
	C06E04.xlsx
	C06E04 - Solution.xlsx
	C06E04 - Solution.pbix
	C06E05.xlsx
	C06E05 - Solution.xlsx
	C06E05 - Solution.pbix
	C06E06.xlsx
	C06E06 - Solution.xlsx
	C06E06 - Solution.pbix
Chapter 7: Advanced Unpivoting and Pivoting of Tables	C07E01.xlsx
	C07E01 - Solution.xlsx
	C07E01 - Solution.pbix
	C07E02.xlsx
	C07E02.pbix
	C07E03 - Solution.xlsx
	C07E03 - Solution.pbix
	C07E04.xlsx
	C07E04 - Solution.xlsx
	C07E04 - Solution.pbix
	C07E05 - Solution.xlsx
	C07E05 - Solution.pbix

Chapter	File(s)
Chapter 8: Addressing Collaboration Challenges	C08E01.xlsx
	C08E01 - Alice.xlsx
	C08E01 - Alice.pbix
	C08E01 - Solution.xlsx
	C08E01 - Solution.pbix
	C08E02 - Solution.pbix
	C08E02 - Solution.pbit
	C08E02 - Solution 2.pbit
	C08E03 - Solution.xlsx
	C08E03 - Solution 2.xlsx
	C08E04 - Solution.xlsx
	C08E04 - Solution.pbix
	C08E05.xlsx
	C08E05.pbix
	C08E05 - Folder.zip
	C08E05 - Solution.xlsx
	C08E05 - Solution.pbix
Chapter 9: Introduction to the Power Query M Formula Language	C09E01 – Solution.xlsx
	C09E01 – Solution.pbix
Chapter 10: From Pitfalls to Robust Queries	C10E01.xlsx
	C10E01 - Solution.xlsx
	C10E02 - Solution.xlsx
	C10E02 - Solution.pbix
	C10E03 - Solution.xlsx
	C10E03 - Solution.pbix
	C10E04 - Solution.xlsx
	C10E04 - Solution.pbix
	C10E05.xlsx
	C10E05 - Solution.xlsx
	C10E05 - Solution.pbix
	C10E06.xlsx
	C10E06 - Solution.xlsx
	C10E06 - Solution.pbix
	C10E06-v2.xlsx
Chapter 11: Basic Text Analytics	Keywords.txt
	Stop Words.txt
	C11E01.xlsx
	C11E01 - Solution.xlsx
	C11E01 - Solution.pbix
	C11E02 - Solution.xlsx
	C11E02 - Refresh Comparison.xlsx
	C11E02 - Solution.pbix

Chapter	File(s)
	C11E03 - Solution.xlsx
	C11E04 - Solution.xlsx
	C11E04 - Solution.pbix
	C11E05 - Solution.xlsx
	C11E05 - Solution.pbix
	C11E06 - Solution.xlsx
	C11E06 - Solution.pbix
	C11E07 - Solution.pbix
Chapter 12: Advanced Text Analytics: Extracting Meaning	C12E01 - Solution.xlsx
	C12E01 - Solution.pbix
	C12E02.xlsx
	C12E02 - Solution.xlsx
	C12E02 - Solution.pbix
	C12E02 - Solution.pbit
	C12E03 - Solution.xlsx
	C12E03 - Solution.pbix
	C12E04.xlsx
	C12E04.pbix
	C12E04 - Solution.xlsx
	C12E04 - Solution.pbix
	C12E05 - Solution.pbix
	C12E06 - Solution.xlsx
	C12E06 - Solution.pbix
Chapter 13: Social Network Analytics	C13E01 - Solution.xlsx
	C13E01 - Solution.pbit
	C13E02 - Solution.xlsx
	C13E02 - Solution.pbit
	C13E03 - Solution.xltx
	C13E03 - Solution.pbit
	C13E04 - Solution.xlsx
	C13E04 - Solution.pbix
	C13E05 - Solution.xlsx
	C13E05 - Solution.pbix
	C13E06 - Solution.xlsx
	C13E06 - Solution.pbix
Chapter 14: Final Project: Combining It All Together	C14E01 - Goal.xlsx
	C14E01.zip
	C14E01 - Solution.xlsx
	C14E01 - Solution.pbix
	C14E02 - Compromised.xlsx
	C14E02 - Solution.xlsx
	C14E02 - Solution.pbix

System requirements

You need the following software and hardware to build and run the code samples for this book:

- Operating System: Windows 10, Windows 8, Windows 7, Windows Server 2008 R2, or Windows Server 2012

- Software: Office 365, Excel 2016 or later versions of Excel, Power BI Desktop, Excel 2013 with Power Query Add-In, or Excel 2010 with Power Query Add-In

How to get support & provide feedback

The following sections provide information on errata, book support, feedback, and contact information.

Errata & book support

We've made every effort to ensure the accuracy of this book and its companion content. You can access updates to this book—in the form of a list of submitted errata and their related corrections—at

https://www.microsoftpressstore.com/powerquery

If you discover an error that is not already listed, please submit it to us at the same page.

If you need additional support, email Microsoft Press Book Support at mspinput@microsoft.com.

Please note that product support for Microsoft software and hardware is not offered through the previous addresses. For help with Microsoft software or hardware, go to http://support.microsoft.com.

Stay in touch

Let's keep the conversation going! We're on Twitter: http://twitter.com/MicrosoftPress.

CHAPTER 1

Introduction to Power Query

Sure, in this age of continuous updates and always-on technologies, hitting refresh may sound quaint, but still when it's done right, when people and cultures re-create and refresh, a renaissance can be the result.

—*Satya Nadella*

IN THIS CHAPTER, YOU WILL

- Get an introduction to Power Query and learn how it was started

- Learn the main components of Power Query and the Power Query Editor

- Explore the tool and prepare sample data for analysis

In this book you will learn how to harness the capabilities of Power Query to resolve your data challenges and, in the process, save up to 80% of your data preparation time. This chapter begins with a formal introduction. Power Query deserves it. You see, as you are reading these lines, there are probably half a million users, right now, at exactly this moment, who are clenching their teeth while manually working their way through repetitive but crucial data preparation tasks in Excel. They do it every day, or every week, or every month.

By the time you finish reading this book, about 50 million people will have gone through their rigorous manual data preparation tasks, unaware that a tool hiding inside Excel is just waiting to help them streamline their work. Some of them have already resorted to learning how to use advanced tools such as Python and R to clean their data; others have been relying on their IT departments, waiting months for their requests to be fulfilled; most of them just want to get the job done and are resigned to spending hundreds or thousands of hours preparing their data for analysis. If you or your friends are among these 50 million, it's time to learn about Power Query and how it will change your data analytics work as you know it.

Whether you are new to Power Query or are an experienced practitioner, this chapter will help you prepare for the journey ahead. This journey will empower you to become a master data wrangler and a self-made discoverer of insight.

What Is Power Query?

Power Query is a game-changing data connectivity and transformation technology in Microsoft Excel, Power BI, and other Microsoft products. It empowers any person to connect to a rich set of external data sources and even local data in a spreadsheet and collect, combine, and transform the data by using a simple user interface. Once the data is well prepared, it can be loaded into a report in Excel and Power BI or stored as a table in other products that incorporate it. Then, whenever the data is updated, users can refresh their reports and enjoy automated transformation of their data.

> **See Also** Power Query has been used by millions of users since its release. Due to its significant impact to empower information workers and data analysts, Microsoft has decided to incorporate it into more products, including the following:
>
> Microsoft SQL Server Data Tools (SSDT) for SQL Server 2017 Analysis Services and Azure Analysis Services (see https://docs.microsoft.com/en-us/sql/analysis-services/what-s-new-in-sql-server-analysis-services-2017)
>
> Common Data Service for Apps, which is used by Microsoft PowerApps (see https://docs.microsoft.com/en-us/powerapps/maker/common-data-service/data-platform-cds-newentity-pq)

As you prepare your data using Power Query Editor, the main interface of Power Query, the tool records a sequence of transformation instructions, enabling you to repeat the data preparation sequence in the future. Advanced Excel users often compare it to macro recording, but it is much simpler than that. When you finish the transformation steps, you can load the prepared data to a report. From that point on, any time you refresh the report, the sequence of transformation steps runs, saving you many hours and days of repetitive manual data preparation work.

Power Query is truly simple to use. It shares a unified user experience—no matter what data source you import the data from or which format you have. Power Query enables you to achieve complex data preparation scenarios via a sequence of small steps that are editable and easy to follow. For advanced user scenarios, power users can modify each step via the formula bar or the Advanced Editor to customize the transformation expressions (using the M query language, which is explained in Chapter 9, "Introduction to the Power Query M Formula Language"). Each sequence of transformations is stored as a query, which can be loaded into a report or reused by other queries to create a pipeline of transformation building blocks.

Before examining each of the main components of Power Query, let's go back a few years and learn how it started. A short history lesson on Power Query will help you understand how long this technology has been out there and how it has evolved to its current state.

A Brief History of Power Query

Power Query was initially formed in 2011 as part of Microsoft SQL Azure Labs. It was announced at PASS Summit in October 2011 under the Microsoft codename "Data Explorer." Figure 1-1 shows its initial user interface.

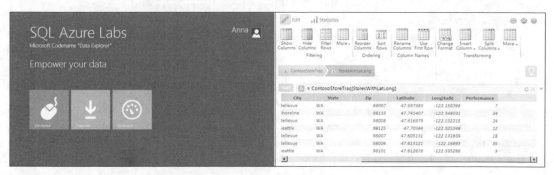

FIGURE 1-1 Microsoft codename "Data Explorer" was an early version of Power Query.

In February 27, 2013, Microsoft redesigned the tool as an Excel add-in and detached it from SQL Azure Labs. Now called Data Explorer Preview for Excel, the tool was positioned to enhance the self-service BI experience in Excel by simplifying data discovery and access to a broad range of data sources for richer insights.

Right at the start, as an Excel add-in, Data Explorer provided an intuitive and consistent experience for discovering, combining, and refining data across a wide variety of sources, including relational, structured and semi-structured, OData, web, Hadoop, Azure Marketplace, and more. Data Explorer also provided the ability to search for public data from sources such as Wikipedia (a functionality that would later be removed).

Once installed in Excel 2010 or 2013, Data Explorer Preview for Excel was visible in the Data Explorer tab. This tab in Excel had the same look and feel as the Power Query add-in today. The Power Query Editor was called New Query at that point, and it lacked the ribbon tabs of Power Query. To review the announcement of Data Explorer and see its initial interface as an Excel add-in, you can watch the recorded video at https://blogs.msdn.microsoft.com/dataexplorer/2013/02/27/announcing-microsoft-data-explorer-preview-for-excel/.

Figure 1-2 shows statistics on the increasing adoption of Data Explorer and its transition from SQL Azure Labs to Excel. According to the MSDN profile of the Data Explorer team at Microsoft (https://social.msdn.microsoft.com/Profile/Data%2bExplorer%2bTeam), the team started its first community activity in October 2011, when Data Explorer was first released in SQL Azure Labs. In February 2013, when Data Explorer was released as an Excel add-in, the community engagement had significantly increased, and the move to Excel had clearly paid off.

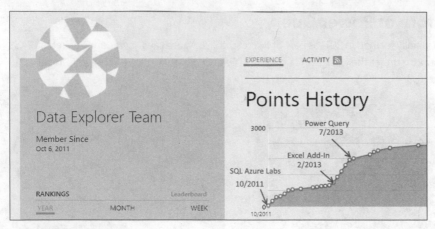

FIGURE 1-2 The Points History of the Data Explorer team on MSDN shows the increasing adoption of Data Explorer after the team pivoted from SQL Azure Labs to Excel.

As you can see in the Points History trend line in Figure 1-2, in July 2013, the activity of the Data Explorer team started to lose momentum. However, it wasn't a negative moment in the history of Data Explorer—just a rebirth of the tool under a new name. In July 2013, Microsoft announced the general availability of the add-in under its new name, Power Query add-in for Excel. At that time, the add-in provided much the same user experience as the latest version of Power Query.

The Power Query team began to release monthly updates of the Power Query add-in. This development velocity led to rapid innovation and constant growth of the community. Many users and fans helped to shape the product through direct feedback, forums, and blogs.

The Power Query add-in is still constantly updated, and it is available for download as an add-in for Excel 2010 and Excel 2013. Once it is installed, you see Power Query as a new tab in Excel, and you can connect to new data sources from its tab.

In December 2014, Microsoft released a preview of Power BI Designer (https://powerbi.microsoft.com/en-us/blog/new-power-bi-features-available-for-preview/). The Power BI Designer was a new report-authoring client tool that enabled business intelligence practitioners to create interactive reports and publish them to the Power BI service, which was still under preview. Power BI Designer unified three Excel add-ins—Power Query, Power Pivot, and Power View—and was important to the success of Power BI. Inside Power BI Designer, Power Query kept all the functionality of the Excel add-in. While most of the user experiences were the same, the term Power Query was no longer used in Power BI Designer. Seven months later, in July 2015, Microsoft changed the name of Power BI Designer to Power BI Desktop and announced its general availability (https://powerbi.microsoft.com/en-us/blog/what-s-new-in-the-power-bi-desktop-ga-update/).

At this stage, the Power Query team kept delivering monthly updates of Power Query for Excel and Power BI Desktop while working with the Excel team to completely revamp the default Get Data experience in Excel.

While the Power Query add-in was initially separate from Excel, Microsoft decided to incorporate it as a native component and use the Power Query engine as the primary data stack in Excel. In September

2015, Microsoft released Excel 2016 with Power Query integrated as a first-class citizen of Excel rather than an add-in. Microsoft initially placed the Power Query functionality inside the Data tab, in the Get & Transform section, which has since been renamed Get & Transform Data.

Power Query technology was available for the first time for mass adoption, supporting native Excel functionalities such as Undo and Redo, copying and pasting of tables, macro recording, and VBA. To read more about Power Query integration in Excel 2016, see https://blogs.office.com/en-us/2015/09/10/integrating-power-query-technology-in-excel-2016/.

In March 2017, Microsoft released an update to Office 365 that included further improvements to the data stack. The Power Query technology has truly become the primary data stack of Excel (https://support.office.com/en-us/article/unified-get-transform-experience-ad78befd-eb1c-4ea7-a55d-79d1d67cf9b3). The update included a unification of experiences between queries and workbook connections, and it improved support for ODC files. In addition, it placed the main Power Query entry point, the Get Data drop-down menu, as the first command in the Data tab, in the Get & Transform Data section.

In April 2017, Microsoft released SQL Server Data Tools (SSDT) and announced its modern Get Data experience in Analysis Services Tabular 1400 models (https://blogs.msdn.microsoft.com/ssdt/2017/04/19/announcing-the-general-availability-ga-release-of-ssdt-17-0-april-2017/). With SSDT 17.0, you can use Power Query to import and prepare data in your tabular models in SQL Server 2017 Analysis Services and Azure Analysis Services. If you are familiar with Analysis Services, you can learn how to start using Power Query at https://docs.microsoft.com/en-us/sql/analysis-services/tutorial-tabular-1400/as-lesson-2-get-data?view=sql-analysis-services-2017.

> **Note** While this book is focused on Excel and Power BI Desktop, you will find most of the chapters and exercises of the book quite relevant for working with Analysis Services, especially in early stages of your projects, when you need to deal with messy datasets.

In March 2018, Microsoft announced the Common Data Service (CDS) for Apps (https://power-apps.microsoft.com/en-us/blog/cds-for-apps-march/) and incorporated Power Query as one of its main data import tools, along with Microsoft Flow (see Figure 1-3). Microsoft extended Power Query beyond its original purpose to address BI scenarios, so that Power Query can now be used as a simple ETL (Extract Transform Load) tool that enables business users to develop business applications for Microsoft Office 365 and Dynamics 365, using PowerApps without requiring development skills.

Also in March 2018, Microsoft reinstated the term Power Query in Power BI Desktop and Excel by changing the title of the Query Editor dialog box to Power Query Editor. To launch it, you can now select Launch Power Query Editor from the Get Data drop-down menu. In July 2018, Microsoft announced that the online version of Power Query will be part of a new self-service ETL solution, dataflows, that will enable you to easily perform data preparations in Power Query, store the results on Azure, and consume it in Power BI or other applications (https://www.microsoft.com/en-us/businessapplicationssummit/video/BAS2018-2117).

FIGURE 1-3 Power Query in CDS for Apps, which was announced in March 2018.

Where Can I Find Power Query?

Finding Power Query in Excel and Power BI Desktop can be challenging if you don't know what to look for. At this writing, there is no single entry point with the name "Power Query" to launch the Power Query Editor. Figure 1-4 summarizes the main entry points for Power Query in Excel and Power BI.

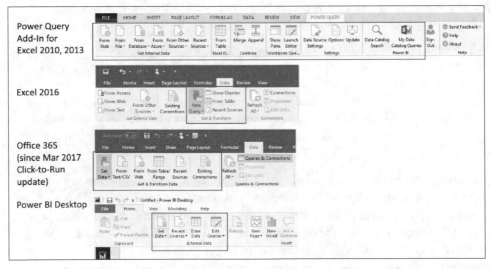

FIGURE 1-4 A number of entry points in Excel and Power BI Desktop can be used to initiate Power Query.

To start importing data and reshape it in Excel 2010 and 2013, you can download the Power Query add-in from https://www.microsoft.com/en-us/download/details.aspx?id=39379. This add-in is available in Excel Standalone and Office 2010 and 2013. Once it is installed, the Power Query tab appears. To start importing data, you can select one of the connectors in the Get External Data section. To edit existing queries, you can select Show Pane and select the relevant query you wish to edit; alternatively, you can select Launch Editor and select the relevant query in the Queries pane.

> **Note** Importing data by using the Get External Data section in the Data tab of Excel 2010 and 2013 leads you to the legacy Get Data experiences and not Power Query.

To get and transform data in Excel 2016 by using Power Query technology, you can first check the Data tab. If you see the Get & Transform section, select the New Query drop-down menu and then select the relevant data source type you wish to use. If you use a later version of Excel, you will find the Get & Transform Data section, where you can start importing data via the Get Data drop-down menu. To edit existing queries, you can select Show Queries in Excel 2016 (in the older versions) or select Queries & Connections, under the Queries & Connections section in the Data tab.

> **Note** If you use Excel 2016 and see both the Get External Data and Get & Transform sections in the Data tab, keep in mind that the first section will lead you to the legacy import scenarios. To use Power Query technology, you should select the New Query drop-down menu under Get & Transform. In the latest Excel 2016, 2019, and Office 365 versions, this functionality is under the Get Data drop-down menu.

In Power BI Desktop, you can select Get Data in the Home tab. The Get Data dialog box then opens, enabling you to select your data source. In the Get Data drop-down menu, you can select one of the common sources, such as Excel, Power BI Service, SQL Server, or Analysis Services. To edit your existing queries in the report, you can select Edit Queries in the Home tab to launch the Power Query Editor. From here, you can find the Queries pane on the left side of the Power Query Editor and select the query you wish to edit.

Now you know the main entry points for Power Query. In the next section you will learn the main components of Power Query.

Main Components of Power Query

In this section, you will be introduced to the main components of Power Query and the core user interfaces: the Get Data experience and connectors, the Power Query Editor, and the Query Options dialog box.

Get Data and Connectors

Connecting to a data source is the first step in the life cycle of a corporate report. Power Query enables you to connect to a wide variety of data sources. Often, data sources are referred to as *connectors*. For example, when you select Get Data in Excel, select From Database, and then select From SQL Server Database, you choose to use the SQL Server connector in Power Query. The list of supported connectors is often updated monthly through Power BI Desktop updates and later updated in Excel in Office 365 and the Power Query add-in for Excel 2010 and 2013.

To view the currently supported connectors in Excel, go to Get Data in the Data tab and review the different options under From File, From Database, From Azure, From Online Services, and From Other Sources, as illustrated in Figure 1-5.

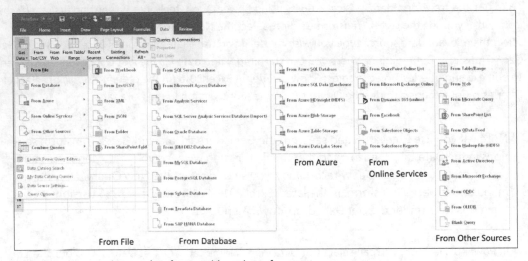

FIGURE 1-5 You can import data from a wide variety of connectors.

Many connectors are released in Power BI Desktop but do not immediately find their way into Excel; this may be due to the maturity of the connector, its prevalence, or the business agreement between Microsoft and the data source provider. In addition, the following connectors appear in Excel if you use Excel Standalone, Office Pro Plus, or Office Professional editions:

- **Databases:** Oracle, DB2, MySQL, PostgreSQL, Sybase, Teradata, and SAP Hana

- **Azure:** Azure SQL Server, Azure SQL Data Warehouse, Azure HDInsight (HDFS), Azure Blob Storage, Azure Table, and Azure Data Lake Store

- **Other sources:** SharePoint, Active Directory, Hadoop, Exchange, Dynamics CRM, and Salesforce

- **Data Catalog:** Data Catalog Search and My Data Catalog Queries

For more details, visit https://support.office.com/en-us/article/where-is-get-transform-power-query-e9332067-8e49-46fc-97ff-f2e1bfa0cb16.

In Power BI Desktop, you can select Get Data to open the Get Data dialog box. From there, you can search for the connector you want to use or navigate through the views All, File, Database, Azure,

Online Services, and Other to find your connector. For a full list of the connectors in Power BI Desktop, see https://docs.microsoft.com/en-us/power-bi/desktop-data-sources.

If you want to reuse an existing data source, you don't need to go through the Get Data interface. Instead, you can select Recent Sources from the Get & Transform Data section of the Data tab in Excel or from the Home tab of Power BI Desktop. In the Recent Sources dialog box, you can find the specific data sources that you have recently used. You can also pin your favorite source to have it always shown at the top when you open the Recent Sources dialog box.

Many of the data sources you connect to, such as databases and files on SharePoint, provide built-in authentication methods. The credentials you provide are not stored in a report itself but on your computer. To edit the credentials or change the authentication method, you can launch Data Source Settings from the Home tab of the Power Query Editor or select Options & Settings from the File tab. When the Data Source Settings dialog box opens, you can select your data source and choose to reset the credentials. To learn more about Data Source Settings, see https://support.office.com/en-us/article/data-source-settings-power-query-9f24a631-f7eb-4729-88dd-6a4921380ca9.

The Main Panes of the Power Query Editor

After you connect to a data source, you usually land in the Navigator. In the Navigator, you typically select the relevant tables you want to load from the data source, or you can just get a preview of the data. (You will walk through using the Navigator in Exercise 1-1.) From the Navigator, you can select Edit to step into the heart and center of Power Query: the Power Query Editor. Here is where you can preview the data in the main pane, explore the data, and start performing data transformations. As illustrated in Figure 1-6, the Power Query Editor consists of the following components: the Preview pane, ribbon, Queries pane, Query Settings pane, Applied Steps pane, and formula bar. Let's quickly review each part.

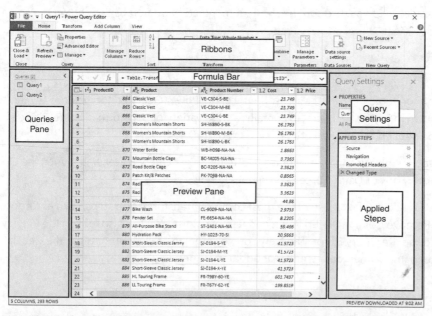

FIGURE 1-6 The Power Query Editor includes a number of user interface components.

Preview Pane

The Preview pane, which is highlighted as the central area of Figure 1-6, enables you to preview your data and helps you explore and prepare it before you put it in a report. Usually, you see data in a tabular format in this area. From the column headers you can initiate certain transformations, such as renaming or removing columns. You can also apply filters on columns by using the filter control in the column headers.

The Preview pane is context-aware. This means you can right-click any element in the table to open a shortcut menu that contains the transformations that can be applied on the selected element. For example, right-clicking the top-left corner of the table exposes table-level transformations, such as Keep First Row As Headers.

> **Tip** Using shortcut menus in the Preview pane of the Power Query Editor helps you to discover new transformations and explore the capabilities of Power Query.

Remember that the Preview pane does not always show the entire dataset. It was designed to show only a portion of the data and allow you to work on data preparation with large datasets. With wide or large datasets, you can review the data by scrolling left and right in the Preview pane, or you can open the Filter pane to review the unique values in each column.

Beyond data exploration, the most common action you will take in the Preview pane is column selection. You can select one or multiple columns in the Preview pane and then apply a transformation on the selected columns. If you right-click the column header, you see the relevant column trans-formation steps that are available in the shortcut menu. Note that columns have data types, and the transformations available to you through the shortcut menu and ribbon tabs depend on the column's data type.

The Ribbon

Following the common look and feel of Microsoft Office, the Power Query Editor includes several ribbon tabs, as shown in Figure 1-7. Each tab contains a wide variety of transformation steps or other actions that can be applied to queries. Let's review each of the tabs:

- **File:** This tab enables you to save a report, close the Power Query Editor, and launch the Query Options dialog box or Data Source Settings dialog box.

- **Home:** In this tab you find some of the most common transformation steps, such as Choose Columns, Remove Columns, Keep Rows, and Remove Rows. You can also refresh the Preview pane and close the Query Editor. The New Source command takes you through the Get Data experience to import new data sources as additional queries.

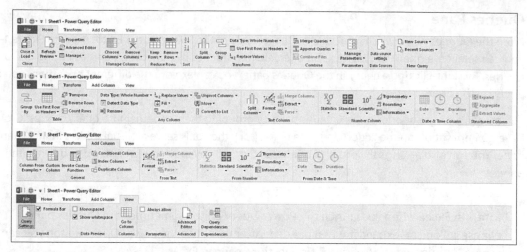

FIGURE 1-7 The Power Query Editor has several useful ribbon tabs.

Note You can work on multiple queries in the Power Query Editor. Each query can be loaded as a separate table or can be used by another query. Combining multiple queries is an extremely powerful capability that is introduced in Chapter 3, "Combining Data from Multiple Sources."

- **Transform:** This tab enables you to apply a transformation on selected columns. Depending on the data type of the column, some commands will be enabled or disabled; for example, when you select a Date column, the date-related commands are enabled. In this tab you can also find very useful transformations such as Group By, Use First Row As Headers, Use Headers As First Row, and Transpose.

- **Add Column:** This tab enables you to add new columns to a table by applying transformations on selected columns. Two special commands enable you to achieve complex transformations on new columns through a very simple user interface. These commands, Column From Examples and Conditional Column, are explained and demonstrated in more detail throughout the book. From this tab, advanced users can invoke Custom Column and Custom Functions, which are also explained in later chapters.

- **View:** From this tab, you can change the view in the Power Query Editor. From this tab you can enable the formula bar, navigate to a specific column (which is very useful when your table contains dozens of columns), and launch Query Dependencies.

Throughout this book, you will be introduced to the most common and useful commands in the Power Query Editor through hands-on exercises that simulate real-life data challenges.

Queries Pane

From the Queries pane, which is located on the left side of the Power Query Editor (refer to Figure 1-6), you can select the query you wish to edit or create new queries by duplicating or referencing one of the queries. By right-clicking a query in the Queries pane, you can explore the different operations you can apply on the query.

You can arrange queries in the Queries pane by grouping them together into query groups. Groups have no implication on the underlying data or a report; they only serve as visual folders in the Queries pane. You can also arrange the order of queries and groups by moving elements up or down in the pane.

> **Note** In Excel, when you launch the Power Query Editor, sometimes the Queries pane is collapsed. You can expand it when needed. After you close the Power Query Editor, you can manage queries via the Queries & Connections pane in Excel.

Query Settings and Applied Steps

From the Query Settings pane on the right side of the Power Query Editor, you can rename a query, launch the Query Properties dialog box to provide a description, and manage the transformation steps. In the Applied Steps pane you can review a query's transformation steps.

Power Query enables you to create a sequence of transformations on imported data before the data lands in a report. As you apply transformation steps, those steps are appended in the Applied Steps pane. At any time you can select one of the steps in Applied Steps, change it, or insert a new step between two existing steps or at the end.

The Formula Bar, the Advanced Editor, and the M Query Language

The formula bar in the Power Query Editor is turned off by default. You can enable it from the View tab by selecting the Formula Bar check box. While you are not required to use the formula bar in many data transformation scenarios, you will see in this book that there are many scenarios in which the formula bar can be helpful.

Whereas Excel's formula bar shows Excel formulas, the formula bar in the Power Query Editor shows M formulas. Each transformation step that you create in the Power Query Editor, starting from the initial import of the data, generates a formula in this bar. This formula is part of the M query language, a special programming language developed by Microsoft for Power Query that enables you to extend the transformation capabilities of this tool.

From the Home tab or the View tab, you can launch the Advanced Editor, which shows the entire M expression that was generated by the steps you took in the Power Query Editor. From here, advanced users can customize the expression to create complex transformations. For most of the exercises in this book, you will not need to open the Advanced Editor. However, if you are curious about M, you can launch the Advanced Editor and explore the M syntax of your queries. You will be introduced to M in the exercises throughout this book whenever a customization of the code in the formula bar or in the Advanced Editor will help you resolve data challenges. Chapter 9 gives you an opportunity to dive deep into M and focus on its core syntax and built-in functions.

> **Note** If programming is not your cup of tea, don't worry. Most of the challenges in this book do not require you to use M.

Query Options in Excel and Options in Power BI

The Query Options dialog box in Excel and the Options dialog box in Power BI Desktop enable you to set various settings for Power Query. In Excel, the options are grouped in Global and Current Workbook sections. In Power BI Desktop, the options are grouped in Global and Current File sections. Some of the options are available only in Excel. Other options are available only in Power BI desktop. The latter product includes additional settings for Power BI Desktop beyond Power Query.

The Global options, which are stored on your computer, affect all the reports that you create from that computer. The Current Workbook options and Current File options are stored in the file and are not propagated to other files. As shown in Figure 1-8, each of the option groups is divided into the multiple subgroups. The Data Load and Privacy subgroups are represented in both the Global and Current groups.

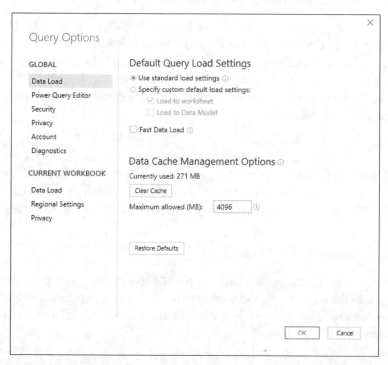

FIGURE 1-8 The Query Options dialog box in Excel contains Global properties stored on the computer and Current workbook properties stored in the report.

To launch the Query Options dialog box in Excel, go to the Data tab, select Get Data, and then select Launch Power Query Editor. You can also open the Query Options dialog box from the Power Query Editor: In the File tab, select Options and Settings and then select Query Options. To open the Query Options dialog box from Power BI, go to File, select Options and Settings, and select Options.

You don't need to configure options very frequently. The default options will typically meet your needs. If you are an advanced Excel user and usually work with Data Models, you can change the default Data Load options by selecting the Specify Custom Default Load Settings and then selecting Load to Data Model under Default Query Load Settings.

Exercise 1-1: A First Look at Power Query

Now that you have learned about the main components of Power Query, it's time to start a quick exercise to get better acquainted with the various components of Power Query. You can follow this exercise by using Excel or Power BI Desktop.

To start this exercise, download the workbook C01E01.xlsx from https://aka.ms/DataPwrBIPivot/downloads and save it in a new folder: *C:\Data\C01*. Now is a good time to download all the resources. All the file names will follow the same naming conventions: as *CxxEyy.xslx* or *CxxEyy.pbix*, where *C* stands for "chapter," *xx* is a two-digit number that corresponds to the chapter number, *E* stands for "exercise," and *yy* is a two-digit number that corresponds to the exercise number.

> **Note** To follow the exercises in the book, you will be asked to save source data files in a subfolder under C:\Data. For each chapter, you will create a dedicated subfolder under C:\Data, from C01 for Chapter 1 to C14 for Chapter 14. Most of the exercises include solution files. The queries in the solution files assume that the source data is located under C:\Data\C*XX*, where *XX* is the chapter number.

After you have saved the workbook C01E01.xlsx, you can open it to review its main table. This table contains a product catalog with product identifier number, product name, product number, cost, and price. In the next chapter, you will work on the product number column to extract the product color, size, and category. In this exercise, you will just use this dataset to explore the Power Query Editor's user interfaces.

1. Start a blank Excel workbook or Power BI report.

2. In Excel 2016 or later versions, go to the Data tab and select Get Data in the Get & Transform Data section. Explore the different menus and submenus under Get Data. As illustrated in Figure 1-5, you have many data sources to choose from. For this exercise, select From File and then select From Workbook.

   In Excel 2010 or 2013, with Power Query installed, go to the Power Query tab and select From File and then From Workbook.

In Power BI Desktop, in the Home tab, select the Get Data drop-down menu and then select Excel. Alternatively, select Get Data. The Get Data dialog box opens. Explore the different data source types (also called connectors). You can enter the names of data source types in the search box to do this exploration. When you are done, select Excel.

3. In the Import Data dialog box that opens, navigate to *C:\Data\C01* and select the workbook *C01E01.xslx*. Press Enter or select Open to close the dialog box.

4. In the Navigator dialog box that opens (see Figure 1-9), navigate to the table you need to import. This dialog box always opens when you connect to data sources that contain multiple tables. When you connect to relational databases, such as SQL Server or Access databases, the left pane includes more options, but most of the user interfaces here look the same.

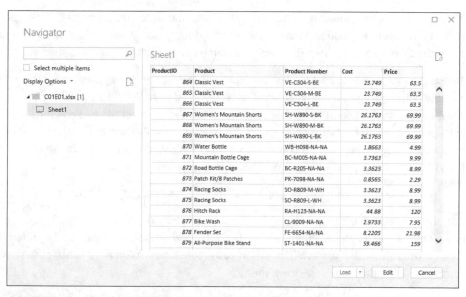

FIGURE 1-9 The Navigator dialog box enables you to select the tables to load.

You can see in Figure 1-9 that Load, rather than Edit, is the default button. Many users may miss Power Query altogether by moving through the default flow. By selecting Load you skip the data preparation step and load the table to your report as-is.

Note If you don't see the Edit button as the second button after Load in the Navigator dialog box (refer to Figure 1-9), you may find it under a different name (such as Transform Data). Microsoft is evaluating different button names to see what resonates best with clients. In this book, when you are instructed to select Edit in the Navigator, and you cannot find it, select Transform Data or the second button after Load.

> **Tip** Even if your data is in good shape, it is recommended that you select Edit and not Load in the Navigator dialog box. This will open the Power Query Editor, where you can preview the data, explore it, and confirm that the data is in the expected format.

5. Select Sheet1, and then select Edit. The Power Query Editor opens. It is a good time to go over Figure 1-6 and ensure that you can find all the components in the Power Query Editor. Note that the Power Query Editor in Excel and Power BI Desktop share the same user interface. There are only minor differences between the two products.

   If you cannot find the formula bar, you can activate it by going to View tab and selecting Formula Bar. From now on, the formula bar will always be visible.

6. In the Queries pane or in the Query Settings dialog box, where the query is named Sheet1, rename it Products. To rename the query in the Queries pane, double-click it and rename it. To rename the query in the Query Settings dialog box, edit the Name text box in the Properties section.

7. In the Preview pane, notice that the last two columns are Cost and Price. Say that you want to add a new column for profit that contains Cost subtracted from Price. To add a new column that is based on the calculation of two other columns, you need to select the two columns first. To select a column in Power Query, you can click its header in the Preview pane. Alternatively, you can use the cursor keys to select a column. To select multiple columns, you can use the Shift or Ctrl keys (Shift for adjacent columns and Ctrl for non-adjacent columns).

   Select the Price column. Then, while pressing Ctrl or Shift, select the Cost column.

8. To add the new column, look for the relevant transformation in the Add Column tab. Go to Add Column, review the different commands, and select Standard. You can now see the different arithmetic operations that are available when you create a new column. To subtract cost from price, select Subtract in the drop-down menu.

9. When the Subtraction column is added in the Preview pane, rename it *Profit*. To rename a column, you can double-click its name in the header of the column and rename it. Alternatively, you can right-click the column header to open the shortcut menu, where you can find a wide variety of transformation options you can apply on the selected column(s). You should also see the Rename option in the shortcut menu.

10. Look at the values in the Profit column. Do you see negative numbers in this column? You should not. If you do, it is because of the way you implemented step 7. If you see negative numbers in the column, it means you first selected the Cost column and then the Price column in step 7 instead of selecting Price and then Cost. To fix it (or simply to ensure that the formula is correct), follow these steps:

    a. Check out the Applied Steps pane on the right side of the Power Query Editor. You can see all the steps that were generated. Select any of the steps and review their output in the Preview pane. The data you see in the Preview pane is only a cached preview of the actual data. None of the intermediate tables are stored in the report itself.

b. In Applied Steps, select the Inserted Subtraction step.

c. In the formula bar, look for a long formula and find the following code inside it:

```
[Cost] - [Price]
```

Change it to the following:

```
[Price] - [Cost]
```

Here is what the full formula should end up looking like:

```
= Table.AddColumn(#"Changed Type", "Subtraction", each [Price] - [Cost],
type number)
```

> **Note** At this stage, if you are new to Power Query, don't try too hard to understand the syntax in the formula bar. This formula is part of the M language. Throughout this book, you will learn when and how to modify such formulas, without needing to master M syntax. By the time you reach Chapter 9, you will be ready to dive deep into M and explore its secrets.

11. Remove the Product Number column by selecting the column and pressing the Delete key. Alternatively, in the Home tab, select Remove Columns.

12. Try filtering the data. Say that you only need to keep rows whose product contains the text "Mountain". To do this, you can select the filter control in the header of the Product column. In the Filter pane that opens, review the different products.

Select Text Filters, and then select Contains. In the Filter Rows dialog box that opens, enter *Mountain* in the text box to the right of Contains and click OK.

> **Note** By default, Power Query handles text in a case-sensitive manner. If you enter *mountain* in the text box in step 12, you will miss all the "Mountain" products, as there are no lowercase "mountain" products. To apply a case-insensitive filter, you can modify the M formula. Here is the original formula that opens in the formula bar:
>
> ```
> = Table.SelectRows(#"Removed Columns", each Text.Contains([Product], "Mountain"))
> ```
>
> By adding *Comparer.OrdinalIgnoreCase* as a third argument to the *Text.Contains* function, you can achieve case-insensitive filtering. Here is the modified formula that will apply a case-insensitive filter:
>
> ```
> = Table.SelectRows(#"Removed Columns", each Text.Contains([Product], "mountain",
> Comparer.OrdinalIgnoreCase))
> ```
>
> You may be concerned that this modification is too advanced for you at this stage, but don't worry. You can achieve most of your data preparation challenges without needing to modify formulas. Throughout this book, you will learn when such changes can help you, and you will also learn how to make these changes—and you will not need to learn the entire M syntax. Chapter 10, "From Pitfalls to Robust Queries," will help you become more experienced and lead you to a deeper understanding of M.

13. Finally, load the query to the report. If you are using Power BI Desktop, select Close & Apply in the Home tab. From here you can start building the visualization of the transformed table. If you are using Excel, select Close & Load in the Home tab to load the transformed table as a table in the worksheet.

> **Note** Unlike in Power BI, in Excel you have multiple load options to support different Excel features. You can load the transformed data into a table in a worksheet, load it to the Data Model, or just keep it as a connection for later use. In Excel 2016 or later versions, you also can load the data into a PivotTable or PivotChart directly from the Import Data dialog box.

14. Open the source file C01E01.xlsx and make some changes. After you save the file, refresh the report and notice how your query handles the modified data. To refresh the query in Excel, select Refresh All in the Data tab. To refresh the query in Power BI Desktop, select Refresh in the Home tab.

This is the core of automation, and it is a tremendous time-saving element in Power Query. You can prepare your data once and then trigger a refresh to automatically prepare your data any time.

> **See Also** You can also enjoy scheduled refreshes of reports if you use the Power BI service, including on-premises data sources. Learn more at https://docs.microsoft.com/en-us/power-bi/refresh-scheduled-refresh.

15. Edit the query by following these steps:

a. In Excel, select Queries & Connections in the Data tab and double-click the Products query. Alternatively, in Power BI Desktop, select Edit Queries in the Home tab.

b. Select any of the steps in Applied Steps, modify or delete existing steps, and insert new steps. To insert a step between two steps, select the first step and use any of the transformations in the ribbon or shortcut menus.

c. To save the changes and refresh the data, select Close & Load in Excel or Close & Apply in Power BI Desktop.

You have now imported and transformed the original source table. You can download the solution files C01E01 - Solution.xlsx and C01E01 - Solution.pbix from https://aka.ms/DataPwrBIPivot/downloads.

This exercise provided a warmup for the wide variety of data challenges you will face—and learn how to resolve—in the rest of the book.

Summary

In this chapter you were introduced to Power Query and got a quick glimpse of its capabilities. You have learned about the short history of the tool and how it has evolved from an exploratory tool to a prevalent data preparation technology in Excel, Power BI, Analysis Services, CDS, and PowerApps. By the time you read this section, there is a good chance that Power Query will have taken an even more prominent role, with a new web interface that can be integrated into many solutions and services in the Microsoft stack.

In the first exercise in this book, you imported a table and learned about some basic transformations. In the next chapter, you will learn how to resolve basic data preparation challenges in the Power Query Editor, which will allow you to start saving significant time and avoid repetitive data preparation efforts.

CHAPTER 2

Basic Data Preparation Challenges

Before anything else, preparation is the key to success.

—*Alexander Graham Bell*

IN THIS CHAPTER, YOU WILL

- Learn how to split and extract valuable information from delimiter-separated values

- Learn how to enrich your data from lookup tables in a single table or by using relationships between fact tables and lookup tables

- Learn how Add Column from Examples can help you extract or compute meaningful data from columns and use it to explore new transformations

- Learn how to extract meaningful information, such as hyperlinks, from text columns

- Handle inconsistent date values from one or more locales

- Learn how to extract date or time elements from *Date* columns

- Split a table into a fact table and a lookup table by using the Reference and Remove Duplicates commands

- Learn how to avoid refresh failures when a lookup table contains duplicate values, even when you are sure you removed them

- Split delimiter-separated values into rows to define group/member associations

Working with messy datasets can consume a lot of time for a data analyst. In the past, analysts needed to tackle badly formatted data with painful manual cleansing efforts. Excel power users could also use advanced formulas and VBA to clean and prepare data. Those who knew programming languages such as Python and R could harness their power to aid in the cleansing effort. But in many cases, data analysts eventually abandoned their exploration of messy datasets, uncertain of the return on investment they would get from cleaning the badly formatted data.

In this chapter, you will learn a wide variety of techniques in the Power Query Editor in Excel and Power BI for cleaning badly formatted datasets. These techniques will enable you to prepare your data in a matter of minutes. If you are new to Power Query, this chapter is the key to achieving a lot as a data analyst. The simple techniques that you will learn here will significantly reduce your data preparation time and enable you to tackle bigger challenges more quickly.

You may need to prepare messy data for an ad hoc analysis, or you might need to periodically prepare and circulate reports for large audiences. This chapter introduces the most common and basic data preparation techniques that will save your time and enable you to automate and streamline your efforts to gain insights.

Extracting Meaning from Encoded Columns

One of the most common challenges in unprepared data is to extract meaning from columns that are badly formatted. If you have a sequence of delimiter-separated codes or values in a single column, you might want to split them into multiple columns.

Excel provides native formula functions for extracting values from badly formatted text. You can use a combination of the functions *LEFT*, *MID*, *RIGHT*, *FIND*, *SEARCH*, and *LEN* to extract any substring from text. But often, the logic to extract the information you seek requires complex formulas and is hard to maintain over time, requiring you to expand the formulas to new rows when your source data changes.

The Text to Columns wizard in the Data tab of Excel enables you to easily split a column into multiple columns. Unfortunately, if you need to load a new table and apply the same type of split, you need to repeat the steps or use macros and VBA. In this section you will learn how you can use Power Query to tackle this challenge. You will find that the Power Query Editor in Excel and Power BI is extremely helpful, especially if you need to repeat the same tasks often, work with large datasets, or maintain a report over the long term.

AdventureWorks Challenge

In this chapter, you will work with the product catalog of a fictitious bike manufacturer company, AdventureWorks Cycles, in the *AdventureWorks* database.

> **See Also** AdventureWorks Cycles is a fictitious company invented by Microsoft to demonstrate the implementation of Microsoft applications in close-to-real-life business scenarios. The AdventureWorks database can be deployed on an Azure SQL Database server for learning purposes. You can create an Azure SQL Database server that contains AdventureWorks data by following the steps in the article https://docs.microsoft.com/en-us/azure/sql-database/sql-database-get-started-portal. You are not required to do this to follow the exercises in this book, but doing so will give you more data samples to practice Power Query.

Imagine that you are a new analyst in the fictitious company AdventureWorks. Your first task is to analyze the company's product catalog and find out how many products the company manufactures by category, product size, and color. The list of products is provided in an Excel workbook that is manually exported from a legacy data warehouse. You can download the workbook C02E01.xlsx from https://aka.ms/DataPwrBIPivot/downloads.

Unfortunately, the product catalog is missing the Category, Size, and Color columns. Instead, it contains a Product Number, containing dash-separated values that include the information on category, size, and color. Figure 2-1 shows the mapping between the Product Number column and the missing columns.

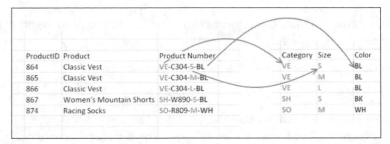

FIGURE 2-1 The AdventureWorks product catalog has category, size, and color values encoded inside the product number.

Your predecessor, who was recently promoted and now leads the Business Intelligence team, had solved this challenge by using Excel formulas. In the next exercise, you will learn how he implemented the solution.

Exercise 2-1: The Old Way: Using Excel Formulas

Download the workbook C02E01 - Solution.xlsx from https://aka.ms/DataPwrBIPivot/downloads. This workbook, which was implemented by your predecessor, uses Excel formulas to extract the product category, color, and size. In this exercise, you can follow his notes and learn how he implemented the solution—without using Power Query.

> **Note** Your goal in Exercise 2-1 is to review a typical solution in Excel, without using Power Query. You are not required to implement it or even fully understand it. As you will soon learn, the Power Query solution is simpler.

1. Open the workbook C02E01 - Solution.xlsx in Excel.

2. Review the first three worksheets: Products, Categories, and Colors. Products contains the main catalog table. In the Categories worksheet, you can see the mapping between category codes and values. For example, *VE* stands for *vests*, *SH* stands for *shorts*, *WB* stands for *bottles*, and *BC* stands for *cages*. In the Colors worksheet, you can see the mapping between color codes and values. For example, *BE* stands for *blue*, and *BK* stands for *black*.

   The fourth worksheet contains three PivotTables with the kind of analysis you would expect to do. All the PivotTables are fed from the data in the Products worksheet.

3. In the Products worksheet, select the cell F2. In the formula bar, notice that this cell contains the following formula:

   ```
   =LEFT(C2, 2)
   ```

The formula returns the two leftmost characters from column C, which contains the product number. These two characters represent the category code.

4. Select cell G2. In the formula bar, you can see the following formula:

```
=RIGHT(C2, 2)
```

The formula returns the two rightmost characters from column C, which contains the product number. These two characters represent the color code.

5. Select cell H2. In the formula bar you can see the following formula:

```
=SUBSTITUTE(MID(C2, SEARCH("-", C2, 8), 3), "-", "")
```

This formula returns the code that represents the product size. This is where things become difficult. The inner formula searches for the character "-" in the product number at cell C2, starting from character 8. It returns the location of the character. Then, the *MID* function returns a three-digit substring. The substring may contain a leading or trailing dash character. The *SUBSTITUTE* function trims away the dash character.

6. Select cell I2. In the formula bar you can see the following formula:

```
=VLOOKUP(F2, Categories!A:B, 2, FALSE)
```

This formula returns the category value from the Categories worksheet, whose product code matches the value in F2.

7. Select cell J2. In the formula bar you can see the following formula:

```
=VLOOKUP(G2, Colors!A:B, 2, FALSE)
```

This formula returns the color value from the Colors worksheet, whose color code matches the value in G2.

If you are an Excel power user, it will not be difficult for you to implement the same formulas just described on a new dataset, such as in C02E01.xlsx. If you are not a power user, you can copy and paste the dataset from C02E01.xlsx to the relevant columns in the Products worksheet of C02E01 - Old Solution.xlsx, and then copy down all the formulas in columns F to J.

But what do you do if you need to update this workbook on a weekly basis? As you get constant product updates, you will need to perform a repetitive sequence of copies and pastes, which may lead to human errors and incorrect calculations. In the next two exercises, you will learn a better way to achieve your goals—by using Power Query.

Exercise 2-2, Part 1: The New Way

In this exercise, you will use the Power Query Editor to create a single Products table. Maintaining this new solution will be much easier than with C02E01 - Old Solution. A single refresh of the workbook will suffice, and you will no longer have many formulas in the spreadsheet to control and protect.

You can follow this exercise in Excel, Power BI Desktop, or any other product that includes the Power Query Editor.

Download the workbook C02E02.xlsx from https://aka.ms/DataPwrBIPivot/downloads and save it in a new folder: *C:\Data\C02*. The workbook contains the *AdventureWorks* database Products, Categories, and Colors worksheets. You will start the exercise by importing the three tables to the Power Query Editor.

1. Start a new blank Excel workbook or a new Power BI Desktop report.

2. Follow these steps to import C02E02.xlsx to the Power Query Editor:

   a. **In Excel:** In the Data tab, select Get Data, From File, From Workbook.

> **Note** Due to variations in the ribbons in the older versions of Excel, the instructions throughout the book from now on will assume you use Excel 2016 or later. (As a result, all entry points will be through the Get Data drop-down in the Data tab.) You can still follow these steps in the Power Query add-in for Excel 2010 and 2013 as well—the differences will be minuscule, and will only be applicable to the initial steps in the Data/Power Query ribbons. The ribbon differences among the Power Query versions is described in Chapter 1, "Introduction to Power Query," in the section, "Where Can I Find Power Query?"

   In Power BI Desktop: In the Get Data drop-down menu, select Excel.

   b. Select the file C02E02.xlsx and select Import.

   c. In the Navigator dialog box that opens in Excel, select the Select Multiple Items check box. In either Excel or Power BI Desktop, select the worksheets Categories, Colors, and Products and select Edit. (As explained in Chapter 1, If you don't find the Edit button in the Navigator dialog box, select Transform Data, or the second button that is right to Load.)

3. In the Power Query Editor that opens, to the left you can see the Queries pane, which contains three queries—one for each of the worksheets you selected in the Navigator in step 2. By selecting each of the queries, you can see a preview of the data in the Preview pane. To the right, you can see the Query Settings pane and the Applied Steps pane, which shows you the sequence of transformation steps as you make changes to your query. Follow these steps to prepare the Categories and Colors queries:

   a. In the Queries pane, select the Categories query. In the Preview pane, you will notice that the headers are Column1 and Column2. The first row contains the column names: Category Code and Product Category Name. To promote the first row, on the Transform tab, select Use First Row As Headers.

> **Tip** If you prefer working with shortcut menus, you can click on the table icon in the top-left corner of the table in the Preview pane of the Power Query Editor and select Use First Row As Headers.

b. In the Queries pane, select the Colors query, which requires the same preparation step as the Categories query. Its column names are Column1 and Column2. The first row contains the actual column names, Color Code and Color. To promote the first row, on Transform tab, select Use First Row As Headers.

4. In the Queries pane, select the Products query.

5. Select the Product Code column either by clicking its header or by selecting the Choose Columns drop-down menu on the Home tab and then selecting Go to Column. When the Go to Column dialog box opens, select the Product Code column in the list and click OK to close the dialog box.

6. On the Transform tab, select Split Column and then select By Delimiter. You can also right-click the header of the Product Code column and select Split Column from the shortcut menu, and then select By Delimiter.

7. In the Split Column by Delimiter dialog box that opens, by default, the correct settings are selected, and you could simply click OK to close the dialog box, but before you do, review the elements of the dialog (see Figure 2-2):

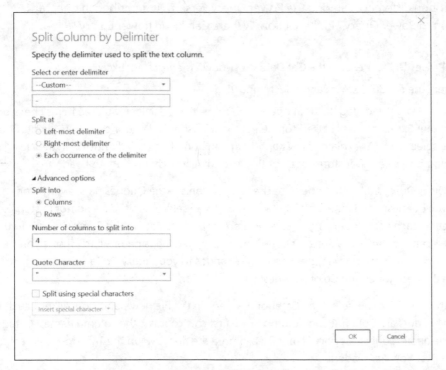

FIGURE 2-2 The Split Column by Delimiter dialog box is automatically set to split by the dash delimiter. More options can be found under Advanced Options. It is recommended that you review them and ensure that the default choices are correct.

- The Custom option is selected in the dialog box, and the dash character is specified as a delimiter. This selection is recognized by Power Query because all the values in the columns are dash-separated.

- Each Occurrence of the Delimiter is selected because there are multiple dash characters.

- If you expand the Advanced Options section, you can see that Power Query detected that Product Number values can be split into four columns.

> **Tip** When you have a fixed number of delimiters, the split into columns is effective. When you have an unknown number of delimiters, you should consider splitting the column into rows. Later in this exercise, you will learn when splitting into rows can be helpful.

- You can see that the quote character is also set. Why do you need it? How will you split dash-separated values if one of the values contains a dash that should not be used as a delimiter? The owner of your data can use double quotes at the beginning and end of text that contains a dash. Power Query will not split the dash characters inside the quoted string. The only caveat is that when you have a double quote at the beginning of a value, but you are missing an ending double quote, the entire text starting from the double quote will be kept intact. To ignore quotes, select None as the quote character.

8. After you close the Split Column by Delimiter dialog box, you can see in the Preview pane that the Product Number column is split into four columns: Product Number.1, Product Number.2, Product Number.3, and Product Number.4. Rename them *Category Code, Short Product Number, Size,* and *Color.* To rename a column, double-click the column name and type a new name. Alternatively, you can select the column and then select Rename in the Transform tab. The column name is then selected, and you can enter the new column name.

    At this stage, you have extracted the size column, and you have separate codes for the product category and color. You will now learn two approaches for adding the actual category and color values instead of their codes. In Exercise 2-2, Part 2, you will learn how to merge the category and color values into the Products table, and in Exercise 2-2, Part 3, you will learn how to keep the three tables as fact and lookup tables.

9. To save the workbook or Power BI report follow these steps:

    In Excel:

    a. In the Home tab of the Power Query Editor, select the Close & Load drop-down menu and then select Close & Load To. The Import Data dialog box opens.

    b. Select Only Create Connection and ensure that Add This Data to the Data Model is unselected. (In the third part of this exercise, you will select this check box.)

    c. Save the workbook as C02E02 - Solution - Part 1.xlsx.

    In Power BI Desktop: Select Close & Apply and save the report as C02E02 - Solution - Part 1.pbix.

Exercise 2-2, Part 2: Merging Lookup Tables

In this part of Exercise 2-2, you will merge the category and color values from the Categories and Colors queries into the Products query, according to their corresponding codes. Recall from Exercise 2-1 that mapping between the codes and the values can be done using *VLOOKUP* in Excel. In this exercise, you will learn an equivalent method using the Power Query Editor.

1. **In Excel:** Open the file C02E02 - Solution - Part 1.xlsx. In the Data tab, select Get Data and then select Launch Power Query Editor.

    In Power BI Desktop: Open the file C02E02 - Solution - Part 1.pbix and select Edit Queries from the Home tab.

2. In the Power Query Editor that opens, in the Queries pane, select the Products query. On the Home tab, select Merge Queries.

3. In the Merge dialog box that opens, you can merge between two tables according to matching values in specified columns. You will merge the category names from the Categories query into the Products query, according to the matching category code. Figure 2-3 illustrates the following steps you need to take in the Merge dialog box:

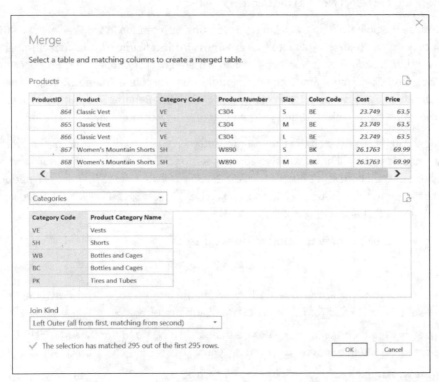

FIGURE 2-3 You can merge categories into products by category code in the Merge dialog box.

a. Select the Category Code column in the Products table, and in the drop-down menu below the Products table, select Categories. Then select Category Code in the second table (refer to Figure 2-3).

b. In the Join Kind drop-down, make sure Left Outer (All from First, Matching from Second) is selected, and click OK.

In the Power Query Editor, you can see that a new Categories column is added as the last column, with Table objects as values.

4. Expand the Categories column (by clicking on the control at the right side of its header or by selecting the Categories column, and then selecting Expand in the Transform tab).

5. In the Expand pane, deselect Category Code and deselect Use Original Column Name As Prefix. Then click OK. The new Categories column is transformed to a new column called Product Category Name, with the matching category values in each row.

6. Now that you have the actual category name, remove the Category Code column by selecting it and pressing the Delete key.

Note   Step 6 may seem a bit awkward for new users, who are accustomed to Excel formulas. You may be surprised to find that Product Category Name remains intact after the removal of Category Code. But keep in mind that the Power Query Editor does not work like Excel. In step 3, you relied on Category Code, as you merged categories into products by using the matching values in the Category Code column. However, in step 6 you removed the Category Code column. Whereas a spreadsheet can be perceived as a single layer, Power Query exposes you to a multi-layered flow of transformations, or states. Each state can be perceived as a transitory layer or a table, whose sole purpose is to serve as the groundwork for the next layer.

7. To merge the colors into the Products query, on the Home tab, select Merge Queries again. When the Merge dialog box opens, follow these steps (see Figure 2-4):

a. Select the Color Code column in the Products table, and in the drop-down menu below the Products table, select Colors. Then select the Color Code column in the second table.

b. In the Join Kind drop-down, ensure that Left Outer (All from First, Matching from Second) is selected and click OK.

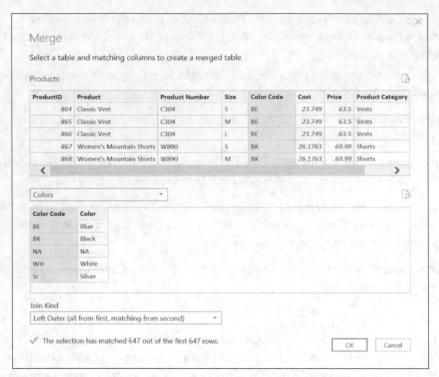

FIGURE 2-4 You can merge colors into products by color code in the Merge dialog box.

In the Power Query Editor, a new Colors column is added as the last column, with Table objects as values. Let's pause for a moment and learn about the Table object and how to interact with it. In addition to the expand control located on the right side of the column, you have three common interactions with the Table objects:

- You can drill down to a single Table object by clicking on any of the table hyperlinks. When you do so, a new step is added to Applied Steps, and from here you could potentially continue preparing your data, which is based on the selected Table object. Try it now.

  Select any of the Table objects in the Colors column. The table in the Preview pane is transformed into a single-row table with the specific color code and color value that was merged in the cell that you selected. Delete this step from Applied Steps so you can get back to the Products table.

- You can also drill down to a single Table object as a new query. This can allow you to explore the data of a single table, while keeping the original table intact. To drill down to a single Table object as a new query, right-click any of the Table objects and select Add As New Query. A new query is created, with all the transformation steps in Products, including the new drill-down step, which is equivalent to the drill-down in the preceding example. If you tried it, you can now delete the new query.

- For temporary inspection of a specified table object, you can click on the space of any cell that contains a Table object. At the bottom of the Preview pane, you see a preview of the table. Now that you've learned a bit more about the Table objects, let's expand the Colors column.

 Note You will find that working with other structured objects in the Power Query Editor—such as Record, List, and Binary objects—is similar: You can drill down to single object, add the object as a new query, or preview its content by clicking anywhere in the cell's space.

8. Expand the Colors column (by clicking on the control at the right side of its header or by selecting the Colors column and then selecting Expand in the Transform tab).

9. In the Expand pane, deselect Color Code and deselect Use Original Column Name As Prefix. Then click OK. The new Colors column is transformed to Color, with the matching color values in each row.

10. Now that you have the actual color values, remove the Color Code column. The Products query is ready, and it's time to load it to the report.

11. **In Excel:** Follow these steps to load Products into the Data Model:

    a. In the Home tab of the Power Query Editor, select Close & Load.

    b. In Excel, on the Data tab, select Queries and Connections to open the Queries pane. Right-click Products and select Load To.

    c. In the Import Data dialog box that opens, select Add This Data to the Data Model and click OK.

    d. You can now create a PivotTable that uses the Data Model and analyzes the distribution of colors or categories. On the Insert tab, select PivotTable. The Create PivotTable dialog box opens. Ensure that the option Use This Workbook's Data Model is selected and click OK to close the dialog box.

    In Power BI Desktop: Follow these steps:

    a. In the Queries pane, right-click Categories and deselect the Enable Load check box.

    b. Right-click the Colors query and deselect the Enable Load check box.

    The last two steps allow you to treat specific queries as stepping-stones for other queries. Because you have extracted the category and color values from Categories and Colors, you can keep Products as the single table in your report. Deselecting Enable Load ensures that these queries are not loaded to the Power BI report. These steps are equivalent in Excel to step 9b, in Exercise 2-2, Part 1, where you selected Only Create Connection in the Import Data dialog box.

    c. On the Home tab, select Close & Apply.

The Products table is now loaded and ready, with categories, colors, and sizes. To review the solution, including an example of a PivotTable with the distribution of products by color, download the workbook C02E02 - Solution - Part 2.xlsx from https://aka.ms/DataPwrBIPivot/downloads. To review the Power BI solution, download the report C02E02 - Solution - Part 2.pbix.

Exercise 2-2, Part 3: Fact and Lookup Tables

In Part 2 of Exercise 2-2, you merged the category and color values from the Categories and Colors queries into the Products query. While this approach enables you to have a single table with the necessary information for your report, there is a better way to do it, using relationships.

> **Note** When you import multiple tables, relationships between those tables may be necessary to accurately calculate results and display the correct information in your reports. The Excel Data Model (also known as Power Pivot) and Power BI Desktop make creating those relationships easy. To learn more about relationships in Power BI, see https://docs.microsoft.com/en-us/power-bi/desktop-create-and-manage-relationships.

In Part 3 of Exercise 2-2, you will start where you left off in Part 1 and load the three queries as separate tables in the Data Model.

1. **In Excel:** Open the file C02E02 - Solution - Part 1.xlsx. In the next steps you will load all the queries into the Data Model in Excel, which will enable you to create PivotTables and PivotCharts from multiple tables. On the Data tab, select Queries & Connections.

   a. In the Queries & Connections pane that opens, right-click the Categories query and select Load To.

   b. In the Import Data dialog box that opens, select Add This Data to the Data Model and close the dialog box.

   c. Right-click the Colors query and select Load To.

   d. In the Import Data dialog box that opens, select Add This Data to the Data Model and close the dialog box.

   e. Right-click the Products query and select Load To.

   f. In the Import Data dialog box that opens, select Add This Data to the Data Model and close the dialog box.

   At this stage, you have the three tables loaded to the Data Model. It's time to create the relationship between these tables.

   g. On the Data tab, select Manage Data Model. The Power Pivot for Excel window opens.

   h. On the Home tab, select the Diagram view.

   In Power BI Desktop: Open the file C02E02 - Solution - Part 1.pbix and select the Relationships view from the left-side menu.

2. Drag and drop Category Code from the Categories table to Category Code in the Products table.

3. Drag and drop Color Code from the Colors table to Color Code in the Products table.

   Your Data Model now consists of a fact table with the product list and two lookup tables with the supplementary information on categories and colors. As shown in Figure 2-5, there are one-to-many relationships between Category Code in the Categories table and Category Code in the Products table, as well as between Color Code in the Colors table and Color Code in the Products table.

> **See Also** The topic of modeling is not the focus of this book. To learn more about Power Pivot, Data Models, and relationships in Excel and Power BI, see *Analyzing Data with Power BI and Power Pivot for Excel* by Alberto Ferrari and Marco Russo (Microsoft Press).

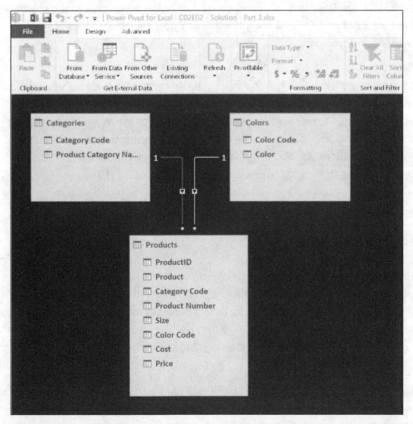

FIGURE 2-5 The Diagram view shows the Data Model relationships in Excel between Categories and Products and between Colors and Products.

4. After you have established the relationships between the tables, hide the columns Category Code and Color Code in the tables to ensure that these fields will no longer be selected in PivotTables, PivotCharts, and Power BI visualizations. By hiding these fields, you help report consumers enjoy a cleaner report. In other scenarios where you have multiple fact tables connected to a lookup table by the same column, hiding the column in the fact tables can lead to a more extendable report, in which a single column in the lookup table can be used in a slicer or a visual to filter data coming from the multiple fact tables.

In Excel, right-click Color Code in the Colors table and select Hide from Client Tools. Repeat this step on Color Code in the Products table and Category Code in the Categories and Products tables.

In Power BI, right-click Color Code in the Colors table and select Hide in Report View. Repeat this step on Color Code in the Products table and Category Code in the Categories and Products tables.

You can now create PivotTables, PivotCharts, and visualizations as demonstrated in the solution files C02E02 - Solution - Part 3.xlsx and C02E02 - Solution - Part 3.pbix, which are available at https://aka.ms/DataPwrBIPivot/downloads.

> **Tip** While the solution in Exercise 2-2, Part 2 simplifies your report, as it leaves you with a single table, in real-life reports that have multiple tables, the solution in Exercise 2-2, Part 3 will provide more opportunities for insight, as your model will become more complex. For example, having a single Categories lookup table connected to multiple fact tables with Product Category codes will allow you to compare between numerical columns across the different fact tables, using the shared categories.

Using Column from Examples

Often, the first command you see on the left side of the ribbon can reveal the importance of a feature. That is why, for example, you can find PivotTable as the first command in the Insert tab of Excel. In the Power Query Editor, you can find one of the most important capabilities as the first command in Add Column tab. Column from Examples is a powerful feature that enables you to extract meaning from existing columns into a new column, without any preliminary knowledge of the different transformations available in the Power Query Editor.

By using Column from Examples, you can add new columns of data in the Power Query Editor by simply providing one or more sample values for your new column. When you provide these examples, Power Query tries to deduce the calculation needed to generate the values in the new column. This capability can be used as a shortcut to extract new meaning from data. This is a very powerful feature, especially for new users because it means you are not required to explore for the necessary transformation in the ribbons or memorize the M formulas to extract the meaningful data into the new column. If you simply provide a few examples in the new column, Power Query tries to do the work for you.

Exercise 2-3 provides a quick demonstration of Column from Examples with the dataset from Exercise 2-2.

Exercise 2-3, Part 1: Introducing Column from Examples

In Exercise 2-2, you learned how to split the product code into four elements. But imagine that you just need to extract the product size from the code. In this exercise you will learn how to do this by using Column from Examples.

If you didn't follow Exercise 2-2, download the workbook C02E02.xlsx from https://aka.ms/ DataPwrBIPivot/downloads and save it in the folder *C:\Data\C02*.

1. Start a new blank Excel workbook or a new Power BI Desktop report.

2. Follow these steps to import C02E02.xlsx to the Power Query Editor:

   a. **In Excel:** On the Data tab, select Get Data, From File, From Workbook.

      In Power BI Desktop: In the Get Data drop-down menu, select Excel.

   b. Select the file C02E02.xlsx and select Import.

   c. In the Navigator dialog box that opens, select Products and then select Edit.

3. In the Power Query Editor, you can now see in the Preview pane that the Product Number column contains four dash-separated codes (for example, VE-C304-S-BE). The challenge is to extract the third value, which reflects the size of the product.

   Select the Product Number column, and on the Add Column tab, select the Column from Examples drop-down menu, where you see two options:

   - From All Columns
   - From Selection

   In this exercise, you need to extract the size of the product from Product Number, so select From Selection.

 Tip In many cases, if you know in advance which columns should contribute to the new column, selecting the relevant input columns and then selecting From Selection in the Column from Examples drop-down menu will improve the chances that Power Query will provide a useful recommendation.

The Power Query Editor now enters a new state. The Preview pane is pushed down, and a new section is shown on top of the Preview pane, with the message Enter Sample Values to Create a New Column. In the bottom-right part of this new section are OK and Cancel buttons to exit from this special state.

On the right side of the Preview pane is an area with a new empty column. This is where you can enter your examples. Before you do so, rename Column1 to *Size* by double-clicking the header of the new column.

4. Double-click the first blank cell of the Size column in the Preview pane. A drop-down menu shows a few recommended examples that you can select from to create the new column. The values in the drop-down menu can provide some ideas of transformation that can be used to populate the new column.

5. In the first blank cell, enter *S*, which represents the bolded size value in the product number VE-C304-**S**-BE. Press Enter, and Power Query populates the new Size column with all the suggested values, as illustrated in Figure 2-6. Press Ctrl+Enter or click OK to create the column.

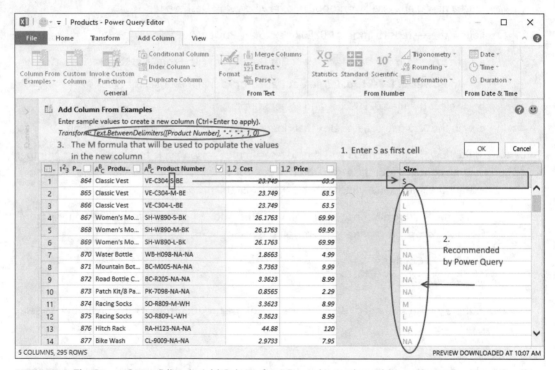

FIGURE 2-6 The Power Query Editor in Add Column from Examples mode enables you to easily extract the size code from Product Number column.

6. You can now see the new Size column, calculated as expected. Load the data to your workbook or to a Power BI report and save.

You can download the solution files C02E03 - Solution.xlsx and C02E03 - Solution.pbix from https://aka.ms/DataPwrBIPivot/downloads.

Practical Use of Column from Examples

Column from Examples is a very useful tool to discover new transformations that are available in the user interface and in M. Let's demonstrate how a new transformation can be discovered, using the output of Column from Examples. In step 6 of Exercise 2-3, Part 1, you can see that in the Applied Steps pane of the Power Query Editor, the last step, Inserted Text Between Delimiters, contains a settings control (in the shape of a cog) at the right side of the step. By clicking the settings control you can open the Text Between Delimiters dialog box. This dialog box allows you to extract text between delimiters. Now, when you know that such a dialog box exists, you can explore the Power Query Editor to find which ribbon command can trigger it, outside the Column from Examples flow. Exploring the Transform tab reveals the command Text Between Delimiters inside the Extract drop-down menu.

For intermediate Power Query users, a great way to improve knowledge of M is to use Column from Examples and review the suggested code that is shown in the top pane (highlighted in Figure 2-6). You may find some useful functions, such as *Text.BetweenDelimiters*, which is used in Exercise 2-3, Part 1.

Column from Examples can help you achieve a wide variety of transformations on text, dates, times, and numbers. You can even use it to create bucketing/ranges and conditional columns, as you will see in Exercise 2-3, Part 2.

> **See Also** To find the latest list of the functions supported by Column from Examples, go to https://docs.microsoft.com/en-us/power-bi/desktop-add-column-from-example.

Exercise 2-3, Part 2: Converting Size to Buckets/Ranges

In this part of Exercise 2-3, you will use Column from Examples to group numeric size values into buckets. You can download the solution files C02E03 - Solution.xlsx and C02E03 - Solution.pbix from https://aka.ms/DataPwrBIPivot/downloads to follow the steps of this exercise.

1. Open C02E03 - Solution.xlsx or C02E03 - Solution.pbix and launch the Power Query Editor. To launch the Power Query Editor in Excel, go to the Data tab, select Get Data, and then select Launch Power Query Editor. To launch the Power Query Editor in Power BI Desktop, select Edit Queries on the Home tab.

    You can see that the Size column contains a combination of alphabetic and numeric size values. In the next two steps you will learn how to ignore the textual values and focus only on numeric values in the Size column by creating a new column with the numeric representation for sizes. There are several ways to achieve this goal. In step 2, you will do it using the error-handling features in Power Query. In step 3, you will do it using Column from Examples.

2. To extract all the numeric sizes from the Size column by using error handling, follow these steps:

    a. Select the Size column. On the Add Column tab, select Duplicate Column.

    b. Rename the new column *Size - Numbers* and change its type to Whole Number by selecting the ABC control in the header and Whole Number in the drop-down menu.

c. You now see Error values in all the cells that contained textual size codes (S, M, L, X, and NA), but you want to work on numbers only, so you need to replace the errors with nulls. To do this, select the Size - Numbers column, and on the Transform tab, select the Replace Values drop-down menu and then select Replace Errors. An easier way to find the Replace Errors transformation is by right-clicking on the column header and finding the transformation in the shortcut menu.

d. In the Replace Errors dialog box that opens, enter *null* in the Value box and click OK to close the dialog box.

3. To extract the numeric size values by using Column from Examples, instead of replacing errors with null, follow these steps:

a. If you applied step 2, delete the last four steps that were created in Applied Steps. Your last step should now be Inserted Text Between Delimiter.

b. Select the Size column. On the Add Column tab, select the Column from Examples drop-down menu and then select From Selection.

c. When the Add Column from Examples pane opens, showing the new column, rename it *Size - Numbers*.

d. Double-click the first blank cell in the Size - Numbers column. You can see that the value in the Size column is S. Because you are not interested in textual size values, enter *null* in the first blank cell and press Enter.

e. When you see that the second and third values in the Size column are M and L, enter *null* in both the second and third cells of Size - Numbers and press Enter.

f. Move to the cell in row 7. You can see that the value in the Size column is NA. Enter null in the seventh cell of the Size - Numbers column and press Enter.

g. Move to row 21. You can see that the value in the Size column is X. Enter *null* in the corresponding cell of the Size - Numbers column and press Enter.

h. Now, in row 22, you see the value 60. Enter *60* in the corresponding cell of the Size - Numbers column and press Enter. Power Query populates the new Size column with all the suggested values. You can now press Ctrl+Enter to create the new Size - Numbers column.

In Applied Steps, you can now see the new Added Conditional Column step. Select the settings icon or double-click this step, and the Add Conditional Column dialog box opens. This dialog box allows you to create a column based on conditions in other columns. You could also have reached this point, and created a new column for the numeric size values, by applying a conditional column instead of by using Column from Examples. Close the Add Conditional Column dialog box. You will learn about this dialog box In Exercise 2-4.

4. Change the type of the Size - Numbers column to Whole Number by selecting the ABC control in the header of the column in the Preview pane and Whole Number in the drop-down menu.

In the next part of this exercise, you will create a separate table for the products with numeric sizes and will classify them into four size buckets (S = Small, M = Medium, L = Large, and X = Extra Large) by using Column from Example.

5. In the Queries pane, right-click Products and select Reference. Rename the new query *Numeric-Size Products*. To rename the query, right-click the query in the Queries pane and select Rename in the shortcut menu, or rename the query in the Query Settings pane, under Properties, in the Name box.

> **Tip** Using Reference is a very useful technique for branching from a source table and creating a new one, starting from the last step of the referenced query.

6. In the new query, remove all the products whose Size - Numbers value is null. To do so, click the filter control in the Size - Numbers column and select Remove Empty.

7. Say that you want to convert the numeric sizes into the buckets of X, L, M, and S as follows: Numbers equal to or greater than 70 will be assigned to the X bucket. Numbers equal to or greater than 60 will be assigned to L. Numbers equal to or greater than 50 will be assigned to M, and numbers equal to or greater than 40 will be assigned to S. Here are the steps to achieve this by using Column from Examples (see Figure 2-7 to ensure you follow the steps correctly):

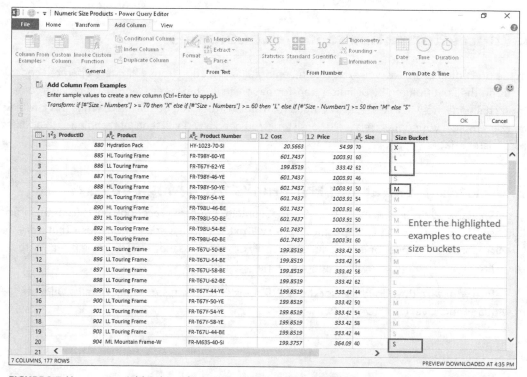

FIGURE 2-7 You can use Add Column from Examples to create size buckets.

a. Select the Size - Numbers column, and in the Add Column tab, select the Column from Examples drop-down menu and then select From Selection.

b. Rename the new column *Size Bucket.*

c. Enter *X* in row 1 (because Size - Numbers is 70).

d. Enter *L* in rows 2 and 3 (because the Size - Numbers values are 60 and 62, respectively).

e. Enter *M* in row 5 (because Size - Numbers is 50).

f. Enter S in row 20 (because Size - Numbers is 40).

g. Press Ctrl+Enter to create the new Size - Bucket column. The Size - Bucket column now contains the required bucket names for the relevant ranges.

8. For learning purposes, double-click the Added Conditional Column step in the Applied Steps pane. The Add Conditional Column dialog box opens. Review the conditions that defined the ranges for each bucket, and close the dialog box.

9. Review the M formula in the formula bar for a quick glimpse into the M syntax, which is discussed in more detail throughout the book, specifically in Chapter 9, "Introduction to the Power Query M Formula Language."

You can download the solution files C02E03 - Solution - Part 2.xlsx and C02E03 - Solution - Part 2.pbix from https://aka.ms/DataPwrBIPivot/downloads.

Extracting Information from Text Columns

In the preceding exercises, you extracted meaningful information from delimiter-separated codes by using the Split Column by Delimiter transformation. In the next exercise, you will tackle a common challenge: how to extract meaningful data from unstructured textual data. While this challenge can be simple if your data is relatively consistent, you need a wider arsenal of techniques to address inconsistent data.

Exercise 2-4: Extracting Hyperlinks from Messages

In this exercise you will work on a workbook that contains imported Facebook posts from the official Microsoft Press Facebook page. Specifically, you will extract the hyperlinks from posts that were shared by Microsoft Press. While some hyperlinks are easily extracted, as they start with the prefix "http://", there are plenty of edge cases that cannot be easily addressed.

Before you start, download the workbook C02E04.xlsx from https://aka.ms/DataPwrBIPivot/downloads and save it in *C:\Data\C02.*

> **Note** While some elements in this exercise may be a bit advanced, requiring lightweight manipulation of formulas that are not explained in detail in this chapter, you will still find these elements extremely useful, and you will be able to apply them to your own data even if you do not fully understand them yet. Chapter 9 explains M in more detail, and it will help you feel more comfortable with the type of changes you encounter here.

1. Start a new blank Excel workbook or a new Power BI Desktop report.

2. Follow these steps to import C02E04.xlsx to the Power Query Editor:

   a. **In Excel:** On the Data tab, select Get Data, From File, From Workbook.

   In Power BI Desktop: In the Get Data drop-down menu, select Excel.

   b. Select the file C02E04.xlsx and select Import.

   c. In the Navigator dialog box that opens, select Sheet1 and then click Edit.

   The Power Query Editor opens, and you see that the Message column contains free text. Before you extract the hyperlinks from the Message column, to achieve your goal, as illustrated in Figure 2-8, you first need to duplicate the column to keep the original message intact, so select the Message column, and from the Add Column tab, select Duplicate Column.

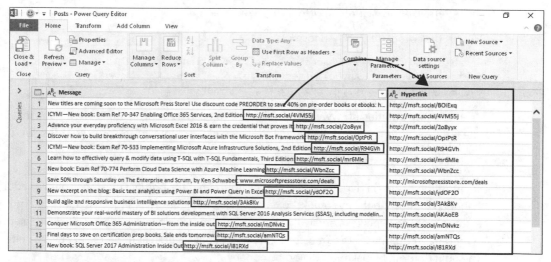

FIGURE 2-8 You can extract hyperlinks from Microsoft Press Facebook posts.

3. Rename the new column *Hyperlink*.

4. To extract the hyperlink from the new column, you can use the hyperlink prefix "http://" as a delimiter and split the column, so select the Hyperlink column, and on the Transform tab, select Split Column and then select By Delimiter.

5. In the Split Column by Delimiter dialog box that opens, do the following:

   a. Enter *"http://"* in the text box below Custom.

   b. Select the Left-Most Delimiter option at Split At radio buttons and click OK to close the dialog box.

You can now see that the Hyperlink column has been split into two columns: Hyperlink.1 and Hyperlink.2. But how can you extract hyperlinks that start with "https://" or perhaps just "www."?

6. In Applied Steps, select the step Split Column by Delimiter.

7. Ensure that your formula bar in the Power Query Editor is active. If you don't see it, go to the View tab and select the Formula Bar check box. Now, you can see the following formula, which was generated in step 7:

```
= Table.SplitColumn(#"Renamed Columns", "Hyperlink",
Splitter.SplitTextByEachDelimiter({"http://"},
QuoteStyle.Csv, false), {"Hyperlink.1", "Hyperlink.2"})
```

8. To split the Hyperlink column by additional delimiters, you can change the function name from *Splitter.SplitTextBy**Each**Delimiter* to *Splitter.SplitTextBy**Any**Delimiter*. Now, you can add the new delimiters "https://" and "www.". You can see in the formula above that "https://" is wrapped in double quotes inside curly brackets. Curly brackets represent lists in the M language of Power Query. You can now add multiple items to the list by adding double-quoted comma-separated delimiters, like this: *{"http://", "https://", "www."}*.

Here is the complete modified formula:

```
= Table.SplitColumn(#"Renamed Columns", "Hyperlink",
Splitter.SplitTextByAnyDelimiter({"http://", "https://", "www."},
QuoteStyle.Csv, false), {"Hyperlink.1", "Hyperlink.2"})
```

9. Thanks to the addition of "www." as a delimiter, you can now see in the Preview pane that in line 8 a new hyperlink was detected in the Hyperlink.2 column: microsoftpressstore.com/deals.

10. Go back to the last step in Applied Steps.

11. To audit the results in Hyperlink.2, in row 15, notice that the original message contains additional text following the hyperlink. To remove the trailing text from the hyperlink, you can assume that the hyperlinks end with a space character and split Hyperlink.2. To do it, select the Hyperlink.2 column. On the Transform tab, select Split Column and then select By Delimiter. The Split Column by Delimiter dialog box opens.

    a. Select Space from the Select or Enter Delimiter drop-down.

    b. Select the Left-Most Delimiter option for Split At radio buttons and click OK to close the dialog box.

12. Remove the Hyperlink.2.2 column.

To continue auditing the results in Hyperlink.2, scroll down until you find the first null value, in row 29. A null value means that you couldn't detect any hyperlink in the message. But if you take a closer look at the message in the Hyperlink.1 column, you can see that it contains the bolded hyperlink, as shown in the line *Discover Windows containers in this free ebook. Download here:* **aka.ms/containersebook**.

The next challenge is to extract the hyperlinks whose domain name is *aka.ms* and include them in the Hyperlink column. This challenge is rather complex because after you split the Message column by the delimiter *aka.ms*, the domain name will be removed from the split results. When you applied "www." in step 8, "www." was removed from the hyperlink, but that was a safe manipulation. You were taking the risk that the resulted hyperlink will work well without the "www." prefix because it is common to omit this prefix from hyperlinks (e.g., www.microsoft.com and microsoft.com lead to the same website).

You need to find a way to split by aka.ms, and you must find a way to return the domain name, but only for rows that contain that domain. You will soon learn how to do it by using a conditional column. But first, you need to add aka.ms to the list of delimiters.

13. In Applied Steps, select again the first Split Column by Delimiter step, which you modified in step 8, and add aka.ms to the list of delimiters. Here is the modified formula:

```
= Table.SplitColumn(#"Renamed Columns", "Hyperlink",
Splitter.SplitTextByAnyDelimiter({"http://", "https://", "www.", "aka.ms"},
QuoteStyle.Csv, false), {"Hyperlink.1", "Hyperlink.2"})
```

You can now see in row 29 that the hyperlink is /containersebook. In the next steps, you will add a conditional column that will return the missing domain name aka.ms if the values in the Hyperlink column start with /.

14. In Applied Steps, go back to the last step. Remove the Hyperlink.1 column, and rename Hyperlink.2.1 to *Hyperlink Old*.

15. On the Add Column tab, select Conditional Column. When the Add Conditional Column dialog box opens, follow these steps (see Figure 2-9):

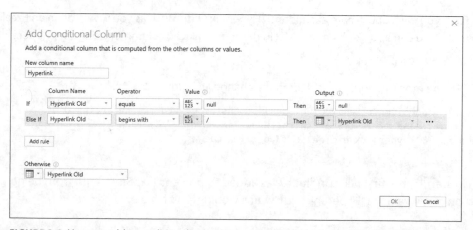

FIGURE 2-9 You can add a conditional column as a preliminary step in adding back the domain name aka.ms. Note that the conditions in the dialog box are used as a stepping-stone to the final conditions.

Note The use of the Add Conditional Column dialog box will help you set the stage for the final conditions. The user interface is limited, and you are using it as a shortcut to generate part of the required conditions. The final touch will require a lightweight modification of the formula in the formula bar in step 16.

    a. Enter *Hyperlink* in the New Column Name box.

    b. Select Hyperlink Old from the Column Name drop-down for If.

    c. Select Equals from the Operator drop-down and enter *null* in both the Value and Output text boxes.

    d. Click the Add Rule button to add a new condition line.

    e. Select Hyperlink Old from the Column Name drop-down for Else If.

    f. Select Begins With as the operator in the second line.

    g. Ensure that Enter a Value is selected in the ABC123 drop-down menu in the second line, under Value, and enter / in the Value box.

    h. In the drop-down menu after the Then label for Else If, select Select a Column and then select Hyperlink Old.

    i. In the drop-down menu below the Otherwise label, select Select a Column and then select Hyperlink Old.

    j. Ensure that your settings match those in Figure 2-9 and click OK to close the dialog box.

16. Now look at the formula bar. It's time to modify the M formula to add the prefix aka.ms if a hyperlink starts with /. Here is the original formula, following step 15:

```
= Table.AddColumn(#"Renamed Columns1", "Custom", each if [Hyperlink Old] = null
then null else if Text.StartsWith([Hyperlink Old], "/") then [Hyperlink Old] else
[Hyperlink Old])
```

To fix it, you can concatenate aka.ms and [Hyperlink Old]. Much as you would do in an Excel formula, you can add aka.ms as a prefix in the Hyperlink Old column by using the *&* operator:

```
"aka.ms" & [Hyperlink Old]
```

Here is the modified formula, including the change, in bold:

```
= Table.AddColumn(#"Renamed Columns1", "Custom", each if [Hyperlink Old] = null
then null else if Text.StartsWith([Hyperlink Old], "/") then
"aka.ms" & [Hyperlink Old] else [Hyperlink Old])
```

Note In step 15, the first null condition was added to prevent *Text.StartsWith* from being applied on a null value in [Hyperlink Old], which would result in an error.

17. Remove the Hyperlink Old column.

You are almost done, but there are few more surprises waiting for you. Continue auditing the results in the Hyperlink column by scrolling down to row 149. The Hyperlink cell is blank, but looking at the original Message column, you can see the following hyperlink inside the message: *https://www.microsoftpressstore.com/Ignite*.

Why is the Hyperlink cell blank in this case? When you split this message in step 14, both "https://" and "www." participated in the split as delimiters. As a result, the split included three separated values, but only the first two were loaded. The next steps help you resolve this problem.

18. In Applied Steps, select the first Split Column by Delimiter step. Change the bolded section in the formula below from *{"Hyperlink.1", "Hyperlink.2"}* to *3*:

```
= Table.SplitColumn(#"Renamed Columns", "Hyperlink",
Splitter.SplitTextByAnyDelimiter({"http://", "https://", "www.", "aka.ms"},
QuoteStyle.Csv, false), {"Hyperlink.1", "Hyperlink.2"})
```

Here is the complete modified formula:

```
= Table.SplitColumn(#"Renamed Columns", "Hyperlink",
Splitter.SplitTextByAnyDelimiter({"http://", "https://", "www.", "aka.ms"},
QuoteStyle.Csv, false), 3)
```

> **See Also** Here you use the argument 3 instead of the list of column names *{"Hyperlink.1", "Hyperlink.2", "Hyperlink.3"}*. The results are the same. The *Table.SplitColumn* function accepts either the column names or the number of new columns to use in the split. The fact is, you miss crucial data when you use only the default split; this is discussed in more detail in Chapter 10, "From Pitfalls to Robust Queries."

Now, as shown in Figure 2-10, you have the hyperlink values either in Hyperlink.2 (in most of the rows) or in Hyperlink.3 (in row 149). If you merge the two columns, you can retrieve the missing hyperlinks and fix the query.

19. While the Split Column by Delimiter step is still selected in Applied Steps, insert the following steps into the transformation sequence:

a. Select the two columns Hyperlink.2 and Hyperlink.3.

b. On the Transform tab, select Merge Columns.

c. When the Insert Step dialog box opens, warning you that this step will be inserted between the existing steps and may break your subsequent steps, select Insert.

d. In the Merge Columns dialog box that opens, keep the default settings and click OK to close the dialog box.

e. Rename the Merged column *Hyperlink.2*.

f. When the Insert Step dialog box opens again, select Insert.

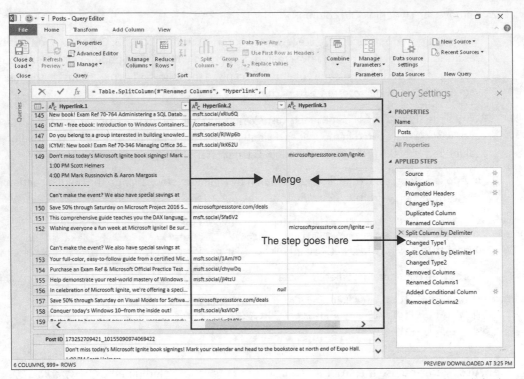

FIGURE 2-10 You can merge the Hyperlink.2 column with the Hyperlink.3 column to extract hyperlinks that start with https://www.

20. You can now select the last step in Applied Steps to ensure that the preceding steps work as expected.

    There are still two cases that have not been handled correctly. First, in row 149 you can see that the hyperlinks don't end with a space but with other punctuation, such as a dot. As a result, in step 11, when you applied space as a delimiter, you were not able to clean the trailing message from the hyperlink value. To fix it, you should trim the punctuation from all hyperlinks.

21. Select the Hyperlink column, and on the Transform tab, select Format and then select Trim. Alternatively, right-click the Hyperlink column, and in the shortcut menu, select Transform and then select Trim.

    By default, Trim removes whitespace from the beginning and end of text values. You can manipulate it to also trim the trailing punctuation. This requires some changes in the formula bar. You can see that the formula includes the bolded element *Text.Trim*:

    ```
    = Table.TransformColumns(#"Removed Columns1",{{"Hyperlink", Text.Trim, type text}})
    ```

    The M function *Text.Trim* accepts a list of text items as its second argument to trim leading and trailing text other than spaces. In M, the punctuation list—dot, comma, and closing parenthesis—can be defined with curly brackets and comma-separated double-quoted values, as shown here:

    ```
    { ".", ",", ")" }
    ```

To feed the list as the second argument to *Text.Trim*, you should also feed its first argument, which is the actual text in the Hyperlink column. To get the actual text, you can use the combination of the keyword *each* and the underscore character. (Chapter 9 explains this in more details.) Copy this modified formula to the formula bar to trim the punctuations from the Hyperlink column:

```
= Table.TransformColumns(#"Removed Columns1",{{"Hyperlink", each Text.Trim(_,
{".",",",")"}), type text}})
```

22. Notice the final issue in row 174, where you can see that the hyperlink ends with a new line, followed by more text. When you applied the second Split Text By Delimiter using a space, you didn't extract the hyperlink correctly. To fix it, select the second Split Text By Delimiter in Applied Steps.

23. In the formula bar, notice the following code:

```
= Table.SplitColumn(#"Changed Type1", "Hyperlink.2",
Splitter.SplitTextByEachDelimiter({" "}, QuoteStyle.Csv, false),
{"Hyperlink.2.1", "Hyperlink.2.2"})
```

Change it to the following (where changes are highlighted in bold):

```
= Table.SplitColumn(#"Changed Type1", "Hyperlink.2",
Splitter.SplitTextByAnyDelimiter({" ", "#(lf)"}, QuoteStyle.Csv, false),
{"Hyperlink.2.1", "Hyperlink.2.2"})
```

The value "*#(lf)*" describes the special line-feed character. In the preceding formula, you used the advanced split function *Splitter.SplitTextByAnyDelimiter* instead of *Splitter.SplitTextByDelimiter* to split by both spaces and line feeds.

24. Finally, to include the prefix "http://" in all the Hyperlink values, in Applied Steps, go back to the last step. Select the Hyperlink column, and on the Transform tab, select Format and then select Add Prefix. When the Prefix dialog box opens, enter *"http://"* in the Value box and close the dialog box.

25. In the preceding step, you added the prefix "http://" in all the rows, even where there are no URLs. But there are legitimate cases in which the Hyperlink column should be empty (for example, row 113). To remove "http://" from cells without hyperlinks, follow these steps:

   a. Select the Hyperlink column. Then, on the Home tab, select Replace Values.

   b. When the Replace Values dialog box opens, enter *"http://"* in the Value to Find box.

   c. Leave the Replace With box empty.

   d. Expand Advanced Options and select the Match Entire Cell Contents check box. (This step is crucial. Without it, Power Query removes "http://" from all the values.)

   e. Click OK to close the dialog box and select Close & Load in Excel or Close & Apply in Power BI Desktop to load the messages and their extracted hyperlinks to the report.

By now, you have resolved most of the challenges in this dataset and extracted the required hyperlinks. You can download the solution files C02E04 - Solution.xlsx and C02E04 - Solution.pbix from https://aka.ms/DataPwrBIPivot/downloads.

> **See Also** There are still a few hyperlinks in the Message column. These hyperlinks do not start with "www.", "http", "https", or "aka.ms". Can you find them? In Chapter 11, "Basic Text Analytics," you will learn advanced techniques for detecting keywords in messages. These techniques will help you detect a wider list of domain names and extract the hyperlinks.

Handling Dates

One of the most common data preparation challenges is dealing with data types. While text columns are easy to handle, numbers and dates can make even the simplest datasets daunting for analysis. In this section you will learn how to handle dates and times. You will start with a common challenge—converting text to dates—and then move on to more challenging cases involving invalid dates. At the end of this section you will learn how to extract specific date or time elements from date/time values.

When you load a table with dates or date/time values, Power Query converts the relevant columns to their correct date/time format. In Exercise 2-4, you imported a dataset with a Date/Time column. Power Query automatically converted the *Date* column to *Date/Time*. Exercise 2-5 shows how Power Query handles a column with mixed date formats.

Exercise 2-5: Handling Multiple Date Formats

Download the workbook C02E05.xlsx from https://aka.ms/DataPwrBIPivot/downloads and save it in *C:\Data\C02*. This workbook contains the AdventureWorks product catalog, with the release date of each product in the last column. Imagine that different data entry teams had typed the products' release dates in five different formats:

- 7/1/2018

- 2018-07-01

- 7.1.2018

- Jul 1, 2018

- 1 July, 2018

For the sake of simplicity, assume that all the teams use the English/United States Locale in their regional settings, so the first date, 7/1/2018, is July 1 (not January 7).

When you try to work with these different formats and apply date calculations, you see that Excel does not recognize the dates in all the cells, and for some cells, it returns a #*VALUE!* error.

1. Open a copy of the workbook C02E05.xlsx. (Be sure to use a copy rather than the original workbook.)

2. In cell H2, add the following formula:

   ```
   = G2 + 1
   ```

   This formula should increment the release date by one day, but the result is 43283. This is because Excel stores dates as sequential serial numbers, so that they can be used in calculations. By default, January 1, 1900, is serial number 1, and July 1, 2018, is serial number 43282 (indicating the number of days since 1/1/1900).

3. To view the dates correctly, change the format of column H to Date. After you make this change, copy and paste the formula from step 2 into the next four rows: H3, H4, H5, and H6.

   Cells H4 and H6 return a #*VALUE!* error because Excel cannot find a way to convert them to dates or numbers to increment them by one.

4. It's time to learn how Power Query can help in this scenario, so open a new workbook or launch Power BI Desktop. Because your input data is based on English (United States) regional settings, you need to ensure that you use this locale in this exercise.

   In Excel: While you are still in the Power Query Editor, select File. Select Options and Settings, and then select Query Options. Under Current Workbook, select Regional Settings and then select English (United States) from the Locale drop-down.

   In Power BI Desktop: Select File, Options and Settings, Options. Under Current File, select Regional Settings and then select English (United States) from the Locale drop-down.

5. Click OK to close the Options dialog box.

6. Import the workbook C02E05.xlsx into the Power Query Editor:

   a. **In Excel:** On the Data tab, select Get Data, From File, From Workbook.

      In Power BI Desktop: In the Get Data drop-down menu, select Excel.

   b. Select the file C02E05.xlsx and select Import.

   c. When the Navigator dialog box opens, select Sheet1 and then select Edit.

7. When the Power Query Editor opens, notice that all the date values in the Release Date column are detected correctly, as shown in Figure 2-11.

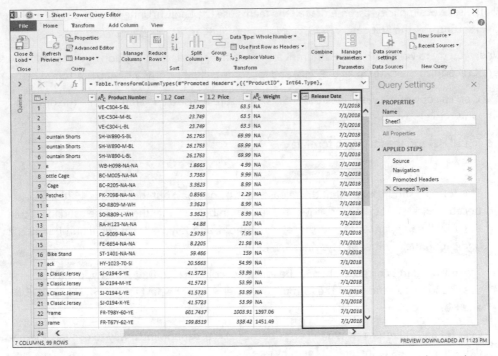

FIGURE 2-11 Power Query automatically changes the column type from *Text* to *Date* and correctly converts the different date formats.

8. Close the Power Query Editor and load the data to your report.

> **Tip** If you import dates of a different locale than the one defined for your Microsoft Windows operating system, you can define the specific locale in the Query Options dialog box, as shown in step 4. After you refresh the preview in the Power Query Editor, you see that the dates are recognized correctly.

Exercise 2-6: Handling Dates with Two Locales

In Exercise 2-5, you had multiple date formats, but you assumed that all dates were used by the same locale. In this exercise, you will learn how to handle cases where your dates are for multiple locales, and the months and days values should be swapped for some of the rows.

Download the workbook C02E06.xlsx from https://aka.ms/DataPwrBIPivot/downloads and save it in *C:\Data\C02*. For simplicity, the workbook contains only two rows from the AdventureWorks product catalog—each row for a product with a different country and release date formatted by the specific country's locale:

- Country: United States, Release Date: 7/23/2018

- Country: United Kingdom, Release Date: 23/7/2018

As you can see in Figure 2-12, the Release Date column, when changed to the *Date* type, returns an error value for the UK row if your locale in the Power Query Options dialog box is set to English (United States); it returns an error value for the US row if your locale is English (United Kingdom) in that dialog box.

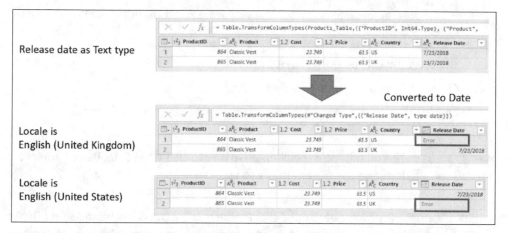

FIGURE 2-12 Converting the Release Date column from *Text* to *Date* yields different errors, depending on the workbook's or file's locale.

To resolve this issue, you cannot rely on the locale in the Options dialog box. Instead, you can use the Split Column by Delimiter and then apply a conditional column, as described in this exercise.

1. Start a new blank Excel workbook or a new Power BI Desktop report.

2. Import C02E06.xlsx to the Power Query Editor:

   a. **In Excel:** On the Data tab, select Get Data, From File, From Workbook.

      In Power BI Desktop: In the Get Data drop-down menu, select Excel.

   b. Select the file C02E06.xlsx and select Import.

   c. In the Navigator dialog box that opens, select Products, and then select Edit.

3. Select the Release Date column. On the Transform tab, select Split Column and then select By Delimiter. The Split Column by Delimiter dialog box that opens detects the forward slash (/) as the delimiter. Click OK to close the dialog box.

   You can now see that Release Date is split into three columns: Release Date.1, Release Date.2, and Release Date.3. When Country is UK, Release Date.1 is the day, and Release Date.2 is the month. When Country is US, Release Date.1 is the month, and Release Date.2 is the day. In the next step, you will learn how to create a new column with the correct date, using an M formula and a custom column. Then, in steps 6–10, you will learn an alternative way that doesn't require you to know M but that involves more interactions with the user interface of the Power Query Editor.

4. On the Add Column tab, select Custom Column. The Custom Column dialog box opens.

    a. Enter *Date* in the New Column Name box.

    b. Enter the following formula in the Custom Column Formula box:

```
if [Country] = "US" then
    #date([Release Date.3], [Release Date.1], [Release Date.2])
else
    #date([Release Date.3], [Release Date.2], [Release Date.1])
```

    Then click OK to close the dialog box.

    c. Change the type of the Date column to *Date*.

    d. Remove the columns Release Date.1, Release Date.2, and Release Date.3.

> **Note** In steps 6–10, you will learn the alternative way to create the date. Before you proceed, you should duplicate the current query so you can keep both versions.

5. To duplicate the Products query, right-click Products in the Queries pane and select Duplicate. A new query, Products (2), is created. Select it and in Applied Steps, delete the last three steps (including Added Custom).

6. Using the Ctrl key, select the three split date columns in this order: Release Date.1, Release Date.2, and Release Date.3. Now, on the Add Column tab, select Merge Columns. The Merge Columns dialog box opens.

    a. Select --Custom as the separator and then enter a forward slash character (/) in the box below.

    b. Enter *US Date* in the New Column Name box and click OK to close the dialog box.

7. Now, create a date column for the UK locale. Using the Ctrl key, select the three split date columns in this order: Release Date.2, Release Date.1, and Release Date.3. Now, on the Add Column tab, select Merge Columns. The Merge Columns dialog box opens.

    a. Select --Custom as the separator and then enter forward slash character (/) in the box below.

    b. Enter *UK Date* in the New Column Name box and click OK to close the dialog box.

    You now have the columns US Date and UK Date with different date formats. It's time to select which date format to choose for each row.

8. On the Add Column tab, select Conditional Column. The Add Conditional Column dialog box opens. Follow these steps to set the dialog as shown in Figure 2-13:

    a. Enter *Date* in the New Column Name box.

    b. Select Country from the Column Name drop-down.

    c. Select Equals as the operator and enter *US* in the box under Value.

d. In the drop-down menu below Output, select Select a Column and then select US Date.

e. In the drop-down menu below the Otherwise label, select Select a Column and then select UK Date.

f. Ensure that your settings match the screenshot in Figure 2-13 and click OK to close the Add Conditional Column dialog box.

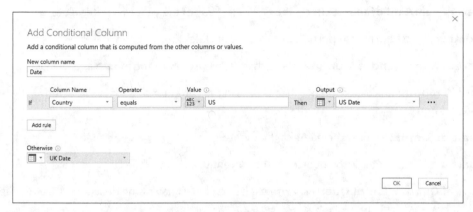

FIGURE 2-13 You can add a conditional column to select the correct date by country.

9. Change the type of the Date column to Date.

10. Remove the columns Release Date.1, Release Date.2, Release Date.3, US Date, and UK Date.

11. Load the query to your Excel workbook or Power BI report. The dates are displayed according to your Windows Locale settings, and you do not have any errors.

You can download the solution files C02E06 - Solution.xlsx and C02E06 - Solution.pbix from https://aka.ms/DataPwrBIPivot/downloads.

Extracting Date and Time Elements

Now you have Date or DateTime columns in your queries, and the format is consistent. How can you extract meaningful elements from such values? The Power Query Editor includes a wide variety of functions, as well as transformations in the Transform and Add Column tabs, to enable you to extract years, quarters, months, days, and many other calculated elements in order to enrich your dataset with time intelligence.

Here are some of the useful transformation steps, which are available on the Transform and Add Column tabs, under the Date drop-down menus when you select a Date or Date/Time column:

- **Age:** You assign this transformation on a selected Date or Date/Time column to calculate the elapsed time since the specific date. This is implemented by subtracting the current Date/Time from the specific value.

- **Date Only:** Extracts the date portion from the selected Date/Time column. Combined with the transformation Time Only, you can transform a Date/Time column into two separate columns, of types Date and Time, which simplifies your model and reduces the size of your report and memory consumption.

- **Year:** Extracts the year portion from a Date or Date/Time column.

- **Start of Year/End of Year:** Extracts the first or last day of the year as a Date value.

- **Month:** Extracts the month portion from a Date or Date/Time column.

- **Start of Month/End of Month:** Extracts the first or last day of the month as a Date value.

- **Days in Month:** Calculates the number of days in the current month of the selected Date column.

- **Name of Month:** Returns the name of the month.

- **Quarter of Year:** Returns the quarter of the current year.

- **Start of Quarter/End of Quarter:** Extracts the first or last day of the quarter as a Date value.

- **Week of Year/Week of Month:** Calculates the number of the week in the year or month.

- **Start of Week/End of Week:** Extracts the first or last day of the week as a Date value.

- **Day:** Extracts the day portion from a Date or Date/Time column.

- **Start of Day/End of Day:** Extracts the first or last date and time of the day from a Date/Time column.

- **Day of Week/Day of Year:** Calculates the number of the current day in the week or year.

- **Name of Day:** Returns the name of the day (for example, Sunday, Monday).

When you select multiple Date or Date/Time columns, you can also apply Subtract Days to calculate the elapsed time between the two dates or compute the earliest or latest dates.

Preparing the Model

Data preparation is key to the success of data analysis. To set the stage for effective analysis, you often need to split tables into multiple tables to ensure that you have a single flat table for facts or transactions (for example, Sales Order) and supplementary tables to support your facts (for example, Products, Clients).

In Exercise 2-2, Part 3, you learned how to create relationships between fact tables and lookup tables. While the modeling elements in Power Pivot and Power BI are not the focus of this book, the capability to shape your tables to meet your needs is indeed the focus. In the next three chapters, you will learn how to combine multiple tables to simplify your model. In Chapter 6, "Unpivoting Tables," you will learn how to break down complex table structures to better support your analysis.

In this section, you will learn the imperative preparation steps that allow you to split an aggregated table into multiple tables, to build star schemas, and to control the granularity of your entities.

Exercise 2-7: Splitting Data into Lookup Tables and Fact Tables

In this exercise, you will import sample data from another fictitious company: Wide World Importers. This dataset, which is richer and newer than the AdventureWorks dataset, is also provided by Microsoft for learning purposes. To learn more about this data sample, go to https://blogs.technet.microsoft.com/dataplatforminsider/2016/06/09/wideworldimporters-the-new-sql-server-sample-database/.

The workbook C02E07.xlsx which can be downloaded from https://aka.ms/DataPwrBIPivot/downloads, summarizes Wide World Importers orders. The goal of this exercise is to show you how easy it is to use Power Query to split a table into a fact table and a lookup table by using the Reference and Remove Duplicate options.

1. Download the workbook C02E07.xslx and save it in the folder *C:\Data\C02*.

2. Open a new blank Excel workbook or a new Power BI Desktop report and import the workbook C02E07.xslx to the Power Query Editor.

3. In the Navigator dialog, select the Sales_Order table and then select Edit.

4. Rename the Sales_Order query *Sales Order - Base*.

   Your goal here is to split the original table into two tables, with the correct granularity levels, as shown in Figure 2-14. One of the tables (the bottom left table in Figure 2-14) is for the orders and their stock item identifiers (the fact table), and the second (the bottom right table in Figure 2-14) is for the stock items (the lookup table).

OrderID	Order Date	Quantity	Unit Price	Stock ID	Stock Item	Stock Lead Time
1	1/1/2013	10	230	67	Ride on toy sedan car (Black) 1/12 scale	14
2	1/1/2013	9	13	50	Developer joke mug - old C developers never die (White)	12
2	1/1/2013	9	32	10	USB food flash drive - chocolate bar	14
3	1/1/2013	3	30	114	Superhero action jacket (Blue) XXL	12
4	1/1/2013	2	13	50	Developer joke mug - old C developers never die (White)	12
4	1/1/2013	5	32	130	Furry gorilla with big eyes slippers (Black) S	12
4	1/1/2013	96	2.7	206	Permanent marker black 5mm nib (Black) 5mm	14
5	1/1/2013	3	32	121	Dinosaur battery-powered slippers (Green) XL	12

OrderID	Order Date	Quantity	Unit Price	Stock ID
1	1/1/2013	10	230	6
2	1/1/2013	9	13	5
2	1/1/2013	9	32	1
3	1/1/2013	3	30	11
4	1/1/2013	2	13	5
4	1/1/2013	5	32	13
4	1/1/2013	96	2.7	20

Stock ID	Stock Item	Stock Lead Time
1	USB missile launcher (Green)	14
2	USB rocket launcher (Gray)	14
3	Office cube periscope (Black)	14
4	USB food flash drive - sushi roll	14
5	USB food flash drive - hamburger	14
6	USB food flash drive - hot dog	14
7	USB food flash drive - pizza slice	14

FIGURE 2-14 You can split the Sales Order table into a fact table and a lookup table.

5.   Right-click Sales Order - Base and select Reference. Rename the new query *Stock Items*. (To rename the query, right-click the query in the Queries pane and select Rename in the shortcut menu, or rename the query in the Query Settings pane, under Properties, in the Name box.)

6.   Select the Stock Items query, and in Home tab, select Choose Columns.

7.   In the Choose Columns dialog box that opens, deselect all columns and then select the columns Stock ID, Stock Item, and Stock Lead Time. Click OK to close the dialog box.

8.   Select the Stock ID column, and on Home tab, select Remove Rows and then Remove Duplicates.

You now have a lookup table for the stock items, with unique stock items on each row.

> **Note** If you have multiple Stock ID values in the stock items table, you will not be able to create the relationship in step 13. This exercise deliberately avoids two crucial steps that are explained at the end of this exercise. Without these steps, Remove Duplicates by itself will not be sufficient to ensure that your lookup table has unique Stock ID values, and, as a result, the refresh will fail.

9.   To create a new fact table for the orders, in the Queries pane, right-click on the Sales Order - Base query and select Reference.

10. Rename the new query *Sales Orders*. (To rename the query, right-click the query in the Queries pane and select Rename in the shortcut menu, or rename it in the Query Settings pane, under Properties, in the Name box.)

11. Select the Sales Orders query, and on the Home tab, select Choose Columns. The Choose Columns dialog box opens. Deselect the columns Stock Item and Stock Lead Time. Click OK to close the dialog box.

12. **In Excel:** On the Home tab, select Close & Load To to avoid loading the base query into your worksheet or Data Model. Then, in the Queries and Connections pane, select Sales Orders and Stock Items and load them into the Data Model, using the Load To option, as you did in Exercise 2-2, Part 2 step 11.

     In Power BI Desktop: Disable the loading of Sales Order - Base, as you did in Exercise 2-2, Part 2 step 11.

13. Create a relationship between the two tables through the Stock ID columns.

When a Relationship Fails

When you create lookup tables in Power Query, as you did in Exercise 2-7, and you use text columns as keys in the relationship, two additional steps must be performed before you remove the duplicate keys in step 8 to ensure that your report does not fail to refresh.

In Exercise 2-7, in step 8 you removed the duplicate Stock ID values from the lookup table. Unfortunately, Power Query was designed differently than the Data Model in Excel and Power BI. While Power

Query is always case sensitive, the Data Model is not. As a result, if your Stock ID value, *"Stock_1"*, will include a lowercase or uppercase variant (e.g. *"STOCK_1"*) or will include a trailing space (e.g. *"Stock_1 "*), Power Query will keep the two instances as unique values, but the Data Model will consider them duplicates and will issue the following error:

```
Column 'Stock ID' in Table 'Stock Items' contains a duplicate value 'Stock_1' and this is
not allowed for columns on the one side of a many-to-one relationship or for columns that
are used as the primary key of a table.
```

To experience this error, open the workbook C02E07.xslx, and modify two of the Stock ID values. Change one of the values to uppercase, and add a space character at the end of another value. Then save the workbook and try to refresh your Exercise 2-7 solution workbook or Power BI report.

To fix this issue, apply the following steps on the Sales Orders - Base query:

1. Launch the Power Query Editor and select the Sales Orders - Base query.

2. Select the Stock ID column, and in the Transform tab, select Format and then select Lowercase or Uppercase or Capitalize Each Word. Any of these three options will ensure that the keys are normalized, so variations of lowercase/uppercase values will be removed as duplicate values by Power Query.

3. Select the Stock ID column, and on the Transform tab, select Format and then Trim.

4. Refresh the workbook or report, and the error does not occur again.

Referencing and removing duplicates to create lookup tables are common steps. Many users who apply the Remove Duplicates step are not aware of the potential refresh failures that could occur for a dataset that contains lowercase/uppercase variations or trailing spaces. Oftentimes, the errors even appear sooner, as the users try to build the relationship. Handling the case-sensitive values and trimming the spaces before the removal of duplicates will resolve these issues.

Download the solution files C02E07 - Solution.xlsx and C02E07 - Solution.pbix from https://aka.ms/DataPwrBIPivot/downloads.

> **See Also** The pitfall of failing to apply these steps to prevent relationship refresh failures, is described at my blog at https://datachant.com/2017/02/14/power-bi-pitfall-10/. In Chapter 10, you will learn about more common pitfalls, or common errors that expose your reports to serious failures.

Exercise 2-8: Splitting Delimiter-Separated Values into Rows

In the preceding section, you learned how to split tables into fact and lookup tables. In this exercise, you will learn about a special case of fact and lookup tables. Imagine that your fact table acts as a mapping table that associates between members' entities and their group unique identifiers. The lookup table in this scenario describes the group entities.

In this exercise, you will again use the AdventureWorks product table. Each product can be shipped in one or more colors. The associated colors are represented in comma-separated values, as illustrated in Figure 2-15, in the table to the left. In this exercise, you will learn how to split the products table into two tables: one for the entities (in this case, the products entities, without the colors) and the other one for the associations between groups and their members (in this case, product codes and colors).

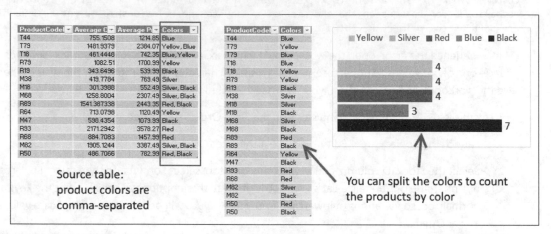

FIGURE 2-15 You can split the comma-separated AdventureWorks product colors column to find how many products are released by color.

For this exercise, you will use the sample workbook C02E08.xlsx, which can be downloaded from https://aka.ms/DataPwrBIPivot/downloads. The sample workbook summarizes AdventureWorks product codes by average cost, average price, and comma-separated colors. To create a report that shows the number of products of each color, as shown in Figure 2-15, do the following.

1. Download the workbook C02E08.xslx and save it in the folder *C:\Data\C02*.

2. Open a new blank Excel workbook or a new Power BI Desktop report and import the workbook C02E08.xslx from *C:\Data\C02* to the Power Query Editor.

3. In the Navigator dialog, select Products and then select Edit.

4. In the Queries pane, right-click Products and select Reference. Your goal is to create a new table with a mapping between the product codes and the colors.

5. Rename the new query *Products and Colors*. (To rename the query, you can right-click the query in the Queries pane and select Rename in the shortcut menu, or you can rename the query in the Query Settings pane, under Properties, in the Name box.)

6. With the new query selected, on the Home tab, select Choose Columns.

7. In the Choose Columns dialog box that opens, select ProductCodeNew and Colors and click OK to close the dialog box.

8. Select the Colors column, and on the Transform tab, select Split Column and then select By Delimiter.

9. In the Split Column by Delimiter dialog box that opens, note that the comma delimiter is selected by default, along with the option Each Occurrence of the Delimiter (see Figure 2-16). Expand the Advanced Options section and switch the Split Into option from Columns to Rows. Click OK to close the dialog box.

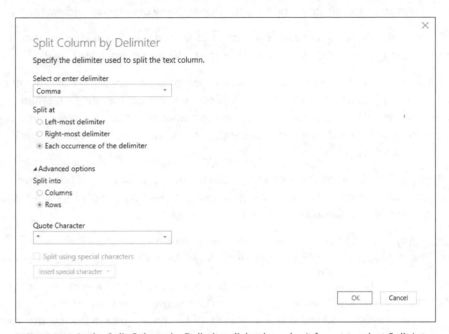

FIGURE 2-16 In the Split Column by Delimiter dialog box, don't forget to select Split Into, and then select Rows under Advanced Options.

10. In the Colors and Products query, select the Colors column. On the Transform tab, select Format and then select Trim. This step removes the leading spaces from the color values.

You can now load the two tables into the Data Model in Excel or Power BI Desktop and create a relationship between ProductCodeNew in Products and ProductCodeNew in Products and Colors. You can download and review the solution files C02E08 - Solution.xlsx and C02E08 - Solution.pbix from https://aka.ms/DataPwrBIPivot/downloads.

Tip To minimize the size of your report, you should remove the Colors column from the final Products table. However, if you try to do it now, you will get errors, as the Products query is referenced by Products and Colors. To resolve this issue and make it possible to remove Colors from Products, you need to create a new reference from Products and remove the Colors column from the referencing query. Then ensure that the original Products query is used only as a base query and will not get loaded to the Data Model or report. (In Exercise 2-2, Part 2, you learned how to disable the loading.)

Summary

Data preparation can be extremely time-consuming. But with the rich transformation capabilities available in the Power Query Editor, you can clean and prepare any dataset for analysis. This chapter introduced you to common data challenges and the ways Power Query provides to address them.

In Exercise 2-2 you learned how Power Query can extract codes and how to associate meaning with these codes, without the complex and difficult-to-maintain formulas presented in Exercise 2-1.

In Exercise 2-3, you were introduced to a very useful capability to extract meaning from columns, using examples. You saw that Column from Examples enables you to extract text, date, time, and numbers and offers a variety of transformations, based on the output examples you provide. You saw how this feature can be used to extract text between delimiters, apply a conditional column, and create buckets from ranges of numbers.

In Exercise 2-4, you learned how to parse hyperlinks from textual feed and apply different transformation techniques to achieve your goals. One of the most important lessons from this exercise is that you should audit your queries as often as possible and look for edge cases.

A common and highly time-consuming challenge involves handling inconsistent dates in your datasets. In Exercises 2-5 and 2-6, you learned how simple it is address inconsistent dates in Power Query.

Finally, in Exercises 2-7 and 2-8, you learned how to split a table into a fact table and a lookup table by using the Reference and Remove Duplicates options. You also learned how to avoid refresh errors by using Lowercase and Trim transformations, as well as how to split comma-separated values into rows to build group/members tables.

Even though you are still close to the beginning of this book, based on the exercises you have completed so far, you can probably reduce your data cleansing efforts by thousands of hours. In the next chapter, you will learn how to combine multiple tables and further reduce your time to insight.

CHAPTER 3

Combining Data from Multiple Sources

The attempt to combine wisdom and power has only rarely been successful and then only for a short while.

—Albert Einstein

IN THIS CHAPTER, YOU WILL

- Append tables from a few specified data sources

- Append multiple Excel workbooks from a folder

- Append multiple worksheets from an Excel workbook

While Albert Einstein's quote may be correct, and wisdom and power have only rarely been combined successfully, with Power Query you have the power to combine multiple sources to gain a lasting wisdom. In this chapter you will learn how to combine multiple tables in various levels of complexity to gain insights from the combined datasets.

Chapter 2, "Basic Data Preparation Challenges," discusses different scenarios of badly formatted and unprepared data. Often the data you need to deal with will be well formatted but dispersed over multiple data sources. In such scenarios, the main challenge is to combine the data together to bring the separate silos into a single source of wisdom. Appending multiple tables is the focus of this chapter.

This chapter starts with basic append scenarios for a small number of tables with a common format and moves on to tackle real-life challenges such as ever-changing data sources.

Appending a Few Tables

One of the most common features in Power Query is Append Queries, which is available on the Home tab of the Power Query Editor. It enables you to append together a predefined set of tables. For simplicity, this chapter starts with appending two tables that share the same format (that is, they both have the same column names).

Appending Two Tables

Before we jump to how to append two tables together, let's review the rationale for appending the two tables together to perform the analysis rather than keeping them separated. Why shouldn't you just copy and paste the two tables into a new Excel workbook, each one pasted into a separate worksheet, and use a third worksheet for the required computations? While this approach might be simple for tables with few rows and columns, performing such calculations on larger and ever-changing tables is a completely different ballgame.

Here is how you would approach this challenge in Excel without Power Query: You would need to copy and paste the tables and append them manually into a single table. Whenever the data changed, you would need to copy and paste the table again. Alternatively, you would need to create complex calculations to summarize the ranges in the different worksheets. Whenever the dataset size changed, you would need to update the ranges in your formulas. Fortunately, you can use Power Query to automate this rigorous process. Next time you have new data in your tables, a mere refresh will do the work for you.

Exercise 3-1: Bikes and Accessories Example

This exercise involves two tables from the fictional AdventureWorks bike company, introduced in Chapter 2. To help place the problem in a business context, imagine that AdventureWorks, whose main product line is bikes, acquires a new company that enriches the product portfolio with accessories products. As the chief analyst for AdventureWorks, you are asked to create a new report based on the unified product lines (see Figure 3-1).

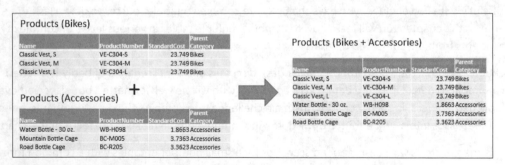

FIGURE 3-1 Your business problem is how to append the Bikes and Accessories tables into a single Products table.

To append the Bikes and Accessories tables, you can start from a new Excel workbook or a Power BI Desktop report and import the two tables as separate queries. You can follow the steps of this exercise after you download the files C03E01 - Bikes.xlsx and C03E01 - Accessories.xlsx from https://aka.ms/DataPwrBIPivot/downloads.

1. Open a blank new Excel workbook or a Power BI Desktop.

    In Excel: On the Data tab, select Get Data, From File, From Workbook.

    In Power BI Desktop: Select Get Data, Excel, Connect.

2. Select the file C03E01 - Bikes.xlsx and select Import.

3. In the Navigator, select Bikes and select Edit.

4. In the Power Query Editor, select Close & Load To. If you use Power BI Desktop, select Close & Apply and skip step 5.

5. In the Import Data dialog box, select Table and click OK. You now have all the Bikes data imported to your new workbook or Power BI Desktop. Whenever the data in C03E01 - Bikes.xlsx changes, and new bikes are added to the product line, you can obtain the latest data by clicking Refresh All on the Data tab of Excel or by pressing Ctrl+Alt+F5. If you use Power BI Desktop, you can simply select Refresh on the Home tab.

It's time to import Accessories into the workbook or Power BI report.

6. **In Excel:** On the Data tab, select Get Data, From File, From Workbook.

   In Power BI Desktop: On the Home tab, select Get Data, select Excel, and select Connect.

7. Select the file C03E01 - Accessories.xlsx and select Import.

8. In the Navigator, select Accessories and select Edit.

9. To append Bikes to Accessories in the Power Query Editor, ensure that the Accessories query is selected and select Append Queries on the Home tab. Note that the Append Queries drop-down also includes the option Append Queries as New, which will be described in Exercise 3-2.

10. When the Append dialog box opens, select Bikes as the table to append, and click OK.

11. **In Excel:** Expand the Queries pane (the pane on the left side of the Power Query Editor).

    In Power BI Desktop: Ensure that the Queries pane is expanded (the pane on the left side of the Power Query Editor).

    Notice that you have two queries in the Queries pane: Bikes and Accessories. As you have just appended the query Bikes into Accessories, the query name doesn't represent the appended data. You should therefore rename the Accessories query and ensure that this query, and not Bikes, will be loaded to the Excel workbook or Power BI report. To rename it, right-click the query Accessories, select Rename, and rename it *Products*. You can also rename the query in the Properties section of the Query Settings pane.

12. Follow these steps to unload Bikes:

    In Excel:

    a. Select Close & Load To.

    b. In the Import Data dialog box, select Table and click OK.

    c. To unload Bikes from the workbook, in the Queries & Connections pane, right-click the query Bikes and select Load To.

d. In the Import Data dialog box, select Only Create Connection and click OK.

e. When the Possible Data Loss dialog box opens, click OK to unload the query and delete the table.

f. Finally, delete Sheet2 if this is where you initially loaded the Bikes table, and rename the last sheet *Products*.

In Power BI Desktop: Right-click Bikes in the Queries pane, deselect Enable Load, and select Close & Apply.

You now have an appended Products table that contains the combined data from Bikes and Accessories. But if you take a closer look at the Queries pane, you will notice the asymmetrical nature of the append step. You now have the Bikes query and the combined Products query. But where is Accessories? Recall that right after importing Accessories, you appended Bikes to it and renamed it Products. In the future, if you want to apply some changes to the Accessories table, it will be difficult to find the right step to modify, as you now have a query with the combined transformation steps of Accessories and the appended Products table. A cleaner approach would be to have Accessories as a separate query—and this is why the Append Queries transformation has a sibling transformation called Append Queries as New.

Exercise 3-2, Part 1: Using Append Queries as New

The Home tab of the Power Query Editor enables you to append multiple queries in the Combine section in two ways: by using Append Queries or Append Queries as New (see Figure 3-2).

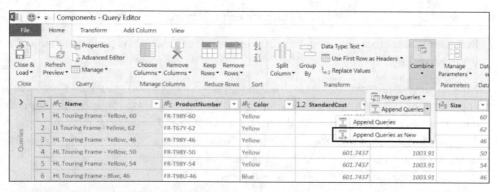

FIGURE 3-2 The transformation Append Queries as New enables you to have separate queries for the appended table and its parts.

In the preceding exercise you appended two tables by using the **Append Queries** transformation, which appends the second query to the current one. **Append Queries as New** creates a third query that combines the two queries, and thus, the two queries remain unaffected.

Instead of repurposing Accessories to include all the products, in this exercise you will keep Accessories as a separate query and create a new one for the products.

1. Follow steps 1–8 in Exercise 3-1 to load the queries Bikes and Accessories into the Power Query Editor.

2. In the Power Query Editor, ensure that the Accessories query is selected, and select Append Queries as New in the Append Queries drop-down on the Home tab.

3. When the Append dialog box opens, select Bikes as the table to append to the primary table and click OK. You now have a new query, Append1, with the combined Bikes and Accessories data.

4. Rename the new query *Products* and follow Exercise 3-1 step 12 to unload Bikes. To unload Accessories, you can again follow step 12, but this time apply the instructions on Accessories instead of Bikes.

5. Save your workbook or Power BI report. Next you will learn another method to append Bikes and Accessories into a new query—by using the Reference option. You will also compare the underlying M expression of the two methods.

> **Tip** When you append a small set of tables, it is recommended to use Append Queries as New instead of Append Queries so that in the future you can easily edit the separate building blocks of the appended table.

Exercise 3-2, Part 2: Query Dependencies and References

In Exercise 3-2 Part 1, you applied Append Queries as New, which resulted in a new query that combined Bikes and Accessories. The new query referenced the other two queries and used their output as its input. When a query is referencing another query, a dependency between the queries is established. When a query has dependencies on other queries, you cannot delete it. (If you try to delete Bikes, for example, you will get a prompt that prevents you from deleting it, as Products is dependent on it.)

To view dependencies between queries, open the Excel workbook or Power BI report that you created in Exercise 3-2 Part 1 and launch the Power Query Editor. On the View tab, select Query Dependencies. The Query Dependencies dialog box opens, as shown in Figure 3-3.

The Query Dependencies dialog box shows a flow diagram, which starts from the bikes and accessories files as the data sources, flows through the intermediate queries Bikes and Accessories, and finally ends at Products, where you appended the two tables. This view will come in handy when you work on complex data preparation scenarios.

Now that you know how to view the dependencies between queries, you're ready to learn about references, which enable you to create rich and reusable data transformation flows and tackle real-life data challenges. A reference can be used to create a new query whose source, or input data, is the output of another query.

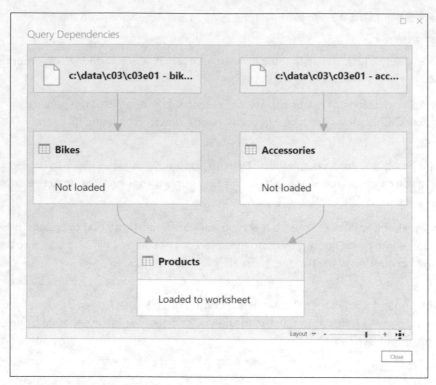

FIGURE 3-3 Query Dependencies dialog box shows the references and dependencies between the queries of a report.

Earlier, in Exercise 3-2 Part 1, you loaded Bikes and Accessories as queries and applied Append Queries as New to create a new query with the appended results. An alternative method to reach the same outcome can be achieved by using a combination of Append Queries and Reference:

1. Follow steps 1–8 in Exercise 3-1 to load the queries Bikes and Accessories into the Power Query Editor.

2. Open the Queries pane and right-click Accessories. Select Reference and notice that you now have a new query, Accessories (2), which starts with the output of Accessories.

3. Rename Accessories (2) to *Products*.

4. With the Products query selected, select Append Queries on the Home tab to append Bikes to Products: When the Append dialog box opens, select Bikes as the table to append and click OK.

Now you can examine how Power Query handled the Reference and Append Queries steps in the underlying M formulas and compare the output of the Reference and Append Queries combination with the output of Exercise 3-2 Part 1. Let's examine the underlying M code.

> **See Also** Recall that Chapter 1, "Introduction to Power Query," introduces M code, which is generated by Power Query to execute the transformation steps. Each transformation step that you create in the Power Query Editor is translated into a line of code, which can be seen in the formula bar.

On the View tab, select Formula Bar and then select Source in Applied Steps of the Query Settings pane. Here is the M formula you see:

```
= Accessories
```

This code represents the output of the Accessories query, which is used as the input for the new query. As you might guess, this code was generated by applying Reference on Accessories.

Click Advanced Editor on the Home tab to review the M expression:

```
let
    Source = Accessories,
    #"Appended Query" = Table.Combine({Source, Bikes})
in
    #"Appended Query"
```

Chapter 9, "Introduction to the Power Query M Formula Language," covers this syntax in more detail and explains the meaning of *let* and *in*, but for now, you can just focus on the two lines between *let* and *in*.

The first line after *let* places the output of the query Accessories in Source. (You can see that Source is also the first step in the Applied Steps pane.) The second line uses *Table.Combine* to append between Source and Bikes—and this is an append operation between Accessories and Bikes. (You may have noticed that the queries are wrapped in curly brackets, which are explained in the next section. Hint: Curly brackets are used to create a list.)

If you now look at the M code that was generated when you followed Exercise 3-2 Part 1 using Append Queries as New, you find the following code in the Advanced Editor:

```
let
    Source = Table.Combine({Accessories, Bikes})
in
    Source
```

If you look closely at these two sections of code, you will see that the two expressions return the same output: the combined tables of Accessories and Bikes.

To conclude this exercise, you can use a combination of Reference and Append Queries to get the same results as when you use Append Queries as New. While the latter technique leads to fewer lines of codes and takes only a single user interface step instead of two, there is no real difference between the two methods. So why did we introduce the Reference option? As you will see in later chapters, Reference can be very helpful in creating a pipeline of transformation queries or multiple transformation branches of the same base query.

Appending Three or More Tables

So far in this chapter, you learned how to append two tables. It's time to move to a more generic challenge: how to append three tables or more. One approach to this challenge is to start by appending two tables and then to append the output of the two tables with a third table. Next, you can append the output of these steps with a fourth table, and so forth. While this approach can work well, it is difficult to maintain, as it requires the creation of intermediate queries. When you need to append three or four tables, it is not a significant price to pay, but with a larger number of queries, a better approach is required.

Exercise 3-2, Part 3: Bikes + Accessories + Components

Let's return to our fictional story. After the successful integration of the accessories product line with bikes, AdventureWorks decides to acquire a new company and extend its portfolio to components. Your goal as the chief analyst is to append the product lines into a single table.

For this exercise, you can download the following three workbooks from https://aka.ms/ DataPwrBIPivot/downloads:

- C03E01 - Bikes.xlsx

- C03E01 - Accessories.xlsx

- C03E01 - Components.xlsx

Open a new blank Excel or a new Power BI Desktop and import the three Excel workbooks into the Power Query Editor. Each workbook contains a single worksheet with a corresponding name (that is, a Bike worksheet in C03E01 - Bikes.xlsx, an Accessories worksheet in C03E01 - Accessories.xlsx, and a Components worksheet in C03E01 - Components.xlsx). If you're not sure how to import these workbooks, see Exercise 3-1 for the steps to load Bikes and Accessories. Then apply similar steps for Components.

1. In the Queries pane of the Power Query Editor, select Components.

2. On the Home tab, select Append Queries as New.

3. When the Append dialog box opens, select Three or More Tables. The Available Table(s) and Tables to Append lists appear, as shown in Figure 3-4. You can find Bikes and Accessories under Available Table(s).

4. Add Bikes and Accessories to the Tables to Append list and click OK.

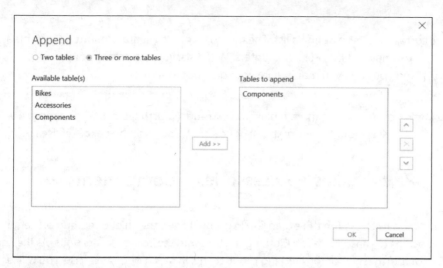

FIGURE 3-4 The Append dialog box with the Three or More Tables option enables you to select multiple queries to append.

You now have a new query, Append1, with the combined product line. From here, you can rename it *Products* and unload the intermediate queries as you learned in Exercise 3-1.

> **Tip** In the Append dialog box, shown in Figure 3-4, you can control the order of the tables in the appended table. You can select a table and change its order in the list by clicking the up and down arrows on the right side of Tables to Append. You can even add a table multiple times to Tables to Append to duplicate the data in the appended table.

Now that you have appended Bikes, Accessories, and Components, you can see how easy it is to apply the same transformation in the formula bar of the Power Query Editor. When the Products query is selected, you can see the following formula:

```
= Table.Combine({Components, Bikes, Accessories})
```

Do you find this familiar? Earlier, when you appended two tables, the formula bar included the following code:

```
= Table.Combine({Accessories, Bikes})
```

From the syntax of this formula, you can see that *Table.Combine* is the function that is used to execute the append transformation of multiple tables. The function can hold multiple tables inside curly brackets.

> **Note** M uses curly brackets to define a list. The members of the list are separated by commas. You will see more examples of lists in later chapters. With lists, you can create powerful transformations, and you can even manipulate your query at runtime.

Now that you know how to append three tables, you can add a fourth table, but this time you will do it by using code only. (Keep your Excel workbook or Power BI report for the next exercise.)

Exercise 3-2, Part 4: Bikes + Accessories + Components + Clothing

Let's return to our fictional story. With the expansion in product lines, the chief operating officer of AdventureWorks decides to consolidate the Clothing division with the core business units. As the chief analyst, you receive a fourth table for the clothing product line. In part 4 of this exercise, you will learn how to append the four tables together—this time using M and without the Append dialog box.

For this exercise, you can download the workbook C03E01 - Clothing.xlsx from https://aka.ms/ DataPwrBIPivot/downloads. Open the Excel workbook or Power BI Desktop report from Exercise 3-2 Part 3 and import Clothing as a new query. (See Exercise 3-1 for the steps to load Bikes and Accessories. Then apply similar steps for Clothing.) Rename the new query *Clothing*.

In the Power Query Editor, select the Products query. Look at the formula bar. You should see the following formula:

```
= Table.Combine({Components, Bikes, Accessories})
```

You need to modify it by adding *Clothing* anywhere inside the curly brackets. Make sure that all four tables are comma separated inside the curly brackets. When you are done, press Enter. Your formula can look like any of the following:

```
= Table.Combine({Clothing, Components, Bikes, Accessories})
```

Or

```
= Table.Combine({Components, Clothing, Bikes, Accessories})
```

Or

```
= Table.Combine({Components, Bikes, Accessories, Clothing})
```

To verify that the *Table.Combine* worked, click the filter control in the header of the ParentProduct-CategoryName column. When the Filter pane opens, you should see four values: Accessories, Bikes, Components, and Clothing. Checking the values in the Filter pane is an easy and practical method to audit your transformation steps.

Now that you have appended Clothing to the products, you're ready to move to new scenarios and learn how to append multiple tables on a larger scale.

Appending Tables on a Larger Scale

In the preceding section you learned how to append multiple tables by using Append Queries and Append Queries as New in the Power Query Editor. While these transformations come in handy when you have a predefined set of table names, in some common scenarios, you cannot know in advance which table names are available, and you are required to create a report of the combined data on a frequent basis. So a manual manipulation of the queries to include the current table names each time they change, may be a time-consuming effort you would better avoid.

Appending Tables from a Folder

The most common scenario, and its challenge, can be demonstrated in this example: Imagine that you have multiple tables that you need to append. Each table is in a separate Excel workbook whose name includes a different year and month:

- Jan2018.xlsx

- Feb2018.xlsx

- Mar2018.xslx

- Apr2018.xslx

Each month, a new Excel workbook is added to a shared folder, and you are asked to prepare an updated report that appends all the tables from the folder. Say that you have already created a report that separately imports each of the tables and appends them using the preceding technique. When a new file is added (for example: May2018.xlsx), you would need to follow a sequence of manual steps to modify the queries: First you would import the Excel file as a new query, named May2018. Then you would edit the append step in Applied Steps in the Power Query Editor to include the new query. You could add the query in the following formula (with the change highlighted in bold):

```
= Table.Combine({Jan2018, Feb2018, Mar2018, Apr2018, May2018})
```

This method will ultimately become very tedious if you need to repeat it each month. Wouldn't it be better if you could create an improved query that will automatically append any workbook from the folder—with a single refresh of the workbook and with no manual edits to the query? This is possible, thanks to the import from Folder option.

Exercise 3-3: Appending AdventureWorks Products from a Folder

Let's return to AdventureWorks for an illustration of the challenge at hand. Say that an IT VBA developer created a script that updates an Excel file whenever a new product is released. Each year, a new Excel file is created, and it is updated on the fly with newly released products. The product files are aggregated in a shared folder, as shown in Figure 3-5. As the chief analyst, you would like to create a report that combines all products.

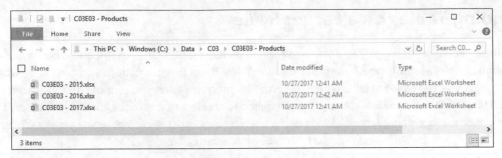

FIGURE 3-5 In this example, AdventureWorks collects Excel workbooks with products by their release year in a shared folder.

To follow the steps in this exercise, you can download the file C03E03 - Products.zip from https://aka.ms/DataPwrBIPivot/downloads and extract the Excel files into the folder *c:\Data\C03\C03E03 - Products*).

1. Open a blank new workbook in Excel or a new Power BI Desktop report.

   In Excel: On the Data tab or on the Home tab, select Get Data, From File, From Folder.

   In Power BI Desktop: On the Home tab, select Get Data, File, Folder and select Connect

2. In the Folder dialog box that opens, browse to the folder created earlier (refer to Figure 3-5) or copy and paste its path to the Folder path and click OK.

3. In the new dialog box that opens (titled with the name of the folder name you selected in step 2), select Combine and then select Combine and Edit.

> **Tip** It is not recommended to use the Combine and Load option, which combines all files and loads the appended result to the report, without the opportunity to edit it. As a good practice, when you are not sure which files should be combined, select Edit in the dialog box described in step 3. The Power Query Editor opens with a preview of the folder and enables you to apply filters on the files you want to combine. For example, if you have other types of documents in the folder, you can filter the files by the extension .xlsx to combine only the Excel files and ignore the other types. You can then combine the files in the Power Query Editor by selecting the Combine Files in the header of the Content column.

4. In the Combine Files dialog box that opens, select Sheet1, as shown in Figure 3-6, and click OK.

> **Note** The Combine Files dialog box is equivalent to the Navigator dialog box that opens when you load a single Excel workbook. In the Navigator you can select the worksheet or table to edit or load to the report, in the Combine Files dialog box you can select the worksheet or table to use from all the files in the folder. You need to apply your selection on a sampled workbook and worksheet, and then that selection will be applied to all the other workbooks in the folder.

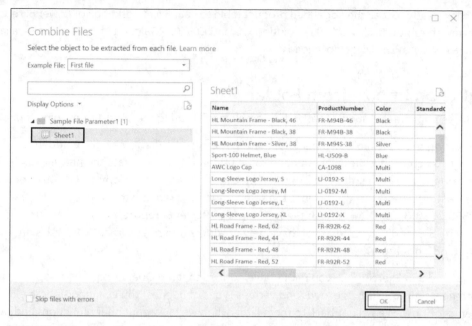

FIGURE 3-6 Combine Files enables you to select the worksheet or table to combine. Once selected, all worksheets or tables with the same name in each Excel workbook in the folder will be combined.

5. In the Power Query Editor that opens, look in the preview pane, and see that the first column, Source.Name, contains the file names. Click in the filter control of the Source.Name header. In the Filter pane, you will notice that the values in this column are the same as the actual file names in the folder.

The Source.Name column can sometimes be of significant value. In the preceding example, the column SellStartDate shows the release date of each product in AdventureWorks. The release year can be extracted from this column if years are needed in the report. However, in many cases you wouldn't have such a column, and the contextual information will be available only in the file name. Fortunately, you can extract this contextual information from Source.Name.

To extract the year 2017 from C03E03 - 2017.xlsx in Source.Name, you can apply different transformation techniques. Chapter 2 provides a detailed walkthrough on similar scenarios, so we highlight just a few of them in this context. The file names in this case contain the prefix C03E03 - and the suffix .xlsx, with the year in between. You can extract the year from Source.Name in two ways:

- Replace C03E03 - with an empty string, and then replace .xlsx with an empty string. You learned how to use Replace Values in Chapter 2.

- Alternatively, split Source.Name at 9 characters from the left (using Split by Number of Characters), and then split the second column with a dot, or alternatively split the second column by position at 4 characters from the right. Remove the first and third columns and keep the second column, which contains the extracted years.

You are now ready to load the appended product table to your Excel workbook or Power BI report. You can review the solution files C03E03 - Solution.xlsx and C03E03 - Solution.pbix, which are available at https://aka.ms/DataPwrBIPivot/downloads.

Thoughts on Import from Folder

There are three important elements involved in combining files using the Import from Folder option:

- Importing multiple tables from a folder is very powerful. When a new file is added, the query you created earlier will not need to be updated to incorporate the new file into the append transformation. To prove it, you can run a small test. Copy and paste one of the existing source workbooks into the same folder and rename the duplicated file C03E03 - 2018.xlsx. Now refresh the workbook or Power BI report that you have created in Exercise 3-3 and confirm that you have new products from the year 2018. Isn't this an outstanding feature?

- After step 5 in Exercise 3-3, you might have noticed that the Queries pane was populated with new artifacts such as groups and various types of queries. You can ignore these elements for now. We will get back to them later, when we talk about query functions and other advanced topics.

- You can combine multiple files from shared folders on a network or on SharePoint sites. Using shared folders enables you to share an Excel workbook or Power BI report with other report authors and refresh it. If you use Power BI, you can publish the report to the Power BI service and enjoy a scheduled refresh. When the folder is located on your SharePoint Online or OneDrive for Business, the Power BI service will have direct access to the data and can be configured to refresh it periodically. When the shared folder is local, you can use the Power BI On-Premises Gateway, so the Power BI service will have access to the folder to perform periodic refreshes.

Appending Worksheets from a Workbook

Let's look at one last large-scale table append scenario: combining tables from multiple worksheets. In the preceding example, you combined AdventureWorks products that were separated in different workbooks. Each workbook had its own products, by their release year. Imagine, however, that the same tables are stored on separate worksheets in the same Excel workbook. Can you append all worksheets into a single table, while keeping the context of the release year for each product, as shown in Figure 3-7? Can you also ensure that each year, you will not need to update the query when a new worksheet is added? How can you ensure that next year's products are automatically combined into your report when you click Refresh?

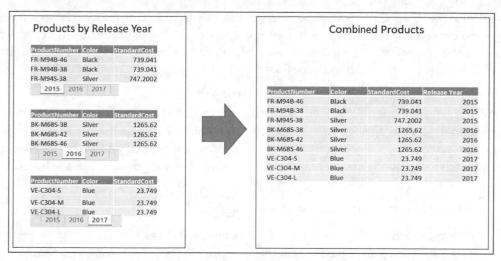

FIGURE 3-7 Your goal with the AdventureWorks products divided into separate worksheets by their release year is to append them, while keeping their release year context, and avoid further modification of the query for future years.

Exercise 3-4: Appending Worksheets: The Solution

To follow the solution for this challenge, you can download the file C03E04 - Year per Worksheet.xlsx from https://aka.ms/DataPwrBIPivot/downloads.

1. Open a blank new workbook in Excel or a new Power BI Desktop report.

    In Excel: On the Data tab, select Get Data, From File, From Workbook.

    In Power BI Desktop: On the Home tab, select Get Data, select File, Excel and select Connect.

2. Select the file C03E04 - Year per Worksheet.xlsx and select Import.

3. In the Navigator dialog box, select the line with the folder icon (in this example, C03E04 - Year per Worksheet.xlsx).

> **Note**   Do not select any of the specific worksheets in the Navigator dialog box. While you can do so, and can then append the worksheets as you did in Exercise 3-1, this solution will lead to undesired results for the long term. When new worksheets are added to the workbook, you will need to modify the queries and add the new worksheets. Instead, in step 3, you selected the entire workbook, which will allow you to build a robust solution.

    In Excel: Click Edit.

    In Power BI Desktop: If Edit is disabled, right-click C03E04 - Year per Worksheet.xlsx and select Edit from the shortcut menu.

4. When the Power Query Editor opens, rename the query *Products*. In the main Preview pane, you can see a table with each worksheet in a separate row. The actual content from each worksheet is encapsulated in the Data column. Before you combine the worksheets, you can remove the three columns: Item, Kind, and Hidden.

> **Tip** If you have hidden worksheets in your source workbook or specific worksheets with unrelated data, you can filter them out before all worksheets are appended in step 5; this is a good time to apply the necessary filters. For example, you can apply a filter on the Hidden column to keep only the rows containing the value FALSE to exclude hidden worksheets.

5. On the header of the Data column, click the expand button.

6. When the Expand pane opens, showing the columns you can expand, click OK to expand all columns. When you expand the Data column, the combined table has meaningless header names (Column1, Column2, and so forth) and contains both headers and rows from each worksheet, as shown in the first table in Figure 3-8.

> **Note** If your product tables in each worksheet consisted of Table objects, in step 6 you could expand the actual product column names, instead of having Column1, Column2, and so on. (To convert a range in Excel to tables, select the range or a single cell in a range and click Table on the Insert tab, or press Ctrl+T.)

The transformation flow diagram in Figure 3-8 outlines the three transformation steps that are required to clean the combined table. In the first step, you move up the first row, which was the headers row of table 2015, to become the headers of the combined table. Then, in the next step, you remove all the headers of worksheets 2016 and 2017. Finally, in the third step, you rename the 2015 column *Year* to represent the release year of each product. Throughout the book, we may use this type of diagram to depict the sequence of main transformations steps and capture the rationale for solving advanced data preparation problems. Next we look at the steps in more detail.

7. On the Transform tab, select Use First Row as Headers. This enables you to preserve the column headers from the first worksheet as the column headers for the appended table.

8. In the Preview pane, notice that the column headers of worksheets 2016 and 2017 are interspersed as rows throughout the appended table. These rows include the value Name in the Name column and should be removed from the table. To filter out these rows, click on the filter control in the left side of the Name header. When the Filter pane opens, type *Name* in the search box and deselect the value Name. Then click OK.

9. Double-click the first column header named 2015, and rename it *Release Year*.

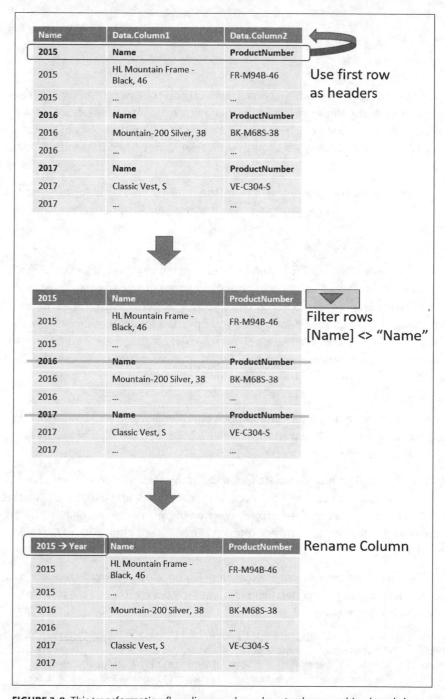

FIGURE 3-8 This transformation flow diagram shows how to clean combined worksheets.

Note Steps 7-9 may fail you in the long term. You will shortly learn why and how to resolve it.

You can now load the combined table to your Excel workbook or Power BI report. You have successfully combined the three worksheets by their release year and have extracted the release year of each product from the worksheet names. It's time to test the scalability of the solution and see if it will refresh correctly when a fourth worksheet is added with the products released in 2018.

10. With your Excel workbook or Power BI report with the combined products still open, open the source Excel file C03E04 - Year per Worksheet.xlsx that was used in this exercise. Duplicate the 2017 worksheet as a fourth worksheet and rename it *2018*.

Tip If you have the Power Query Editor open in Excel (and not in Power BI Desktop), you may have noticed that you cannot access other open workbooks or open more Excel workbooks via the File tab in Excel while the Power Query Editor is open. Hence, in step 10, you may need to close the Power Query Editor before you open the source workbook. To work around this limitation, you can start a new Excel instance via the taskbar or Start menu and open C03E04 - Year per Worksheet.xlsx. The new Excel instance will not be blocked by the current Power Query Editor window.

11. Refresh the Products query in your Excel workbook or Power BI report and ensure that the duplicated products from the 2018 worksheet are now appended with the value *2018* as their release date. You should find that it works!

   Add a 2014 worksheet with historical data for products released in 2014 as the first worksheet. To do it, you can duplicate one of the existing worksheets, and add it as the first worksheet in C03E04 - Year per Worksheet.xlsx. Now, when the leftmost worksheet is 2014 instead of 2015, the refresh fails, with this error: "*Expression.Error: The column '2015' of the table wasn't found.*"

12. For a short-term fix of this error, launch Power Query Editor, select the Products query in the Power Query Editor and select the step Changed Types in Applied Steps. In the formula bar, you see the following formula:

```
= Table.TransformColumnTypes(#"Promoted Headers",{{"2015", Int64.Type}, {"Name",
type text}, {"ProductNumber", type text}, {"Color", type text}, {"StandardCost",
type any}, {"ListPrice", type any}, {"Size", type text}, {"Weight", type any},
{"ParentProductCategoryName", type text}, {"ProductCategoryName", type text}})
```

Find the text "2015" in the preceding formula and replace it with "2014".

13. Select the step Renamed Columns in Applied Steps. In the formula bar, you see the following formula:

```
= Table.RenameColumns(#"Filtered Rows",{{"2015", "Release Year"}})
```

Find the text "2015" in the preceding formula and replace it with "2014".

14. Close the Power Query Editor and refresh the report. The products released in 2014 are now correctly combined into your report.

You can review these steps in the solution files C03E04 - Solution 01.xlsx or C03E04 - Solution 01.pbix, which are available at https://aka.ms/DataPwrBIPivot/downloads.

If you could assume that the first worksheet will always be 2015, or now, after the fix, 2014, and if you can ensure that new products will always be added as new worksheets to the right, your mission is accomplished. But what should you do if this assumption cannot be made? How can you improve the query to ensure that you will not need to repeat steps 12–14 whenever a new worksheet is added as the first worksheet?

In the following and final part of this chapter, you will learn how to improve the query to support the scenario where you cannot know which worksheet will be the first one.

A Robust Approach to Combining Multiple Worksheets

This section briefly introduces new concepts to improve the robustness of your queries and avoid refresh errors. In Exercise 3-4, you combined three worksheets of AdventureWorks products by their release year. While you could append the three worksheets in a scalable way and incorporate a combined table from the new worksheets as they are added to the data source, you found out that the query will fail when an unknown worksheet is added as the first worksheet.

In Exercise 3-4 you followed three steps (7–9) to combine the worksheets into a single table. In Chapter 10, "From Pitfalls to Robust Queries," you will learn in more details how each one of these steps could have been done differently to avoid potential errors. For now, this section just briefly introduces the mistakes and how to resolve them in this particular scenario:

- In step 7, you used First Row as Headers and allowed Power Query to automatically change the column types for you. As a result, the year 2015 was explicitly referenced in the formula. You kept the formula as is and, as a result, exposed the query to future refresh failures. Chapter 10 refers to this mistake as the *changed types pitfall*.

- In step 9, you renamed the header 2015 to *Release Year*. This action triggered an explicit reference to column 2015 in the formula bar and exposed the query to refresh failures, as observed when you added 2014 as the first worksheet. Chapter 10 refers to this mistake as the *rename columns pitfall*.

> **See Also** You should note that in step 8, you almost fell for another pitfall, the search in filters pitfall, when you applied the filter through the Search pane instead of selecting Text Filters and then defining the filter condition explicitly. You will learn about this pitfall and the others in Chapter 10.

To correct these two pitfalls, follow these steps:

1. Open the Products query in the Power Query Editor and delete the step Changed Types from Applied Steps. (You will explicitly apply the correct types later.)

2. Select the step Renamed Columns in Applied Steps. In the formula bar, you see the following formula:

   ```
   = Table.RenameColumns(#"Filtered Rows",{{"2015", "Release Year"}})
   ```

3. Replace "2015" in the preceding formula with the code **Table.ColumnNames(#"Filtered Rows"){0}**. The final formula line with the modified code in bold is as follows:

   ```
   = Table.RenameColumns(#"Filtered Rows",{{Table.ColumnNames(#"Filtered Rows"){0},
   "Release Year"}})
   ```

   Chapter 9 covers the M language in depth. You should feel completely comfortable at this stage if you don't understand its syntax. You do not need to fully master M to resolve 99% of data challenges you will ever face. However, because you modified the M formula here, let's briefly examine what happened.

   In a nutshell, instead of telling Power Query "Please rename column 2015 to Release Year," you changed the instructions to "Please rename the *first* column to Release Year."

   How did you refer to the first column? By using the function *Table.ColumnNames*. This function returns the list of column names of the table it receives as an argument. In this case, the table is #"Filtered Rows", which was named by the preceding step in which you filtered the table. Finally, to direct Power Query to the first element in the column names list, you can use the index zero inside curly brackets. This method in M allows you to access specific elements in a list or a specific row in a table. The index in M starts at zero instead of one. So the index of the first element is 0, and the *n*th element is *n*–1. In Chapter 10, you will use the function *Table.ColumnNames* to avoid referring to columns by their hardcoded names—and therefore avoid refresh errors when column names change.

4. You can conclude the creation of a robust query by explicitly changing the column types as follows:

   a. Make the Release Year column a Whole Number column.

   b. Make the StandardCost column a Decimal Number column.

   c. Make the ListPrice column a Decimal Number column.

You can now close the Power Query Editor and refresh the report. The products will be combined correctly, no matter which year is placed as the first worksheet.

You can review the preceding steps in the solution files C03E04 - Solution 02.xlsx or C03E04 - Solution 02.pbix, which are available at https://aka.ms/DataPwrBIPivot/downloads.

Summary

In this chapter, you have been introduced to one of the most common transformations in Power Query. Combining tables that have the same format will simplify your analysis and avoid the reporting complexities that tend to result in working with silos of separated datasets.

This chapter starts with the basic transformations Append Queries and Append Queries as New, which enable you to combine two or more tables. It discusses the difference between the two methods and the importance of Reference and Query Dependencies to reviewing your transformation flow.

The second part of the chapter moves to real-life scenarios in which the number of tables and their names are unknown. You learned about import from Folder, which combines tables from a folder and allows you to append the tables while keeping the context from their file names (available in the column Source.Name).

In this chapter you have also learned how to append tables from multiple worksheets while keeping the original worksheet names as an additional context and ensuring that new worksheets will be appended to the query without further modification.

Finally, in this chapter you have learned about a few of the common pitfalls that are discussed in more detail in Chapter 10, and you have learned how to improve a query by using the M function *Table.ColumnNames*, which helps you avoid refresh failures when the name of the first worksheet is changed.

This chapter assumes that the appended tables share the same format—an assumption that made your job relatively easy—but in Chapter 4, "Combining Mismatched Tables," you will examine common scenarios in which even slight variations in format between tables can make the combination of tables impossible without proper data preparation. You will find Chapter 4 crucial to obtaining everlasting wisdom from your newly acquired knowledge. With Power Query, in contrast to Einstein's argument, it is not rare to combine power and wisdom. What would Einstein do if he had Power Query?

CHAPTER 4

Combining Mismatched Tables

Combine the extremes, and you will have the true center.

—*Friedrich Schlegal*

IN THIS CHAPTER, YOU WILL

- Learn the impact of combining mismatched tables incorrectly

- Correctly combine tables with mismatched column names

- Correctly combine mismatched tables from a folder

- Learn how to normalize column names by using a conversion table

- Learn different solutions for table normalization with varied levels of complexity and performance constraints

In Chapter 3, "Combining Data from Multiple Sources," you learned how to combine multiple tables in Power Query and append them together to simplify your analysis and reporting capabilities. Oftentimes, tables come to you in different formats, or they gradually change as different owners manipulate them, unaware of the potentially disastrous impact on your reports.

This chapter focuses on a big challenge: how to combine mismatched tables. To understand this challenge, let's use socks as an analogy for tables. The work you did in Chapter 3 was like learning how to wear a pair of socks. In this chapter, you will learn how to handle your mismatched socks. As you will surely agree, when your socks are matching, the wearing part is easy. It is the matching part that can be excruciating. And sometimes finding the right sock in a large pile of washed clothes is simply impossible. Can you combine the extremes and wear mismatched socks? In real life, when you're really talking about tables, yes. This chapter looks at how you can live with mismatched tables in Power Query, no matter their extreme mismatched formats.

The Problem of Mismatched Tables

In Chapter 3 you appended multiple tables using a variety of techniques: You manually loaded multiple tables and selected Append Queries or Append Queries as New on the Home tab of the Power Query Editor to consolidate them into a single table. You also imported the tables from multiple files from a folder and appended all tables from multiple worksheets of a single workbook. As you worked through the different exercises, there was a single consistent theme throughout the chapter—an implicit assumption that was not articulated in detail: All the tables shared the same format.

It is perfectly reasonable to expect that your tables will have a consistent format before you combine them together. However, although this may be a reasonable requirement in ideal scenarios, it is seldom feasible in real life. You may need to work with tables that have different formats or, even worse, that may gradually become different. This section defines the main scenarios of mismatched tables and how to identify their impact.

What Are Mismatched Tables?

Mismatched tables, in the context of this chapter, are tables that describe the same semantic entities and their facts but have mismatched column names. For example, say that Table1 consists of the column names employee, age, and gender. Table2 consists of the column names Name, Age, and F/M. Table 4-1 illustrates the differences between the column names in these two tables.

TABLE 4-1 Examples of Mismatched Column Names

	Table1	*Table2*	**Mismatch Reason**
Column1	*employee*	*Name*	Different column names
Column2	*age*	*Age*	Different column names due to case sensitivity
Column3	*gender*	*F/M*	Different column names

The Symptoms and Risks of Mismatched Tables

Now that you understand what mismatched tables are in the context of this chapter, you are ready to learn about the main symptoms you encounter when you try to combine mismatched tables or refresh an existing report that was created on tables that did have the same format but that have changed and become mismatched since the report was created.

When you combine two tables in the Power Query Editor, each matching column will be correctly appended in the combined table. For each row in the first table, the values in the matching columns will be copied to the combined table. The same logic will be applied for the second table: For each row in the second table, the values in the matching columns will be copied to the combined table.

So, how does Power Query handle mismatched columns? In most cases, Power Query combines the tables into a new table that contains a superset (or a union) of all the columns from the source tables. Each row from the first table is copied to the combined table, and blank values appear in the columns that exist only in the second table. Each row from the second table will be copied in the same manner, with blank values in the columns that are exclusive to the first table. We refer to this symptom, which is illustrated in Figure 4-1, as *split data*. Instead of converging the values from the two tables into a single column, Power Query keeps the original columns, with their inherited disjointed data.

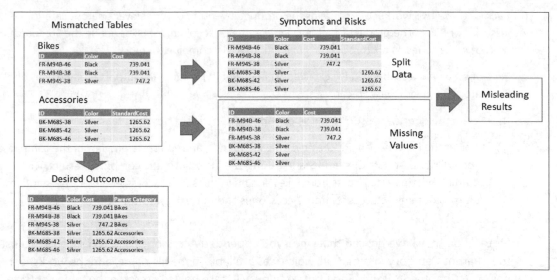

FIGURE 4-1 Mismatched tables can have two types of symptoms: split data and missing values, that lead to misleading results.

The second symptom that can occur when you combine mismatched tables, also illustrated in Figure 4-1, is *missing values*. It happens when the mismatched columns from the first table are chosen for the combined table, and all the mismatched columns from the second table are blatantly ignored. As a result, for each row in the second table, in the combined table, you find empty values in the mismatched column. Later in this chapter, you will learn more about this symptom and ways to resolve it.

When the preceding symptoms are ignored or undetected, the risks are clear. Split data and missing values can lead to inaccurate and misleading results. Fortunately, now you know how to detect the symptoms of mismatched tables that are badly combined, and you understand how important it is to look for these symptoms. It's time to learn how to resolve these problems so you can successfully combine mismatched tables.

Exercise 4-1: Resolving Mismatched Column Names: The Reactive Approach

In this exercise you will learn how to resolve mismatched column names and avoid the split data and missing values symptoms described in the preceding section (refer to Figure 4-1). This exercise uses Excel workbooks with AdventureWorks data to demonstrate the problem and its solution.

Let's first look at the split data symptom in a simple scenario and examine how you can reactively fix it by matching the column names. For this exercise, you can download the following workbooks from https://aka.ms/DataPwrBIPivot/downloads:

- C04E01 - Accessories.xlsx

- C04E01 - Bikes.xlsx

Each of these two workbooks contains the product inventory of the relevant parent category—Accessories or Bikes. The product cost is available in the Cost column of Bikes and in the StandardCost column of Accessories. Work through this exercise to try to combine them.

1. Open a new workbook in Excel or report in Power BI Desktop and import the two workbooks into the Power Query Editor.

2. Select the query Accessories and select Append Queries as New.

3. Look at the Preview pane of the new query Append1, and you see a preview of the combined tables. Note that both Cost and StandardCost are included in the combined results. The Cost column contains actual costs from Bikes and null values from Accessories, and the StandardCost column contains actual costs from Accessories and null values from Bikes.

Note You may have noticed that when you appended Accessories and Bikes, you have lost their Parent Category information, which was available in the file name, and the worksheet name. In Chapter 5, "Preserving Context," you will learn how to preserve the table context.

4. Select the Accessories query and rename the StandardCost column *Cost*. Now when you again select Append1, you see that the split data symptom is resolved as the mismatched columns have been converged.

The solution described here is simple, and you can often take this approach to resolve mismatched column names. But sometimes, you will not be able to use manually renaming to resolve mismatched column names. For example, say that you have two tables with 100 columns to match. Taking the ad hoc manual renaming approach presented here would become a repetitive and time-consuming task. Even worse, in most cases, when you combine tables from a folder, manual renaming of columns does not work, as you will see in the next section.

Combining Mismatched Tables from a Folder

In the preceding section, you learned how to manually change mismatched column names before you append the tables. When you have multiple tables in a folder with mismatched column names, the situation becomes more challenging. On one hand, manually appending them together would not be a good approach, especially if you have a large number of files. On the other hand, combining the files together from a folder would not allow you to apply different logic for each file.

Facing this challenge, you might be tempted to go to the source code and rename the columns in its source. But say that you have a table with 20 columns in each of 60 workbooks in a folder to. You would need to go over 1,200 columns to ensure that their name are matching and rename them manually in the source code. This approach would not be practical, especially if you don't own the source files, and will continue to get them periodically, often with mismatched column names.

Recall that in Chapter 3 you learned how to combine multiple tables from a folder. As you followed the steps in that chapter, Power Query used the headers of the first table as the headers of the combined table. When you combine tables with mismatched column names from a folder, you soon start to see the missing values symptom. The next section demonstrates this symptom and shows how to successfully combine mismatched tables from a folder.

Exercise 4-2, Part 1: Demonstrating the Missing Values Symptom

Let's return to our fictional company, AdventureWorks. Each of the company's four product line managers owns an Excel workbook of the product inventory. As chief analyst, you have been asked to combine the four tables and share your analysis, but when you access the different workbooks, you discover that the product line managers have become creative and have changed many column names in their product tables (see Figure 4-2). As you try to combine the tables from the folder, you discover that it doesn't work well. This exercise walks through the steps of dealing with this issue.

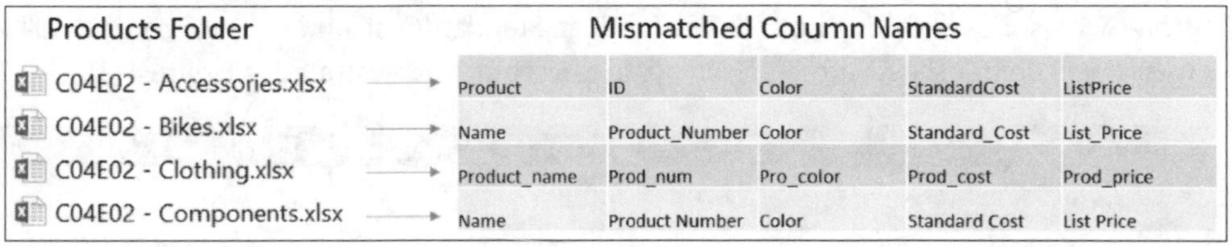

Products Folder	Mismatched Column Names				
C04E02 - Accessories.xlsx	Product	ID	Color	StandardCost	ListPrice
C04E02 - Bikes.xlsx	Name	Product_Number	Color	Standard_Cost	List_Price
C04E02 - Clothing.xlsx	Product_name	Prod_num	Pro_color	Prod_cost	Prod_price
C04E02 - Components.xlsx	Name	Product Number	Color	Standard Cost	List Price

FIGURE 4-2 In the AdventureWorks Products folder, the workbooks have mismatched column names.

1. Download the file C04E02 - Products.zip from https://aka.ms/DataPwrBIPivot/downloads.

2. Extract the contents of this ZIP file to a new folder: *C:\Data\C04\C04E02 - Products*. The folder now contains the following files:

    a. C04E02 - Accessories.xlsx

    b. C04E02 - Bikes.xlsx

    c. C04E02 - Components.xlsx4

    d. C04E02 - Clothing.xlsx

3. Review the files, and notice that the column names are too different and it will not be practical to start fixing them one by one.

4. Let's import the four mismatched tables from the folder and encounter the missing values symptom:

    In Excel: Open a new workbook and on the Data tab, select Get Data, From File, From Folder.

    In Power BI Desktop: Start a new report, select Get Data, and in the Get Data dialog box, select File and then select Folder.

5. In the Folder dialog box that appears, select the folder *C:\Data\C04\C04E02 - Products* and click OK.

6. In the next dialog box, which is titled the same as the folder you selected in step 5, in the Combine drop-down menu, select Combine and Edit.

7. When the Combine Files dialog box opens, in the Example File drop-down menu, select any one of the options and then select Sheet1 and click OK.

> **Note** The Example File drop-down menu enables you to choose the workbook to use and apply its format on all the files in the folder. As part of this choice, you need to decide which column names will be inherited by the combined table. Each file contains different column names, and you will soon see the full impact of the missing values symptom.

8. When the Power Query Editor opens, scroll down the main Preview pane until the rows change from Accessories to Bikes. The columns Product, StandardCost, and ListPrice contain null values (which will be translated into blank values in the report), as illustrated in Figure 4-3.

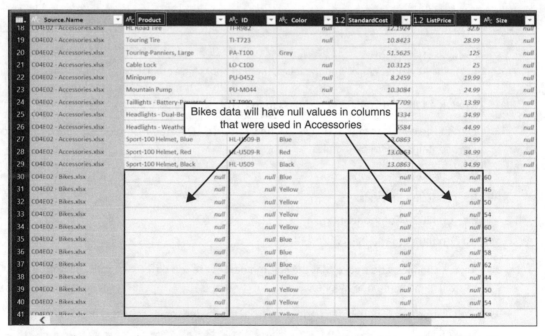

FIGURE 4-3 The missing values symptom is triggered when you import from a folder multiple tables with mismatched columns.

Before you can resolve the missing values symptom, you need to open the Queries pane and select the query Transform Sample File from C04E02 - Products, which this book refers to as the *sample query*. It was generated when you combined the files from the folder. When the sample query is selected, you can see in the main Preview pane of the Power Query Editor that the Accessories data is correctly displayed. Solving the missing values symptom always starts with the sample query.

Tip When you combine files from a folder, Power Query creates a query function, a sample query, a file query, and a parameter. Those artifacts help you combine multiple files from a folder, based on the selected data. The main transformation for each file is implemented in the function. To help you to customize the transformation on each file, you can make changes on the sample query. These changes will be propagated to the function and will be applied to all the files. Whenever you combine files from a folder, look for the sample query that starts with the text *Transform Sample File from* to make changes on each file before it gets appended.

Exercise 4-2, Part 2: The Same-Order Assumption and the Header Generalization Solution

To solve the missing values problem, let's assume that all the product tables share the same order of columns, even if their column names are different. With this assumption, you can use arbitrary column names—such as the default generic column names Column1, Column2, and so on—and you can use the column order to correctly append the tables. The following steps should be applied after steps 1–8 of Exercise 4-2 Part 1:

9. With the Power Query Editor still open from step 8, select the query Transform Sample File from C04E02 - Products in Queries pane and rename it *Products Sample*.

10. In Applied Steps, delete the last step, Promote Headers. Without that step, the combined table has the generic column names Column1, Column2, Column3, and so forth. When all tables have the same generic column names, you can see the correct data in the appended table.

11. Select the query C04E02 - Products and review the combined table. Notice the following error:

    `Expression.Error: The column 'Product' of the table wasn't found.`

12. In Applied Steps, delete the last step, Changed Type. Now the combined table doesn't have any missing values. You can confirm that this is so by scrolling down again and ensuring that all the values for Accessories are included.

13. Now with all the data appended correctly in C04E02 - Products, you can promote the first row as headers by selecting Use First Row as Headers on the Transform tab.

    Unfortunately, the headers from each table are now added as rows in the appended table. In Chapter 3, you resolved a similar issue by filtering out the headers. This time, you have different column names as rows, and you cannot easily determine which values you should explicitly exclude in the filter. To resolve this challenge, you can mark the headers by adding an index column before the combine step. The index will serve as your cue to identify the embedded headers.

14. In the Queries pane, select Products Sample. On the Add Column tab, select Index Column. You can see that the sample data includes an incrementing index number for each row, and the first row, which contains the original column names of the table, is now indexed as zero.

15. Go back to the query C04E02 - Products and remove all headers by filtering out the rows with zero index. To do this, click on the filter control of the last column, which is labeled 0. Deselect the value 0 in the Filter pane and click OK.

16. Remove the first column (C04E02 - Accessories.xlsx column) and the last column (the 0 column). After you removed these columns, you can tweak the formula to gain query robustness, as shown at the last section of Chapter 3, "Combining Data from Multiple Sources." In this case, replace the static reference to the column name C04E02 - Accessories.xlsx with a dynamic one using **Table.ColumnName(...){0}**.

Change the **code** in the formula bar from the following:

```
= Table.RemoveColumns(#"Filtered Rows",{"C04E02 - Accessories.xlsx", "0"})
```

To this:

```
= Table.RemoveColumns(#"Filtered Rows",{Table.ColumnNames(#"Filtered Rows"){0}, "0"})
```

You can now load the combined products table to start the analysis.

The solution to this exercise is available in the Excel workbook C04E02 - Solution.xlsx and the Power BI report C04E02 - Solution.pbix, which are available at https://aka.ms/DataPwrBIPivot/downloads.

Recall that in step 10 you demoted the headers of the first table, to use the generic columns Column1, Column2, and so forth. This step was possible because you assumed that all tables share the same order of columns. Imagine what would happen if one of those tables were ordered differently. For example, what would happen if the product line manager of the Bikes division of AdventureWorks decided to switch the position of the columns Name and Product_Number. Applying the technique described in this section would mess up the combined table. All the rows from Bikes would have product ID values as product names and product name values as product IDs. To avoid this chaos, you would need to establish a data contract with your product line managers to ensure that the column order will never change in the source files. Another approach would be to combine the tables using a different method and normalize all headers before the tables are combined. The following section explores this approach.

Exercise 4-3: Simple Normalization Using *Table.TransformColumnNames*

Matching and renaming column names across multiple tables in an automatic way is an important part of combining mismatched tables. When you have many mismatched columns, manual renaming of specific columns, as demonstrated in Exercise 4-1, is not practical and will not scale with frequent updates or large numbers of files that need to be combined. If you can assume that the column names will have a consistent order in the tables, the header generalization solution demonstrated in Exercise 4-2 will do the job. When you cannot rely on consistent order, however, you will find the normalization of column names a powerful tool.

At its core, column normalization is a simple text manipulation. In many cases, you just need to apply minor text manipulations on all the mismatched columns names to ensure that their format is consistent. For example, you might want to replace all underscore characters with space characters or capitalize each word in every column name.

Simple text manipulation such as lowercasing, uppercasing, or capitalizing each word may be a very effective step in matching column names. Power Query is, by design, case sensitive, so, for example, column1 and Column1 would be handled as two different columns. If your tables tend to change frequently, and if their column names may change from lowercase to uppercase and vice versa, converting them all to the same case will reduce mismatches.

To transform column names by using a simple text manipulation, you can apply the M formula *Table.TransformColumnNames* on a table. For example, if the last step in the Applied Steps pane is named Previous Step, you can apply the following formula to capitalize each word of the column names:

```
= Table.TransformColumnNames(#"Previous Step", Text.Proper)
```

And you can use the following to replace underscores with spaces:

```
= Table.TransformColumnNames(#"Previous Step", each Replacer.ReplaceText(_, "_", " "))
```

In this exercise, you will put these two formulas to use when you combine AdventureWorks Products tables.

> **Note** You should note that at this stage, you don't need to understand the syntax of these formulas. We will cover the syntax in Chapter 9, "Introduction to the Power Query M Formula Language." For now, you should know that both *Text.Proper* and *Replacer.ReplaceText* are M functions that help you transform text. You can use any function inside *Table.TransformColumnNames*. In the preceding examples, *Text.Proper* capitalizes each word in the text and *Replacer.ReplaceText* replaces all instances of the second argument with the third argument in the text.

1. Download the file C04E03 - Products.zip from https://aka.ms/DataPwrBIPivot/downloads.

2. Extract the content of the ZIP file into a new folder: *C:\Data\C04\C04E03 - Products*. The folder now contains the following files:

    a. C04E03 - Accessories.xlsx

    b. C04E03 - Bikes.xlsx

    c. C04E03 - Components.xlsx

    d. C04E03 - Clothing.xlsx

    The files here are the same as in Exercise 4-2 but with two intentional changes. First, the mismatched column names can all be resolved if you capitalize each word and replace underscores with spaces. Second, for Bikes, the first two columns are swapped to ensure that you cannot effectively use the header generalization technique of Exercise 4-2 to combine the tables.

3. Open a blank new workbook in Excel or a new report in Power BI desktop, and follow these steps:

   In Excel: On the Data tab, select Get Data, From File, From Folder.

   In Power BI Desktop: On the Home tab, select Get Data, and in the Get Data dialog box, select File and then select Folder.

4. In the Folder dialog box that appears, select the folder *C:\Data\C04\C04E03 - Products* and click OK.

5. In the next dialog box, named the same as the folder you selected in step 4, in the Combine drop-down menu, select Combine and Edit.

6. When the Combine Files dialog box opens, in the Example File drop-down menu, select any one of the options and then select Sheet1 and click OK.

   As expected, when the Power Query Editor opens, confirm that the appended results suffer from the missing values symptom.

7. Select the sample query Transform Sample File from C04E03 - Products and rename it *Products Sample*.

8. While Products Sample is selected, click the fx icon in the formula bar (see Figure 4-4).

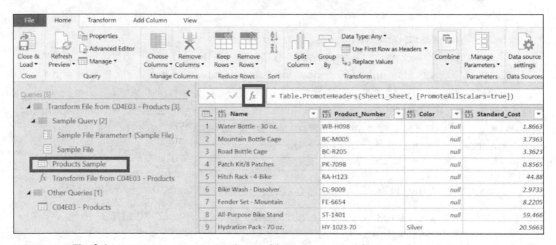

FIGURE 4-4 The fx icon creates a custom step that enables you to apply a formula of a new transformation on the previous step.

9. Notice that a new step, Custom1, is created in the Applied Step pane, and it has the following formula:

   ```
   =  #"Promoted Headers"
   ```

   Promoted Headers was the last step in Applied Steps before you clicked the fx button. #"Promoted Headers" is the variable used for the output of that step. Because this variable returns the table with the mismatched column names, you can apply the

Table.TransformColumnNames function on it with *Text.Lower* to lowercase the column names. To do it, modify the formula as follows:

```
= Table.TransformColumnNames(#"Promoted Headers", Text.Lower)
```

10. Press Enter and notice that all the column names are lowercased. If you prefer to use capitalized column names, you can replace Text.Lower with Text.Proper in the preceding formula.

> **Note**   Even if you work with datasets whose headers are in the desired and matching column names, you can apply this formula to prevent future cases in which the owner of the source table might decide to move from capitalized headers to lowercased, uppercased, or a combination of the three.

11. To replace the underscores in the column names with spaces, click the fx icon in the formula bar again.

12. Notice that a new step, Custom2, is created in the Applied Step, and it has the following formula:

```
=   Custom1
```

Apply *Table.TransformColumnNames* with Custom1 with *Replacer.ReplaceText* to replace underscores with spaces in the column names by modifying the formula as follows:

```
= Table.TransformColumnNames(Custom1, each Replacer.ReplaceText(_,"_", " "))
```

13. Press Enter and notice that all the column names contain spaces instead of underscores. The column names have become user friendly.

14. Select the C04E03 - Products query and remove the last step, Changed Types, from the Applied Steps pane. You can now see that all the column names contain spaces instead of underscores, and the files have been appended together correctly, without any further evidence of the missing values symptom.

You can download the solution files C04E03 - Solution.xlsx and C04E03 - Solution.pbix from https://aka.ms/DataPwrBIPivot/downloads.

The Conversion Table

In Exercise 4-3, you applied simple text manipulations on mismatched column names and replaced underscores with spaces. In real-life scenarios, simple text manipulations will, unfortunately, not suffice.

To demonstrate this, let's go back to our fictional company, AdventureWorks, and the dataset used in Exercise 4-2. This time, as in Exercise 4-3, the first two columns are swapped, so the header generalization technique shown in Exercise 4-2 will not work.

For the next series of exercises, you will use the dataset C04E04 - Products.zip, which is located at https://aka.ms/DataPwrBIPivot/downloads.

In the Products folder are different tables with the columns ID, Product_Number, Product_num, and Product Number that are used by different product line managers to represent the same column. You cannot apply a simple text manipulation to normalize these column names. Instead, you can build a conversion table with pairs of mismatched column names and their desired normalized names. Figure 4-5 illustrates the mismatched column names and how they can be represented in a conversion table. The Source column represents the mismatched column name that you would like to replace; the Target column represents the desired and normalized column name.

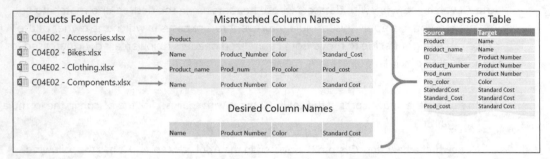

FIGURE 4-5 In the conversion table, each mismatched column name is paired with a target column name.

Creating a conversion table can be time-consuming. However, you don't need to create in it a row for each column name in your source files. In the example shown in Figure 4-5, the conversion table doesn't include the pair Name → Name, and it doesn't need to. Only the pairs of mismatched columns and their desired replacements should be included. If you have hundreds of columns, only the few that are mismatched should be included in the conversion table.

To review the actual conversion table you will use in Exercise 4-4, you can download the workbook C04E04 - Conversion Table.xlsx from https://aka.ms/DataPwrBIPivot/downloads.

> **Tip** When you use an external Excel workbook as your conversion table, you can start with a small table of few mismatched column names and gradually add new mismatched columns and their desired replacements. When you hook the conversion table to your queries, you do not need to edit the query any longer to refine the normalization of new mismatched column names. Instead, simply modify the external conversion table and refresh the report.

Now that you know how to manually create a conversion table, you can learn how to use it to replace the mismatched columns. To do this, you can use the Merge Queries transformation that is available on the Power Query Editor's Home tab. As demonstrated in Chapter 2, "Basic Data Preparation Challenges," Merge Queries enables you to join between multiple tables, based on shared values of specified columns.

Before you learn how to use the Merge Queries to apply the conversion table, let's pause to discuss one of the main challenges in column name normalization. In the last part of this chapter, you will learn how to apply *Table.TransformColumnNames*, as demonstrated in Exercise 4-3, and use a conversion table inside a custom function to replace the column names. As that technique requires a deeper knowledge of M, this chapter first shows three other UI-driven approaches to applying the conversion table that do not require the use of advanced M formulas.

The user interface of the Power Query Editor is rich with text transformations on columns but not on headers. Exercises 4-4, 4-5, and 4-6 focus on the normalization of column names, using three techniques that are UI driven and minimize the need to know M. These exercises do not use *Table.TransformColumnNames*, as it requires building a custom function. Instead, these exercises show how to use the Power Query Editor user interface controls.

> **Tip** If you are already comfortable using M, you will enjoy the fourth technique that awaits you in the last section of this chapter. You will likely find the solution in Exercise 4-7 to be the best method for combining mismatched tables and applying normalization on their column names. You should still follow along with the other exercises so you can appreciate the power of these and learn their pros and cons. In addition, you may find them useful in other data challenges.

Exercise 4-4: The Transpose Technique Using a Conversion Table

To normalize mismatched columns using a conversion table, you need to temporarily transform the column names into a single-column table, merge the conversion table, replace the mismatched column names with the target ones, and transform the column names back as headers. In this exercise you will learn the first of three techniques to do this. But first, you will start with the same sequence that you used in Exercises 4-2 and 4-3 to load the tables from a folder.

1. Download the archive C04E04 - Products.zip and extract it into the folder *C:\Data\ C04\C04E04 - Products*.

2. Download the workbook C04E04 - Conversion Table.xlsx from https://aka.ms/DataPwrBIPivot/ downloads and save it in *C:\Data\C04*. The folder *C:\Data\C04\C04E04 - Products* now contains the following files:

   a. C04E04 - Accessories.xlsx

   b. C04E04 - Bikes.xlsx

   c. C04E04 - Components.xlsx

   d. C04E04 - Clothing.xlsx

3. Import the conversion table to a new workbook or Power BI report:

   In Excel: Open a new workbook and on the Data tab, select Get Data , From File, From Workbook. Select the file C04E04 - Conversion Table.xlsx. Then, in the Navigator, select Header_Conversion and select Edit. Finally, select Close & Load To and select Connection Only.

   In Power BI Desktop: Start a new report, select Get Data, and in the Get Data dialog box, select File and then select Excel. Select the file C04E04 - Conversion Table.xlsx. Then, in the Navigator, select Header_Conversion and select Edit. Finally, select the query in the Queries pane, and deselect Enable Load. Then select Close & Apply.

Now that you have your conversion table as a new query, it's time to load the Products folder.

4. Import the product tables from the folder:

   In Excel: On the Data tab, select Get Data, From File, From Folder.

   In Power BI Desktop: On the Home tab, select Get Data, and in the Get Data dialog box, select File and then select Folder.

5. In the Folder dialog box, select the folder *C:\Data\C04\C04E04 - Products* and click OK.

6. In the next dialog box, named the same as the folder you selected in step 5, in the Combine drop-down menu, select Combine and Edit.

7. When the Combine Files dialog box opens, in the Example File drop-down menu, select any one of the options and then select Sheet1 and click OK.

8. In the Queries pane, select the query Transform Sample File from C04E04 - Products and rename it *Products Sample*. Recall that this query is the sample query. Applying changes here will affect the appended table in the C04E04 - Products query.

9. Rename the C04E04 - Products query *Appended Products* and save the workbook or Power BI report. Then create three copies of it; you will need these copied files for Exercises 4-5, 4-6, and 4-7.

Transpose

The first technique for normalizing the column names is to use the Transpose transformation, which is available on the Transform tab of Power Query Editor. With Transpose, each cell in column X and row Y will be placed in column Y and row X.

When you want to manipulate the values of column names, it is much easier to do it in the Power Query Editor if these column names are represented vertically in a column. This is where Transpose is useful.

However, if you try to transpose a table, you will find out that the original column names are not preserved after the transformation. To preserve the column names, you need to demote the column names to being the first row before you transpose the table. To do this, open your saved workbook or Power BI report from the preceding steps (1–9) and launch the Power Query Editor. In the Queries pane, select the Products Sample query and then follow these additional steps:

10. In Applied Steps, while Products Sample query is selected, delete the step Promoted Headers. Now the headers of the sampled table are in the first row.

11. On the Transform tab, select Transpose. Column1 now contains the column names that need to be normalized.

The Merge Sequence

You have reached the point in the normalization where you merge the conversion table into the transposed table to execute the bulk replacement of mismatched column names. Follow these additional steps:

12. With Products Sample selected, select Merge Queries from the Home tab.

13. When the Merge dialog box opens, select Column1 in Products Sample, and in the drop-down menu located below Products Sample, select Header_Conversion (see Figure 4-6). Then select the Source column of Header_Conversion.

14. Ensure that the Join Kind drop-down is set to Left Outer (All from First, Matching from Second), and click OK.

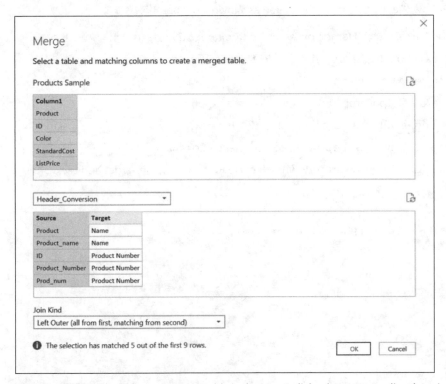

FIGURE 4-6 You can apply a conversion table in the Merge dialog box to normalize the mismatched column names.

15. In the Power Query Editor, when a new Header_Conversion column is added as the last column, with table objects as values, expand the Header_Conversion column (by clicking the control at the right side of its header) or select the Header_Conversion column and then select the Expand in Transform tab.

16. To retrieve the Target value from Header_Conversion table, in the Expand pane, deselect Source and click OK. The new column is transformed to the new column Header_Conversion.Target, with the Target values in rows where Column1 and Source had the same column name or with null value in rows where there were no Source values that matched the values in Column1. Now, whenever you have null values in Header_Conversion.Target, you will use the original column names in Column1.

In the next step you will add a conditional column to copy the target values from rows that need to be normalized and the source values from rows where Header_Conversion.Target is null. The new column will contain the normalized column names or the original column names if the original column names are not found in the conversion table.

17. On the Add Column tab, select Conditional Column. The Add Conditional Column dialog box opens. Follow these steps to set the dialog as shown in Figure 4-7:

   a. In the New Column Name box, enter *New Column Names*.

   b. In the Column Name drop-down, select Header_Conversion.Target.

   c. In the Value box, enter *null*.

   d. In the left Output drop-down, select Select a Column.

   e. In the right Output drop-down, select Column1.

   f. In the left Otherwise drop-down, select Select a Column.

   g. In the right Otherwise drop-down, select Header_Conversion.Target and click OK.

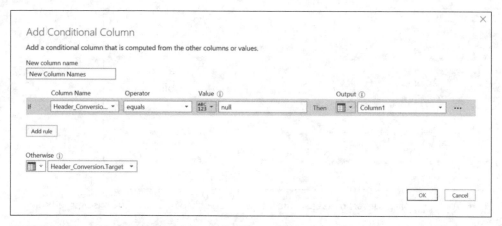

FIGURE 4-7 The Add Conditional Column dialog box can help you create a new column with mixed values from multiple columns depending on defined conditions. In this case, the new column will contain the normalized column names or the original column names if the original column names are not found in the conversion table.

18. Delete Column1 and Header_Conversion.Target.

19. Move New Column Names to be the first column in the table (by simply dragging and dropping it from the right side to the left side or following the advice in the next tip).

> **Tip**   When you have too many columns in a table and need to move a column to the beginning, instead of dragging and dropping the column, you can select the column and, on the Transform tab, select Move and then To Beginning. You can also right-click the column header and select Move and then select To Beginning in the shortcut menu.

> **Note**   Reordering columns in tables can be tricky in Power Query. In Chapter 10, "From Pitfalls to Robust Queries," you will learn how to avoid the related risks. When you move a column, the underlying M formula that references all the columns in the table creates a vulnerable query that will fail to refresh when any one of the columns is missing or renamed.

Transpose Back

Recall that in step 11, you transposed the table and moved the demoted header names into Column1. Transpose enabled you to merge between the original table headers in Column1 and the Source table headers in the conversion table. Then you extracted the Target headers from the merged conversion table and, by using a conditional column, you replaced the original mismatched headers with the target headers. Now, looking at the values of Column1, you can see that you have the normalized values that will be needed as the correct column names. It's time to transpose the table back to restore the column names from Column1. Follow these additional steps:

20. On the Transform tab, select Transpose. The transpose restores the headers from Column1, but now they are stored as the first row of the table, so it's time to promote them back as headers.

21. On the Transform tab, select Use First Row as Headers.

22. Select the Appended Products query in the Queries pane and review the combined table. If you notice an error, remove the last Changed Types step in Applied Steps, and you are done.

You can find the solution files C04E04 - Solution - Transpose.xlsx and C04E04 - Solution - Transpose.pbix at https://aka.ms/DataPwrBIPivot/downloads.

Unfortunately, the transpose technique works only on small datasets. Large datasets with large numbers of rows consume a lot of memory. Power Query supports tables with 16,384 columns. If you transpose a table with more than 16,384 rows, you will face errors, slow imports, and high memory consumption when you turn these rows into columns in the Transpose step. Even if you try this method on 15,000 rows, the memory consumption and the slow refresh rate justify using an alternative technique. In such a case, you need a better solution to normalize the column names—one that will not fail with large tables.

Exercise 4-5: Unpivot, Merge, and Pivot Back

A better method to transform column names into a column and set the stage for the merge of the conversion table is to use the Unpivot transformation. In this exercise you will learn how you can apply it and how to reverse it with the normalized column names by using the Pivot transformation.

See Also Chapter 6, "Unpivoting Tables," walks through a wide variety of applications of the Unpivot transformation. Chapter 7, "Advanced Unpivoting and Pivoting of Tables," describes useful scenarios for using Pivot.

You start this exercise right after the import of the files from the folder that was done in steps 1–9 of Exercise 4-4.

1. Start from the saved workbook or Power BI report from Exercise 4-4 step 9. Open the file with Excel or Power BI Desktop and launch the Power Query Editor.

2. On the Add Column tab, select Index Column. You will understand why you need the index in the next step.

3. Select the Index column, right-click the header of the Index column, and select Unpivot Other Columns. Power Query flattens the table by creating a new table with the trio of columns Index, Attribute, and Value. The Index column will keep the original row ID, which will help you in step 6 to reverse the table back to its original state. The Attribute column will include the column name, and the Value column will include the original values you had in the table. Now you can apply the text manipulation on the Attribute column.

4. Rename the Attribute column *Column1* to ensure that the next steps are consistent.

5. Apply the merge sequence described in Exercise 4-4 steps 12–19 to replace the mismatched column names.

6. To reverse the unpivot step, select the column New Column Names and select Pivot Column on the Transform tab.

See Also The Pivot Column transformation is a very useful step. In Chapter 7, you will learn how it can help you to solve badly structured datasets.

7. When the Pivot dialog box opens, select Value in the Values Column and expand the Advanced Options drop-down. Then select Don't Aggregate, and click OK.

8. Remove the Index column.

9. Select Appended Products in the Queries pane and review the combined table. If you notice an error, remove the last Changed Types steps, and you are done.

You can review the solution files C04E05 - Solution - Unpivot.xlsx and C04E05 - Solution - Unpivot.pbix at https://aka.ms/DataPwrBIPivot/downloads.

While Unpivot technique can be applied on large datasets, the Pivot technique that is used to reverse the table back can consume memory and significantly slow down the refresh time because Power Query needs to go all over the dataset to identify the unique values in Column1 and then construct the new columns from these unique values. As a result, this technique is not ideal if you have large datasets and want to combine the tables in an optimized way and with a shorter refresh time.

Exercise 4-6: Transposing Column Names Only

A performance-optimized method to transform column names into a column and set the stage for the merge of the conversion table is to transpose only the column names as an intermediate transformation phase and then apply the merge. Figure 4-8 shows how you can transpose the column names, apply the normalization, and transpose the column names back into the original table.

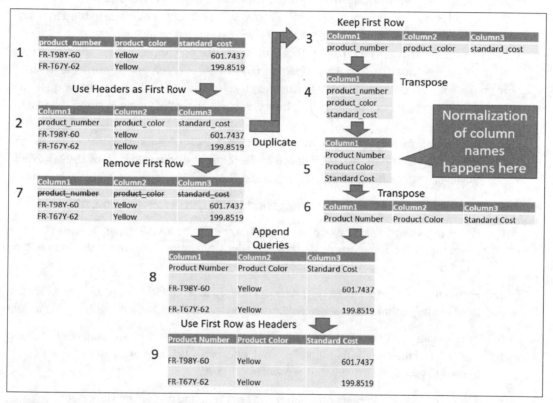

FIGURE 4-8 Normalization of column names involves nine transformation steps.

While the technique illustrated in Figure 4-8 is easy to implement when you combine a few specific files using Append Queries, applying it on a folder is quite advanced, as it relies on custom functions; doing this is therefore recommended here only for learning purposes. You should use this technique if the techniques described already in Exercises 4-4 and 4-5 are not relevant due to performance constraints, and only if you prefer to avoid using the M technique described in Exercise 4-7.

1. Start with the saved queries created in steps 1–9 of Exercise 4-4.

2. In Applied Steps, while the Products Sample query is still selected, delete the step Promoted Headers. Now the headers of the sample table are in the first row.

3. In the Queries pane, right-click Products Sample and select Duplicate. Now, while the new query, Products Sample (2), is selected, select Keep Rows on the Home tab and then select Keep Top Rows. In the Keep Top Rows dialog box, in the Number of Rows box, enter *1* and click OK.

Note When you combine files from a folder, Power Query creates a query function, a sample query, a file query, and a parameter. Those artifacts help you combine multiple files from a folder based on a single file you select. The main transformation for each file is implemented in the function. To help you customize the transformation on each file, you can make changes on the sample query. In this exercise, the sample query is Transform Sample File from Appended Products, and you renamed it *Products Sample*. Changes made in the sample query will propagate to the function and, as a result, will be applied on all the files in the folder. But here is a crucial caveat: If you use Duplicate or Reference on sample queries, the transformations in the new query will not be propagated by Power Query when you combine the files from the folder—unless you apply an advanced technique to "wire" back the new query to the transformation sequence in the sample query. You will apply this wiring in steps 21 and 22.

4. On the Transform tab, select Transpose to set the stage for the normalization. This is the point where you will apply a merge sequence similar to the one described in steps 12–19 of Exercise 4-4. However, in this case, don't follow those steps. There are few variations here that are crucial.

5. While Products Sample (2) is selected, select Merge Queries on the Home tab.

6. When the Merge dialog box opens, select Column1 in Products Sample (2), and in the drop-down below Products Sample (2), select Header_Conversion. Then select the Source column, as you did in Exercise 4-4 (refer to Figure 4-6).

7. Ensure that Join Kind is set to Left Outer (All from First, Matching from Second) and click OK. In the Power Query Editor, the new Header_Conversion column is added, with *table* objects as values.

8. At this stage, you need to add an index column to ensure that the next step will not change the order of the column names in Column1, so on the Add Column tab, select Index Column. In step 13 you will learn why this step was important.

9. Select the Header_Conversion column and select Expand on the Transform tab.

10. In the Expand pane, deselect Source and click OK. The new column is transformed to the new column Header_Conversion.Target, with the Target values in rows where the product column names are mismatched and with null value in rows where you should keep the original product column names.

11. On the Add Column tab, select Conditional Column.

12. When the Add Conditional Column dialog box opens, set it as follows:

   a. In the New Column Name box, enter *New Column Names*.

   b. In the Column Name box, select Header_Conversion.Target.

   c. In the Value box, enter *null*.

d. In the left Output drop-down, select Select a Column.

e. In the right Output drop-down, select Column1.

f. In the left Otherwise drop-down, select Select a Column.

g. In the right Otherwise drop-down, select Header_Conversion.Target and click OK.

13. Ensure that the Index column is still in ascending order. If it isn't, you can sort the Index column in ascending order. The order of the column names is crucial here. In step 9 you expanded the table, and that step can reshuffle the order of the rows. Having the Index column that was added in step 8 helps you preserve the order.

14. Delete the Column1, Header_Conversion.Target, and Index columns and keep only the last column, New Column Names.

15. On the Transform tab, select Transpose. You now have the normalized column names.

    You have finished the normalization part of the Products Sample (2) query, which is illustrated in Figure 4-4 (in step 5 in the figure). From here, you can wrap up the remaining sequence of the transformation steps.

16. To remove the old headers from the table, go back to the original Products Sample query. While Products Sample query is selected in the Queries pane, select Remove Rows on the Home tab and then select Remove Top Rows. In the Remove Top Rows dialog box, in the Number of Rows box, enter *1* and click OK.

17. While Products Sample is still selected in the Queries pane, select Append Queries on the Home tab. The Append dialog box opens. Select Products Sample (2) as Table to Append and click OK.

18. In the Preview pane, you will notice that the normalized column names from Products Sample (2) are now located as the bottom row because you appended Products Sample (2) as the second table. You can switch the tables. In formula bar, note the following formula:

    ```
    = Table.Combine({#"Removed Top Rows", #"Products Sample (2)"})
    ```

    Change the formula by switching the positions of #"Removed Top Rows" and #"Products Sample (2)", as shown here:

    ```
    = Table.Combine({#"Products Sample (2)", #"Removed Top Rows"})
    ```

19. Now that you have the normalized column names in the first row, promote them as headers. To do this, on the Transform tab, select Use First Row As Headers and remove Changed Type from Applied Steps.

> **Note** Removing Changed Type is important here. The Size column for Accessories includes only numbers. Hence, Power Query converted the type of the Size column to Whole Number. But for other products, such as bikes, textual values are valid sizes. If you don't remove the type conversion at this stage, you will receive errors in cells of the Size column that should contain textual values.

20. In the Queries pane, select the query Appended Products to review the combined table. You will notice an error that can be fixed by removing the last step, Changed Type, from Applied Steps.

Now when you scroll down in the Preview pane and reach the rows from C04E04 - Bikes.xlsx, you find out, as shown in Figure 4-9, that the values in the Name column and the Product Number column were swapped. The normalization didn't work well.

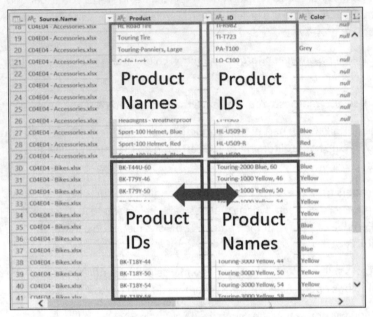

FIGURE 4-9 In the Appended Products query, product IDs and product names are swapped in the Bikes rows.

Tip Auditing the end results is an important step in using Power Query. The Preview pane can often be very misleading, as it shows partial data. In this case, everything worked fine for the Accessories data, but when you take a careful look at the appended results, you find that product ID and product name values are swapped for Bikes. Always take a careful look at the results data.

Let's pause here for a moment to understand what happened and why the normalization hasn't worked. The good news is that the Products Sample (2) query is now performing well on a single file. When you select Products Sample (2), you can see that in the last step in Applied Steps, the headers are normalized as expected. But the bad news is that the header normalization was done on only a single file, and now, when this sample query is reused via the custom function on all the files in the folder, it rigidly transforms all column names by the data in the same single file.

Why is the same single file used? Look at the Products Sample (2) query. When the Source step is selected in Applied Steps, the formula bar shows that the query loads the Excel workbook from the #"Sample File Parameter1" parameter. This parameter was created by Power Query when you combined the files from the folder. You can select this parameter in the Queries pane to find that the parameter's current value is Sample File. You can find the Sample File query below #"Sample File Parameter1" in the Queries pane. This query returns the content of the workbook C04E04 - Accessories.xlsx.

Why were the product ID values and product names swapped for Bikes in the Appended Products query? This happened because the Accessories file, C04E04 - Accessories.xlsx, contains the two columns in the reverse order from C04E04 - Bikes.xlsx. You cannot run the normalization in the Accessories file and apply it on other files if the orders of the columns are different.

To fix this issue, you need to learn how to reuse the logic in Products Sample (2) per file in the folder. Recall from step 3 of this exercise that Products Sample (2) was duplicated from Products Sample, which is a sample query. As a sample query, Products Sample runs on each file in the folder and invokes Products Sample (2). But since Products Sample (2) is currently not a sample query, the files from the folder are not propagated to Products Sample (2). This query always runs its transformation sequence on the same file: C04E04 - Accessories.xlsx.

You need to find a way to convert Products Sample (2) into a reusable query that will accept a file as a parameter from the Products Sample query and normalize the headers for each file. To solve this challenge, you can turn Product Sample (2) into a function (also referred to as a custom function) that can be called and reused for each file in the folder. Carry out the following additional steps to create a function from Products Sample (2):

21. In the Queries pane, right-click Products Sample (2) and select Create Function. The Create Function dialog box opens. In the Function Name box, enter *FnNormalizeColumnNames* and click OK. As shown in Figure 4-10, you now have a new function that can be used on all the files.

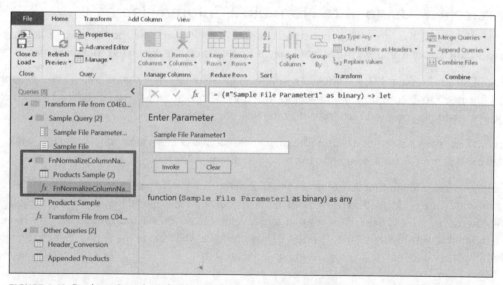

FIGURE 4-10 Products Sample (2) has been converted into the function FnNormalizeColumnNames with Products Sample (2) as its sample query.

Now you have a function, *FnNormalizeColumnNames*, that can be invoked inside the Products Sample query instead of invoking the Products Sample (2) query.

22. In the Queries pane, select the Products Sample query. In Applied Steps, select Appended Query. In the formula bar, replace the following formula:

```
= Table.Combine({#"Products Sample (2)", #"Removed Top Rows"})
```

with the following formula:

```
= Table.Combine({FnNormalizeColumnNames(#"Sample File Parameter1"), #"Removed Top Rows"})
```

The function *FnNormalizeColumnNames* receives an Excel workbook's contents from the folder as an argument and returns the normalized columns. The table #"Removed Top Rows" is the last step in Products Samples, before you applied the append. It includes the original rows without the header.

Why do you use #"Sample File Parameter1" here? Recall that this parameter was always pointing to the Accessories file when it was called inside Sample Products (2). But now, in the context of a function, this parameter is reassigned with the correct file, as Power Query iterates over the files in the folder.

23. Move back to the appended results in the Appended Products query and scroll down the Preview pane to confirm that all the columns of C04E04 - Bikes.xlsx are aligned correctly. Close the Power Query Editor and load the data to your report.

You can download the solution files C04E06 - Solution - Transpose Headers.xlsx and C04E06 - Solution - Transpose Headers.pbix from https://aka.ms/DataPwrBIPivot/downloads.

Exercise 4-7: Using M to Normalize Column Names

This exercise shows the most efficient method to apply a conversion table and normalize column names. In this exercise, you will use M and apply the conversion directly on the column names.

Recall that in Exercise 4-3, you applied a simple text manipulation on the column names by applying the M formula *Table.TransformColumnNames* with the relevant text manipulation as the second argument. For example, you used *Text.Proper* to capitalize each word.

In this final exercise on normalizing column names, you will create a custom function that will normalize the column names according to the rules in the conversion table.

Before you create the function, you need to understand one more transformation change that will simplify your code and speed up the lookup in the conversion table. Recall that earlier your conversion table was constructed as pairs of Source and Target values. Now you will transpose that table and promote the first row as headers. Thus, the new conversion table will include the Source values as headers, and the Target values as the first row, as shown in Figure 4-11.

FIGURE 4-11 Transposing the original conversion table of Source/Destination pairs into a single-row table can be an efficient method of normalizing the column names.

This transformation will allow you to look up Source values as headers in the conversion table and get their Target values in the row by using a simple custom function. To create the transposed conversion table, start with the saved queries from steps 1–9 of Exercise 4-4.

1. Open your workbook or Power BI report and launch the Power Query Editor.

2. In the Queries pane, select the Header_Conversion query.

3. On the Transform tab, select Transpose and then select Use First Row As Headers.

4. In Applied Steps, delete the Changed Type step, which was created automatically. There is no need to have it, and if you keep this step, any changes you make to the Source values in your conversion table may lead to refresh errors in the future.

5. In the Queries pane, select the Products Sample query and click the fx icon, as demonstrated in step 8 of Exercise 4-3.

6. Change the formula in the formula bar from the following:

    ```
    = #"Promoted Headers"
    ```

    to the following:

    ```
    = Table.TransformColumnNames(#"Promoted Headers",
    each try Table.Column(Header_Conversion, _){0} otherwise _)
    ```

7. Press Enter and review the headers in the Preview pane. They were normalized. You can now select the Appended Products query and see that all the mismatched tables were combined correctly.

Let's briefly examine the preceding expression. In Exercise 4-3 you already used *Table.TransformColumnNames*. Here we narrow our explanation and focus on its second argument:

```
each try Table.Column(Header_Conversion, _){0} otherwise _
```

In Chapter 9, you will learn about these types of expressions in more details. The combination of the terms *each* and _ is used as a shortcut to define a function. In this case, *Table.TransformColumnNames* requires a function as a second argument, and because of the use of each and the underscore character, it invokes that function for each column name.

Now, let's go back to some basic syntax and examine the expression above step by step. To access the first row's cell in one of the columns in the conversion table, you used the term {0}. Remember that everything in M is zero-based index, so you use zero instead of one to access the first cell. The curly brackets are used to access a member in a list, by its zero-based index in the list.

Say that you have a Column1 column in the Header_Conversion table. To access the list of values in Column1, you would use the following formula:

```
Header_Conversion[Column1]
```

In this case, the column name is provided as an input parameter to the defined function via the underscore character. To access each of the columns (as lists) by their column names in the Header_Conversion table, you can write the following function:

```
each Table.Column(Header_Conversion, _)
```

Note, that you use the function *Table.Column*. The following formula will not work:

```
each Header_Conversion[_]
```

With this formula, the M engine will search for a column whose actual name is _. As a result, you will get the following error:

```
Expression.Error: The column '_' of the table wasn't found.
```

To avoid getting this error, you use *Table.Column*, which receives a table and a column name and returns the desired column as a list. Combining the formulas together, you can use this formula to access a Target value by Source column in the transposed conversion table that you created in step 3.

```
each Table.Column(Header_Conversion, _){0}
```

So, why do you add the *try/otherwise* elements in step 6? Recall that the conversion table was not designed to hold all the possible column names you have—only the mismatching column names. Therefore, the expression in step 6 includes the *try/otherwise* elements that are bolded in the expression below:

```
each try Table.Column(Header_Conversion, _){0} otherwise _
```

If the Source value is not found in the Header_Conversion table, the *try* part will fail, triggering the *otherwise* part, which will return the Source value.

Here is the entire function again:

```
= Table.TransformColumnNames(#"Promoted Headers",
each try Table.Column(Header_Conversion, _){0} otherwise _)
```

You can read it as the following natural language instructions: "Take the table that resulted at the Promoted Headers step and transform its column names by the following rule: For each column name, try to find it as a column name in the conversion table and return its corresponding value in the conversion table cell. If you fail to do so (which means you don't have such a column name in the conversion table), return the Promoted Headers' column name as an output."

If you didn't follow all the details in this section, don't worry. You can still use the three other methods described in Exercises 4-4, 4-5, and 4-6 to combine mismatched tables with a conversion table. The purpose of Exercise 4-7 is to show you how quickly you can combine mismatching tables by using M. You are encouraged to return to this exercise after you learn more about M in Chapter 9.

The solution files C04E07 - Solution - M.xlsx and C04E07 - Solution - M.pbix are available at https://aka.ms/DataPwrBIPivot/downloads.

Summary

In this chapter, you have learned the implications of combining mismatched tables and the different techniques you can use to match between column names and successfully combine multiple tables.

You have learned how to identify missing values and split data in mismatched tables that are badly combined. You have also learned how to manually rename columns to match the column names before you append the tables.

In cases where multiple tables in a folder all share the same order between columns, you have learned how to apply the header generalization technique to append the tables together. You have also learned about the *Table.TransformColumnNames* function and applied it for simple column name normalization such as to capitalize each word or replace underscores with spaces.

A conversion table helps normalize column names in cases where one-rule text manipulation is irrelevant. You have learned how to merge a conversion table to replace mismatched column names, using three techniques: the transpose, the unpivot, and the transpose of column names only. Finally, you have been introduced to the most effective way to normalize column names: using advanced M code.

The following table summarizes the various techniques and their pros and cons:

Technique	Pros	Cons
1. Header generalization	Simple implementation. No performance penalties.	When the order between columns changes, this method will lead to swapped values.
2. Transpose, merge, and transpose back	Simple implementation. Can handle inconsistent order between columns.	Excessive memory footprint. Will fail when one of the combined tables reaches 16,384 rows.
3. Unpivot, merge, and pivot	Simple implementation. Can work on large datasets. Can handle inconsistent order between columns.	Significantly slower than methods 1, 4, and 5.
4. Transpose column names only	Can handle inconsistent order between columns. Refresh is significantly faster than with methods 2 and 3.	Implementation time is the longest.
5. Use M to normalize column names	Most effective method in terms of performance. Quick implementation time.	Familiarity with M is needed.

The ability to combine mismatched tables can bring significant business value. Imagine that you work for a corporation that constantly acquires new companies. You could apply the techniques in this chapter to quickly mash up different datasets of each acquired company and obtain insights before the data is consolidated by IT. Self-service BI scenarios can truly shine when it comes to combining such siloed datasets together.

CHAPTER 5

Preserving Context

For me context is the key—from that comes the understanding of everything.

—Kenneth Noland

IN THIS CHAPTER, YOU WILL

- Learn how to preserve context from file names and worksheets when you append queries

- Learn how to apply the Drill Down transformation on titles and dynamically preserve their content in tables

- Preserve titles as a pre-append phase by using Drill Down and a custom column to combine multiple tables from a folder

- Preserve titles as a post-append phase by using Drill Down, conditional columns, and the Fill Down transformation to combine multiple worksheets from a workbook

- Learn advanced techniques for preserving specific cells from a grid using index and proximity cues

In Chapters 3, "Combining Data from Multiple Sources," and 4, "Combining Mismatched Tables," you tackled the challenge of combining tables and approached some real-life scenarios of mismatched silos of data that required normalization before they could be combined. But often key contextual information that is stored outside tables is crucial for analysis. Combining tables without their context will yield meaningless results. In this chapter you will learn how to preserve table context and how to combine separate tables with their contextual information. This chapter addresses table context in a variety of scenarios and shows how to dynamically detect and extract key context elements in your data while ignoring irrelevant ones. After all, as Kenneth Noland has pointed out (although probably in a completely different context), with context comes the understanding of everything. Without it, you lose crucial insights.

Preserving Context in File Names and Worksheets

In Chapters 3 and 4 you learned different methods to combine multiple tables. You have used the techniques on product data from the fictional company AdventureWorks. In the exercises in Chapters 3 and 4 you had separate tables for the product parent categories, such as Bikes and Accessories. Luckily (and intentionally), the parent category was provided as a column in the data. Therefore, when you combined the tables, you had the parent category intact. This section goes over a common scenario, in which crucial contextual information is available as a worksheet name or file name but not as a column in the table. The goal here is to find ways to include that data as a column in order to preserve the context.

Let's start with a simple example.

Exercise 5-1, Part 1: Custom Column Technique

In this exercise you will import AdventureWorks product records from two parent categories: Bikes and Accessories, located in two separate workbooks, and append them together. The appended result will not include the product category names, and you would therefore not be able to perform any analysis that compares the performances of the two product lines. In this exercise, you will see how easy it is to preserve the parent categories values in the appended results.

To start the exercise, download the workbooks C05E01 - Bikes.xlsx and C05E01 - Accessories.xlsx from https://aka.ms/DataPwrBIPivot/downloads.

1. Load each of the workbooks to a blank new workbook or Power BI report. For each file, select Sheet1 in the Navigator dialog box before you load it. Then, when the Power Query Editor is open, you should notice that the queries are named Sheet1 and Sheet1 (2), as shown in Figure 5-1. The parent category information is not available as a column.

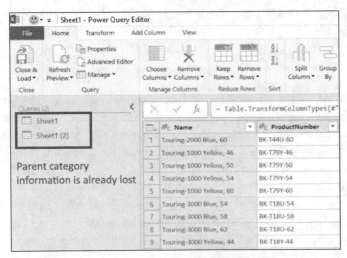

FIGURE 5-1 When you import Bikes and Accessories from Sheet1 of two separate workbooks, the context provided by the file name is lost.

2. Rename Sheet1 to *Bikes* and Sheet1 (2) to *Accessories*. If you don't recall which one of the queries should be Bikes and which one should be Accessories, you can select the first step in Applied Steps and find the relevant parent category referenced as a file name in the formula bar. For example, here is the formula for Bikes:

```
= Excel.Workbook(File.Contents("C:\Data\C05\C05E01 - Bikes.xlsx"), null, true)
```

Alternatively, you can select the settings icon on the right side of the Source step in Applied Steps of each query. In the Excel dialog box that opens, you can look at the File Path setting to determine whether the selected query is Bikes or Accessories.

3. Select the Bikes query in the Queries pane. On the Home tab, from the Append Queries drop-down, select Append Queries As New.

4. In the Append dialog box, select Bikes as Primary Table and Accessories as Table to Append to the Primary Table and click OK.

    The new query Append1 contains the appended data from Bikes and Accessories products, but the parent category context is now lost. Renaming the original queries *Sheet1* and *Sheet1 (2)* to *Bikes* and *Accessories* in step 2 wasn't sufficient to preserve the context, but you can fix it now.

5. Select Bikes in the Queries pane.

6. On the Add Column tab, select Custom Column.

7. When the Custom Column dialog box opens, enter *Parent Category* in the New Column Name box and enter the following line under Custom Column Formula:

    ```
    = "Bikes"
    ```

8. Click OK to close the Custom Column dialog box, and select *Accessories* in the Queries pane.

9. On the Add Column tab, select Custom Column.

10. When the Custom Column dialog box opens, enter *Parent Category* in the New Column Name box and enter the following line under Custom Column Formula:

    ```
    = "Accessories"
    ```

11. Click OK to close the Custom Column dialog box and select the Append1 query in the Queries pane. As you scroll down the Preview pane, you will now notice that the new column, Parent Category, includes the correct context for rows from Bikes and Accessories.

You can download the solution workbook C05E01 - Solution.xlsx and the Power BI report C05E01 - Solution.pbix from https://aka.ms/DataPwrBIPivot/downloads.

Exercise 5-1, Part 2: Handling Context from File Names and Worksheet Names

As a rule, whenever you apply Append Queries or Append Queries As New, you may lose the context that is available in the query names, and if you do, you need to add a preliminary custom column for each table. If you combine multiple files from a folder, and the file names contain the context, you can find the required context in the Source.Name column and do not need to add a custom column. Chapter 3 demonstrates this by preserving the release year of AdventureWorks products (see the section "Appending Tables from a Folder" in Chapter 3).

When dealing with context in worksheet names, you have two ways to preserve the information in these names. If the number of worksheets is small, and their names are not expected to change, you can import each one of the individual worksheets and use the custom column technique described in Exercise 5-1 Part 1 to preserve their context.

You can now download the workbook C05E01 - Bikes & Accessories.xlsx and try it. Import each worksheet, and append the Bikes and Accessories queries by using Append Queries As New. Without adding a custom column for each query, you will not be able to preserve the parent category.

If you need to append many worksheets from a workbook while preserving the worksheet names, you can use the technique explained in Exercise 3-4 in Chapter 3. Here is how you can apply that technique on the file C05E01 - Bikes & Accessories.xlsx:

1. Open a blank new workbook or a new Power BI report.

   In Excel: On the Data tab, select Get Data, From File, From Workbook.

   In Power BI Desktop: On the Home tab, select Get Data, and in the Get Data dialog box, select File and then select Excel.

2. Select the file C05E01 - Bikes & Accessories.xlsx and select Import.

3. In the Navigator dialog box, right-click the workbook item and select Edit from the shortcut menu.

4. In the Power Query Editor, keep the columns Name and Data and extract Data. Thanks to the Name column, you can preserve the parent category context.

5. Use the technique described in Exercise 3-4 to handle the column names that are embedded as rows.

You can download the solution workbook C05E01 - Solution 2.xlsx or the Power BI report C05E01 - Solution 2.pbix from https://aka.ms/DataPwrBIPivot/downloads.

Pre-Append Preservation of Titles

In Part 2 of Exercise 5-1, you were able to combine Bikes and Accessories and preserve their parent category attribute from the file or worksheet names. Unfortunately, in real life you will encounter many scenarios in which key contextual information is stored outside tables and not as file or worksheet names.

Recall from Exercise 5-1 Part 1 that before you appended Bikes and Accessories, you added a custom column in each table with the parent category value. You will now learn an advanced variation of that technique to preserve titles which are available in the data source before the tables' rows.

We will refer to this technique as *pre-append* because you apply it before the append step. The pre-append technique is very useful when you append a few tables using Append Queries or Append Queries As New. It is also very useful when you combine multiple files from a folder, as you will see later. Figure 5-2 illustrates the transformation steps that are necessary to extract the information from the title in the grid and combine it as a new column.

> **Note** Unlike the technique in Exercise 5-1 Part 1, where you applied the keywords Bikes and Accessories as a new column to each query in a hard-coded way, here you need a generic way to extract the value from the title—because you don't know the value in the title, and you need a dynamic method to work with many tables with different titles.

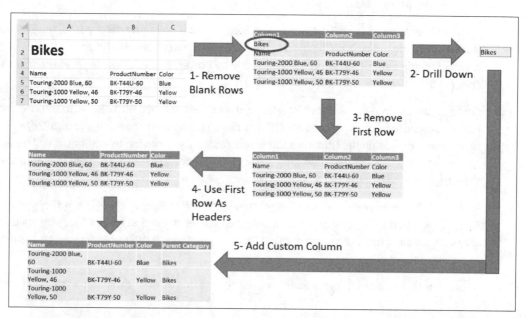

FIGURE 5-2 Pre-append context preservation of titles is illustrated on AdventureWorks products. This method enables you to dynamically extract the table titles and add them in the appended results.

Exercise 5-2: Preserving Titles Using Drill Down

In this exercise you will follow the sequence illustrated in Figure 5-2 to extract the Bikes title from the Excel cell and combine it as a new column on the Bikes table. Then in the proceeding exercise, you will learn how to generalize this technique and apply it on multiple files before you append all tables from a folder.

> **Note** This technique can also work on text and CSV files in a folder when the context is stored as a leading line prior to the lines with the data.

To start the exercise, download the workbook C05E02 - Bikes.xlsx from https://aka.ms/ DataPwrBIPivot/downloads.

1. Open a blank new workbook or a new Power BI report.

   In Excel: On the Data tab, select Get Data, From File, From Workbook.

   In Power BI Desktop: On the Home tab, select Get Data, and in the Get Data dialog box, select File and then select Excel.

2. Select the file C05E02 - Bikes.xlsx and select Import.

3. Select Sheet1 in the Navigator dialog box. Select Edit to open the Power Query Editor and rename the query *Bikes*.

4. Remove the step Changed Type in Applied Steps. (This is not a mandatory step, but it is pointless to apply the automatic Changed Type step at this stage because the column types of the products table cannot be recognized correctly by Power Query at this stage, as the first rows contain the title and blank rows.)

5. On the Home tab, select Remove Rows, and then select Remove Blank Rows to remove the blank rows from your imported date. Why is this step important? Because you will often find blank lines separating the title from the actual tables. By removing these lines, it will be easier to import the product table rows later, after you extract and preserve the parent category in the title in the next steps.

6. Right-click the Bikes query in the Queries pane, and select Reference from the shortcut menu. Bikes (2) is created. Select it and notice that the first cell in the first row includes the value Bikes. Right-click that cell and select Drill Down. This step will show you the word Bikes in the Preview pane.

   Keep your report open to proceed to step 7 after the drill down is explained in the next section.

Drilling Down on a Table Cell Explained in M

Following the selection of Drill Down in the last step in the preceding section, you can see the following line in the formula bar:

```
= Source{0}[Column1]
```

This M formula extracts the value Bikes from the table. In the preceding formula, Source is the name of the table that was provided in the preceding step. You can also see that Source is used as the first step in the Applied Steps pane.

Source{0} returns the first row in the Source table (and *Source{1}* would return the second row and so on). You use a zero-based index from 0 to n–1 to access 1 to n rows. You may find this confusing in the beginning, but will get used to it. In most scenarios, you can just use the user interface and apply Drill Down to access single cells.

In Power Query, rows are represented as records. A record is a list of key/value pairs, where the keys are the column names and values are the corresponding values in the relevant rows. To access a value by a given key in a record, you can use the formula *record[key]*, where *record* is the record name and *key* is the key name. Hence, when the formula is *Source{0}[Column1]*, you access the first row in Source and then access the value in Column1. Figure 5-3 illustrates how the drill-down formula *Source{0}[Column1]* accesses the value Bikes in two steps: from a table to a record and then from a record to cell.

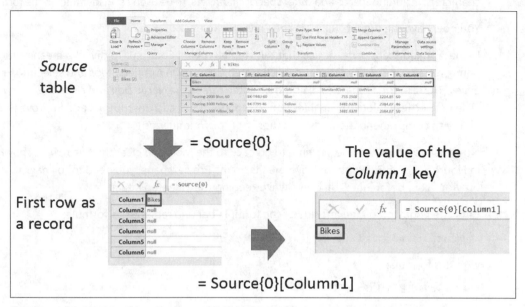

FIGURE 5-3 The Drill Down option generates an M formula. Its logic is explained in two steps.

> **Tip** You don't need to know the M syntax to access rows, columns, or cells. You just need to apply a Drill Down transformation and review the formula bar to get a reminder of the syntax. You should also note that you can access a single cell by first accessing the column and then the row. For example, the code `Source{0}[Column1]` will return the same value as the code `Source[Column1]{0}`. The latter syntax works a bit differently: It first returns a list of all the items in Column1, and then it returns the first element in the list.

Combining the Drill Down Result in the Query

Follow these additional steps to continue Exercise 5-2:

7. Now that you know how to apply a Drill Down to extract a cell, delete Bikes (2) and select the Bikes query.

Here you will apply another Drill Down but this time on the Bikes query.

8. Right-click the cell that contains the value Bikes and select Drill Down.

9. In the formula bar, notice the following formula:

```
= #"Removed Blank Rows"{0}[Column1]
```

You should now recognize the syntax. This time, it is used on the Removed Blank Rows step in Applied Steps, which is represented as #"Removed Blank Rows" in the M formula. (The format #"…", which is called a quoted-identifier in M, is used to allow any sequence of zero or more Unicode characters, including spaces and other special characters, to be used as an identifier in the formula.)

You now have the output "Bikes" in the Preview pane.

10. In the Applied Steps pane, notice that this step is labeled Column1. To give it a meaningful name, rename it *Title*, by right-clicking the step Column1 in Applied Steps and selecting Properties. Then, in the Properties dialog box, enter *Title* in the Name box and close the dialog box. (The Properties dialog box enables you to rename steps, add description, and improve the ability to comprehend the transformation logic of your queries.)

    Now that you have the title, it's time to go back to the table and clear the title row, as shown in Figure 5-2 step 3. But as you have the title in the Preview pane, you need to roll back to the previous step before the Drill Down while keeping the Title step intact.

11. Click the fx button on the left side of the formula bar and replace this formula:

    ```
    = Title
    ```

    with this formula:

    ```
    = #"Removed Blank Rows"
    ```

    This approach allows you to skip the Title step and go back to the preceding step. You now see the table in the Preview pane, instead of the word Bikes. But as you can see, the Title remained in Applied Steps. You will use it shortly.

12. To remove the first row, as illustrated in step 3 of Figure 5-2, on the Home tab, select Remove Rows. Then select Remove Top Rows. When the Remove Top Rows dialog box opens, enter *1* in the Number of Rows box and click OK to close the dialog box.

> **Note** Removing a predefined number of top rows (such as one row in the current exercise) is not a good practice. Later in this chapter, in the section "Using Context Cues," you will learn how to ignore context and remove the top rows by the location of the table in the grid instead of removing a hard-coded number of rows.

13. Following step 4 in Figure 5-2, promote the product column names to become the headers: On the Transform tab, select Use First Rows As Headers.

14. Finally, to follow the last step shown in Figure 5-2, create a custom column with Bikes as the parent category by going to the Add Column tab and selecting Custom Column. When the Custom Column dialog box opens, enter *Parent Category* in the New Column Name box and enter the following formula under Custom Column Formula:

    ```
    = Title
    ```

    Then click OK to close the Custom Column dialog box.

You should now see that Bikes has been added as a new column. You were able to dynamically extract the word Bikes from the cell that was used as the title of the worksheet, and follow the steps in Figure 5-2 to preserve it in your table. You will find this technique extremely useful in real-life data challenges and can apply it in many scenarios, data sources, and data formats—beyond titles in Excel cells.

> **Note** The ability to diverge the transformation into two flows and then converge them together into a single flow is a powerful technique in Power Query. As you become more familiar with M, you will be able to apply such manipulations directly in the Advanced Editor instead of creating custom steps, as you did in this exercise.

You can download the solution workbook C05E02 - Solution.xlsx and the Power BI Report C05E02 - Solution.pbix from https://aka.ms/DataPwrBIPivot/downloads.

Exercise 5-3: Preserving Titles from a Folder

In Exercise 5-2 you preserved the title from a single worksheet. It's time to generalize this technique and apply it on multiple workbooks in a folder.

1. Download C05E03 - Products.zip from https://aka.ms/DataPwrBIPivot/downloads.

2. Extract the content of the ZIP file into a new folder: *C:\Data\C05\C05E03 - Products*. The folder now contains the following files:

    a. C05E03-01.xlsx

    b. C05E03-02.xlsx

    c. C05E03-03.xlsx

    d. C05E03-04.xlsx

3. Review the files and notice that each file contains a table of products with a different title, as shown in Figure 5-4. Intentionally, the files have meaningless names, so the only way to preserve the parent categories of the products in each workbook is by extracting the titles.

4. Open a blank new workbook or a new Power BI report.

    In Excel: On the Data tab, select Get Data, From File, From Folder.

    In Power BI Desktop: On the Home tab, select Get Data, and in the Get Data dialog box, select File and then select Folder.

5. In the Folder dialog box, select the folder *C:\Data\C05\C05E03 - Products* and close the dialog box.

6. In the next dialog box, named the same as the folder you selected in step 5, in the Combine drop-down menu, select Combine and Edit.

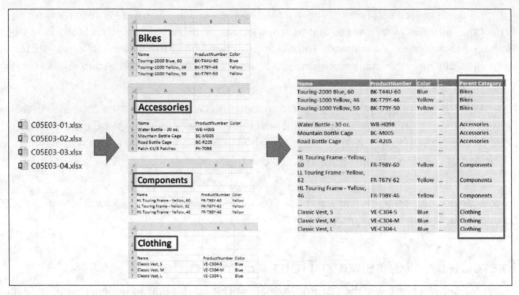

FIGURE 5-4 It is possible to combine multiple tables and preserve their titles.

7. When the Combine Files dialog box opens, in the Example File drop-down menu, select any one of the options and then select Sheet1 and click OK.

8. When the Power Query Editor opens, notice in the Preview pane that the combined products table lacks the parent category context. Again, this is the result of the meaningless filenames. Select the query Transform Sample File from C05E03 - Products and rename the query *Products Sample*.

9. On the Home tab, while Products Sample is selected, select Remove Rows, and then select Remove Blank Rows to apply the first step in Figure 5-2.

10. To extract the title from the Bikes table as you did in Exercise 5-2 (steps 8–14) and preserve all titles in the new Parent Category column, follow these steps on the Products Sample query:

    a. Right-click the cell that contains the value Bikes, and select Drill Down.

    b. In the formula bar, notice the following formula:

       = #"Removed Blank Rows"{0}[Column1]

    c. In the Applied Steps pane, notice that this step is labeled Column1. Right-click the step Column1 in Applied Steps and select Properties. Then, in the Properties dialog box, enter *Title* in the Name box and click OK to close the dialog box.

    d. Click the fx button on the left side of the formula bar and replace this formula:

       = Title

       with this formula:

       = #"Removed Blank Rows"

e. On the Home tab, select Remove Rows. Then select Remove Top Rows. When the Remove Top Rows dialog box opens, enter *1* in the Number of Rows box, and click OK to close the dialog box.

   f. On the Transform tab, select Use First Rows As Headers.

   g. On Add Column tab, select Custom Column. When the Custom Column dialog box opens, enter *Parent Category* in the New Column Name box, and enter the following formula under Custom Column Formula:

   ```
   = Title
   ```

   Then click OK to close the Custom Column dialog box.

11. With the Products Sample query selected, in Applied Steps delete the Changed Type step. (The Changed Type step will lead to errors in the Size column, and you can explicitly change the types of the columns later.)

12. In the Queries pane, select C05E03 - Products.

13. In Applied Steps, delete the last step, Changed Type.

14. Select the filter control on the Parent Category column header to ensure that the titles from the four workbooks were extracted correctly in the pre-append phase of the Products Sample query. The appended results should include all four parent categories.

You can now download the solution workbook C05E03 - Solution.xlsx and the Power BI report C05E03 - Solution.pbix from https://aka.ms/DataPwrBIPivot/downloads.

In the next section you will learn how to apply a post-append context preservation of titles. This will allow you to apply the transformations on the appended results in the C05E03 - Products query instead of applying the changes on Products Sample. You will find this technique especially useful when you combine multiple worksheets, as you will see in Exercise 5-4.

Post-Append Context Preservation of Titles

In the preceding section you applied the pre-append technique to dynamically extract the value of a title and add it as a custom column before the append step. This approach is effective when you have a limited number of tables to append or when you apply it to combine multiple tables from a folder. However, in some scenarios it would be easier to extract the titles from the appended table. We can refer to this technique as *post-append* because you apply it *after* the append step. The post-append technique is especially useful when you append multiple worksheets from a workbook or when your data source includes multiple tables in the same text file—each table separated from its preceding table by a title line.

Exercise 5-4: Preserving Titles from Worksheets in the same Workbook

This exercise demonstrates the use of the post-append method to extract AdventureWorks parent categories from the title in each worksheet of the same workbook. In real-life scenarios, you may have dozens of worksheets in a single workbook, all with the same contextual data stored as titles at the top of each table, as illustrated in Figure 5-5. Note that in this scenario, like the file names in Exercise 5-3 the worksheet names don't hold any meaningful context about their tables.

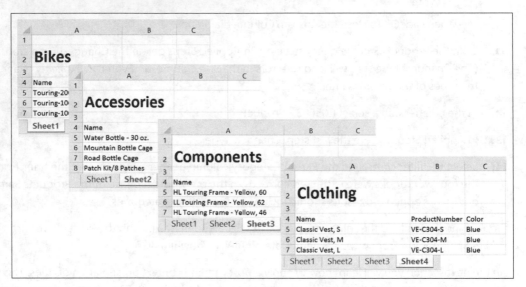

FIGURE 5-5 AdventureWorks products are stored on separate worksheets of the same workbook, with the parent categories as table titles (not worksheet names).

This exercise shows how to extract the titles after you append all the worksheets together.

1. Download the file C05E04 - Products.xlsx from https://aka.ms/DataPwrBIPivot/downloads and save it to *C:\Data\C05*.

2. Open the workbook and review its content. Notice that AdventureWorks products are divided by parent category into four worksheets: Sheet1, Sheet2, Sheet3, and Sheet4, with the table titles Bikes, Accessories, Components, and Clothing as cells above the tables (as shown in Figure 5-5).

3. Open a new blank workbook in Excel or a new report in Power BI Desktop.

    In Excel: On the Data tab, select Get Data, From File, From Workbook.

    In Power BI Desktop: Select Get Data and then select File, Excel, Connect.

4. Select the file C05E04 - Products.xlsx and click Import.

5. In the Navigator dialog box, right-click C05E04 - Products.xlsx and select Edit from the shortcut menu.

6. In the Preview pane, notice that there is no way to determine the parent category of the product. When you combined multiple tables from multiple worksheets in Chapter 3, you had a significant context as the name of each worksheet. It was easy to preserve that context by keeping the Name column. Unfortunately, in this exercise, the worksheet names have no context. You can ignore all the columns except Data. Right-click the header of the Data column and select Remove Other Columns.

7. Expand the Data column by clicking on the expand icon on the right side of the header or by selecting the Data column and then selecting Expand on the Transform tab. Click OK in the Expand pane.

    The first table in Figure 5-6 shows the appended results. The titles Bikes, Accessories, Components, and Clothing are embedded in the appended table. You will need to follow the transformation sequence that is highlighted in Figure 5-6 to extract the titles and pass it into a Parent Category column.

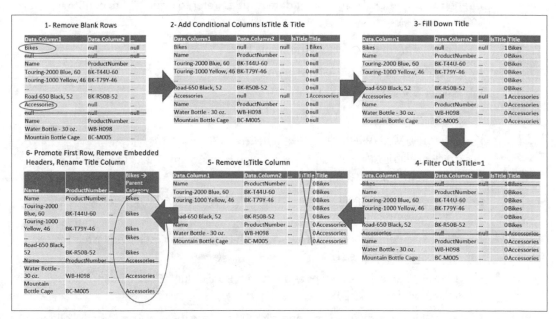

FIGURE 5-6 Post-append context preservation of titles, illustrated on AdventureWorks products, enables you to append multiple worksheets in a workbook while preserving the table titles.

8. On the Home tab, select Remove Rows and then select Remove Blank Rows. The rationale of this step is clear; you applied it in Exercise 5-3 as well. As titles tend to be followed by blank rows for cosmetic purposes, in this step you remove them.

9. On the Add Column tab, select Add Conditional Column.

    Your task is to create a conditional column that will help you identify rows with titles.

There are two approaches to identifying the titles:

a. In the naive approach, you can determine whether the first column is equal to Bikes, Accessories, Components, or Clothing, and you set the new column as 1 if it does, or 0 otherwise. The naive approach is not recommended because it uses hard-coded values to determine the titles. In the future, you may have new parent categories as titles, and you cannot predict their values at this stage. So, each time you get a new worksheet with a new parent category, you will have to modify the query to include it.

b. In the robust approach you identify the titles in the sample data as rows with null values in all the columns except Column1. This approach allows you to create the query once, without the need to modify it whenever worksheets are added with new parent categories.

Tip You will often find multiple methods to extract contextual information. Making explicit assumptions about your data will help you select the best method.

10. Taking the robust approach, follow these steps in the Add Conditional Column dialog box to define the conditional column that detects titles (refer to Figure 5-7 to confirm you follow the steps correctly):

a. Enter *IsTitle* in the New Column Name box.

b. Set Data.Column2 as the first Column Name.

c. Select Does Not Equal as the operator.

d. Enter *null* in the Value text box.

e. Enter *0* in the Output box.

f. Click Add Rule. Repeat steps a–e but with Data.Column3 selected instead of Data.Column2 in step b.

g. Click Add Rule. Repeat steps a–e but with Data.Column4 selected instead of Data.Column2 in step b.

h. Click Add Rule. Repeat steps a–e but with Data.Column5 selected instead of Data.Column2 in step b.

i. Click Add Rule. Repeat steps a–e but with Data.Column6 selected instead of Data.Column2 in step b.

j. Enter *1* in the Otherwise box, and click OK to close the Add Conditional Column dialog box.

Next, you will add a new conditional column with the actual title when IsTitle is 1 and null otherwise. This will set the stage for the Fill Down step to follow, as illustrated in Figure 5-6, step 3.

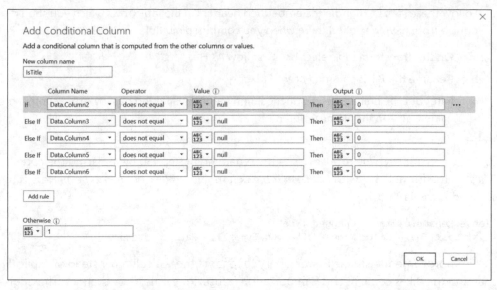

FIGURE 5-7 You can set the Add Conditional Column dialog box to dynamically identify titles.

11. On the Add Column tab, select Add Conditional Column. In the Add Conditional Column dialog box that opens, follow these steps:

   a. Enter *Title* in the New Column Name box.

   b. Enter *IsTitle* in the first Column Name box.

   c. Select Equal as the operator.

   d. Enter *1* in the Value box.

   e. Select the drop-down menu below Output and click Select a Column.

   f. Select Data.Column1 from the Output drop-down.

   g. Enter *null* in the Otherwise box, and click OK to close the Add Conditional Column dialog box.

   You now have the titles in the Title column for rows with titles and nulls in the product rows. This is where the Fill Down transformation comes in handy.

12. Right-click the header of the Title column, select Fill, and then select Down. This step enables you to preserve the parent category in the correct context and in each row.

   You can now filter out the title rows, and the IsTitle column will help you to do it.

13. Click the filter control in the header of the IsTitle column. When the Filter pane opens, deselect the value 1 and then click OK.

14. Remove the IsTitle column. (Once you have used it to remove the title rows, you no longer need it.)

15. Follow these steps to handle the embedded headers in the table rows which you should recognize from having applied them when you combined multiple worksheets in Chapter 3:

    a. On the Transform tab, select Use First Row As Headers.

    b. Rename the Bikes column *Parent Category*.

    c. Filter out the embedded product column names by filtering out rows that contain the value Name in the Name Column.

Tip You can improve the robustness of the renaming in step 15b by replacing the code *"Bikes"* in the formula bar with *List.Last(Table.ColumnNames(#"Changed Type"))*. Here is the modified formula:

```
= Table.RenameColumns(#"Changed Type",
{{List.Last(Table.ColumnNames(#"Changed Type")), "Parent Category"}})
```

This improvement instructs Power Query to rename the last column instead of explicitly renaming the Bikes column. This is important because, in real life, data changes. The original query will fail to refresh if the Bikes table no longer is the first workbook in your source folder. Instructing Power Query to rename the last column will ensure that your query will not fail to refresh. In Chapter 9, "Introduction to the Power Query M Formula Language," you will learn more about the syntax used here, and in Chapter 10, "From Pitfalls to Robust Queries," you will learn how to optimize your queries in similar manners, including in the context of renaming columns.

16. Close the Power Query Editor and load the appended table.

You can download the solution workbook C05E04 - Solution.xlsx and the Power BI report C05E04 - Solution.pbix from https://aka.ms/DataPwrBIPivot/downloads.

Using Context Cues

In Exercise 5-4, you were able to extract and preserve the titles from AdventureWorks worksheets after the append step and use them as the parent category. Because the appended tables included the titles as embedded rows, you used a conditional column to detect the titles. To dynamically identify rows with titles, you assumed that the titles exist in rows in which the first column is not blank and all the other columns are blank. But what do you do if you cannot make this assumption? Is there a way to identify titles by their proximity to specific cells?

In this section you will learn how to identify context by its location and proximity to specific "anchor" cells. These anchor cells will be used as cues to help you find the context you need. You will also learn how to ignore irrelevant context.

You will use a new variation of the AdventureWorks Products workbook. Unlike the sample workbook used in Exercise 5-4, this time the parent category is located inside a small table, on top of the Products table, as shown in Figure 5-8.

You will identify the parent category value by using the location of the text Parent Category.

	A	B	C	D	E	F	G	H
1								
2	Parent Category	Report Date						
3	Bikes	1/1/2018						
4								
5	Name	ProductNumber	Color	StandardC	ListPrice	Size		
6	Touring-2000 Blue, 60	BK-T44U-60	Blue	755.1508	1214.85	60		
7	Touring-1000 Yellow, 46	BK-T79Y-46	Yellow	1481.938	2384.07	46		
8	Touring-1000 Yellow, 50	BK-T79Y-50	Yellow	1481.938	2384.07	50		
9	Touring-1000 Yellow, 54	BK-T79Y-54	Yellow	1481.938	2384.07	54		
10	Touring-1000 Yellow, 60	BK-T79Y-60	Yellow	1481.938	2384.07	60		
11	Touring-3000 Blue, 54	BK-T18U-54	Blue	461.4448	742.35	54		
12	Touring-3000 Blue, 58	BK-T18U-58	Blue	461.4448	742.35	58		
13	Touring-3000 Blue, 62	BK-T18U-62	Blue	461.4448	742.35	62		
14	Touring-3000 Yellow, 44	BK-T18Y-44	Yellow	461.4448	742.35	44		

FIGURE 5-8 Your challenge is to extract the parent category from the top table and preserve it as a new column in the appended bottom tables.

Exercise 5-5: Using an Index Column as a Cue

In this exercise you will use different techniques to preserve the parent category. You will import each worksheet with a cue that will help you combine the tables and preserve the parent category.

1. Download the workbook C05E05 - Products.xlsx from https://aka.ms/DataPwrBIPivot/ downloads and save it in the folder *C:\Data\C05*.

    Open the workbook and review its content. You can see that AdventureWorks products are split into four worksheets. As shown in Figure 5-8, each parent category—Bikes, Accessories, Components, and Clothing—is stored in a separate small table above the product table of each worksheet. The worksheets are named Sheet1, Sheet2, Sheet3, and Sheet4 and cannot help you differentiate between the parent categories.

2. Open a blank new workbook in Excel or a new report in Power BI Desktop.

    In Excel: On the Data tab, select Get Data, From File, From Workbook.

    In Power BI Desktop: Select Get Data and then select File, Excel, Connect.

3. Select the file C05E05 - Products.xlsx and click Import.

4. In the Navigator dialog box, right-click C05E05 - Products.xlsx and select Edit from the shortcut menu.

5. Right-click the header of the Data column, and select Remove Other Columns from the shortcut menu. As in Exercise 5-4, now you should find a way to detect the rows with the parent category values. Expanding this table in the Data column at this stage will be premature. You first need to extract some cues from each table: their row numbers.

In Exercise 5-4, you assumed that the parent category is located as a title in rows that have no other values. Following that assumption, you added a conditional column to detect rows with values in the first column and blank values in the rest. In this exercise, you can no longer make this assumption. As illustrated in Figure 5-8, the parent category value (cell A3) is located next to the Report Date value (cell B3).

Then, how can you identify the parent category? While you can assume that rows with parent category values always have values in the first two columns, and empty in all the other columns, this assumption is too risky. What would happen if one of the worksheets contained new information in cells C3 and C4?

You can resolve the current challenge by making a new assumption: After you remove blank rows, the parent category value in each worksheet will always be in the cell at the intersection of the second row and first column. (In Exercise 5-6, you will learn a different method of extracting the parent category.)

To identify the parent category value, you first need to mark the second row of each worksheet (after the blank rows were removed). To do it, you will take advantage of the Index Column and apply it on each table of Data column.

6. On the Add Column tab, select Index Column and ensure that you select the default option and create a zero-based index. Then copy this formula from the formula bar:

```
= Table.AddIndexColumn(#"Removed Other Columns", "Index", 0, 1)
```

Now that the formula is copied, you can delete this step from the Applied Steps pane. You just need the formula to set the stage for the next steps.

7. On the Add Column tab, select Custom Column. The Custom Column dialog box opens.

8. As shown in Figure 5-9, paste the formula from step 6 under Custom Column Formula, and modify the formula as follows:

   a. Remove the equal sign. By default, an equal sign is added in the Custom Column Formula box.

   b. Replace #"Removed Other Columns" with [Data]. You can do this by selecting the text #"Removed Other Columns" and then selecting Data in the Available Columns box.

   This is the resulting formula:

```
= Table.AddIndexColumn([Data], "Index", 0, 1)
```

> **Tip** Clicking on one of the columns in the Available Columns box of the Custom Column dialog box generates the code in M to access the value of that column in each row and use it in the results of the new custom column. In this case, clicking Data generates [Data] in the formula box.

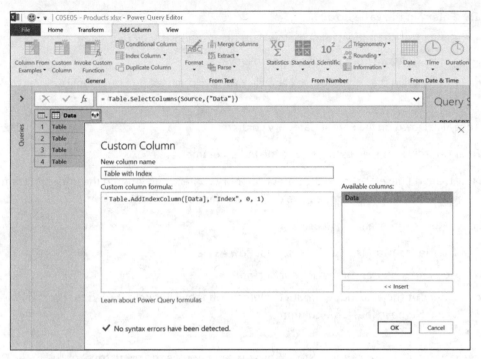

FIGURE 5-9 Adding an index column to each worksheet table object will enable you to get the right cue to preserve the parent categories.

9. Still in the Custom Column dialog box, in the New Column Name enter *Table with Index* and click OK. You now have two columns in the Preview pane: the Data column with the original table objects for each imported worksheet and the Table with Index column with the same table objects and the newly added index column.

10. Remove the Data column. You can now work with the Table with Index column.

11. Expand the Table with Index column by clicking the expand icon on the right side of the header. Deselect Use Original Column Name As Prefix and click OK.

    You can now see that the parent category is always available in rows where the index column has the value 1. The context headers Parent Category and Report Date are always in rows where the index column has the value 0. From here, the data preparation steps are easy.

12. To mark the rows with the Parent Category values, on the Add Column tab, select In Add Column and then select Add Conditional Column. In the Add Conditional Column dialog box that opens, make the following changes:

    a. Enter *Parent Category* in the New Column Name box.

    b. Select Index as the first column name.

    c. Select Equal as the operator.

d. Enter *1* in the Value box.

   e. Select the drop-down menu below Output and choose Select a Column.

   f. Select Column1 from the Output drop-down.

   g. Enter *null* in the Otherwise box and click OK to close the Add Conditional Column dialog box.

13. Apply Fill Down on the Parent Category column.

14. Filter out rows with values 0, 1, or 2 in the Index column.

Now that you have preserved the parent category context, and ignored the irrelevant context in rows with Index 1, you can remove the Index column.

15. Follow these three familiar steps:

   a. On the Transform tab, select Use First Row As Headers.

   b. Rename the Bikes column *Parent Category*.

   c. Filter out the embedded product column names by filtering out rows that contain the value Name in the Name column.

> **Tip** As you recall in Exercise 5-4 (step 15b), you can improve the robustness of the renaming in step 15b of this exercise by replacing the code *"Bikes"* in the formula bar with *List.Last(Table.ColumnNames(#"Changed Type")).*

You can now load the query to your report. The parent category context has been preserved in the appended results, thanks to the cue you used in the pre-append step—in this case, the cue was the Index column of each worksheet.

You can download the solution workbook C05E05 - Solution.xlsx and the Power BI report C05E05 - Solution.pbix from https://aka.ms/DataPwrBIPivot/downloads.

Exercise 5-6: Identifying Context by Cell Proximity

In Exercise 5-6, you assumed that the parent category value is always located in the second row and first column of each sheet (after blank rows are removed). Now you will change your assumption, and assume that the row location of the parent category value can change and no longer be used to detect the context you need to extract.

For the sake of this exercise, you can assume that the parent category value (as shown in Figure 5-10 in cell A6) can always be found below the cell with the value Parent Category in Column1 (as shown in Figure 5-10 in cell A5). You can use the location of the cell with the hardcoded text Parent Category as an "anchor" or a cue for the location of the parent category value. Anchoring your context to fixed elements can help you to make robust assumptions and will enable you to create robust queries that will better last through the changes to data over time.

To make the challenge more interesting, in this exercise you will find arbitrary values above Parent Category. Therefore, you can no longer assume that the parent category is in a specific row. Moreover, you can no longer assume that the product table will always be in a specific row. Figure 5-10 illustrates the challenge at hand.

	A	B	C	D	E	F	G	H
1	irrelevant data	we should ignore it						
2	irrelevant data							
3	irrelevant data	we don't know how many of these irrelevant rows will be included here						
4								
5	Parent Category	Report Date						
6	Bikes	1/1/2018						
7								
8	Name	ProductNumber	Color	StandardC	ListPrice	Size		
9	Touring-2000 Blue, 60	BK-T44U-60	Blue	755.1508	1214.85	60		
10	Touring-1000 Yellow, 46	BK-T79Y-46	Yellow	1481.938	2384.07	46		
11	Touring-1000 Yellow, 50	BK-T79Y-50	Yellow	1481.938	2384.07	50		
12	Touring-1000 Yellow, 54	BK-T79Y-54	Yellow	1481.938	2384.07	54		
13	Touring-1000 Yellow, 60	BK-T79Y-60	Yellow	1481.938	2384.07	60		
14	Touring-3000 Blue, 54	BK-T18U-54	Blue	461.4448	742.35	54		
15	Touring-3000 Blue, 58	BK-T18U-58	Blue	461.4448	742.35	58		
16	Touring-3000 Blue, 62	BK-T18U-62	Blue	461.4448	742.35	62		

FIGURE 5-10 Your challenge is to extract the parent category from the top table and preserve it as a new column in the appended bottom tables while ignoring all irrelevant data.

In this exercise you will learn a new technique to dynamically find the row indices of the context and product table headers, and this will enable you to ignore irrelevant context in each worksheet, extract only the parent category, and append all the product tables together. The technique requires you to use the M function *List.PositionOf*. This function receives a list as an input and a value to find its position, and it returns the index (starting from zero) of the position of the value in the list.

1. Download the workbook C05E06 - Products.xlsx from https://aka.ms/DataPwrBIPivot/ downloads. Save the workbook in the folder *C:\Data\C05*.

2. Either repeat steps 2–9 in Exercise 5-5 or start from the workbook C05E06 - Jump Start.xlsx or the report C05E06 - Jump Start.pbix, both from https://aka.ms/DataPwrBIPivot/downloads.

   When you are done, you should have two columns in the Preview pane: the Data column with the original table objects for each imported worksheet and the Table with Index column with the same table objects and the index column.

3. In the Power Query Editor, on the Add Column tab, select Custom Column. When the Custom Column dialog box opens, follow these steps:

   a. Enter *Row Index of Parent Category* in the New Column Name box.

   b. Copy the following formula to the Custom Column Formula box, and click OK to close the Custom Column dialog box:

   ```
   List.PositionOf([Data][Column1], "Parent Category")
   ```

   This formula applies *List.PositionOf* on Column1, which is represented as a list and provided as the first argument [Data][Column1]. The second argument, "Parent Category", is the value you would like to find in the list in order to return its position in the list, which represents the row index where "Parent Category" is hardcoded.

You will find out that the returned column "Row Index of Parent Category" contains varying numbers. Each number represent the location of the "Parent Category" cell in a zero-based index.

You will now create a new custom column. This time, you will drill down on each table object in the Data column by using the index found in the preceding step to retrieve the actual parent category values. Recall that the parent category value is located below Parent Category. You can use the index in Row Index of Parent Category and increment it by one to get the parent category value.

4. On the Add Column tab, select Custom Column. When the Custom Column dialog box opens, make the following changes:

   a. Enter *Parent Category* in the New Column Name box.

   b. Copy the following formula to the Custom Column Formula box, and click OK to close the Custom Column dialog box:

   ```
   [Data]{[Row Index of Parent Category] + 1}[Column1]
   ```

Earlier in this chapter, in the section "Drilling Down on a Table Cell Explained in M," you encountered a simpler version of this formula:

```
Source{0}[Column1]
```

The syntax here is the same. You can refer to a single cell in a table by using this syntax:

```
Table{row_index}[column_name]
```

Recall that curly brackets are used to access the row in the table by zero-based index. The square brackets are used to access the column name. In the formula in step 4b, you first access the table object in each row of the Data column by calling [Data]. Then you access the row index by the value that is available in the Row Index of Parent Category column, after incrementing the index by 1. Finally, in the specified row you access the cell in Column1.

You have preserved the parent category in the Parent Category column. It's time to detect the row index of the headers of the main table—the AdventureWorks products. The next step is similar to step 3, but this time you search for "Name" instead of "Parent Category".

5. On the Add Column tab, select Custom Column. When the Custom Column dialog box opens, follow these steps:

   a. Enter *Row Index of Name* in the New Column Name box.

   b. Copy the following formula to the Custom Column Formula box, and click OK to close the Custom Column dialog box:

   ```
   List.PositionOf([Data][Column1], "Name")
   ```

6. You can now remove the columns Row Index of Parent Category and Data. In the next step you will work on the Table with Index column, which you created in Exercise 5-5.

7. Expand the Table with Index column by clicking the expand icon on the right side of the header. Deselect Use Original Column Name As Prefix in the Expand pane and click OK.

   At this stage, you have preserved the parent category in the appended results. Your next challenge is to use the two cues you have in the columns Index and Row Index of Name. All the rows whose index is below Row Index of Name should be filtered out because they don't belong to the product table. You can do this in two steps: You will first create a conditional column and then filter the table by the results in the new column.

8. On the Add Column tab, select Conditional Column. When the Add Conditional Column dialog box opens, set it up as shown in Figure 5-11, following these steps:

   a. Enter *Index* in the Column Name box.

   b. Set Is Greater Than or Equal To as the operator.

   c. In the drop-down menu below Value, click Select a Column.

   d. Select Row Index of Name in the Value drop-down.

   e. Enter *1* in the Output box.

   f. Enter *0* in the Otherwise box, and click OK to close the Add Conditional Column dialog box.

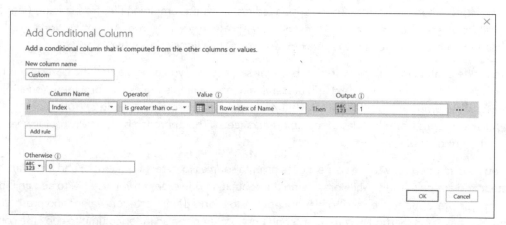

FIGURE 5-11 To filter out rows before the product table, follow step 8 and ensure that the Add Conditional Column dialog box is set as shown in this screenshot.

9. Filter the rows with the value 1 in the Custom column, and remove the columns Index, Row Index of Name, and Custom.

10. Follow these three familiar steps to remove the embedded product headers:

    a. On the Transform tab, select Use First Row As Headers.

    b. Rename the Bikes column *Parent Category*.

    c. Filter out the embedded product column names by filtering out rows that contain the value Name in the Name column.

Tip As in Exercise 5-4 and 5-5, you can improve the robustness of the renaming in step 10b by replacing the code *"Bikes"* in the formula bar with *List.Last(Table.ColumnNames(#"Changed Type"))*.

You can download the solution workbook C05E06 - Solution.xlsx and the Power BI report C05E06 - Solution.pbix from https://aka.ms/DataPwrBIPivot/downloads.

Summary

In this chapter you have learned how to preserve context, which is typically located outside tables. You have learned about a variety of context-preservation scenarios, with a focus on the ability to combine contexts and tables from multiple sources.

You started by using the basic Append Queries technique with file names or worksheet names that include key contextual information about the data. You applied a custom column on each query to preserve the context.

You have learned how to use the pre-append technique to dynamically detect and extract titles in worksheets and combine them into the appended results when combining files from a folder. Using the Drill Down step, you were able to preserve parent category values from AdventureWorks product tables, and you also learned the M syntax for accessing specific cells in a table.

To tackle context in multiple worksheets on the same folder, you have learned the post-append technique for detecting the context and preserving it after multiple tables are combined. You applied conditional columns and used the Fill Down transformation to preserve AdventureWorks parent product categories from the titles of multiple worksheets. (This approach is especially useful when pre-append is not possible.)

You have learned how to use context cues on data sources to detect both crucial and irrelevant context and append results while preserving the context. In one exercise, you used M to add an index column in a pre-append step and to identify AdventureWorks parent category values and preserve them. You have also learned how to apply conditional columns on an index column to copy the context to a new column—and how to apply Fill Down to preserve the context.

At the end of this chapter, you used pre-append cues to identify context by its proximity to "anchor" cells. Anchoring valuable data to fixed elements in your data can improve the robustness of your queries. You have learned how to use the M function *List.PositionsOf* to find relevant anchors and how to drill down in M, based on the found position index.

In Chapter 6, "Unpivoting Tables," you will see some common scenarios in which the context is well preserved in tables but misrepresented and badly structured so that it slows you down and prevents you from reaching the real business potential of the data.

While context is the key to gaining understanding, if you deliver it poorly, you lock away many insights.

CHAPTER 6

Unpivoting Tables

Give me a lever long enough and a fulcrum on which to place it, and I shall move the world.

—Archimedes

IN THIS CHAPTER, YOU WILL

- Learn how to identify badly structured context in tables

- Learn the basics of Unpivot transformations, including Unpivot Columns, Unpivot Other Columns, and Unpivot Only Selected Columns

- Apply basic Unpivot transformations to improve table context

- Learn why it is important to remove totals when you import a source table and how to do it effectively

- Learn how to unpivot summarized tables with 2x2 levels of hierarchy in rows and columns

- Learn how to filter out subtotals from summarized tables

So far in this book, you have learned how to tackle a wide variety of challenges to analyze unprepared data. You have learned the basics of data cleansing for individual columns and the art of combining multiple tables. In Chapter 5, "Preserving Context," you learned about the importance of context and how to preserve it. Now that you understand how to format your data well, aggregate it from multiple data sources, and fully preserve its context, it's time to learn how to resolve a subtler challenge.

Your tables are manifestations of the context they represent. Preserving the context is a well-defined problem, but deciding what is the best representation of your context is a completely different challenge. In this chapter, you will learn how to improve the table structure in your reports in order to better represent the data's subject matter and improve the ability to analyze that data. The Unpivot transformation is a cornerstone technique in addressing badly designed tables, and it is pivotal to your success as a data wrangler. With Unpivot, Power Query will become your Archimedes lever and fulcrum to move data in all shapes and forms.

Identifying Badly Designed Tables

In the study of linguistics, scholars distinguish between syntax, semantics, and pragmatics. Whereas *syntax* focuses on the relationships between words, and *semantics* deals with the meaning of the sentences, *pragmatics* focuses on the way different context can influence the interpretation of a message. We can use syntax, semantics, and pragmatics as metaphors for data preparation and transformation.

In earlier chapters, you learned how to improve the "syntax" of your data by cleaning badly formatted data. You enriched the "semantics" of your data by combining disjoint datasets and preserving their context. In this chapter, you will focus on a subtler challenge and learn the "pragmatics" of data preparation. The way you design your tables significantly affects the way your data will be interpreted. As in pragmatics, where different social context or tone of voice can affect the way a communicated message is interpreted, in data analytics, the way you design your tables can significantly impact the way your data is analyzed and interpreted.

If your tables are well designed, you can effectively use them in PivotTables and PivotCharts in Excel or in Power BI visuals. Poor table design leads to overly complex implementation of the necessary analytics calculations.

In this chapter, you will learn how to restructure badly designed tables to improve the way your data is represented, which will enable you to tap into more insights using PivotTables in Excel and visuals in Power BI. A badly designed table, in this context, is a table that doesn't represent well the real-life entities whose data is tracked and represented in your reports. It is not always easy to identify badly designed tables. One way to get an initial sense of whether a table is well structured is to see if each row in the table intuitively represents the real-life subject matter.

Data that is structured in a table or in a set of interconnected tables is always a representation of real entities. They can be the sales transactions in your company, scientific measurements of your experiments, student test results in a school, or game statistics for your favorite basketball group. All these entities and the facts that you have collected about them are represented in a collection of textual and numeric values in tables. You know that a table is well designed when each of its rows represents a unique entity.

To see the difficulty involved in identifying badly design tables, let's explore four tables that were differently designed to describe the same subject matter: the total revenues for the fictional company AdventureWorks. As illustrated in Figure 6-1, each one of the four tables has a different schema for showing the total revenue by customer account and the product's parent category.

Table 1 in Figure 6-1 is structured as a typical Excel PivotTable. The account is set as a row field, the parent category is a column field, and the revenue is set as the values of the pivot. While Table 1 might make a good visual in your final report, you will find it ineffective if you use this structure as the source of PivotTables in Excel or visuals in Power BI.

Table 2 in Figure 6-1 is also structured as a PivotTable. Both the account and the parent category are set as column fields, and revenue is set as the values of the pivot. If you are familiar with PivotTables, you know that both Table 1 and Table 2 could be manifestations of the same source table.

Table 1: Pivot with Account in Rows and Parent Category in Columns

Account	Accessories	Bikes	Clothing	Components
Action Bicycle Specialists	1,299.89	76,613.65	2,461.66	9,494.08
Aerobic Exercise Company				1,732.89
Bulk Discount Store	730.46	70,597.28	851.56	1,980.92

Table 2: Pivot with Account, and Parent Categories in Columns

Action Bicycle Specialists				Aerobic Exercise Company	Bulk Discount Store			
Accessories	Bikes	Clothing	Components	Components	Accessories	Bikes	Clothing	Components
1,299.89	76,613.65	2,461.66	9,494.08	1,732.89	730.46	70,597.28	851.56	1,980.92

Table 3: Accounts as Multiline Records

Attribute	Value
Account	Action Bicycle Specialists
Accessories	1,299.89
Bikes	76,613.65
Clothing	2,461.66
Components	9,494.08
Account	Aerobic Exercise Company
Components	1,732.89
Account	Bulk Discount Store
Accessories	730.46
Bikes	70,597.28
Clothing	851.56
Components	1,980.92

Table 4: Fact Table

Account	Category	Revenues
Action Bicycle Specialists	Accessories	1,299.89
Action Bicycle Specialists	Bikes	76,613.65
Action Bicycle Specialists	Clothing	2,461.66
Action Bicycle Specialists	Components	9,494.08
Aerobic Exercise Company	Components	1,732.89
Bulk Discount Store	Accessories	730.46
Bulk Discount Store	Bikes	70,597.28
Bulk Discount Store	Clothing	851.56
Bulk Discount Store	Components	1,980.92

FIGURE 6-1 With these four variations of AdventureWorks revenues by account and parent category, can you guess which tables are badly designed?

Table 3 in Figure 6-1 shows an extreme case where the table structure becomes a generic container of attribute/value pairs. While you might find this table clear enough to read and to identify the context of individual values, this table design is not readable by PivotTables in Excel or visuals in Power BI.

Table 4 is the best-designed table in Figure 6-1. Its format represents the revenues of Adventure-Works by account and parent category in a consumable way that PivotTables in Excel and visuals in Power BI can use. In fact, when you use Table 4 as your source for a PivotTable in Excel, you can easily create Table 1 and Table 2 by dragging and dropping Account, Category, and Revenues Columns, Rows, and Values sections in the PivotTable Fields pane. Tables that are structured like Table 4 are sometimes called *fact tables*. They represent the facts of the entities involved. In this case, the entities are the total revenues, summarized by account and parent category levels.

See Also Fact tables are often explained along with lookup/dimension tables and the star schema. Chapter 2, "Basic Data Preparation Challenges," describes how to create a fact table and a lookup table by applying references and removing duplicates. To learn more about fact tables in the context of modeling in Power BI and Power Pivot, read *Analyzing Data with Power BI and Power Pivot for Excel* by Alberto Ferrari and Marco Russo (Microsoft Press).

Tables 2 and 3 can easily be identified as unintuitive representations of AdventureWorks revenues and, therefore, badly designed. However, it may be less easy to see that tables like Table 1 are badly designed. Unlike Tables 2 and 3, which will not fit into an Excel PivotTable or a Power BI visual, tables like Table 1 can fit them. So, what is wrong with the design of Table 1? It includes four columns of the same type—all are revenues by different product parent categories.

If you detect that your source tables include multiple numeric columns with different contexts for the same attribute, you should suspect that there is a better way to represent the tables. For example, a common poor design for a table is to have multiple years as separate columns, with each column having the same type of numeric value. In Table 1, the revenues of four product parent categories are represented in separate columns. To determine the total revenue by account, you would have to sum up the four columns of each row—and this task will not lead to a practical solution in Excel PivotTables or in Power BI visuals.

So, of the options in Figure 6-1, Table 4 is the best option for representing AdventureWorks revenues. But what can you do if your source data is already formatted like the data in Table 1, Table 2, or Table 3? Can you transform any of these other tables into a table like Table 4 for better analysis capabilities? In the wild you will find many examples of badly designed tables that resemble the first three tables in Figure 6-1—and, yes, you can transform them. This chapter shows you how to transform them into fact tables that can be better consumed by PivotTables in Excel and visuals in Power BI.

The next section introduces the Unpivot transformation and explains how to apply it on summarized tables such as Table 1 in Figure 6-1.

Introduction to Unpivot

The Unpivot transformations are available on the Transform tab of the Power Query Editor or in the shortcut menu when you right-click a header of one or more selected columns. There are three Unpivot options in the shortcut menu and Transform tab:

- Unpivot Columns

- Unpivot Other Columns

- Unpivot Only Selected Columns

These three options yield the same result on a table, but they may act differently as new columns are added to your table in the future. You will learn about the differences among the three options in the next section.

When you apply Unpivot on selected columns, Power Query restructures your table by creating a separate row for each cell in the columns that are unpivoted. The row of each such cell will include the columns that were not unpivoted and an additional two columns: Attribute and Value. The Attribute column will contain the original column name of the cell, and the Value column will contain the original value in that cell. Figure 6-2 illustrates how each cell in the unpivoted columns is placed after the unpivot transformation.

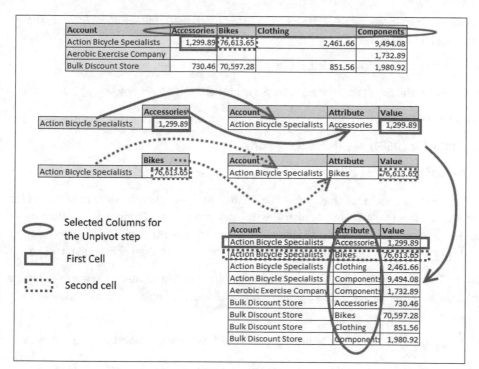

FIGURE 6-2 The positions of specific values in the original table and in the unpivoted table are demonstrated in this diagram.

The Unpivot transformation may be confusing when you encounter it for the first time. Basically, when you apply Unpivot, you divide the table into two types of columns:

- **Anchor columns:** The anchor columns are columns that are not unpivoted. They represent attributes you want to keep on your entities. In Figure 6-2 the only anchor column is the Account column. Later in this chapter you will see examples that have multiple anchor columns.

- **Unpivoted columns:** The Unpivoted columns are columns that have different manifestations of the same attribute. For example, Accessories, Bikes, Components, and Clothing are all revenues. While each of these columns has a different manifestation of a product parent category from AdventureWorks, the values are all of the same attribute: the revenues.

Unpivot takes any cell in the unpivoted columns and represents it in a row that contains the anchor columns and two new columns: Attribute and Value for the cell's corresponding original column name and value.

Exercise 6-1: Using Unpivot Columns and Unpivot Other Columns

In this exercise you will practice using the two main Unpivot transformations: Unpivot Columns and Unpivot Other Columns. To follow this exercise, you will use an AdventureWorks workbook sample that is in the same format as Table 1 in Figure 6-1.

1. Download the workbook C06E01.xlsx from https://aka.ms/DataPwrBIPivot/downloads and save it in *C:\Data\C06*.

2. Open a blank new workbook in Excel or a new report in Power BI Desktop.

   In Excel: On the Data tab, select Get Data, From File, From Workbook.

   In Power BI Desktop: In the Get Data drop-down menu, select Excel.

3. Select the file C06E01.xlsx and select Import.

4. In the Navigator dialog box, select Revenues and then select Edit.

5. In the Power Query Editor that opens, notice that the Preview pane contains revenues for AdventureWorks by Account, Accessories, Bikes, Clothing, and Components. Select the last four columns either by pressing the Ctrl key as you keep clicking the headers or using Shift+right arrow or by selecting the Accessories column and then pressing Shift+End.

6. On the Transform tab, select Unpivot Columns. Alternatively, right-click one of the selected columns and then select Unpivot Columns. The table is now unpivoted, like Table 4 in Figure 6-2.

In the formula bar, notice that the M function uses the *Table.UnpivotOtherColumns* function:

```
= Table.UnpivotOtherColumns(#"Changed Type", {"Account"}, "Attribute", "Value")
```

You can now delete the Unpivoted Columns step from Applied Steps and select the first column, Account. Now, on the Transform tab, select the Unpivot Columns drop-down and then select Unpivot Other Columns. Alternatively, you can right-click the header of Account and select Unpivot Other Columns from the shortcut menu. You will notice that the results in the Preview pane are the same as in step 6. Review the formula bar, and see that it contains the same *Table.UnpivotOtherColumns* function. The only lasting difference is that the transformation step in Applied Steps is now called Unpivoted Other Columns instead of Unpivoted Columns.

So, what is the actual difference between Unpivot Columns and Unpivot Other Columns, if the underlying M function is the same? There is no difference. It's only a matter of ease of use. When you have more anchor columns than columns to unpivot, you can select the columns to unpivot and apply Unpivot Columns. When you have more columns to unpivot than anchor columns, you can select the anchor columns and then apply Unpivot Other Columns.

At this stage, you may wonder why Unpivot Columns acts like Unpivot Other Columns in the underlying M formula. The two user interfaces trigger the same transformation because of a common assumption: It is most common for your anchor columns to remain unchanged and your unpivoted columns to change over time. For example, the source table in Exercise 6-1 includes four product parent categories. In the future, if AdventureWorks enters new markets or acquires a new company that ships new products, the source table will include new revenue columns with new parent categories. By using *Table.UnpivotOtherColumns*, you allow a query to scale over time to unpivot the new columns, without the need to change the query.

A common scenario where *Table.UnpivotOtherColumns* makes a lot of sense is when your source table includes multiple columns of the same attribute by different time periods, such as years, quarters, or months. In such cases, the current design of the Unpivot transformation enables your query to be robust enough to unpivot the new periods as expected and without further modifications as new columns are added in the next time periods.

> **Tip** Because both Unpivot Columns and Unpivot Other Columns perform at the formula level as Unpivot Other Columns, it is recommended that you ensure that your anchor columns are not going to change when you apply these transformations.

When you apply Unpivot Columns and Unpivot Other Columns, the M formula explicitly refers to the anchor columns by name. For example, in the preceding formula, the Account column is the anchor column. If an anchor column is renamed in the data source, it will fail during the next refresh. Even worse, when a new anchor column is added to the data source, the new column will be unpivoted along the other columns, which will break your table in an unexpected way.

Figure 6-3 demonstrates how Unpivot will fail in Exercise 6-1 if a new column is added for account addresses in the source table. With Unpivot, Power Query thinks the Address column should be unpivoted along with the Accessories, Bikes, Clothing, and Components columns. Because Address is not a product parent category, and the address values do not represent revenues, you will receive errors if you try to change the type of the Value column to *Decimal Number*.

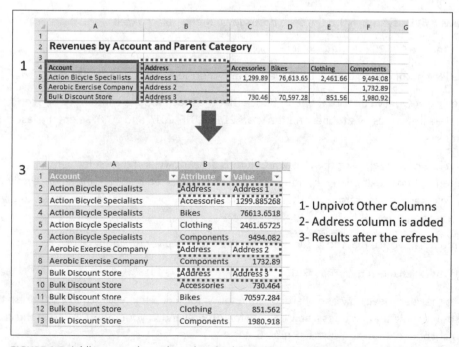

FIGURE 6-3 Adding an anchor column breaks the unpivoted table when using Unpivot Other Columns or Unpivot Columns.

An even worse problem arises if the newly added anchor column includes numbers. Imagine that in the source table of AdventureWorks revenues in Exercise 6-1, a new column is added with the total number of sales per account. Now, during the next refresh, the new column is unpivoted along the product parent categories, and all the sales counts are treated as revenues. The consequences can be misleading and even devastating to your final reports.

So, what should you do if you expect your source table to have new anchor columns? You'll find the answer in the next section.

Exercise 6-2: Unpivoting Only Selected Columns

As explained in the preceding section, when anchor columns change, Unpivot Other Columns fails. It is not sufficient to apply Unpivot Columns from the user interface in such scenarios because that step is translated to Unpivot Other Columns in the formula bar (*Table.UnpivotOtherColumns*). Instead, you should use the third Unpivot option in the Power Query Editor: Unpivot Only Selected Columns. In this exercise you will try this option on a new source table. This time, you will use a data sample from the fictional company Wide World Importers and unpivot the total revenues in 2015, 2016, 2017, and 2018.

1. Download the workbook C06E02.xlsx from https://aka.ms/DataPwrBIPivot/downloads and save it in *C:\Data\C06*.

2. Open a blank new workbook in Excel or a new report in Power BI Desktop.

   In Excel: On the Data tab, select Get Data, From File, From Workbook.

   In Power BI Desktop: In the Get Data drop-down menu, select Excel.

3. Select the file C06E02.xlsx and select Import.

4. In the Navigator dialog box, select Revenues and then select Edit.

5. In the Power Query Editor that opens, notice that the Preview pane contains Wide World Importers' revenues by supplier and the years 2015, 2016, 2017, and 2018. Select the last four columns.

6. On the Transform tab, click the Unpivot Columns drop-down and then select Unpivot Only Selected Columns. Alternatively, right-click one of the selected columns and select Unpivot Only Selected Columns from the shortcut menu. You can now see that the table was unpivoted as expected.

In the formula bar, notice that the M function uses the *Table.Unpivot* function:

```
= Table.Unpivot(#"Changed Type", {"2015", "2016", "2017", "2018"}, "Attribute", "Value")
```

Notice that the years have now been hardcoded in the M formula. Next year, when you refresh the report on a source table that includes a new column for 2019 revenues, your report will treat the 2019 column as an anchor column, as shown in Figure 6-4.

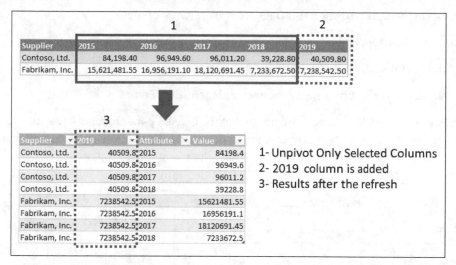

FIGURE 6-4 Having a new year column breaks the unpivoted table when Unpivot Only Selected Columns was used on the previous years.

To avoid having the 2019 column treated as an anchor column, it is recommended to use Unpivot Other Columns in this scenario. Given the limitations of Unpivot Only Selected Columns, you are encouraged to use it only when your unpivoted columns are not expected to change and when the only changes expected should occur in your anchor columns.

Handling Totals

When you unpivot summarized tables, you often find total columns and rows. While you may be tempted to import these elements to a query, you are encouraged not to do so but to instead remove these elements during the import phase. Having totals in your data will impact your ability to have simple and reusable reports. Exercise 6-3 demonstrates this scenario.

> **See Also** As with totals, having subtotals in unpivoted data is not recommended. Handling subtotals is discussed later in this chapter.

Exercise 6-3: Unpivoting Grand Totals

This exercise demonstrates the impact of including grand totals when you unpivot the source table. It also shows the best way to remove the Grand Totals column and row using Power Query.

1. Download the workbook C06E03.xlsx from https://aka.ms/DataPwrBIPivot/downloads and save it in *C:\Data\C06*.

2. Open a blank new workbook in Excel or a new report in Power BI Desktop.

In Excel: On the Data tab, select Get Data, From File, From Workbook.

In Power BI Desktop: In the Get Data drop-down menu, select Excel.

3. Select the file C06E03.xlsx and select Import.

4. In the Navigator dialog box, select Revenues and then select Edit.

In the Power Query Editor that opens, notice that the Preview pane contains AdventureWorks' revenues by account and the parent categories: Accessories, Bikes, Clothing, and Components. The last row and last column contain Grand Total values, as shown in Figure 6-5.

Account	Accessories	Bikes	Clothing	Components	Grand Total
Action Bicycle Specialists	1,299.89	76,613.65	2,461.66	9,494.08	89,869.28
Aerobic Exercise Company				1,732.89	1,732.89
Bulk Discount Store	730.46	70,597.28	851.56	1,980.92	74,160.23
Central Bicycle Specialists				31.58	31.58
Channel Outlet	216.00		308.66		524.66
...					
Vigorous Sports Store				858.90	858.90
West Side Mart				63.90	63.90
Grand Total	6,915.14	574,611.56	16,087.72	111,075.73	708,690.15

FIGURE 6-5 Unpivoting row and column grand totals may lead to undesired results in your unpivoted data. Look for such rows and columns and remove them in the query.

5. Select the Account column, and on the Transform tab, click the Unpivot Columns drop-down and select Unpivot Other Columns. Alternatively, right-click the Account column header and select Unpivot Other Columns from the shortcut menu.

The table is unpivoted. Notice that for each Account entity, there is a row with Grand Total in the Attribute column, and when you scroll down the table, the last five rows include Grand Total in the Account column.

If you import the Grand Totals row and column into your workbook or Power BI report and summarize the entire unpivoted Value column, you end up quadrupling the actual revenues—because each revenue by a specific account and parent category will be summarized four times. To understand why, you can count the number of times the same revenue is accounted for in the original source table, before the unpivot. The revenue of a specific account/parent category is summarized in four locations of the table: once in the specific inner cell, once in the row of the specific account in the Grand Total column, once in the Grand Total row and the column of the specific parent category, and finally at the bottom-right corner of the Grand Total cell.

Including the total column or row in the unpivoted results will overcomplicated your calculations and visuals. It will also make your report prone to errors. You will need to filter out Grand Total from the Account and Parent Category columns in your visual filters or create a complicated DAX measure that filters them out.

Let's look at a DAX measure you could use in this case. (You can download the sample Power BI report C06E03 - Wrong Solution.pbix from https://aka.ms/DataPwrBIPivot/downloads.)

To sum up all revenues, you could use the following formula in DAX (assuming that your table is Revenues and the revenue amount is in the Revenue column):

```
Total Revenue = SUM ( Revenues[Revenue] )
```

Unfortunately, this data is quadrupled, so you need to apply the following DAX formula:

```
Total Revenue = CALCULATE (
  SUM ( Revenues[Revenue] ),
  FILTER (
    Revenues,
    Revenues[Account] <> "Grand Total" && Revenues[Parent Category] <> "Grand Total"
  )
)
```

While this measure can help you if you are forced to work with data containing grand totals, it would be best to ensure in the first place that grand totals will be filtered out at the query level.

Removing Grand Totals

While you can continue the preceding exercise and filter out the Grand Total values immediately after the Unpivot step, when considering performance and load time, this approach is not very efficient. You could reduce the time it takes to perform the unpivot operations by removing the unnecessary Grand Total column and row before the unpivot. To properly remove the Grand Totals, continue the exercise with the following steps:

6. Delete the Unpivot Other Columns step from the Applied Steps pane.

7. Select the Grand Total column and press Delete.

In this exercise, Grand Total is a column name, and it is safe to remove it by using the user interface. In the next exercise you will see a case where the grand total column is named Column10. Removing such a generically named column could lead to unexpected results if your table expands (and the grand total column shifts to right). Exercise 6-4 shows how to remove the grand total column when it's the last column by using M.

8. On the Home tab, select Remove Rows and then select Remove Bottom Rows.

9. When the Remove Bottom Rows dialog box opens, enter *1* in the Number of Rows box, and click OK to close the dialog box.

While using the Remove Bottom Rows dialog box is indeed the easiest way to remove the grand total row, oftentimes, when you deal with uncleaned data—and especially when you work with spreadsheets as your source data—you need to remove additional rows from the bottom of the table. To scale up your query to remove the grand totals along with additional rows at the bottom, you can apply an M formula that dynamically detects the location of the grand total row and removes it along with the other irrelevant rows.

In the sample data, you would use the following formula to perform the removal of the bottom row:

```
= Table.RemoveLastN(#"Removed Columns",1)
```

You can use the following formula instead:

```
= Table.FirstN(#"Removed Columns", List.PositionOf(#"Removed Columns"[Account],
"Grand Total"))
```

Press Enter, and you should get the same transformation: The grand total row is removed. Now, however, your query ignores any trailing rows in your data.

Let's look at the formula you just used. *Table.FirstN* keeps the first N rows in a table. It receives two arguments: the table and the number of rows to keep. *#"Removed Columns"* is the quoted identifier of the table. The second argument should contain the number of rows you want to keep. You already used the *List.PositionOf* function in Chapter 5. In this case, you access the Account column as a list and search for the keyword *"Grand Total"*. The result is a zero-based index of the Grand Total row, and it is exactly the number of rows you would like to keep.

Now when Grand Total row is removed, you can proceed with the unpivot step.

10. Select the Account column, and on the Transform tab, click the Unpivot Columns drop-down and then select Unpivot Other Columns. Alternatively, right-click Account column header and select Unpivot Other Columns from the shortcut menu. You can now rename the Attribute column to *Parent Category* and the Value column to *Revenue*.

As shown in this exercise, it is important to remove grand totals when you use Unpivot. Removing the grand total columns is straightforward, and you can apply smart logic in M to remove the grand total from the bottom row, along with any irrelevant trailing data that is in your worksheet.

You can download the solution files C06E03 - Solution.xlsx and C06E03 - Solution.pbix from https://aka.ms/DataPwrBIPivot/downloads.

Unpivoting 2×2 Levels of Hierarchy

In the preceding section you learned how to use the Unpivot transformation on simple tables. In many other cases, you will encounter source tables formatted as simple summary tables, and the Unpivot transformation in Power Query will be one of your most useful tools. This is especially true with spreadsheet sources that are not as well-prepared as the data in your company's data warehouse.

Because most Excel users are not familiar with PivotTables, they tend to share static summarized reports instead of fact tables. If you need to consume their already summarized data in your own reports, you can use Unpivot to break down these summarized tables and transform the data into a format that is consumable by Excel PivotTables and Power BI visuals. In real life, however, you confront much more complicated tables that include multiple levels of aggregations in columns and rows.

The next two exercises take you one step further and show how to unpivot the most common nested tables. Mastering this section will enable you to unpivot many structured tables and transform them into fact tables that can fit into Excel PivotTables and PivotCharts and Power BI visuals.

Exercise 6-4: Unpivoting 2×2 Levels of Hierarchy with Dates

To begin unpivoting complex tables, let's consider an example: The fictional company Wide World Importers plans to expand and seek new funding. As the chief analyst of an investment company, you were asked to evaluate the performance of Wide World Importers. You received a report with summarized revenues by year, month, supplier categories, and suppliers, as shown at the top of Figure 6-6.

You immediately identify the opportunity to unpivot the data and transform the summarized table into a fact table, as illustrated at the bottom of Figure 6-6.

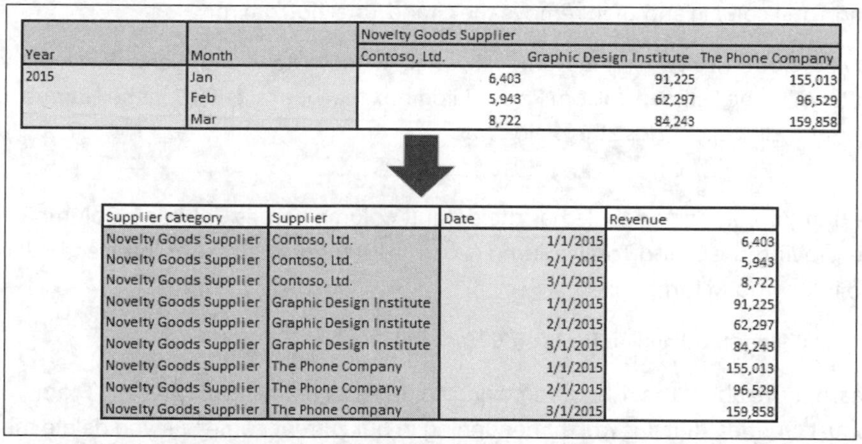

		Novelty Goods Supplier		
Year	Month	Contoso, Ltd.	Graphic Design Institute	The Phone Company
2015	Jan	6,403	91,225	155,013
	Feb	5,943	62,297	96,529
	Mar	8,722	84,243	159,858

Supplier Category	Supplier	Date	Revenue
Novelty Goods Supplier	Contoso, Ltd.	1/1/2015	6,403
Novelty Goods Supplier	Contoso, Ltd.	2/1/2015	5,943
Novelty Goods Supplier	Contoso, Ltd.	3/1/2015	8,722
Novelty Goods Supplier	Graphic Design Institute	1/1/2015	91,225
Novelty Goods Supplier	Graphic Design Institute	2/1/2015	62,297
Novelty Goods Supplier	Graphic Design Institute	3/1/2015	84,243
Novelty Goods Supplier	The Phone Company	1/1/2015	155,013
Novelty Goods Supplier	The Phone Company	2/1/2015	96,529
Novelty Goods Supplier	The Phone Company	3/1/2015	159,858

FIGURE 6-6 You can use Power Query to unpivot complex tables like this Wide World Importers revenues summary table. The bottom unpivoted table will better suit for analysis.

Before going over the necessary steps to unpivot this table, let's focus on the main challenges involved. You can identify the anchor columns as Year and Month, but the Year column includes null values in the Power Query Editor. In addition, you see null values in the Supplier Category row. Trying to unpivot the columns with the revenues will fail, as you need to have the pair Supplier Category and Supplier as attributes. If you apply Unpivot on all the columns by year and month, the suppliers will be shown in the Value column instead of the Attribute column.

To set the stage for the Unpivot to work, you need to perform a sequence of transformations which don't seem trivial: Fill Down on the Year column, Merge on the Year and Month columns, Transpose the table, Fill Down on the Supplier Category, Apply First Row as Headers, and Unpivot. This exercise shows the steps in more detail:

1. Download the workbook C06E04.xlsx from https://aka.ms/DataPwrBIPivot/downloads and save it in *C:\Data\C06*.

2. Open a blank new workbook in Excel or a new report in Power BI Desktop.

   In Excel: On the Data tab, select Get Data, From File, From Workbook.

   In Power BI Desktop: In the Get Data drop-down menu, select Excel.

3. Select the file C06E04.xlsx and select Import.

4. In the Navigator dialog box, select Revenues and then select Edit.

5. In the Power Query Editor that opens, notice that the Preview pane contains Wide World Importers' revenues by year, month, supplier category, and supplier, as illustrated in the top table of Figure 6-6.

6. It's time to remove grand totals as you have learned in Exercise 6-3. You can simply remove the Grand Total column and then remove the Grand Total bottom row.

   To remove the bottom row, on the Home tab, select Remove Rows and then select Remove Bottom Rows. In the Remove Bottom Rows dialog box that opens, enter *1* in the Number of Rows box, and click OK to close the dialog box.

Tip Notice that your imported table has the default column names Column1, Column2, and so on. Removing the Grand Total column (Column10) through the user interface will generate the following M formula:

```
= Table.RemoveColumns(#"Changed Type",{"Column10"})
```

You will learn more about the risks of removing columns by name in Chapter 10, "From Pitfalls to Robust Queries," but it is worth mentioning in our current context. If you delete the Grand Total column in this case, when new suppliers are added to the source table, Column10 will no longer represent the grand total. A better alternative to remove the Grand Total column is to remove the Changed Type step from Applied Steps and then remove the last column by using M. Here is the code to do so:

```
= Table.RemoveColumns(Revenues_DefinedName,
List.Last(Table.ColumnNames(Revenues_DefinedName)))
```

In this formula, you apply *Table.ColumnNames* to get the list of column names from the table, whose identifier is *Revenues_DefinedName*. Then you get the name of the last column by applying the formula *List.Last* on the list of column names.

---

7. Select Column 1, and on the Transform tab, select Fill, Down. This step fills down the Year column and replaces null values with the correct years in each row. In Chapter 5 you learned

about the importance of Fill Down in context preservation. In this case you use it to preserve the correct year value in each row.

Next you need to consolidate the Year and Month columns into a Date column to reduce the year/month hierarchy into a single cell. (You will see in a minute how effective this step is.)

8. Select Column1 and Column2, and on the Transform tab, select Merge Columns. In the Merge Columns dialog box that opens, select Space as Separator, and then click OK to close the dialog box.

Looking at the Supplier Category values in the first row, at this stage, you might wish for a Fill Right transformation to fill the null values of the Supplier Category row. You don't have such a functionality, but you can transpose the table and then apply Fill Down on the Supplier Category column. Recall from Chapter 4, "Combining Mismatched Tables," that Transpose allows you to reconstruct a table so that, for example, each cell in the ith row and jth column will now be positioned in the jth row and ith column.

9. On the Transform tab, select Transpose.

10. Now you can fill down the supplier categories and remove the nulls. Select the first column, and on the Transform tab, select Fill, Down.

11. On the Transform tab, select Use First Rows as Headers.

12. Select the first two columns (which are the anchor columns in this case, representing the supplier category and the supplier name). On the Transform tab, click the Unpivot Columns dropdown and select Unpivot Other Columns. Alternatively, right-click one of the selected columns and select Unpivot Other Columns from the shortcut menu.

13. Rename the columns as follows:

    a. First column: *Supplier Category*

    b. Second column: *Supplier*

    c. Third column: *Date*

    d. Fourth column: *Revenue*

14. Change the type of the Date column to Date. Ensure that the Revenue column is set to Decimal Number or Currency.

You can now load the unpivoted data to your workbook or Power BI report.

To review the solution, download the files C06E04 - Solution.xlsx and C06E04 - Solution.pbix from https://aka.ms/DataPwrBIPivot/downloads.

Exercise 6-5: Unpivoting 2×2 Levels of Hierarchy

We can generalize the Unpivot steps that are necessary to transform any summarized tables with 2×2 levels of hierarchy into a fact table. In Exercise 6-4 you had the Year and Month columns as a two-level hierarchy represented in each row. You easily merged the Year and Month columns into a single date column and were able to preserve their context. Let's now look at how to handle cases where a two-level row hierarchy cannot be kept merged.

Figure 6-7 shows a summary table of AdventureWorks revenues with Sales Person, Client Company, Product Parent Category, and Category columns. To begin, you need to take the steps that are necessary to set the stage for the unpivot. These steps will be familiar, as they are a generalization of Exercise 6-4.

SalesPerson	CompanyName	Accessories			Bikes		
		Bike Racks	Bottles and Cages	Cleaners	Mountain	Road Bike	Touring Bikes
jae0	Action Bicycle Specialists	432	31.199476	38.16			76613.6518
	Bulk Discount Store	216	23.952	28.62		70597.28	
	Central Bicycle Specialists						
linda3	Aerobic Exercise Company						
	Eastside Department Store	144	29.94	38.16		51096.05	
	Extreme Riding Supplies						41337.936

Parent Category	Category	Sales Person	Company	Revenue
Accessories	Bike Racks	jae0	Action Bicycle Specialists	432
Accessories	Bike Racks	jae0	Bulk Discount Store	216
Accessories	Bike Racks	linda3	Eastside Department Store	144
Accessories	Bottles and Cages	jae0	Action Bicycle Specialists	31.199476
Accessories	Bottles and Cages	jae0	Bulk Discount Store	23.952
Accessories	Bottles and Cages	linda3	Eastside Department Store	29.94
Accessories	Cleaners	jae0	Action Bicycle Specialists	38.16
Accessories	Cleaners	jae0	Bulk Discount Store	28.62
Accessories	Cleaners	linda3	Eastside Department Store	38.16
Bikes	Road Bikes	jae0	Bulk Discount Store	70597.284
Bikes	Road Bikes	linda3	Eastside Department Store	51096.05481
Bikes	Touring Bikes	jae0	Action Bicycle Specialists	76613.6518
Bikes	Touring Bikes	linda3	Extreme Riding Supplies	41337.936

FIGURE 6-7 You can use Power Query to unpivot complex tables like this AdventureWorks revenues summary table. The bottom unpivoted table is surely better suited for analysis.

1. Download the workbook C06E05.xlsx from https://aka.ms/DataPwrBIPivot/downloads and save it in *C:\Data\C06*.

2. Open a blank new workbook in Excel or a new report in Power BI Desktop.

   In Excel: On the Data tab, select Get Data, From File, From Workbook.

   In Power BI Desktop: In the Get Data drop-down menu, select Excel.

3. Select the file C06E05.xlsx and select Import.

4. In the Navigator dialog box, select Revenues and then select Edit. In the Power Query Editor that opens, notice that the Preview pane contains the AdventureWorks revenues, as shown in the top table in Figure 6-7.

5. Remove the Grand Totals column and row, as suggested in Exercise 6-4.

6. Select Column1, and on the Transform tab, select Fill, Down. This step fills down the SalesPerson column and replaces null values with the correct values in each row.

7. Select Column1 and Column2, and on the Transform tab, select Merge Columns. In the Merge Columns dialog box that opens, select Colon as Separator, and then click OK to close the dialog box.

> **Note** In Exercise 6-4, you merged the columns, and it was an intuitive step, as you converted Year and Month into dates. In this exercise, merging SalesPerson and CompanyName may seem disruptive at first, as you are messing with the values of the first two columns. Nevertheless, this step is crucial for the Unpivot. In step 13, you will fix the temporary mess and split the columns.

Why did we use a colon in the merge? We assume that the values in the columns SalesPerson and CompanyName will never contain a colon character. This way we will be able to split them correctly later on. If you run this technique on your own data, make sure you select a separator that does not exist in the data. You can even select a rare combination of characters as a separator in step 7.

8. On the Transform tab, select Transpose.

9. Select Column1, and on the Transform tab, select Fill, Down.

10. On the Transform tab, select Use First Rows as Headers.

11. Select the first two columns (which are the anchor columns, representing the supplier category and the supplier name).

12. On the Transform tab, click the Unpivot Columns drop-down menu and then select Unpivot Other Columns. Alternatively, right-click one of the selected columns and select Unpivot Other Columns from the shortcut menu.

Next, you need to fix that Attribute column, which consists of the merged SalesPerson and CompanyName columns.

13. Select the Attribute column, and on the Transform tab, select Split Column, By Delimiter. In the Split Column By Delimiter dialog box that opens, set Select or Enter Delimiter to Colon, and then click OK to close the dialog box.

14. Rename the columns as follows:

    a. First column: *Parent Category*

    b. Second column: *Category*

    c. Third column: *Sales Person*

    d. Fourth column: *Company*

    e. Fifth column: *Revenue*

15. Change the type of the last column to Decimal Number or Currency.

You can now load the unpivoted data to your report.

To review the solution, download the files C06E05 - Solution.xlsx and C06E05 - Solution.pbix from https://aka.ms/DataPwrBIPivot/downloads.

Handling Subtotals in Unpivoted Data

Earlier in this chapter, you learned why totals kept in your data can be a source of overcomplication. The same rationale applies to subtotals. For basic summation operations in your PivotTables or Power BI visuals, you need to apply explicit filtering logic to ignore the subtotals and ensure that each cell in the summarized data is added up only once in a report. That is why it is important to filter subtotals at the query level.

In Exercise 6-3, you saw that removing totals is a relatively simple pre-unpivot step. It is rather challenging, however, to remove the subtotals columns and rows from their original locations in a source table. To illustrate the challenge, let's work with the source table from Exercise 6-5 that includes subtotals in rows and columns, as shown in Figure 6-8.

⊿	A	B	C	D	E	F	G	H	I	J	K
1			Accessories			Accessories Total	Bikes			Bikes Total	Grand Total
2	SalesPerson	CompanyName	Bike Racks	Bottles and Cage	Cleaners		Mountain Bike	Road Bikes	Touring Bikes		
3	joe0	Action Bicycle Specialists	432.00	31.20	38.16	501.36			76,613.65	76,613.65	77,115.01
4		Bulk Discount Store	216.00	23.95	28.62	268.57		70,597.28		70,597.28	70,865.86
5		Central Bicycle Specialists				0.00				0.00	0.00
6	joe0 Total		648.00	55.15	66.78	769.93	0.00	70,597.28	76,613.65	147,210.94	147,980.87
7	shu0	Coalition Bike Company				0.00	529.49			529.49	529.49
8		Discount Tours	72.00			72.00		2,041.19		2,041.19	2,113.19
9		Engineered Bike Systems				0.00			2,604.76	2,604.76	2,604.76
10	shu0 Total		72.00	0.00	0.00	72.00	529.49	2,041.19	2,604.76	5,175.44	5,247.44
11	Grand Total		720.00	55.15	66.78	841.93	529.49	72,638.47	79,218.41	152,386.38	153,228.31
12											

FIGURE 6-8 This AdventureWorks source table summarizes revenues, including subtotals for sales person and parent category.

Exercise 6-6: Handling Subtotals

In this exercise, you will learn how to filter out subtotal elements after the Unpivot step. It is useful to remove the subtotals after the Unpivot because the positions of subtotal columns in the source table may change. If you remove subtotals before the Unpivot, you will run into trouble if, in the future, the positions of the subtotals change. For example, you might end up removing a product column instead of a subtotal column. To correctly ignore subtotals, it is recommended to apply an Unpivot and then exclude the subtotals by using a filter. This exercise shows the process:

1. Download the workbook C06E06.xlsx from https://aka.ms/DataPwrBIPivot/downloads and save it in *C:\Data\C06*.

2. Select the file C06E06.xlsx and select Import.

3. In the Navigator dialog box, select Revenues and then select Edit.

4. Follow steps 6–15 of Exercise 6-5 to unpivot the table. (Alternatively, you can open the solution workbook or Power BI report from Exercise 6-5, and in Applied Steps edit the Source step and replace the source file from C06E05.xlsx to C06E06.xlsx. In addition, remove the steps where you deleted the Grand Total column and row—you are going to remove them after the unpivot in this exercise.)

5. In the Power Query Editor, notice that the Parent Category column now includes the subtotals titled Accessories Total, Bikes Total, Clothing Total, and Component Total (see Figure 6-9). You need to filter them out. Select the filter control in the header of the Parent Category column.

You may be tempted at this stage to use the Filter pane and deselect the subtotal labels that are highlighted in Figure 6-9. But if you do so, your query will only filter out the current labels and will miss new labels in the future if new parent categories are added in the source table.

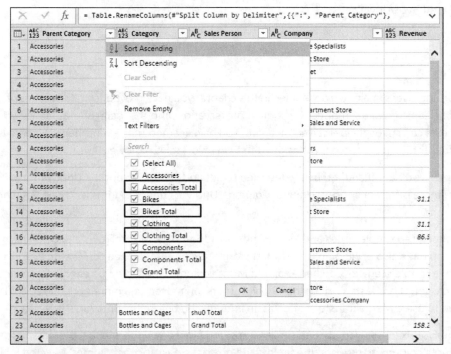

FIGURE 6-9 The Parent Category column labels should be filtered out after the Unpivot. Don't be tempted to filter them by deselecting the values. Use Text Filters instead.

6. To perform the correct filtering, select Text Filters and then select Does Not End With.

7. In the Filter Rows dialog box that opens, enter *Total* in the value box, and then click OK to close the dialog box. You can test your filtering step by again clicking the filter control in the header of the Parent Category column and ensuring that all the Total values highlighted in Figure 6-9, including Grand Total, are now gone.

Applying this filter allows you to remove the parent category subtotals from the columns of the source table. You still have the sales person subtotals from the rows of the source table (refer to Figure 6-8 to review the row and column subtotals).

8. Select the filter control in the header of the Sales Person column. Do you see the total values? To remove them, select Text Filters and then select Does Not End With.

9. In the Filter Rows dialog box that opens, enter *Total* in the value box, and then click OK to close the dialog box. You can test your filtering step by again clicking the filter control in header of the Sales Person column and ensuring that all the Total values are now gone.

10. Load the unpivoted data to your report. Both Grand Total and subtotals have been filtered out.

To review the solution, download the files C06E06 - Solution.xlsx and C06E06 - Solution.pbix from aka.ms/DataPwrBIPivot/downloads.

Summary

Reiterating the linguistics analogy from earlier, in this chapter you have moved from the realms of syntax (or data cleansing) and semantics (or context preservation) into the realm of pragmatics, where different contexts can shape the perceived meaning. You have learned that, even when your data is cleaned and fully intact, it may be badly designed to fit in PivotTables or Power BI visuals.

In this chapter you have identified badly designed tables and learned about the Unpivot transformation and its three different options: Unpivot Columns, Unpivot Other Columns, and Unpivot Only Selected Columns.

You have unpivoted simple tables and learned how to address Grand Total rows and columns in the source table. You have also applied an Unpivot transformation on summarized tables with 2×2 levels of hierarchy. In a simple scenario, you had Year and Month columns that could be easily merged into a single column to simplify the staging for the Unpivot. Then you moved to a more generalized solution, where you had to use a Merge transformation as an interim step before the unpivot.

In these Unpivot exercises, you applied similar steps: you filled down the anchor columns, merged them into a single column, transposed the table, filled down the new anchor columns, selected Use First Row as Headers, unpivot, and split the merged Attribute column.

Finally, in this chapter you have learned a simple technique to filter out subtotals after the Unpivot step and avoid the explicit and risky removal of Subtotal columns and rows before the Unpivot as their position may change.

In Chapter 7, "Advanced Unpivoting and Pivoting of Tables," you will continue your journey with the Unpivot transformation, generalizing a solution that will help you unpivot any summarized table, no matter how many levels of hierarchy there are in the rows and columns. You will also learn about cases where Unpivot is overused and how to fix it by using Pivot, the inverse transformation to Unpivot.

Advanced Unpivoting and Pivoting of Tables

Some painters transform the sun into a yellow spot, others transform a yellow spot into the sun.

—Pablo Picasso

IN THIS CHAPTER, YOU WILL

- Learn how to unpivot summarized tables with 3×3 levels of hierarchies and generalize the transformation steps to unpivot any summarized table

- Learn how to convert the unpivot sequence into a function and apply it on multiple files from a folder and multiple worksheets that require unpivoting

- Learn how to apply Pivot to reverse Unpivot and how to apply Pivot to transform multiline records into fact tables

In this chapter, you will continue learning about the Unpivot transformation by generalizing a solution that will help you unpivot any summarized table, no matter how many levels of hierarchies you have as rows and columns. You will also learn how to handle scenarios where Unpivot is overused and how to fix it by using Pivot, the inverse transformation of Unpivot. With the Pivot transformation, you will learn how to transform multiline records into a table.

Some areas in this chapter require manipulations in M, the Power Query formula language. As we have only briefly introduced M in Chapter 1, "Introduction to Power Query," and lightly touched it in other chapters, you are encouraged to return to this chapter again after reading the detailed review of M in Chapter 9, "Introduction to the Power Query M Formula Language."

The techniques you will learn in this chapter will enable you to perform a wide range of transformations and reshape overly structured datasets into a powerful and agile analytics platform. Many analysts know how to transform insight into static summarized tables, but you will be among the few who can transform any static table into insights.

Unpivoting Tables with Multiple Levels of Hierarchy

In Chapter 6, "Unpivoting Tables," you learned the importance of unpivoting summarized tables and reshaping their table structure so that they are consumable by PivotTables in Excel and visuals in Power BI. You started the journey by unpivoting simple tables and then moved on to more complex tables with two levels of hierarchy.

You will now continue the journey by performing a more complex unpivot in this section, using a summarized table that includes three levels of hierarchy in both rows and columns. In this chapter, you will learn to apply the steps in such a way that you will eventually be able to apply a generalized technique on any summarized table with multiple levels of hierarchies.

The Virtual PivotTable, Row Fields, and Column Fields

To help generalize the transformation steps necessary to unpivot any type of summarized table, you need to understand the terms *Row fields* and *Column fields* and learn how to think of a summarized table as a virtual PivotTable.

When you have a summarized table as your source, you can view it as if it were built as a PivotTable in Excel. While it is not a real PivotTable, and its fields are "hardcoded," visualizing your source table as a PivotTable and identifying the fields that should feed the PivotTable will help you unpivot it. Figure 7-1 demonstrates how a source table would look in a PivotTable and which fields would be dragged and dropped to Rows, Columns, and Values.

The source table shown in Figure 7-1 summarizes the revenues of AdventureWorks products by country, state/region, city, color, parent category, and category. By visualizing it as a PivotTable, you can identify which fields are set as rows and columns in the PivotTable Fields pane.

You can download the source table C07E01.xlsx from https://aka.ms/DataPwrBIPivot/downloads. As shown in Figure 7-1, the source table resembles a PivotTable with the fields Country, State/Region, and City set as Rows and the fields Color, Parent Category, and Category set as Columns. The Revenues field is set as Values.

You may not understand yet why imagining a PivotTable can help at this stage. But for now, we just need to formalize the terms you will see in the next section. Therefore, when you want to unpivot a summarized table, you can imagine how it would look like in a PivotTable and think about how you would drag and drop the columns from the unpivoted table as fields in the Rows and Columns sections of the PivotTable Fields pane. In the next section, we use the term *Row fields* to indicate the columns in the unpivoted table that would be set in the Rows section in our imaginary PivotTable's Fields pane. Following the same logic, we use the term *Column fields* to indicate the columns in the unpivoted table that would be set in the Columns section of the PivotTable's Fields pane.

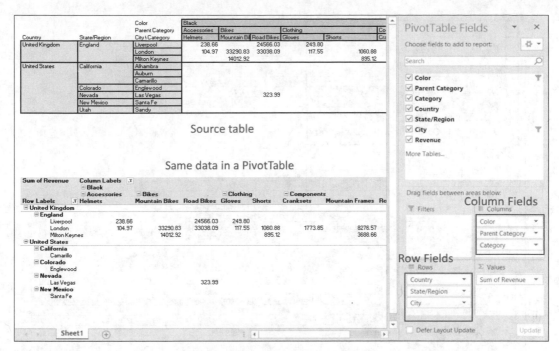

FIGURE 7-1 You can view any summarized table as a virtual PivotTable. The summarized table in this figure is compared to an actual PivotTable that could show the same results.

You are now ready to move to the first exercise, where you will unpivot an AdventureWorks summarized table of 3×3 levels of hierarchy. For the sake of generalizing the steps shown here, we refer to this table as *N×M* instead of 3×3. This generalization will help us later on in this chapter.

Exercise 7-1: Unpivoting the AdventureWorks *N×M* Levels of Hierarchy

You will now follow the transformation steps to unpivot the source table in Figure 7-1. Before you proceed, there are two important themes you should be aware of. If you have gone through the exercises in Chapter 6, you will find the following technique similar as you have already applied it on 2×2 tables. This time, however, we use generic terms, which will allow you to follow these instructions on multiple levels of hierarchy in *N* rows and *M* columns.

The general steps to unpivot any summarized table are illustrated in Figure 7-2, which summarizes the entire sequence of transformations in an intuitive way. You may already find this sequence somewhat familiar from Exercise 6-5: Unpivoting 2×2 Levels of Hierarchy.

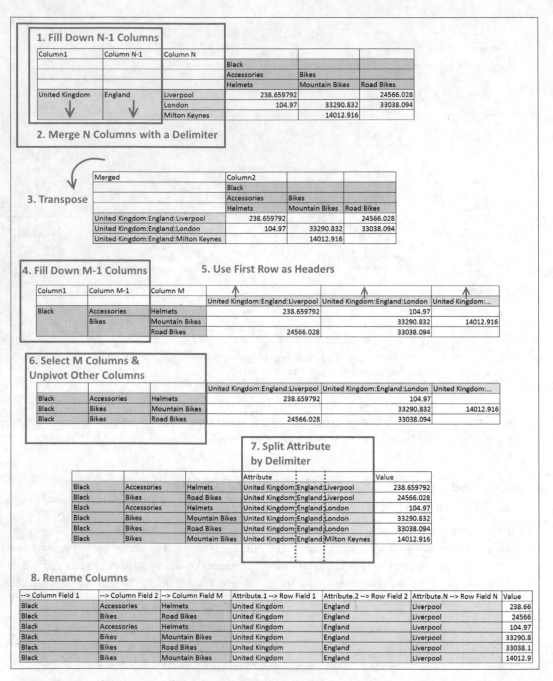

FIGURE 7-2 Using this sequence of transformations you can unpivot any summarized table with *N×M* levels of hierarchy.

1. Download the workbook C07E01.xlsx from https://aka.ms/DataPwrBIPivot/downloads and save it in *C:\Data\C07*.

2. Open a blank new workbook in Excel or a new report in Power BI Desktop.

   In Excel: On the Data tab, select Get Data, From File, From Workbook.

   In Power BI Desktop: In the Get Data drop-down menu, select Excel.

3. Select the file C07E01.xlsx and select Import.

4. In the Navigator dialog box, select Revenues and then select Edit.

   When the Power Query Editor opens, you can visualize in your mind the virtual PivotTable Row fields and Column fields: The Row fields are Country, State/Region, and City. The Column fields are Color, Parent Category, and Category. We will refer to the letter N as the number of Row fields; in this case, $N=3$. We will refer to the letter M as the number of Column fields; in this case, $M=3$.

5. Notice that the first two (N–1) columns in the Preview pane include null values (because of the hierarchical nature of the Row fields). Select the first N–1 columns, and on the Transform tab, select Fill, Down.

   Next, you are going consolidate all the Row fields and merge them together. In Exercise 6-5, you applied the Merge transformation on two columns. This time you will do it on three columns, or, in a more generic way, on N columns.

6. Select the first N columns, and on the Transform tab, select Merge Columns. The Merge Column dialog box opens. Select Colon as Separator and then close the dialog box.

> **Note** Make sure you select a separator that does not already exist in the data. You can even select a rare combination of characters as a separator instead of a colon. Remember the separator you chose, because you are going to need it in step 12.

7. On the Transform tab, select Transpose.

8. To fill down the Column fields and remove the nulls from the higher levels of hierarchy, select the first M–1 columns, and on the Transform tab, select Fill, Down.

9. On the Transform tab, select Use First Row as Headers.

10. Select the first M columns.

11. On the Transform tab, select the Unpivot Columns drop-down and then select Unpivot Other Columns. Alternatively, right-click one of the selected column headers and select Unpivot Other Columns from the shortcut menu.

    Your Attribute column now contains the merged combinations of Row field values (for example, *United Kingdom:England:Liverpool*) that were merged in step 6.

12. Select the Attribute column, and on the Transform tab, select Split Column, By Delimiter. In the Split Column By Delimiter dialog box that opens, set Colon as Select or Enter Delimiter and close the dialog box.

> **Note** As noted in step 6, when your data already contains the Colon character, use the combination of characters that you used as a separator in step 6 and enter them instead of the Colon in step 12.

13. Rename the first *M* columns as the Column fields: *Color, Parent Category, Category*. Name the next *N* columns as the Row fields: *Country, State/Region, City*.

14. Rename the Value column to fit the semantics of the data (in this case, *Revenue*) and explicitly change the column type to Decimal Number or Currency.

15. Load the unpivoted data to your workbook or Power BI report.

To review the solution, download the files C07E01 - Solution.xlsx and C07E01 - Solution.pbix from https://aka.ms/DataPwrBIPivot/downloads.

Generalizing the Unpivot Sequence

In the preceding section you unpivoted a summarized table with 3×3 levels of hierarchy. In this section you will learn how to modify the formulas and convert the query into a function that can be used on different summarized tables. The rationale for using such a function is clear: If you have dozens of different reports, each using a different summarized table as the source data, the function will work on all of them.

With such a function, instead of manually going through the preceding sequence for each type of a summarized table, you will be able to aggregate all the steps into a single transformation step that can be applied on any summarized table. In this section you will improve the query that you created in Exercise 7-1 and generalize the Unpivot sequence to work on any type of summarized table, with any level of hierarchy in rows and columns.

Exercise 7-2: Starting at the End

Before learning how to generalize the Unpivot sequence, this short exercise shows you how to invoke the generalized function, and demonstrates how easy it is to unpivot a different table with it. You will import a different AdventureWorks summarized table, with 2×2 levels of hierarchy (as shown at the top Preview pane in Figure 7-3), and invoke a function that applies the Unpivot sequence of Exercise 7-1 (as shown at the bottom of the Preview pane in Figure 7-3).

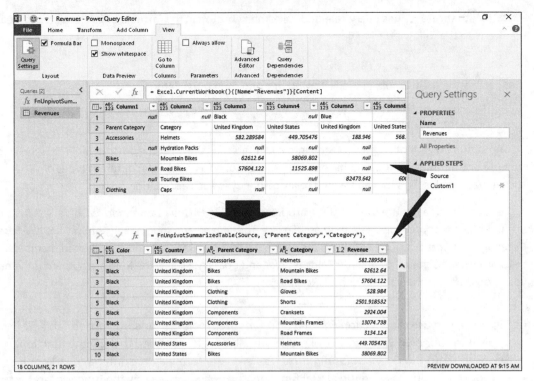

FIGURE 7-3 In this exercise you invoke a function that performs the entire unpivot sequence on a new summarized table.

1. Download the workbook C07E02.xlsx or the Power BI report C07E02.pbix from https://aka.ms/ DataPwrBIPivot/downloads and save it in *C:\Data\C07*.

2. Open the file in Excel or Power BI Desktop and launch the Power Query Editor:

   In Excel: Open the workbook C07E02.xslx, and on the Data tab, select Get Data, Launch Power Query Editor.

   In Power BI Desktop: Open the report C07E02.pbix and on the Home tab, select Edit Queries.

3. In the Power Query Editor that opens, in the Queries pane, select the Revenues query. In the Preview pane, notice that you have imported a different AdventureWorks summarized table, with 2×2 levels of hierarchy (as shown at the top table in Figure 7-3). This time the Row fields in a virtual PivotTables would be Parent Category and Category, and the Column fields would be Color and Country.

   You can see that there is also another item in the Queries pane: *FnUnpivotSummarizedTable*, which is marked with the fx icon. This function was crafted from the query that you created in Exercise 7-1. In the next section you will learn how to create it. For now, you can just learn how to invoke it to unpivot the Revenues query. Instead of following the entire unpivoting sequence in Exercise 7-1, you will be able to unpivot the Revenues table in two simple steps.

4. With the Revenues query selected, click the fx button in the formula bar. A new step is created with the following formula:

```
= Source
```

5. Change the formula to the following one and then press Enter:

```
= FnUnpivotSummarizedTable(Source, {"Parent Category","Category"},
{"Color","Country"}, "Revenue")
```

The summarized table is transformed into a fact table (as shown at the bottom table in Figure 7-3). Isn't it magical? Imagine that you have 50 different reports to create from different types of summarized tables. This function would really be handy in such a scenario.

Let's pause for a minute to look at the arguments used in *FnUnpivotSummarizedTable*. The first argument is the source table—in this case, *Source*. The second argument is a list of Row fields—*Parent Category* and *Category*. The curly brackets define the list and wrap its comma-separated members. The third argument is the list of Column fields—*Color* and *Country*. Finally, the fourth argument is the name you should use for the Value column—*Revenue*.

> **Tip** You can use the function *FnUnpivotSummarizedTable* on any summarized table. To apply it in your own Excel workbooks or Power BI reports, you need to copy the function. Simply referring to *FnUnpivotSummarizedTable* in your formulas in a different workbook or report, without copying the actual function, will not work. To copy the function, you can right-click it in the Queries pane and select Copy. Then, in your destination workbook or Power BI report, right-click the empty space in the Queries pane and select Paste. You can also open the Advanced Editor from the Power Query Editor of C07E02.xslx or C07E02.pbix and copy the source code. Then, create a blank query in your destination report, select Advanced Editor, and paste it.

Exercise 7-3 shows how to create *FnUnpivotSummarizedTable* step by step.

Exercise 7-3: Creating *FnUnpivotSummarizedTable*

You will now learn how to generalize the unpivot sequence that you created in Exercise 7-1 and turn it into a function. The techniques you will apply here will not only be helpful in generalizing the unpivot sequence for a wide variety of summarized tables but will also help you appreciate the power in refining M formulas to generalize and improve the robustness of your data preparation automation.

Part 1: Creating RowFields, ColumnFields, and ValueField

You will start with the results from Exercise 7-1, or you can download the workbook C07E01 - Solution.xlsx or the Power BI report C07E01 - Solution.pbix from https://aka.ms/DataPwrBIPivot/downloads.

1. Open C07E01 - Solution.xlsx or C07E01 - Solution.pbix and launch the Power Query Editor.

2. Open a blank query as follows:

In Excel: Right-click the Queries pane, select New Query, select Other Sources, and select Blank Query.

In Power BI Desktop: Right-click the Queries pane, select New Query, and then select Blank Query.

3. Rename the new query *RowFields*, and copy the following code into the formula bar to create the list of Row fields:

```
= {"Country", "State/Region", "City"}
```

4. Create a new blank query. Rename it *ColumnFields*, and copy the following code into the formula bar to create the list of Column fields:

```
= {"Color", "Parent Category", "Category"}
```

> **Note** It is important that you name the new queries *RowFields* **and** *ColumnFields*. You will soon use them in the code to generalize the steps in Exercise 7-1. Note that in Exercise 7-1, the letter *N* represented the length of RowFields and the letter *M* represented the length of ColumnFields.

5. Create a new blank query. Rename it *ValueField*, and copy the following code into the formula bar:

```
= "Revenue"
```

Part 2: Deleting Changed Type Steps

In this part of the exercise you will delete the Changed Type steps, which are too specific to the current data source and will not help you generalize this query to handle any summarized table.

6. In the Queries pane, select the Revenues query. In Applied Steps, select the third step, Changed Type. In the formula bar you should see the following code:

```
= Table.TransformColumnTypes(Revenues_DefinedName,{{"Column1", type text},
{"Column2", type text}, {"Column3", type text}, {"Column4", type any}, {"Column5",
type any}, {"Column6", type any}, {"Column7", type any}, {"Column8", type any},
{"Column9", type any}, {"Column10", type any}, {"Column11", type any}, {"Column12",
type any}, {"Column13", type any}, {"Column14", type any}, {"Column15", type any},
{"Column16", type any}, {"Column17", type any}, {"Column18", type any}, {"Column19",
type any}, {"Column20", type any}, {"Column21", type any}, {"Column22", type any},
{"Column23", type any}, {"Column24", type any}, {"Column25", type any}, {"Column26",
type any}, {"Column27", type any}, {"Column28", type any}, {"Column29", type any},
{"Column30", type any}, {"Column31", type any}, {"Column32", type any}, {"Column33",
type any}})
```

This step was generated automatically when you imported the source table into the Power Query Editor. If you end up working with smaller tables that do not have one of the columns listed here, such as Column33, the query will fail. The best solution at this stage is to remove this step, so click the Delete icon on the Changed Type in Applied Steps pane, and then, in the Delete Step dialog box, select Delete.

> **See Also** In Chapter 10, "From Pitfalls to Robust Queries," you will learn more details about the rationale of Changed Type and why it is preferred to delete it and explicitly change the types when needed.

7. In Applied Steps, select the Changed Type1 step. Here is an excerpt of the formula that appears in the formula bar:

```
= Table.TransformColumnTypes(#"Promoted Headers",{{"::Color", type text},
{"::Parent Category", type text}, {"Country:State/Region:City \ Category",
type text}, {"United Kingdom:England:Abingdon", type number}, {"United
Kingdom:England:Cambridge", type number}, {"United Kingdom:England:
Gloucestershire", type number}, {"United Kingdom:England:High Wycombe",
type number}, {"United Kingdom:England:Liverpool", type number},
{"United Kingdom:England:London", type number}, …
```

Like the Changed Type step mentioned in step 6, this step was generated when you set First Row as Headers in Exercise 7-1. This formula will be useless, and it will fail to refresh, if you try to apply it on completely different tables. Therefore, you should remove this step as well, so click the Delete icon on the Changed Type1 step, and then, in the Delete Step dialog box, select Delete.

8. In Applied Steps, select the Changed Type2 step. You should see the following line of code in the formula bar:

```
= Table.TransformColumnTypes(#"Split Column by Delimiter",{{"Attribute.1",
type text}, {"Attribute.2", type text}, {"Attribute.3", type text}})
```

This step was generated when you split the Attribute column into three columns. You can delete it as well because it will not apply in some situations. For example, if you were to apply the unpivot on two levels of hierarchy in Rows, there would be no value in having code that changes the types of three columns. Therefore, click the Delete icon on the Changed Type2 *step*, and then, in the Delete Step dialog box, select Delete.

Part 3: *Table.ColumnNames, List.FirstN,* and *List.Count*

In this part of the exercise, you will modify the formulas that explicitly refer to column names, and generalize them to refer to the columns in a dynamic way, relying on the length of RowFields and the length of ColumnFields that were created in part 1. You will use three useful functions: *Table.ColumnNames, List.FirstN,* and *List.Count* to achieve this generalization.

9. In Applied Steps, select the step Filled Down. The formula bar should show the following line:

```
= Table.FillDown(Revenues_DefinedName, {"Column1", "Column2"})
```

This code was generated in step 5 from Exercise 7-1 and filled down the first *N*–1 columns (which are all the Row fields except of the last). You need to modify the code and change the hardcoded list *{"Column1", "Column2"}* to a dynamic list of the first *N*–1 column names in the current table.

Before you do this, let's briefly look at why *Revenues_DefinedName* is used in this formula instead of *Navigation*. By looking at the Applied Steps pane, you can see that the Filled Down step is below the Navigation step. Normally, you would see in the formula bar a reference to a table name that matches the name of the preceding step in Applied Steps. But in this case, you can see that *Revenues_DefinedName* is used in the formula instead of *Navigation*.

To understand why this is the case, select Advanced Editor on the Home tab, and you see the following line:

```
Revenues_DefinedName = Source{[Item="Revenues",Kind="DefinedName"]}[Data],
```

See that the correct identifier to apply the Fill Down transformation is *Revenues_DefinedName* (the identifier used before the first equal sign). Now that you know how to refer to the preceding step, let's look at how to modify the Fill Down step to generically fill down on *N*–1 columns.

Again, here is the original Fill Down formula that is shown in the formula bar:

```
= Table.FillDown(Revenues_DefinedName, {"Column1", "Column2"})
```

Now you should change it to the following formula:

```
= Table.FillDown(Revenues_DefinedName,
    List.FirstN(
        Table.ColumnNames(Revenues_DefinedName),
        List.Count(RowFields) - 1))
```

Let's examine the change. *Table.FillDown* received a static list as the second argument. To turn it into a dynamic list, you first need to get a list of all column names of the table. You do this by using the function *Table.ColumnNames* on the preceding step, *Revenues_DefinedName*:

```
Table.ColumnNames(Revenues_DefinedName)
```

The preceding formula uses *Revenues_DefinedName* to refer to the table provided at the Navigation step.

You have already seen *Table.ColumnNames* in several examples in earlier chapters. In this example, it returns all the column names for the current table: Column1, Column2, Column3, and so on. To return only the first *N*–1 columns, you first need to calculate *N*–1. In this case, *N* represents the count of the *RowFields* list:

```
List.Count(RowFields)
```

Therefore, *N*–1 is simply the following:

```
List.Count(RowFields) - 1
```

Now, when you know how to calculate *N*–1, you can fetch the first *N*–1 column names by applying *List.FirstN*, which returns a list with the first items from the original list. *List.FirstN* has two arguments: the input list and the number of first items to retrieve. You can build the list {"Column1", "Column2"} by using the following code:

```
List.FirstN(Table.ColumnNames(Revenues_DefinedName), List.Count(RowFields) - 1)
```

And this formula is now used as the second argument in the modified *Table.FillDown* formula:

```
= Table.FillDown(Revenues_DefinedName,
    List.FirstN(
        Table.ColumnNames(Revenues_DefinedName),
        List.Count(RowFields) - 1))
```

10. In Applied Steps, select the Merged Columns step. This step was generated when you merged the first *N* column. In the formula bar, you should find the following hardcoded reference to the list {"Column1", "Column2", "Column3"}.

```
= Table.CombineColumns(
    #"Filled Down",
    {"Column1", "Column2", "Column3"},
    Combiner.CombineTextByDelimiter(":", QuoteStyle.None),
    "Merged"
)
```

> **Note** In the formula bar you can see a single-line version of this formula. To make it easier to read, the formula is provided here in a multiline format.

To dynamically refer to the *N* column names of the source table, you can use the same code that you applied in step 8 but this time with *N* as the second argument of *List.FirstN* instead of *N*–1. Here is the modified formula for the Merged Columns step (provided here in a multiline format):

```
= Table.CombineColumns(
    #"Filled Down",
    List.FirstN(
        Table.ColumnNames(#"Filled Down"),
        List.Count(RowFields)
    ),
    Combiner.CombineTextByDelimiter(":", QuoteStyle.None),
    "Merged"
)
```

11. Move to the next step that requires a modification in Applied Steps: Filled Down1. This step was generated for the second fill down (see Exercise 7-1, step 8). Here is the code that appears in the formula bar:

```
= Table.FillDown(#"Transposed Table", {"Column1", "Column2"})
```

You need to change the hardcoded column names into a dynamic version. But this time, because you have transposed the table and handled the Column fields, you need to fill down the first *M*–1 columns of ColumnFields. Here is the modified code:

```
= Table.FillDown(
    #"Transposed Table",
    List.FirstN(
        Table.ColumnNames(#"Transposed Table"),
        List.Count(ColumnFields) - 1
    )
)
```

Unlike the modified *Table.FillDown* in step 9, which used *List.Count* on RowFields, in this step you use *List.Count* on *ColumnFields* to get the number *M*–1.

12. To refine the Unpivot step, in Applied Steps, select Unpivoted Other Columns. You see the following hardcoded columns in the formula bar:

```
= Table.UnpivotOtherColumns(#"Promoted Headers", {"::Color", "::Parent Category",
"Country:State/Region:City \ Category"}, "Attribute", "Value")
```

In Exercise 7-1, you applied Unpivot Other Columns by selecting the first *M* columns. To get the first *M* columns dynamically, you can apply the following modified code:

```
= Table.UnpivotOtherColumns(
    #"Promoted Headers",
    List.FirstN(
        Table.ColumnNames(#"Promoted Headers"),
        List.Count(ColumnFields)
    ),
    "Attribute",
    ValueField
)
```

You apply the same technique here except that you use *M* instead of *M*–1, and you apply *Table.ColumnNames* on the table #*"Promoted Headers"*, which represents the last transformation step.

You also include the query *ValueField* instead of *"Value"* as the new name of the *Value* column. This modification will allow you to use the column name Revenue. You could do this later, in the renaming step, instead.

13. In Applied Steps, select Split Column By Delimiter. You will find the following code, which splits the Attribute column into the *N* columns Attribute.1, Attribute.2, and so forth. Here is its multiline version:

```
= Table.SplitColumn(
    #"Unpivoted Other Columns",
    "Attribute",
    Splitter.SplitTextByDelimiter(":", QuoteStyle.Csv),
    {"Attribute.1", "Attribute.2", "Attribute.3"}
)
```

The third argument of *Table.SplitColumn* defines two important elements: the number of the columns to split and the names of the split columns. Instead of the default Attribute.*X* names, you can use the Row fields (Country, State/Region, City), which are already defined in the RowFields query. Here is the modified indented code:

```
= Table.SplitColumn(
    #"Unpivoted Other Columns",
    "Attribute",
    Splitter.SplitTextByDelimiter(":", QuoteStyle.Csv),
    RowFields
)
```

Part 4: Renaming Columns and *List.Zip*

Now you're ready to refine the most complicated step in Applied Steps: Renamed Columns.

14. Select the Renamed Column step in Applied Steps. When you look at the formula bar, you see the following code:

```
= Table.RenameColumns(#"Split Column by Delimiter",{{"::Color", "Color"},
{"::Parent Category", "Parent Category"}, {"Country:State/Region:City \ Category",
"Category"}, {"Attribute.1", "Country"}, {"Attribute.2", "State/Region"},
{"Attribute.3", "City"}, {"Value", "Revenue"}})
```

This code renames the columns by passing a list of lists as the second argument of *Table.RenameColumns*. Each inner list is a pair of textual values: The first text is the existing column name, and the second text is the new column name.

15. Look at the Preview pane and notice that you have already correctly renamed the Row fields and the Value column in step 13. You just need to rename the first *M* columns. To obtain the list of the first *M* column names, run the following code:

```
List.FirstN(
    Table.ColumnNames(#"Split Column by Delimiter"),
    List.Count(ColumnFields)
)
```

To obtain the new names, you can simply access the ColumnFields query.

But how can you create a list of lists, where each item from the first *M* column names is paired with the Column fields? For that purpose, you can use the *M* function *List.Zip*. This function gets two lists as input and returns a single list of lists, with the pairs from both lists. For example, the following input:

```
List.Zip({"A","B","C"}, {"1", "2", "3"})
```

returns the following list:

```
{{"A","1"}, {"B", "2"}, {"C", "3"}}
```

Thus, when you will apply *List.Zip* on the first *M* column names of the table and on the Column fields as follows:

```
List.Zip(
    {
        List.FirstN(
            Table.ColumnNames(#"Split Column by Delimiter"),
            List.Count(ColumnFields)
        ),
        ColumnFields
    }
)
```

you will get the desired list of lists that is used in the original formula:

```
{{"::Color", "Color"}, {"::Parent Category", "Parent Category"}, {"Country:State/
Region:City \ Category", "Category"}
```

Finally, here is the modified code for the Renamed Columns step:

```
= Table.RenameColumns(
    #"Split Column by Delimiter",
    List.Zip(
        {
            List.FirstN(
                Table.ColumnNames(#"Split Column by Delimiter"),
                List.Count(ColumnFields)
            ),
            ColumnFields
        }
    )
)
```

16. Earlier in this exercise you removed the Changed Type steps. It's time to explicitly change the type of the Revenue column to *Decimal Number*. When you do this through the user interface, the underlying code in the formula bar is as follows:

```
= Table.TransformColumnTypes(#"Renamed Columns",{{"Revenue", type number}})
```

Change the hardcoded *Revenue* to *ValueField*:

```
= Table.TransformColumnTypes(#"Renamed Columns",{{ValueField, type number}})
```

It's time to detach your generalized unpivot sequence from its source. You can see that the first two steps are dependent on a specific workbook and worksheet. You can also generalize these steps and start the unpivot sequence from any input source.

17. In Applied Steps, right-click the Filled Down step and select Extract Previous. In the Extract Steps dialog box, set Source as Extract Query Name and then close the dialog box. A new query that loads the source table from the Excel file is created. The generalized query starts as a reference to the new query.

Part 5: Converting the Query into a Function

You have reached the final stage, where you will convert the query into a function. Chapter 4, "Combining Mismatched Tables," briefly introduced you to functions. In Power Query, you can create parameters, reference them in the formula bar, and then, convert the query into a function by using Create Function in the Queries pane.

Later in the book, you will learn and practice more cases to create functions from queries, using the Create Function user interface. But in this example, you will learn how to create a function using the Advanced Editor, because the Create Function dialog box does not work well on lists.

18. Right-click the Revenues query in the Queries pane and select Advanced Editor. The code already includes the refined and generalized version of the unpivot sequence you have made so far.

19. To convert the unpivot sequence into a function, add the following line as the first line in the Advanced Editor (above the *let* line):

```
(Source, RowFields, ColumnFields, ValueField)=>
```

20. Remove the following line:

```
Source = Source,
```

21. Click Done to close the Advanced Editor dialog box and rename the Revenues query *FnUnpivotSummarizedTable*.

Notice in the Queries pane in Figure 7-4 that the *FnUnpivotSummarizedTable* item is marked with an fx icon. When you select it, you no longer see any preview of the data. Instead, the Preview pane shows the Enter Parameters pane, which can be used to invoke the function. However, in this case, it will not work well, because you cannot feed the function with lists. In Applied Steps, notice that the entire set of steps has been reduced to a single step, and you can no longer edit the function in the user interface.

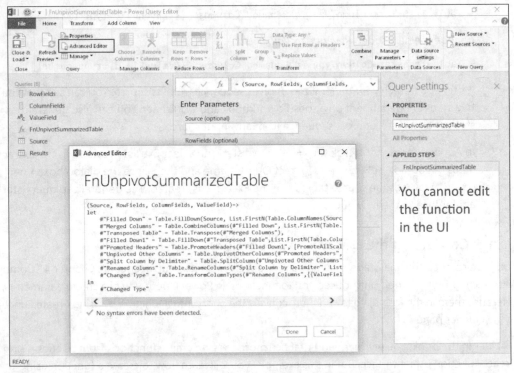

FIGURE 7-4 When a function is created using Advanced Editor, and not via the Create Function user interface, you cannot edit the function outside the Advanced Editor. Once you converted the query into a function, in Applied Steps there is only one uneditable step.

> **Tip** Unlike functions that are created using Create Function in the user interface, which includes an editable sample query, a function created directly in Advanced Editor (as shown in steps 18–21), can no longer be edited outside the Advanced Editor—at least not directly. You can, however, duplicate the function, and in the duplicated query you can remove the first line or comment it out by adding // at the beginning of the line. In this way you can convert the duplicated function to an editable query. You will then be able to see the steps in the Applied Steps pane and make changes through the user interface. When you are done making the changes in the new query, you can copy the code from the Advanced Editor to the original function and modify the function according to the UI changes you have made in the new query.

Let's pause for a minute and examine what you have done. In step 19 you added a line that converts a query into a function.

A function can be written as a standalone query, as you did in this case, or as an inner element inside a query. When invoked with arguments, it produces a new value. You can invoke the function by listing the function's parameters in comma-separated format inside parentheses, following the function name.

These are the arguments you declared in the function:

- *Source*—The input source table you used

- *RowFields*—A list of the Row fields, in this case *{"Country", "State/Region", "City"}*

- *ColumnFields*—A list of the Column fields, in this case *{"Color", "Parent Category", "Category"}*

- *ValueField*—The column name to use for the unpivoted Value column, in this case *"Revenue"*

The goes-to symbol => divides between the function interface declaration and the function's implementation. You already completed the implementation part of the function when you generalized each of the relevant steps using the parameters *Source*, *RowFields*, *ColumnFields*, and *ValueField*.

You should note that the function header can also be defined with the explicit types that are required as input arguments and the expected output type using the *as* element followed by the specific type. Here is the strongly typed function header:

```
(Source as table, RowFields as list, ColumnFields as list, ValueField as text) as table =>
```

You can use this instead of the line in step 19. Having the types declared can ensure that when the function is invoked with wrong types, an error is returned. For example, incorrectly passing the text *"Country, State/Region, City"* instead of a list in the *RowFields* argument will trigger the following error:

```
Expression.Error: We cannot convert the value "Country, State/Region, City" to type List.
Details:
    Value=Country, State/Region, City
    Type=Type
```

Part 6: Testing the Function

You can now use the function to unpivot any summarized table, much as you did in Exercise 7-2. To test it with the source table from Exercise 7-1, follow these steps:

22. Right-click the Source query (which was generated in step 17) and select Reference. Rename the new query *Results*.

23. In the formula bar, modify the code from the following:

```
= Source
```

To this:

```
= FnUnpivotSummarizedTable(Source, RowFields, ColumnFields, ValueField)
```

At this stage, if you wish, you can also delete the queries RowFields, ColumnFields, and ValueField and perform the unpivot as follows:

```
= FnUnpivotSummarizedTable(Source, {"Country", "State/Region", "City"},
{"Color", "Parent Category", "Category"}, "Revenue")
```

Interestingly, but not very practically, the function can even work on a 1x1 summarized table. (It is always good to test your functions and queries on edge cases.) For example, you can load the AdventureWorks revenues source table, which was used in Exercise 6-1 (C06E01.xlsx from https://aka.ms/DataPwrBIPivot/downloads), and apply the following code on the last step (that is, #"Changed Type"):

```
= FnUnpivotSummarizedTable(#"Changed Type", {"Account"}, {"Parent Category"}, "Revenue")
```

How does this work? When the Row fields and the Column fields contain a single element, Fill Down does not fail on an empty list of columns but simply returns its input table. In addition, Merge Columns is also resilient to edge cases and can be applied on a single column, returning the input table as a result. While it may be pointless to apply *FnUnpivotSummarizedTable* on a 1×1 summarized tables, since a simple Unpivot will do the trick, it's nice to have the reassurance that this function is robust to handle such edge cases.

To review the solution to this exercise, download the files C07E03 - Solution.xlsx and C07E03 - Solution.pbix from https://aka.ms/DataPwrBIPivot/downloads.

Conclusions

In this section, you have learned how to generalize the Unpivot sequence to handle complex summarized tables with any number of hierarchy levels in rows and columns. You have also learned how to create functions by using the Advanced Editor. As you refined each step in the query, using *Table.ColumnNames*, *List.FirstN*, or *List.Zip*, you were introduced to the potential to improve your queries in other scenarios in the future and scale up your report to automatically import and transform a wide variety of source tables. In Chapter 9, you will learn more about custom functions, and in

Chapter 10, you will learn about more scenarios where lightweight editing of M formulas can help your queries withstand extreme changes in data format.

The Pivot Column Transformation

So far, in this chapter and in the preceding chapter you have addressed different Unpivot scenarios and learned how to apply Unpivot to transform summarized tables into fact tables. But sometimes a source table is structured in a format that is too flattened—as if someone overused Unpivot and created a source table with multiple rows that should belong to the same entity. This section covers such scenarios and shows how to apply the inverse of an Unpivot: the Pivot Column transformation.

Exercise 7-4: Reversing an Incorrectly Unpivoted Table

This exercise demonstrates how a single Unpivot transformation can harm your data and shows how to reverse it in the Power Query Editor (assuming that you cannot ask for the change at the data source level).

1. Download the workbook C07E04.xlsx from https://aka.ms/DataPwrBIPivot/downloads and save it in *C:\Data\C07*.

2. Open a blank new workbook in Excel or a new report in Power BI Desktop.

   In Excel: On the Data tab, select Get Data, From File, From Workbook.

   In Power BI Desktop: In the Get Data drop-down menu, select Excel.

3. Select the file C07E04.xlsx and select Import.

4. In the Navigator dialog box, select Revenues and then select Edit.

5. In the Power Query Editor that opens, in the Preview pane, look at the table (shown in the top table of Figure 7-5), which contains sales transactions from the fictional company AdventureWorks.

The last four columns represent four numeric attributes in each sale transaction: The *SubTotal* column represents the amount of the sale before tax and freight costs, *TaxAmt* represents the tax amount of the sale, *Freight* represents the shipment cost, and *TotalDue* is the total amount (*TotalDue = SubTotal + TaxAmt + Freight*).

The sales table in the top diagram of Figure 7-5 is well designed. Each of the sales transaction is located on a separate line, and this will enable you to perform simple row-level calculations, such as tax percentage.

In the following steps, you will break the design of this table to demonstrate the impact of an incorrect Unpivot transformation.

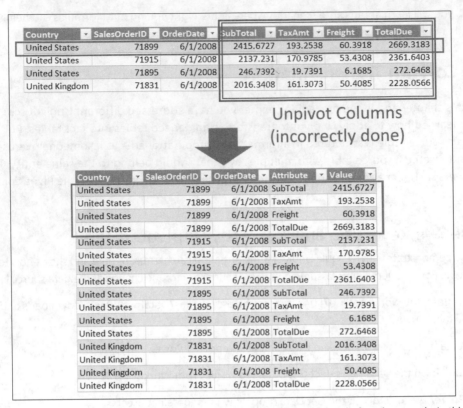

FIGURE 7-5 This exercise shows you how to fix your data when unpivot is done incorrectly. In this example, unpivoting four numeric columns leads to a new table with four rows for each sales order.

6. Select the last four columns and then, on the Transform tab, select Unpivot Columns. As shown at the bottom of Figure 7-5, the unpivoted table is more complicated for analysis than the table at the top of the figure, as the row context now contains only one of the four numeric attributes.

Imagine that this table is your source data, and you need to reverse the Unpivot. The next steps show you how to do it.

7. Select the Attribute column, and on the Transform tab, select Pivot Column.

8. When the Pivot Column dialog box opens, make the following changes:

    a. Ensure that the Pivot Column dialog box states: "Use the names in column "Attribute" to create new columns." You cannot change the selection of the column to pivot at this stage. So, if a different column is mentioned in the text, it means that you didn't select the right column at step 7: You would need to select Cancel in the Pivot Column dialog box and select the correct column before you could again select Pivot Columns.

    b. Set Values Column to Value.

    c. Expand the Advanced options and set Aggregate Value Function to Don't Aggregate as seen in Figure 7-6.

    d. Click OK to close the dialog box.

You can now see that you have regained the former table structure.

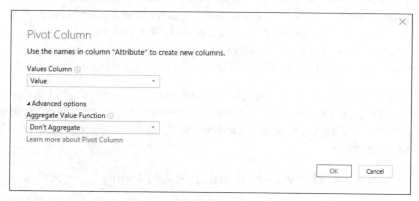

FIGURE 7-6 The Pivot Column dialog box with its Don't Aggregate option enbles you to transform unpivoted tables.

To review the solution, download the files C07E04 - Solution.xlsx and C07E04 - Solution.pbix from https://aka.ms/DataPwrBIPivot/downloads.

Exercise 7-5: Pivoting Tables of Multiline Records

In Exercise 7-5 you applied Unpivot on the numeric columns. The anchor columns (as they are called in Chapter 6) helped you maintain the context of each transaction when you applied the Pivot Columns step. In this exercise you will see what happens when the entire table is unpivoted, and how to resolve it.

1. Repeat steps 1–4 of Exercise 7-4 on a blank workbook or a new Power BI report.

2. Select the first column and then press Ctrl+A to select all columns.

3. In the Transform tab, select Unpivot Columns.

    In the Preview pane, you can see that the unpivoted table contains only the two columns Attribute and Values. Applying Pivot Columns at this stage simply will not work because you have lost your anchor columns.

    Save your query at this stage. You will resume working on it shortly.

Before you will learn how to handle attribute/value pairs, let's pause briefly to discuss the importance of dealing with the attribute/value format. This format is quite common, especially with log files and unstructured data that is not formatted as JSON or XML.

Let's look at why this format is so common. Imagine that you need to import data from a system where a large dataset of entities may contain hundreds of different attributes that can be customized by the users of that system. Few of these attributes are mandatory, and others are optional.

Exporting such a dataset to text files in a regular tabular format would not be efficient. It would create a sparse table with hundreds of columns and empty cells because most of the attributes are optional and empty. To avoid the need to export sparse tables, which will inflate the file with dozens or hundreds of separator characters for empty values, the designers of the relevant system may implement the export as a sequence of multiline records of attribute/value pairs. Thus, you may find this format quite common, especially if you wish to import logs or exported text files.

In the next part of the exercise you will see how to handle the multiline records of attribute/value pairs. You will start with a simple solution, in which you can assume that each multiline record has a fixed number of rows. Then you will apply a generic approach, which assumes that each record will always start with the same attribute.

Part 1: Working with a Fixed Number of Attributes and Using Integer Divide

In step 3 of this exercise, you unpivoted all columns. The unpivoted table contains a sequence of groups, and each group consisted of seven rows of attribute/value pairs. To pivot the table back, you need to regain the context of each group and find a way to use unique numbers for each group before the Pivot operation.

4. In the Queries pane, right-click the Revenues query and select Reference. Rename the new query *Revenues - Fixed Number of Attributes*.

5. On the Add Column tab, select Index Column. The new column includes a running number, starting with zero for the first row.

   In the next step, you will apply integer division of 7 on the running number. Integer division is a division in which the remainder part is discarded. This step will allow you to convert the running index from an individual row index into a group index since each group consists of seven rows.

6. Select the Index column. On the Transform tab, in the Number Column section, select Standard, Integer-Divide. In the Integer-Divide dialog box that opens, enter 7 in the Value box and click OK to close the dialog box. You can now see that the Index column has the value 0 for the first group of 7 rows, 1 for the next group of 7 rows, 2 for the third group of rows, and so forth. You are now ready for the Pivot step.

 Note In step 6, do not add a new column with Integer-Divide. Ensure that you apply Integer-Divide on the existing Index column.

7. Select the Attribute column, and on the Transform tab, select Pivot Column.

8. In the Pivot Column dialog box that opens, make the following changes:

   a. Set Values Column to Value.

   b. Expand Advanced Options.

c. Set Aggregate Value Function to Don't Aggregate.

   d. Click OK to close the dialog box.

9. Remove the Index column. The table is now successfully pivoted. Save your report so you can move on to a more generic technique for pivoting multiline records.

You can review the solution in the files C07E05 - Solution.xlsx and C07E05 - Solution.pbix, which are available to download from https://aka.ms/DataPwrBIPivot/downloads. (This solution can be found in the Power Query Editor as the query, Revenues - Fixed Number of Attributes.)

Part 2: Handling an Unfixed Number of Attributes, with a Conditional Column, and Fill Down

Occasionally, you will need to work with multiline records that have optional attributes. In such situations, you cannot assume that you have a fixed number of rows for each record as you did in Part 1. This part of the exercise describes a more generic technique that enables you to pivot the table. In this case, you need to make the following assumptions: Each record will always start with the same attribute name, and while the rest of the attributes may be optional, the first attribute is mandatory. Figure 7-7 illustrates the transformation steps needed to pivot the multiline records into a fact table.

Start this part of the exercise with the saved file from Part 1 when the Power Query Editor is open.

10. In the Queries pane, right-click the Revenues query and select Reference. Rename the new query *Revenues - Fixed First Attribute*. This new query will be used to pivot the data with the assumption that each new multiline record starts with the Country attribute.

11. On the Add Column tab, select Index Column.

   You will use the running index to represent each row. But now comes a bigger challenge: You need to identify the index of the rows with Country in the Attribute column. For that purpose, you can use Conditional Column and Fill Down transformations, both of which are very helpful for context preservation. You used them extensively in Chapter 5, "Preserving Context," when you needed to preserve context from table titles.

12. On the Add Column tab, select Conditional Column. In the Add Conditional Column dialog box that opens, make the following changes:

   a. Enter *Row ID* in the New Column Name box.

   b. Set Column Name to Attribute.

   c. Keep Equals as the operator.

   d. Enter *Country* in the Value text box.

   e. Set Select a Column as Output and select the Index column.

   f. Enter *null* in the Otherwise box. (You need the null value for the rows with non-Country values to set the stage for the next step: Fill Down.)

   g. Click OK to close the dialog box.

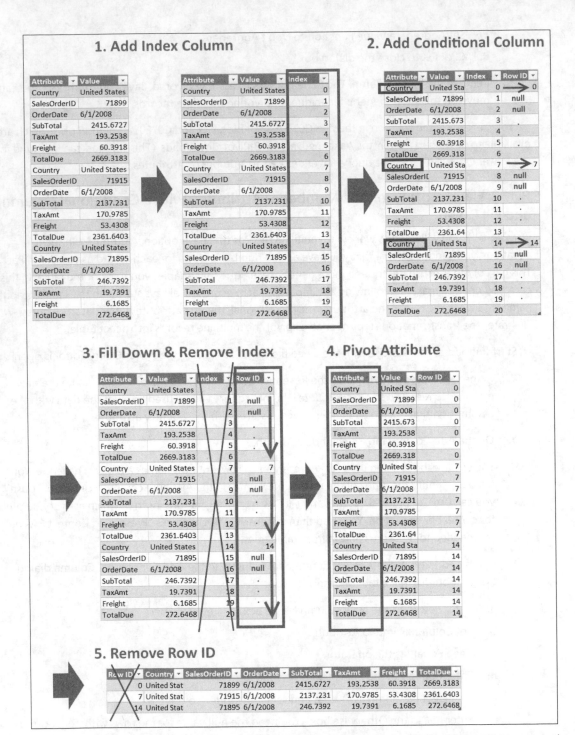

1. Add Index Column

Attribute	Value	Index
Country	United States	0
SalesOrderID	71899	1
OrderDate	6/1/2008	2
SubTotal	2415.6727	3
TaxAmt	193.2538	4
Freight	60.3918	5
TotalDue	2669.3183	6
Country	United States	7
SalesOrderID	71915	8
OrderDate	6/1/2008	9
SubTotal	2137.231	10
TaxAmt	170.9785	11
Freight	53.4308	12
TotalDue	2361.6403	13
Country	United States	14
SalesOrderID	71895	15
OrderDate	6/1/2008	16
SubTotal	246.7392	17
TaxAmt	19.7391	18
Freight	6.1685	19
TotalDue	272.6468	20

2. Add Conditional Column

Attribute	Value	Index	Row ID
Country	United Sta	0	0
SalesOrderID	71899	1	null
OrderDate	6/1/2008	2	null
SubTotal	2415.673	3	.
TaxAmt	193.2538	4	.
Freight	60.3918	5	.
TotalDue	2669.318	6	
Country	United Sta	7	7
SalesOrderID	71915	8	null
OrderDate	6/1/2008	9	null
SubTotal	2137.231	10	.
TaxAmt	170.9785	11	.
Freight	53.4308	12	.
TotalDue	2361.64	13	
Country	United Sta	14	14
SalesOrderID	71895	15	null
OrderDate	6/1/2008	16	null
SubTotal	246.7392	17	.
TaxAmt	19.7391	18	.
Freight	6.1685	19	.
TotalDue	272.6468	20	

3. Fill Down & Remove Index

Attribute	Value	Index	Row ID
Country	United States	0	0
SalesOrderID	71899	1	null
OrderDate	6/1/2008	2	null
SubTotal	2415.6727	3	.
TaxAmt	193.2538	4	.
Freight	60.3918	5	.
TotalDue	2669.3183	6	
Country	United States	7	7
SalesOrderID	71915	8	null
OrderDate	6/1/2008	9	null
SubTotal	2137.231	10	.
TaxAmt	170.9785	11	.
Freight	53.4308	12	.
TotalDue	2361.6403	13	
Country	United States	14	14
SalesOrderID	71895	15	null
OrderDate	6/1/2008	16	null
SubTotal	246.7392	17	.
TaxAmt	19.7391	18	.
Freight	6.1685	19	.
TotalDue	272.6468	20	

4. Pivot Attribute

Attribute	Value	Row ID
Country	United Sta	0
SalesOrderID	71899	0
OrderDate	6/1/2008	0
SubTotal	2415.673	0
TaxAmt	193.2538	0
Freight	60.3918	0
TotalDue	2669.318	0
Country	United Sta	7
SalesOrderID	71915	7
OrderDate	6/1/2008	7
SubTotal	2137.231	7
TaxAmt	170.9785	7
Freight	53.4308	7
TotalDue	2361.64	7
Country	United Sta	14
SalesOrderID	71895	14
OrderDate	6/1/2008	14
SubTotal	246.7392	14
TaxAmt	19.7391	14
Freight	6.1685	14
TotalDue	272.6468	14

5. Remove Row ID

Row ID	Country	SalesOrderID	OrderDate	SubTotal	TaxAmt	Freight	TotalDue
0	United Stat	71899	6/1/2008	2415.6727	193.2538	60.3918	2669.3183
7	United Stat	71915	6/1/2008	2137.231	170.9785	53.4308	2361.6403
14	United Stat	71895	6/1/2008	246.7392	19.7391	6.1685	272.6468

FIGURE 7-7 When each multiline record starts with the same attribute name (in this case "Country"), you can apply this pivot sequence to transform this table into a well-designed fact table.

13. Select the Row ID column, and on the Transform tab, select Fill, Down. You can now remove the Index column.

Row ID now contains the number 0 for the first group, the number 7 for the second group, the number 14 for the third group, and so forth. If you run this technique on multiline records with optional attributes, the numbers in Row ID will not be multiples of 7 or of any other fixed number. It does not really matter which values you have in Row ID. The only important thing is that it consists of unique values for each record or group of rows thanks to the Fill Down.

Now when the context for each record is reconstructed, you are ready for the pivot finale.

14. Select the Attribute column, and on the Transform tab, select Pivot Column.

15. When the Pivot Column dialog box opens, make the following changes:

    a. Set Values Column to Value.

    b. Expand Advanced Options.

    c. Set Aggregate Value Function to Don't Aggregate.

    d. Click OK to close the dialog box.

16. Remove the Row ID column.

You can review the solution in the files C07E05 - Solution.xlsx and C07E05 - Solution.pbix, which are available to download from https://aka.ms/DataPwrBIPivot/downloads. (This solution can be found in the Power Query Editor in the query, Revenues - Fixed First Attribute.)

Summary

In this chapter you have finished your exploration of unpivoting summarized tables. You have learned how to unpivot complex tables with 3×3 levels of hierarchy and how to generalize the steps by replacing hardcoded column names in the M formulas with *Table.ColumnNames* and *List* functions. You have also learned how to convert a generalized query into a function and created *FnUnpivotSummarizedTable*, which you successfully tested on several summarized tables.

In the second part of the chapter, you learned how to reverse the Unpivot step and apply Pivot Columns to improve your table structure. You have also learned about the consequences of unpivoting all columns and why multiline records of attribute/value pairs represent a common data format that you should learn how to pivot. By using Index, Conditional Column, and Fill Down, you have learned the necessary staging sequence for Pivot to work in such cases. With this new technique, you can now handle many scenarios involving multiline records.

CHAPTER 8

Addressing Collaboration Challenges

Great things in business are never done by one person. They're done by a team of people.

—Steve Jobs

IN THIS CHAPTER, YOU WILL

- Learn how to use parameters in Power Query for paths of local data sources

- Use Power BI templates in conjunction with parameters to enable multiple co-authors to import data from local files

- Learn the limitations of parameters in Excel and how to use tables or named ranges as parameters

- Learn how to resolve firewall errors and consolidate queries

- Learn how to connect to shared files on OneDrive for Business and SharePoint

- Learn how to connect to specific subfolders on SharePoint and how to modify queries that connect to local folders so they can import data from SharePoint

- Learn the security considerations involved in sharing workbooks and Power BI report files with colleagues

As you become a proficient report author, you face new challenges when you start co-authoring reports and sharing reports with colleagues. While simultaneous editing of queries is not supported, and it's not possible to compare differences between revisions of reports, there are plenty of basic challenges that surface when you start sharing report "source code" that you can address.

As a report author, you may already work on a team of specialists who share write access to the same Excel workbooks or Power BI report files. You may often modify the reports to fix bugs or provide improvements. There are even cases in which you may share reports in a very traditional and basic way—as a file. The goal of this chapter is to introduce you to some of the basic collaboration challenges and their solutions. This chapter will help you better collaborate with other co-authors and avoid foolish mistakes. It will also help you write better reusable queries and understand how to approach your reports in a new context.

> **Note** This chapter does not focus on sharing experiences that are aimed at report consumers. This topic is rapidly evolving and is very different in Excel than in Power BI. While Excel is more limited in terms of its online sharing and scheduled refresh experiences using Power Query, Excel's younger sibling, Power BI allows you to publish your .pbix files to the PowerBI.com service, run a scheduled refresh, and even use on-premises data gateways to ensure that your local data sources are securely connected to the service so that consumers can enjoy up-to-date reports. The Power BI service includes a variety of sharing experiences (see https://docs.microsoft.com/en-us/power-bi/service-share-dashboards) and collaboration and sharing environments (see https://docs.microsoft.com/en-us/power-bi/service-collaborate-power-bi-workspace).

Local Files, Parameters, and Templates

One of the most common challenges you encounter when you co-author a report in Excel or Power BI, is when your data sources are local Excel or text files. We can illustrate this challenge with a very common story of two report authors. Meet Alice and Bob.

Alice and Bob, two fictitious heroes in this chapter, are accomplished Power Query users. Until recently, they worked on separate teams and were the only Power Query experts on those teams, so they have never had to share their queries with others. Last week they joined forces to create a very complex report that Alice started.

Accessing Local Files—Incorrectly

You can download Alice's workbook, C08E01 - Alice.xlsx, or Power BI report, C08E01 - Alice.pbix, from https://aka.ms/DataPwrBIPivot/downloads. The data source C08E01.xlsx is also available for download from this location.

When Bob receives Alice's report for the first time, he receives the following error when he tries to refresh it:

```
DataSource.Error: Could not find a part of the path 'C:\Users\Alice\Documents
\C08\C08E01.xlsx'.
```

Bob follows these steps to fix the problem, after he saves Alice's dataset C08E01.xlsx in his local folder, *C:\Users\Bob\Documents\C08\C08E01.xlsx*:

1. He opens the workbook or Power BI report and launches the Power Query Editor.

2. For each one of the three queries, Revenues, Categories, and Colors, Bob performs these steps:

<ol type="a">
<li>a. He selects the Source step (first step) in Applied Steps.</li>
<li>b. In the formula bar, he replaces the path in this line:</li>
</ol>

```
= Excel.Workbook(File.Contents("C:\Users\Alice\Documents\C08\C08E01.xlsx"),
null, true)
```

with the following:

```
= Excel.Workbook(File.Contents("C:\Users\Bob\Documents\C08\C08E01.xlsx"),
null, true)
```

The modified line contains the path that Bob used to save the local file C08E01.xlsx.

Applying step 2 on the three queries fixes the refresh error. Bob can start working on the report. A few hours later, Bob sends the report back to Alice, who is annoyed to find that the report is not refreshing. Following Bob's email instructions, she modifies the path in the three queries.

As Alice and Bob keep exchanging the report, over time, they gradually add more queries that import data from local files. Eventually, every time they need to work on the queries and exchange the workbook or report they end up modifying the path name in dozens of queries as they flip from one's path to the other's. Things become much more time-consuming as their team grows and two more developers join the team. One day they discover that there is a better way to handle their problem: using a parameter.

Exercise 8-1: Using a Parameter for a Path Name

Power Query enables you to create parameters and incorporate them inside existing M formulas. When you do this, you can have multiple queries reference the same parameter. You can also control the parameter's value from a single location to affect all the queries. In our story, Bob and Alice can use a parameter for the path name, and it will save them all the trouble they have been having to this point.

In this exercise, you will learn how to use a parameter for the path in Excel and Power BI to fix Alice's and Bob's problem.

1. Download the data source C08E01.xlsx and Alice's workbook, C08E01 - Alice.xlsx, or Power BI report, C08E01 - Alice.pbix, from https://aka.ms/DataPwrBIPivot/downloads and save them in *C:\Data\C08*.

2. Launch the Power Query Editor as follows:

   In Excel: Open Alice's workbook, C08E01 - Alice.xlsx. On the Data tab, select Get Data and then select Launch Power Query Editor.

   In Power BI Desktop: Open C08E01 - Alice.pbix. Select Edit Queries on the Home tab.

3. On the Home tab of the Power Query Editor, select the Manage Parameters drop-down and then select New Parameter. In the Parameters dialog box that opens, follow these steps (as shown in Figure 8-1):

   <ol type="a">
   <li>a. Enter Path in the Name box.</li>
   <li>b. Enter C:\Data\C08 in the Current Value box.</li>
   <li>c. Click OK to close the dialog box.</li>
   </ol>

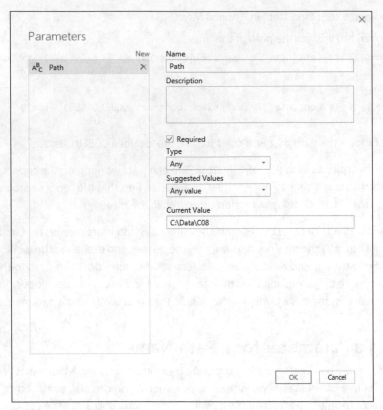

FIGURE 8-1 The Parameters dialog box enables you to create new parameters and edit existing ones. A common use of parameters is to define the path to data source files.

> **Note** In Exercise 8-2, you will refine the parameter to improve the user experience for Alice and Bob and allow them to switch between different predefined path values. For now, this exercise keeps things simple and uses a simple parameter that can accept any value.

4. In the Queries pane, select the queries Revenues, Colors, and Categories one at a time and follow these steps for each query:

   a. In Applied Steps, select the Source step (first step).

   b. In the formula bar, find the following line:

   ```
   = Excel.Workbook(File.Contents("C:\Users\Alice\Documents\C08\C08E01.xlsx"),
   null, true)
   ```

   Using the *Path* parameter and the Ampersand operator sign (&), modify the line to include *Path & "\08E01.xlsx"* instead of *"C:\Users\Alice\Documents\C08\C08E01.xlsx"*.

   Here is the modified line:

   ```
   = Excel.Workbook(File.Contents(Path & "\C08E01.xlsx"), null, true)
   ```

5. To confirm that your three modified queries work as expected, select each query again and make sure there are no longer any errors shown in the Preview pane.

    From now on, Alice, Bob, and their team can make a single change to modify the *Path* parameter value, and they will be able to refresh their reports.

> **Tip** Parameters are helpful in many scenarios. You can use parameters in any context that requires different inputs from the report author. One of the most common scenarios is needing to be able to switch between Development, Test, and Production data sources. In Exercise 8-1, the same user can change the Path value to fit either a Development folder or a Production one. So the advantages of using a parameter are not limited to co-authoring of queries but can help you control and manage the lifecycle of your reports.

You can download the solution files C08E01 - Solution.xlsx and C08E01 - Solution.pbix from https://aka.ms/DataPwrBIPivot/downloads.

Exercise 8-2: Creating a Template in Power BI

Power Query parameters have specific advantages in Power BI Desktop. In this exercise, you will learn about the Power BI template and how you can use it in conjunction with parameters to have a better experience in co-authoring and reusing reports.

A Power BI template is a special file format for a Power BI report. You can export a Power BI template from any existing report. The exported file will be saved as .pbit file, and it will not include the data from the original report. You can share the .pbit file with other co-authors or clients. When they open the template, if your original report included parameters, they will be asked to provide the parameters' values. Once the parameters are set, the report will be loaded—relying on the values they provided during the load.

In this exercise you will create a template of the Power BI report you created in Exercise 8-1. You can download C08E01 - Solution.pbix from https://aka.ms/DataPwrBIPivot/downloads if you didn't follow Exercise 8-1 with Power BI Desktop.

1. Open the Power BI Report C08E01 - Solution.pbix.

2. On the Home tab, select File, Export, Power BI template.

3. In the Export a Template dialog box that opens, enter a description for the template. This text will be shown for any user who opens the template. Here is a possible description:

    ```
    Please provide the path of C08E01.xlsx file. For example: C:\Data\C08
    ```

4. Click OK to close the dialog box.

5. In the Save As dialog box that opens, set the location to save the new template file to *C08E02 - Solution.pbit*, and select Save.

6. Because Power BI Desktop is still open for you on the .pbix report, not the template file, open File Explorer and find the new C08E02 - Solution.pbit file in the location that you set in step 5. You can share this template with other co-authors, and they will no longer need to edit the path from the Power Query Editor as they would with the original solution of Exercise 8-1.

As illustrated in Figure 8-2, when a co-author opens the template, the C08E02 - Solution dialog box opens. After the user enters the path and selects Load, the report loads, and the queries import the data from the local folder.

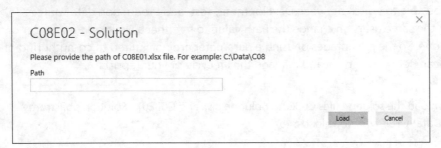

FIGURE 8-2 When a Power BI template file (.pbit) is opened, the user can provide input for all the parameters that were used.

To improve Alice and Bob's user experience, because you already know which paths each of them is using, you can continue this exercise with the next steps.

7. While *C08E01 - Solution.pbix* is still open, on the Home tab, select Edit Queries to go back to the Power Query Editor.

8. On the Home tab, select Manage Parameters. In the Parameters dialog box that opens, in the Suggested Values drop-down, select List of Values.

9. In the table below List of Values, enter the following path values:

   - *C:\Data\C08*
   - *C:\Users\Alice\Documents\C08*
   - *C:\Users\Bob\Documents\C08*

10. In the Default Value drop-down, select *C:\Users\Alice\Documents\C08* to serve as the default path (since Alice was the first person working on this report, you will give her the honor to have her path the default one). You could, however, select any of the three path values you entered in step 9.

11. In the Current Value drop-down, select *C:\Data\C08* since this is where you keep the local data source.

12. To add a description to the parameter, enter the following text in the Description box: *The Path for C08E02.xlsx file*. When you provide a description in this way, an information icon will be added on the right side of the Path label when the template is opened, and when the users hover over it, a tooltip will show the description you provided here.

13. Before you close the Parameters dialog box, ensure that it configured as shown in Figure 8-3.

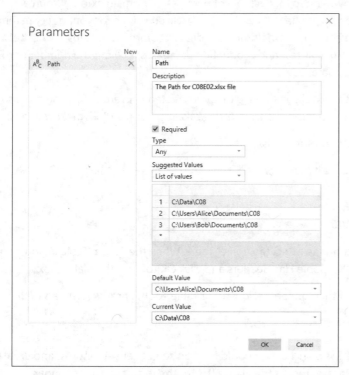

FIGURE 8-3 You can configure the *Path* parameter to include a list of suggested values.

14. Repeat steps 2–5 to create a new Power BI template and name this one *C08E02 - Solution 2.pbit*.

The template is ready to share with Alice and Bob. When one of them opens the template, he or she will be able to select the appropriate path from the drop-down list.

You can download the solution templates C08E02 - Solution.pbit and C08E02 - Solution 2.pbit from https://aka.ms/DataPwrBIPivot/downloads.

Creating a Power BI template is an effective way to reuse a report on different datasets with the same schema. For an example of template reuse, visit https://datachant.com/2016/04/29/power-bi-templates/.

Exercise 8-3: Using Parameters in Excel

Unlike in Power BI Desktop, in Excel you cannot create a dialog box that prompts co-authors to enter parameter values. Excel templates (.xltx) work differently and do not include user input when they load. As a result, when you want to share an Excel workbook that will require a co-author to edit the path, the user will need to launch the Power Query Editor and edit the parameter.

To provide a better user experience, you will learn in this exercise how to use cells in the spread-sheet in conjunction with named ranges or tables to allow users to enter the parameters values without having to launch the Power Query Editor. However, as you will see, there are serious limitations to this technique. Still, this technique allows you to load a table of parameters from an external source, such as a spreadsheet or a configuration file, to have an external centralized source for your query parameters. Such parameters can define certain thresholds in your data transformation steps, switch between multiple predefined data sources (such as test and production databases), or limit the number of rows or the range of dates to pull from a database.

In this exercise, you start with the Excel solution file that you created in Exercise 8-1. You can also download the solution file C08E01 - Solution.xlsx from https://aka.ms/DataPwrBIPivot/downloads.

1. Open the workbook C08E01 - Solution.xlsx.

2. Select New Sheet and rename it *Start Here*.

3. In cell A1, enter *Path*.

4. In cell A2, enter *C:\Data\C08*.

5. Select cells A1 and A2, and on the Insert tab, select Table. When the Create Table dialog box opens, select the box My Table Has Headers and click OK to close the dialog box.

6. Select cell A1 or cell A2 and then on the Design tab of Table Tools, enter *Parameters* in the Table Name box.

Note   As an alternative to steps 5 and 6, you could instead select cells A1 and A2 and create a named range by entering Parameters in the Name Box to the left of the formula bar.

As illustrated in Figure 8-4, at this stage, Path is located as the first cell in a new table and can be easily modified by co-authors of this workbook, without the need to launch the Power Query Editor and find the relevant parameter in the Queries pane. When you share such a workbook with co-authors or colleagues who need to refresh the workbook, you can make their experience easier; in addition, the instructions you may need to share with them (to edit the path) are much simpler.

	A	B	C	D	E	F	G
1	Path						
2	C:\Data\C08						
3							
4							
5							
6							
7							
8							
9							
10							
11							
12							
13							
14							

Start Here   Sheet1   Sheet2   Sheet3   (+)

FIGURE 8-4 You can use a table in Excel for the *Path* parameter.

> **Tip** If you need to pass multiple parameters, you can add more columns, each one with the relevant parameter name in row 1 and its values in row 2. Then, using the Drill Down transformation that is described in step 10, you can access the values of the parameters in the Power Query Editor.

7. When you have the Parameters table ready, to feed the *Path* value into your queries, select any cell (A1 or A2 in this case) in the Parameters table, and on the Data tab, select From Table/Range.

8. When the Power Query Editor opens, expand the Queries pane, and you see the new Parameters query. In the Preview pane you can see the table with the Path column. In the future, if you need additional parameters, you can add them as new columns in the Parameters table in the spreadsheet. For this reason, you can keep Parameters as a standalone query and create a new referencing query for the path.

9. In the Queries pane, right-click Parameters and select Reference. Rename the new query *Path2*. (You still have the old *Path* parameter from Exercise 8-1, but you will remove it soon.)

10. With the Path2 query selected in the Queries pane, right-click its cell *C:\Path\C08* and select Drill Down. The table is transformed into text with the path value.

> **See Also** In Chapter 5, "Preserving Context," you used the Drill Down transformation to extract context from specific cells and preserve it in combined tables. In this exercise, you use the same technique to read parameters.

From here, you can reference Path2 to get the path value from anywhere in your queries. The M function that is generated is simple and easy to use, if you are comfortable with M:

```
= Source{0}[Path]
```

Because the *Source* identifier is equal to *Parameters*, you can avoid steps 9–10 by referencing the following code whenever you need to access the *Path* value:

```
= Parameters{0}[Path]
```

If you have new parameters in the future, you can read a new parameter's value by referencing its column name instead of *Path*. For example, in case you have in a new column for the filename, in the following line, you can access a new parameter called *Filename*:

```
= Parameters{0}[Filename]
```

For the preceding formula, you first selected the first row and then selected the column by name. You can also use the following line to get the same result by selecting the column by its name and then selecting the first cell (by referencing the zero index):

```
= Parameters[Filename]{0}
```

It's time to modify all the queries to load the path from Path2 instead of reading it from the native query parameter *Path* that you created in Exercise 8-1. While the *Path* parameter provided a user-friendly experience in Power BI Desktop when you exported the report to a Power BI template, Path2, which loads the data from the spreadsheet, is more useful in Excel.

11. For each of the queries Revenues, Colors, and Categories, modify the formula in the Source step from *Path* to *Path2*. Here is the modified formula:

    ```
    = Excel.Workbook(File.Contents(Path2 & "\C08E01.xlsx"), null, true)
    ```

    Unfortunately, following this step, you may get the following error in the Preview pane for the Revenues, Colors, and Categories queries:

    ```
    Formula.Firewall: Query 'Colors' (step 'Source') references other queries or steps,
    so it may not directly access a data source. Please rebuild this data combination.
    ```

12. To resolve this error, change the privacy settings of this workbook by following these steps:

    a. In the Power Query Editor, select File, Query and Options, Query Options.

    b. In the Query Options dialog box that opens, in the Current Workbook section, select Privacy in the left pane.

    c. Select the box Ignore the Privacy Levels and Potentially Improve Performance and click OK to close the dialog box.

> **Note** Ignoring privacy levels should be performed with caution. If you don't trust the owner of the workbook, or if you see that the queries are connected to unknown external sources, it is not recommended to apply the settings in step 12. However, there are some cases in which Power Query fails to isolate between the multiple data sources and issues the *Formula.Firewall* error. In part 2 of this exercise, you will learn an advanced technique for resolving the error without needing to ignore privacy levels.

13. Remove the *Path* parameter and rename Path2 to *Path*. Renaming Path2 automatically changes all the references to the new query name in the queries Revenues, Colors, and Categories, so you don't need to repeat step 11 and modify Path2 to Path.

14. On the Home tab, select Close & Apply To.

15. When the Import Data dialog box opens in Excel, select Create Connection Only to ensure that the *Path* query will not be loaded as a new table.

At this stage, as long you use the report, the *Path* parameter can be modified in the workbook followed by a refresh of the workbook to load the data, and you will not need to launch the Power Query Editor to modify the parameter. However, if you share the workbook with colleagues, when they will try to refresh the workbook, they will encounter the same *Formula.Firewall* error you had after step 11. As a result, you would now need to explain to your colleagues how they can turn off the privacy levels in their workbook (as you did in step 12). While ignoring the privacy levels can also be done from Excel without opening the Power Query Editor (by selecting Get Data on the Data tab and then selecting Query Options), you may still prefer to share the solution workbook from Exercise 8-1 and tell your colleagues how to change the parameter in the Power Query Editor, without getting into the sensitive topic of privacy. To get a better use of the Path parameter in the spreadsheet and avoid the privacy discussions with your colleagues, part 2 of this exercise will show how to prevent the *Formula.Firewall* error.

You can download the solution workbook C08E03 - Solution.xlsx from https://aka.ms/ DataPwrBIPivot/downloads. When you open it, you will experience the *Formula.Firewall* error (unless you set privacy levels to be ignored for all workbooks). To resolve the error, Select Get Data on the Data tab, and then select Query Options to follow steps 12b and 12c.

Exercise 8-3 Part 2: Rebuilding the Data Combination

You can avoid the *Formula.Firewall* error altogether by rebuilding the queries in a way that will ensure that all the references to external sources are done in a single query. Whenever you encounter an error that starts with *Formula.Firewall* and ends with the message *Please rebuild this data combination*, you can either cautiously turn off the privacy levels, as explained in step 12 of part 1 of this exercise, or consolidate all the queries that reference queries with external sources into a single query. The Query Dependencies view is a good place to start to understand your challenge.

You can open the workbook C08E03 - Solution.xlsx, launch the Power Query Editor, and on the View tab, select Query Dependencies. Looking at the dependencies (see Figure 8-5), you can immediately see that each of the queries at the bottom is dependent on both Current Workbook and *c:\data\c08\ c08e01.xslx*. But while the latter workbook is referenced directly by Revenues, Colors, and Categories, Current Workbook is not referenced directly by these queries but via Path and Parameters.

By consolidating the references to the dependent external sources in a single query, you can avoid the error. In this example, the consolidation will happen if each of the Revenues, Colors, and Categories queries is directly referring to the current workbook as well as the data source *c:\data\c08\c08e01.xslx*. To do this, select each of the queries, Revenues, Colors, and Categories and in Advanced Editor, add the following line of code after *let*:

```
Path = Excel.CurrentWorkbook(){[Name="Parameters"]}[Content]{0}[Path],
```

The preceding line consolidates all the transformation steps of the Parameters query into a single line. You can now remove the Parameters query, as it is not being referenced anymore in any of the queries.

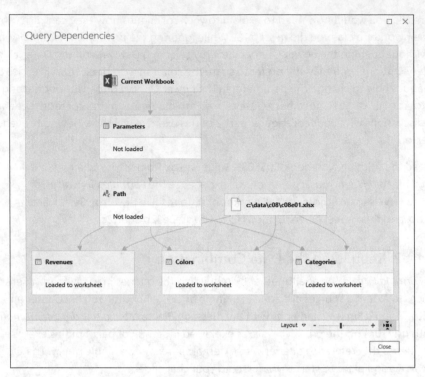

FIGURE 8-5 The Query Dependencies dialog box shows that multiple queries access the external data sources.

An even cleaner approach is to create a new query that returns the Workbook binary and to have Revenues, Colors, and Categories reference the Workbook query. Then, in the Workbook query, you can have the references to the external Excel file and the current workbook.

Here are the steps to do this:

1. Open C08E03 - Solution.xlsx, and on the Data tab, select Get Data and then select Launch Power Query Editor.

2. Ensure that the privacy levels in Query Options, under Current Workbook, are set to Combine Privacy According to Your Privacy Level Settings for Each Source.

3. In the Queries pane, right-click the Colors query and select Duplicate.

4. Rename the new query *Workbook* and delete all the steps in Applied Steps except for the first Source step.

5. On the Home tab, select Advanced Editor and add the following bolded line in the M expression as shown here:

```
let
    Path = Excel.CurrentWorkbook(){[Name="Parameters"]}[Content]{0}[Path],
    Source = Excel.Workbook(File.Contents(Path & "\C08E01.xlsx"), null, true)
in
    Source
```

6. Click Done to close the Advanced Editor. At this stage, you see that the Workbook query returns the same table content of the workbook C08E01.xlsx that you had before step 4.

7. In the Queries pane, select each of the queries Revenues, Colors, and Categories, and for each one of them, select the Source step in Applied Steps and change the line in the formula bar to the following:

   `= Workbook`

8. From Queries pane, remove the Path query and then remove the Parameters query.

9. On the Home tab, select Close & Apply To.

10. In the Import Data dialog box that opens in Excel, select Create Connection Only to ensure that the new Workbook query will not be loaded as a new table.

By following these steps, you have consolidated all the references to the external sources into the Workbook query and avoided the *Formula.Firewall* error. You can now review the Query Dependencies dialog box, as shown in Figure 8-6, to see that Workbook is the only query that accesses the two external data sources (unlike the original more complex dependencies in Figure 8-5).

You can download the solution workbook C08E03 - Solution 2.xlsx from https://aka.ms/ DataPwrBIPivot/downloads. Thanks to the revision you have just made, your colleagues will not have to change or disable their privacy levels.

> **Tip** Rebuilding your queries to prevent firewall errors is not always an easy task. When you consolidate multiple queries into a single query, you lose some flexibility in terms of maintaining and reusing your queries. You should evaluate the pros and cons before you embark on a consolidation effort. As you will see in the next section, sometimes there are just better solutions for altogether avoiding the need to use two data sources.

> **See Also** While there are caveats related to using local Excel spreadsheets as external data sources for Power Query, you can publish Power BI reports to the Power BI service and enjoy scheduled refreshes of your reports, even when they connect to local data sources. The Power BI service can connect to the on-premises local files (or any other on-premises data source) by using on-premises data gateways. Learn more at https://docs.microsoft.com/ en-us/power-bi/service-gateway-onprem.

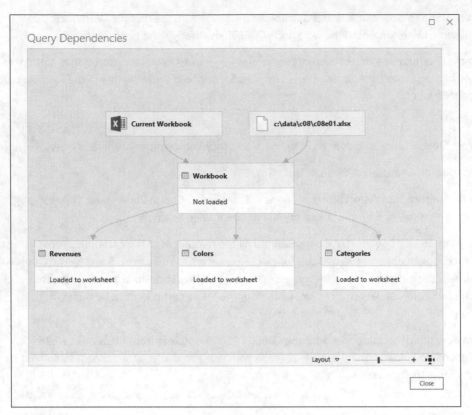

FIGURE 8-6 The Query Dependencies dialog box looks like this after the consolidation effort that fixes the *Formula.Firewall* error.

Working with Shared Files and Folders

In Exercises 8-1, 8-2, and 8-3, you used a variety of techniques to simplify co-authoring experiences when working with local files. Alice and Bob, our fictitious characters, can now easily configure their path and load the data from a local Excel workbook to their shared report.

By now, you are likely thinking that there must be better ways to collaborate between report authors. Can't Alice and Bob use a shared file that is hosted on OneDrive for business or a SharePoint site? You are right. Exercises 8-1, 8-2, and 8-3 introduced you to important techniques involved in using parameters, Power BI templates, worksheet parameters, and the consolidation of queries to avoid refresh errors in common scenarios when local files are used as the data source, but relying on shared files can resolve many team collaboration obstacles.

In this section, you will learn tips and tricks for working with shared files on OneDrive for Business and SharePoint. To follow the exercises in this part, you need a OneDrive for Business account and a SharePoint site on Office 365 where you have access to stored files.

Importing Data from Files on OneDrive for Business or SharePoint

Importing data from source files on OneDrive for Business or SharePoint by using Power Query can be challenging for beginners. Power Query doesn't allow you to navigate to OneDrive for Business or a SharePoint site by using the File Explorer experience, as it does for local files. If you have mapped OneDrive for Business or a SharePoint site as a local folder, you will be able to import the data, as for any other local file, but the source file will not be shareable, as the path will be local and specific to your computer. To overcome this limitation, you can find the correct file URL on OneDrive for Business or SharePoint and use the web connector to import the workbook.

While there are several different ways to obtain the URL that will allow you to access the file, most of these ways lead you to a URL that cannot be used by Power Query. To obtain the correct URL and import the Excel workbook on OneDrive, follow these steps:

1. Log in to OneDrive for Business or SharePoint and navigate to the folder where your workbook is located.

2. Click on the workbook and open it in Excel Online.

3. Select Edit Workbook and then select Edit in Excel.

4. After Excel opens the workbook, on the File tab, select Info and select the path. Then, select Copy Path to Clipboard, as illustrated in Figure 8-7.

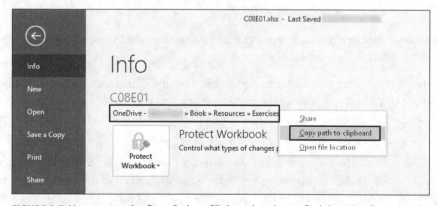

FIGURE 8-7 You can use the Copy Path to Clipboard option to find the URL of your workbook and use it to load the workbook in Power Query.

Note There are many ways to get a URL to open the workbook in the browser, but most of them will not work when you try to use them in Power Query to import the workbook. The Copy Path to Clipboard technique ensures that you obtain the correct URL to allow Power Query to import the workbook.

Here is an example of a URL on OneDrive for Business:

`https://`**`contoso-my`**`.sharepoint.com/personal/`**`alice_contoso_com`**`/Documents/`**`Book/Resources/`** **`Exercises/08/`**`C08E01.xlsx`

This fictitious example was generated by Alice on her OneDrive for Business. The bolded elements in the URL were generated because of the following facts: Alice's company is contoso.com and her email address is alice@contoso.com (this is why you see *alice_contoso_com* in the path). The data source C08E01.xlsx was stored in the folder *Book*, under the subfolders *Resources/Exercises/08*.

Here is an example of the URL on SharePoint Online:

`https://`**`contoso`**`.sharepoint.com/sites/`**`Book`**`/Shared%20Documents/`**`Resources/Exercises/08/`** `C08E01.xlsx`

In this example, the bolded elements in the URL were generated because of the following facts: Alice's company is contoso.com (hence the subdomain in the URL is *contoso*). The data source C08E01.xlsx was stored in a SharePoint site called Book, under the *Documents* folder, in the subfolders *Resources/Exercises/08*.

5. To import the workbook in Power Query, follow these steps:

    In Excel: Open a blank workbook. Then, on the Data tab, select From Web (note that this is not the Web Query option you could select in older versions of Excel) in the Get & Transform Data section.

    In Power BI Desktop: Open a blank report. On the Home tab, select the Get Data drop-down and then select Web.

6. When the From Web dialog box opens, paste the URL from the Clipboard (which was copied in step 4) into the URL box. Then remove the suffix "*?web=1*" and click OK to close the dialog box. (The suffix should be removed because you are not interested in importing the workbook in Excel Online.)

7. If this is your first time accessing OneDrive for Business or SharePoint using Power Query, the Access Web Content dialog box opens. Select Organizational Account in the left pane and then select Sign In. When you complete the login phase, you can click Connect.

8. When the Navigator dialog box opens, go through the familiar user experience to select the relevant worksheets to import, and then click Edit to prepare your data.

Tip To use Power Query to import a text file from OneDrive for Business or a SharePoint site, you can create a temporary Excel workbook in the same folder and follow steps 1–4 to obtain the path. Then continue with steps 5–7 to import the text file.

Exercise 8-4: Migrating Your Queries to Connect to OneDrive for Business or SharePoint

In this exercise, you will modify Alice's queries from connecting to her local computer to connecting instead to your OneDrive for Business folder or SharePoint online site. (You will need to have a OneDrive for Business account, or have access to a SharePoint site in your organization.)

1. Download the data source C08E01.xlsx from https://aka.ms/DataPwrBIPivot/downloads and upload it to OneDrive for Business or SharePoint online.

2. Download Alice's workbook, C08E01 - Alice.xlsx, or Power BI report, C08E01 - Alice.pbix, from https://aka.ms/DataPwrBIPivot/downloads.

3. Open the workbook *C08E01 - Alice.xlsx* or the Power BI report *C08E01 - Alice.pbix*.

4. Follow the steps in the preceding section to track the URL of the Excel workbook C08E01.xlsx that you saved on OneDrive for Business or SharePoint online in step 1.

5. Follow the steps in the preceding section to import the Excel workbook C08E01.xlsx using the From Web dialog box. When the Navigator dialog box opens, select the Colors table and then select Edit.

6. Rename the new query *Workbook*, and with Workbook selected in the Queries pane, delete the last two steps in Applied Steps, keeping only the *Source* step.

7. Much as you did in Exercise 8-3, modify the queries to reference the Workbook query instead of the local file in each query. To do so, follow these steps for each of the queries Revenues, Colors, and Categories:

   a. In Applied Steps, select the Source step.

   b. In the formula bar, change the line from this:

   ```
   = Excel.Workbook(File.Contents("C:\Users\Alice\Documents\C08\C08E01.xlsx"),
   null, true)
   ```

   to the following line:

   ```
   = Workbook
   ```

8. To ensure that the new Workbook query will not be loaded, follow these steps:

   In Excel: On the Home tab of the Power Query Editor, select Close & Apply To. When the Import Data dialog box opens, select Create Connection Only to ensure that the new Workbook query will not be loaded as a new table.

In Power BI Desktop: Right-click the Workbook query in the Queries pane of the Power Query Editor and deselect Enable Load in the drop-down menu.

9. To ensure that you followed the steps correctly, launch the Power Query Editor, and on the View tab, select Query Dependencies. Make sure that the layout of your queries is as shown in Figure 8-8.

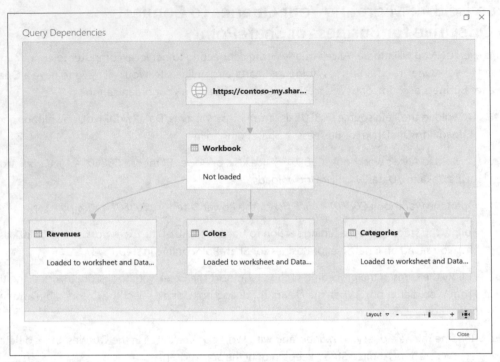

FIGURE 8-8 The Query Dependencies dialog box shows how all the queries are importing the workbook from OneDrive for Business.

You can download the solution files C08E04 - Solution.xlsx and C08E04 - Solution.pbix from https://aka.ms/DataPwrBIPivot/downloads.

The Differences Between OneDrive for Business and SharePoint Online

While OneDrive for Business allows you to move quickly from a local file to a shared file, when you are collaborating with others on a team, it is recommended that you store the shared data source on a SharePoint site. OneDrive for Business is a personal folder, so when the owner of a folder leaves the company, you lose the ability to connect to that source.

If you need to connect to multiple Excel workbooks or text files in a folder, you can store the files on a SharePoint site and use the SharePoint Folder connector. In Exercise 8-5 you will learn how to connect to a SharePoint folder and migrate your queries from a local folder to a SharePoint one.

Exercise 8-5: From Local to SharePoint Folders

In this exercise, you will start with an existing Excel or Power BI report that connects to local data sources in a folder. Then you will upload the data sources to your SharePoint site and modify the queries to import the data sources from SharePoint. The move of the folder to SharePoint, as illustrated in Figure 8-9, is easy. But, as you will find out, the modification of the queries is not trivial.

FIGURE 8-9 Moving a local folder of data sources to SharePoint can improve the collaboration between report authors.

Before you start the exercise, download the following files from https://aka.ms/DataPwrBIPivot/downloads:

- C08E05.xlsx

- C08E05.pbix

- C08E05 - Folder.zip

1. Unzip C08E05 - Folder.zip in your local folder *C:\Data\C08*. After you unzip it, you should have a subfolder named *C08E05 - Folder* that contains three Excel workbooks representing AdventureWorks products by release year. You can review the contents of the Excel workbooks in the folder. Each workbook contains a different release year of AdventureWorks products.

2. Copy the folder *C08E05 - Folder* to a subfolder under the *Documents* folder on a SharePoint site.

3. Open C08E05.xlsx in Excel or C08E05.pbix in Power BI Desktop and launch the Power Query Editor.

   In Excel: On the Data tab, select Get Data and then select Launch Power Query Editor.

   In Power BI Desktop: On the Home tab, select Edit Queries.

4. In the Queries pane, select C08E05 - Folder query. In the Preview pane, you can see the appended AdventureWorks products. You may find these queries familiar. In Exercise 3-3 in Chapter 3, "Combining Data from Multiple Sources," you used the Folder connector to append these workbooks from a folder.

5. Connect to the SharePoint folder to learn the differences between the local and SharePoint folders. To do so, in the Power Query Editor, on the Home tab, select New Source and then do one of the following:

   In Excel: Select File and then select SharePoint Folder.

   In Power BI Desktop: In the Get Data Dialog box that opens, select SharePoint Folder and then click Connect.

6. When the SharePoint Folder dialog box opens, in the Site URL box, enter the root URL of your SharePoint site, without any subfolders. Here is an example of such a URL, if the company subdomain name is contoso and the SharePoint site is Book:

   *https://**contoso**.sharepoint.com/sites/**Book***

> **Note** A key factor in working with SharePoint folders is that you cannot connect directly to a specific subfolder, but only to the main root of the site. To drill down to a specific folder, you need to use filters on the relative path and file names to narrow down the files to the ones you wish to append.

7. If this is your first time accessing SharePoint using Power Query, the Access Web Content dialog box opens. Select Organizational Account in the left pane and then select Sign In. When you complete the login phase, you can click Connect.

8. When a preview of the folder contents opens, select Edit.

9. Because you connected to the root folder of the SharePoint site, you will probably find many irrelevant rows for all the files under the root folder in the Preview pane. To filter the rows and keep only the files in *C08E05 - Folder*, select the filter control in the Folder Path column header.

10. When the Filter pane opens, select Text Filters and then select Contains.

11. When the Filter Rows dialog box opens, in the text box located to the right of the Contains drop-down menu, enter the text */C08E05 - Folder/* and then click OK to close the dialog box. You can now see only the three Excel files in the Preview pane.

12. Rename the query *SharePoint Folder*. It is now time to use it in the existing queries, so in the Queries pane, select the Sample File query.

13. In Applied Steps, select Source. In the formula bar, you can see this formula, which returns the local folder:

    ```
    = Folder.Files("C:\Data\C08\C08E05 - Folder")
    ```

    Replace the formula with the following one:

    ```
    = #"SharePoint Folder"
    ```

14. Repeat step 13 after you select the C08E05 - Folder query in the Queries pane. This query should also be modified to connect to the SharePoint folder instead of the local one.

15. To ensure that the new SharePoint Folder query will not be loaded to the report, follow these steps:

    In Excel: On the Home tab, select Close & Apply To. In the Import Data dialog box that opens, select Create Connection Only to ensure that the new SharePoint Folder query will not be loaded as a new table.

    In Power BI Desktop: Right-click the SharePoint Folder query in the Queries pane and deselect Enable Load from the drop-down menu.

Your queries are now loading the workbooks from SharePoint instead of from local files. Alice and Bob will be happy.

You can download the solution files C08E05 - Solution.xlsx and C08E05 - Solution.pbix from https://aka.ms/DataPwrBIPivot/downloads.

Security Considerations

Power Query was designed with a focus on security. When you build a report in Power Query that connects to an organizational database or any other dataset that requires authentication, your user credentials are stored on your computer to allow you to keep refreshing the report on demand without needing to enter the credentials for each refresh.

When you share the report file with others, the credentials remain on your computer. Your co-authors need to provide their own credentials to connect to the relevant data source. This design protects your credentials and ensures that no other report author can gain access to your credentials.

There are some cases in which you might like to share the queries, model, and visualizations but ensure that the data in the report will be cleaned before you share the report with others. You can do this by using Excel templates or Power BI templates. In Exercise 8-2, you created a Power BI template that enabled the user to enter a parameter value before the data was loaded. Power BI templates can also be created without parameters. The data will still not load to the template, and you can share it with other co-authors without exposing your data. This is usually practical when each report co-author can only access a subset of rows from the same tables in the data sources.

Excel works similarly. To save an Excel workbook as a template and remove the data from the model or tables, select File and then select Save As. Before you save the file, ensure that the file type is changed to Excel Template (.xltx). You see the following prompt before you save the file:

```
The Workbook contains external data. Do you want Microsoft Excel to clear the data
before saving the template, and then automatically refresh the data whenever the template
is opened?
```

Select Yes to remove your data. When your colleague opens the report, Power Query will start the refresh and will prompt the user to provide his or her credentials, if needed. Your data will not be stored in the report.

Removing All Queries Using the Document Inspector in Excel

In some cases, you may want to share transformed data or static charts in worksheets but remove the queries and model from the workbook. While you can manually delete each query and keep the detached tables intact, there is a faster way. You can apply the Document Inspector to instantly remove all the queries in your workbook. To clean all the queries by using the Document Inspector, follow these steps:

1. Go to the File tab in Excel, and in the Info section, select Check for Issues. Then select Inspect Document.

2. When the Document Inspector dialog box opens, select Inspect.

3. Scroll down until you reach the Custom XML Data option, as shown in Figure 8-10.

> **Note** Power Query stores the queries in a special location in the workbook that is known as Custom XML Data. This area in the file is also used by third-party add-ins. Therefore, as a safeguard you should always run the Document Inspector on a copy of the workbook in case the file stores additional data for add-ins, which will be removed by the Document Inspector along with the queries.

4. Select Remove All and then select Close.

5. On the Data tab, select Queries and Connections. You can now see that all the queries have been removed. If you loaded the queries to the Data Model, it will be removed as well.

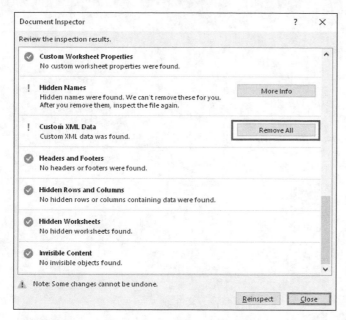

FIGURE 8-10 You can remove all custom XML data in the Document Inspector to delete all the queries.

Summary

In this chapter you have faced new challenges that are common when you start co-authoring reports, sharing reports files with colleagues, and working in team environments.

In Exercises 8-1 and 8-2, you learned how to use parameters and templates to improve your queries when you are collaborating with other report authors and when you import data from local files. In Exercise 8-3, you learned how to create a parameters table in a worksheet and load it as the Parameters query. You then applied Drill Down to load an individual parameter value and resolved *Formula.Firewall* errors by consolidating specific queries.

In Exercises 8-4 and 8-5 you learned how to connect to OneDrive for Business and SharePoint to import data by using Power Query. You also refactored existing queries to load the data from shared workbooks or folders instead of a local source in your file system.

Finally, in this chapter you have learned about some security considerations and techniques that allow you to understand how you can share workbooks and Power BI desktop files and how you can strip the reports from its data or remove all traces of Power Query in the workbook by using the Document Inspector. As you have become more proficient with Power Query, it's time to enter the realms of M, and extend your data-wrangling prowess.

Introduction to the Power Query M Formula Language

You make 'em, I amuse 'em.

—*Dr. Seuss*

IN THIS CHAPTER, YOU WILL

- Learn the maturity stages in learning M

- Learn about online and offline resources for learning M

- Explore the main building blocks of the M language, including the *let* expression

- Understand the main operators and built-in functions for the types in M, including number, time, date, duration, text, null, and logical

- Learn how to build conditions and *if* expressions

- Understand how to define and invoke custom functions

- Learn how to programmatically handle errors

- Learn how to iterate over a loop to achieve complex transformations and how to use recursions and advanced *list* functions

M is the Power Query formula language that is generated by Power Query as you add transformation steps in the user interface of the Power Query Editor. Each transformation step is translated into a single line of M code (or sometimes even a few lines of code) that can be viewed and edited in the formula bar of the Power Query Editor. Together, these steps create the M expression, a block of code that defines the transformation steps in the query and can be edited in the Advanced Editor.

While you can write full M expressions to define queries from scratch in the Advanced Editor, most data challenges can be resolved through the user interface, without the need to write M expressions or even launch the Power Query Editor to edit the expressions. Nevertheless, having a deeper understanding of M will enable you to tackle the most advanced data challenges and extend the use of your queries to address the messiest datasets.

If you are reluctant to learn a new programming language, you will still find this chapter very useful. Unlike with typical programming languages, with M you can achieve a lot by knowing very little.

Learning M

Now that you have stepped through the exercises in earlier chapters, you should feel comfortable starting this chapter to learn more about M, using a direct approach. The following sections dive deeply into M syntax, but this one focuses on learning M as a topic: What does it take to learn M?

So far, you have been casually introduced to M through three user interfaces:

- **The formula bar:** You have seen how to modify an M function in the formula bar to adjust a transformation step to meet your needs. So far in this book, you have usually done this when the user interface has lacked a specific capability (for example, to apply an advanced logical condition when you filter a column).

- **The Custom Column dialog box:** You can use this dialog box to apply some row-level calculations and save the results in the new column.

- **The Advanced Editor:** You can modify multiple steps in a query by using the Advanced Editor, or you can incorporate a code sample from another query or build a custom function to resolve a specific challenge.

Even if you don't understand the syntax or full meaning of the code, the fact that the code is generated using the user interface has helped you understand it to some extent—and this is an important element to remember. The best way for you to learn M is to apply transformation steps in the user interface and then gradually try to understand the underlying code.

Learning Maturity Stages

If you embark on the journey to learn M, you are likely to move through six maturity stages, as illustrated in Figure 9-1. Each stage enables you to resolve new types of data challenges but may keep you locked in a particular comfort zone. Will you be willing to invest significant effort to proceed to the next stage?

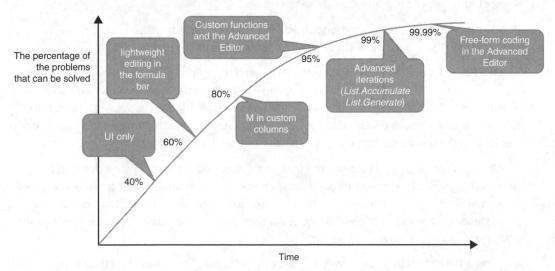

FIGURE 9-1 As you pass through the maturity stages in learning M you can resolve more problems, but most of them can already be resolved when you reach the second stage.

Stage 1: UI Only

If your first exposure to M has been in this book, and you have followed the exercises so far, then you have reached the initial stage of maturity in learning M, and you are already an adept Power Query user. You know that M exists as the underlying language, but you may be reluctant to learn it because the return on investment is not clear. You may also possibly fear learning a programming language or prioritize other languages over M. There are many languages out there—including Excel formulas, VBA, DAX, Python, and R—and you may already practice some of them. Why should you also learn M, which is so different from anything you are used to working with?

The catalyst to move to the next stage comes when you realize that the UI can only help you solve around 40% of the problems you face. When you become motivated to solve more data challenges with Power Query, you will discover that many problems can be overcome with lightweight tweaks of the code. Since this tweaking doesn't require a deep understanding of the syntax, it is a natural stage to attain, even if you are not very advanced in Excel formulas or if you know nothing about software programming.

Stage 2: Lightweight Editing in the Formula Bar

In the second stage of maturity, you apply lightweight modifications to the M code in the formula bar. You may not understand complete formulas, but you can associate some of the elements in the formula with the actions you have taken in the user interface, and you can extend it to meet your needs. At this level, you are able to resolve around 60% of the data challenges you face and a make great impact with your data-wrangling capabilities.

The desire to move to the next stage starts when you have an increasing need to perform more complex calculations in your reports and when you become proficient in other areas, such as DAX in Power BI or Power Pivot in Excel. This is when you discover the power of calculated columns in DAX, and you may think it would be easier to implement a solution by using a custom column in M.

Stage 3: M in Custom Columns

In the third stage, you master the use of custom columns and can write simple but highly effective M formulas in the Custom Column Formula box of the Custom Column dialog box. You master the use of logical conditions in your formulas by using *if/then/else* statements, combined with the Boolean operators *and*, *or*, and *not*. You feel comfortable using the Custom Column dialog box instead of the alternative Conditional Column dialog box and can solve 80% of the data challenges that you encounter.

While some practitioners stay at this stage, many start to understand the power of M and gain the confidence to use the language to address more challenges. This is when they leave the boundaries of the formula bar and start exploring the M expressions in the Advanced Editor to try to apply their knowledge in M and extend their queries to resolve more challenges.

Stage 4: Custom Functions and the Advanced Editor

In the fourth stage, you master the creation of custom functions to reuse your transformation steps. While you appreciate the Create Function feature in the Power Query Editor, you feel comfortable converting queries into custom functions by using the Advanced Editor. You can use the Advanced Editor to perform extensive modification of the code.

At this stage, you can solve 95% of the data challenges you will face. Your reputation as a data-wrangler expands beyond the borders of your team, and you are likely to be approached by many colleagues for help in solving their data challenges.

The catalyst to move to the next stage is no longer driven by critical business needs. After all, you can solve practically any data challenge. The main catalysts to move to the next level are your curiosity and motivation to master M. At this stage, you may start accumulating a library of helpful custom functions, and you might seek new ways to efficiently address problems and reuse your queries in the harshest of situations.

Stage 5: Advanced Iterations (*List.Accumulate* and *List.Generate*)

In the fifth stage, you can approach complex scenarios and generate complex M code to achieve them. While you keep using the Power Query Editor to generate code, you are creating significant and complex code expressions by yourself in the Advanced Editor. You can easily create nested expressions of *let/in* blocks, and you can easily generalize the auto-generated code to do more.

At this stage, you discover the power of *List.Accumulate* and *List.Generate* as useful tools to create iterations of transformations. You can use these functions to create small pieces of M code to be used as arguments in other M functions. Even if the number of use cases where you really need it is very low, the fact that you can write advanced M formulas using *List.Accumulate* and *List.Generate* is a testament to your prowess in M. If you know how to use these functions, you are in Stage 5. In some organizations you may have a reputation of a legendary data-wrangler.

At this stage, you can solve 99% of the data challenges you face. The remaining 1% of the unsolved problems can be handled by using other programming languages besides M. Therefore, your move to the next stage is driven by sheer intellect or your software development experience. If you are not a software developer by background, there is no significant value to moving to the final stage.

Stage 6: Free-Form Coding in the Advanced Editor

In the sixth and final maturity stage, you can write complete M expressions from scratch, without the need to use the Power Query Editor user interface. Free-form coding is a natural thing for you, and you must have a remarkable memory because the Advanced Editor does not have auto-complete or Intelli-Sense capability (at least not yet when these lines were written). You need to remember many function names and their arguments to be in this stage.

Having extensive programming language experience helps you reach this stage, and if you are here, you can seek new ways to make an impact. This is when you may consider writing M for bigger audiences, sharing M functions with your colleagues and even the community, or starting to develop custom data connectors in Visual Studio as the next stage.

> **See Also** If you are a Stage 6 M developer, you are ready to create custom data connectors for Power BI and enable business users to connect to and access data from services and applications that are not provided as out-of-the box connectors by Power BI. Custom data connectors are not described in this book. To learn how to develop such connectors, see https://github.com/Microsoft/DataConnectors.

Online Resources

To move to the next stage in your learning or to understand a new M function, the official Power Query M reference is the resource where you should start. This comprehensive online resource is available on the Microsoft MSDN Library at https://msdn.microsoft.com/query-bi/m/power-query-m-reference.

Often, the official reference site lacks the concrete examples that could help you better understand the use of a function. You are encouraged to search the Internet for relevant blog articles on that topic. These are some of the leading Power Query blogs:

- Chris Webb's BI blog: https://blog.crossjoin.co.uk/category/power-query/

- The Ken Puls (Excelguru) blog: https://www.excelguru.ca/blog/

- Matt Allington's blog (Excelerator BI): https://exceleratorbi.com.au/category/power-query-2/

- Reza Rad's blog (RADACAD): http://radacad.com/category/power-query

- Imke Feldmann's The BICCOUNTANT: http://www.thebiccountant.com/

- DataChant blog: https://datachant.com

Offline Resources

Imagine yourself in an airplane, traveling somewhere far away. Without Internet connectivity, and in a dire need to better understand how a certain M function works, the Power Query Editor includes offline reference pages for all its functions. Sometimes these offline pages include more information or different examples than the MSDN online version, and you are encouraged to check them out.

To review the offline documentation of a function, simply enter an equal sign follows by the function name in the Power Query Editor's formula bar. Don't include any of the parentheses or arguments. After you press Enter, you can see the offline documentation in the Preview pane. For example, if you are using the function *Table.ColumnNames(Source)*, to return the list of column names of the Source table, you can remove the parentheses and Source, as shown here, to get offline documentation of *Table.ColumnNames* (see Figure 9-2):

```
= Table.ColumnNames
```

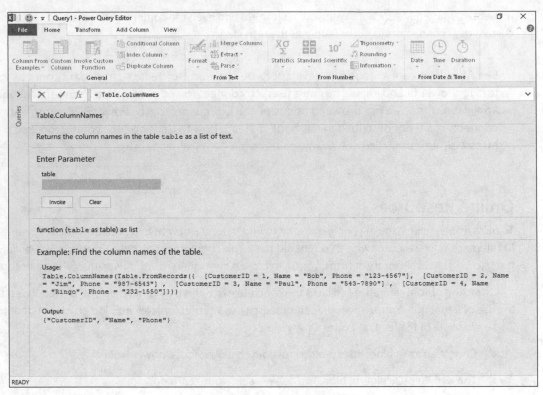

FIGURE 9-2 Enter the function name in the formula bar to read offline documentation of M functions in the Power Query Editor.

Exercise 9-1: Using #*shared* to Explore Built-in Functions

To find new functions and read their offline documentation, you can launch the Power Query Editor, and in the formula bar, enter the following line:

```
= #shared
```

This variable returns a record of all the supported functions in Power Query, including your queries. Let's look at how you can use #*shared* to explore all functions and then drill down to a specific function.

1. Create a blank query, as follows:

   In Excel: On the Data tab, select Get Data and then select From Other Sources and then Blank Query.

   In Power BI Desktop: On the Home tab, select the Get Data drop-down and then select Blank Query.

2. When the Power Query Editor opens, if you don't see the formula bar, enable it on the View tab.

3. Enter the following line in the formula bar and press Enter:

   `= #shared`

   The Preview pane shows a table. It is not a classic table but a record. In its first column is a list of the record's keys (also called field names). In the second column are all the values. Except on the first row, which shows the Query1 key (which is the current query you are working on), all the other values are in the format of functions.

4. Select the blank space in any of the function cells to view at the bottom the offline documentation for that function. Click the Function hyperlink to drill down to the actual function.

5. To find all the *list* functions by using the Power Query user interface, convert the #shared output record into a table by selecting Into Table on the Record Tools Convert tab.

6. Select the filter control of the Name column and select Text Filters. Then select Begins With.

7. When the Filter Rows dialog box opens, enter *List* in the text box to the right of the Begins With drop-down and click OK to close the dialog box.

   You can now see all the *list* functions and explore their offline documentation, as described in step 4.

   You can download the solution files C09E01 - Solution.xlsx and C09E01 - Solution.pbix from https://aka.ms/DataPwrBIPivot/downloads.

M Building Blocks

The central building block in M is the expression. An *expression* is a block of code that is evaluated by the M engine, resulting in a single value. Every transformation step that you have created in the Power Query Editor has generated an M expression. The Preview pane always shows you the value that results from the evaluation of the expression.

In M, each transformation step is a pair consisting of an identifier and its expression. The formula bar enables you to see the expression element of the selected step, and in the Applied Steps pane, you can see the identifier. When you open the Advanced Editor dialog box, you can see the entire M expression of the query. While the code in the Advanced Editor is quite a bit more complex than a single-step M expression in the formula bar, it is still an expression that returns a single value. The following exercise demonstrates this idea in a simple query expression that returns the text *Hello World*.

Exercise 9-2: *Hello World*

In this exercise, you will learn how to map between existing user interfaces in Power Query to expressions and values in M.

1. Launch the Power Query Editor on a blank query. (Not sure how? Follow Exercise 9-1, step 1.)

2. On the Home tab, select Advanced Editor and paste the following code:

```
let
    Source = "Hello",
    Step2 = Source & " ",
    Step3 = Step2 & "World"
in
    Step3
```

3. Click Done to close the Advanced Editor. In the Preview pane, you see the output *Hello World*.

Congratulations. You have written your first "Hello World" program in M. Let's explain the code in M terminology and find out how it is associated with the user interface elements. Figure 9-3 summarizes the main associations between the UI elements—the Advanced Editor, the formula bar, and the Applied Steps pane—and their relevant M building blocks.

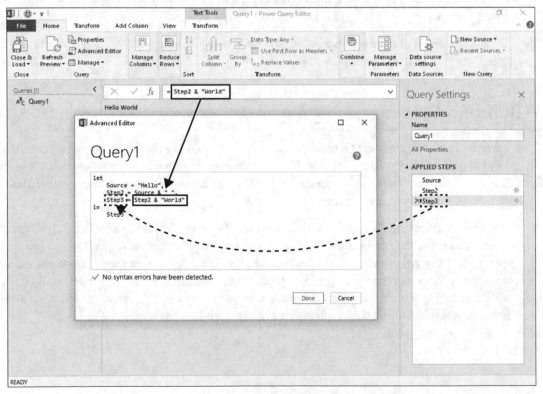

FIGURE 9-3 The Power Query user interface has several M building blocks: the Advanced Editor, the formula bar, and Applied Steps.

In the Preview pane, you can see the *Hello World* value. Usually, you see tables in the Preview pane, but now you see a text value. The expression that you pasted in the Advanced Editor returned the single *Hello World* value. In the formula bar you can see the following line:

```
= Step2 & "World"
```

This code is the expression that is assigned to the *Step3* identifier in the Advanced Editor. It concatenates the value of *Step2* with the text *World*. While the expression is represented in the formula bar, the identifier *Step3* is represented in Applied Steps.

If you select Step2 in Applied Steps, you see the following code in the formula bar:

```
= Source & " "
```

In the Advanced Editor, this expression is represented with its accompanying identifier *Step2*, as follows:

```
Step2 = Source & " ",
```

The trailing comma in this expression is not shown in the formula bar but is needed to separate between identifier/expression pairs that are part of the *let* expression.

While most of the queries are translated into a "linear" sequence of M steps, such as *Source*, *Step2*, and *Step3* (as demonstrated in Exercise 9-2), M enables you to write complex flows and apply conditions that will lead to different flows of execution. You will see this later in this chapter, in the section "An *if* Expression Inside a *let* Expression." But before you dive into such advanced scenarios, it's time to look more closely at the *let* expression. After all, *let* is most likely the first M term you encountered when you opened the Power Query Editor for the first time.

The *let* Expression

Any time you create new queries by using the Power Query Editor and import a dataset to your report following some data preparations, an underlying *let* expression is generated. When you open the Advanced Editor, you see an M expression that starts with *let* and usually ends with *in*, followed by the identifier of the last step.

The *let* expressions allow you to build subsets of smaller expressions that are combined into a single value. Take, for instance, the simple example in Exercise 9-2. In that case, the *let* expression consists of three steps. *Step1* returns the value *Hello*. *Step2* returns the value in *Step1* and a trailing space, and *Step3* returns the value in *Step2* and the trailing value *World*. The *in* defines the second phase of computations that the *let* expression will return. In this basic example, only *Step3* is defined after *in*. As a result, the returned value is the same value in *Step3*: *Hello World*.

A *let* expression enables you to write expressions that are evaluated after the *in* keyword. Here is an example, with code that returns the text *Hello World!!!*:

```
let
  Source = "Hello",
  Step2 = Source & " ",
  Step3 = Step2 & "World"
in
  Step3 & "!!!"
```

In this expression, instead of returning the value in *Step3*, you use a new expression after the *in* keyword that concatenates *Step3* with *!!!*. Here is a similar example, in which you define the *ExclamationMarks* identifier inside the *let* section, and then evaluate it in the *in* expression.

```
let
  Source = "Hello",
  Step2 = Source & " ",
  Step3 = Step2 & "World",
  ExclamationMarks = "!!!"
in
  Step3 & ExclamationMarks
```

A *let* expression can be built as a compound expression made of nested *let* expressions. Here is an example that returns *Hello World!!!*:

```
let
  FirstWord =
  let
    Source = "Hello"
  in
    Source,

  SecondWord =
  let
    Source = "World"
  in
    Source
in
  FirstWord & " " & SecondWord & "!!!"
```

While this expression is completely valid, you will find it rather difficult to maintain in the Power Query Editor. Due to the computation that is needed in the final *in* expression, the entire M expression will be populated in the formula bar, and you will not be able to see the separate steps in the Applied Steps pane. To resolve this issue, and to have separate steps in Applied Steps, as shown in Figure 9-4, you can rewrite the M code by adding a *Result* identifier and moving the expression before the final *in* keyword, as shown here:

```
let
  FirstWord =
  let
    Source = "Hello"
  in
    Source,

  SecondWord =
  let
    Source = "World"
  in
    Source,

  Result = FirstWord & " " & SecondWord & "!!!"
in
  Result
```

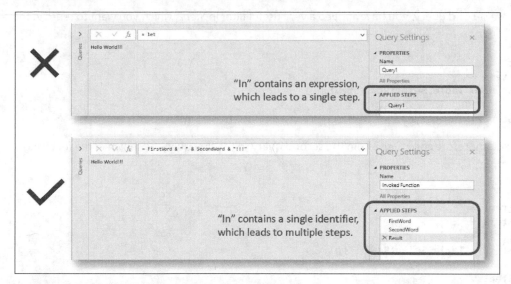

"In" contains an expression, which leads to a single step.

"In" contains a single identifier, which leads to multiple steps.

FIGURE 9-4 Having an expression instead of an identifier after the *in* section in the Advanced Editor leads to a single step in Applied Steps. The preceding M statement demonstrates the solution.

You may have noticed that the identifier *Source* is used twice in the two preceding expressions. Normally, if you use the same identifier twice inside a *let* expression, you get the following error:

```
The variable named 'Source' is already defined in this scope.
```

However, in the two preceding expressions, you have two different *let* expressions, which are nested inside the outer *let* expression. All the identifiers that are defined inside a *let* expression are local and cannot be accessed by the outer *let* expression. When *Source* is evaluated as the value of *SecondWord*, the *Source* in *FirstWord* is not accessible because the two instances of *Source* don't share the same scope.

Merging Expressions from Multiple Queries and Scope Considerations

Understanding the scope in M and how to write *let* expressions can be a handy skill. Oftentimes, you may want to reuse some transformation steps from a query and apply them on a second query. To correctly copy and paste lines of expressions from one query to the other, you usually need to follow three corrective steps in the merged expression. Let's look at this with two queries.

Imagine that you have a query with three transformation steps, as illustrated in this pseudo-code:

```
let
  Step1 = …,
  Step2 = …,
  Step3 = …
in
  Step3
```

In a second query, you have applied a very useful filter in *Step2*, which you want to reuse in the first query:

```
let
  Step1 = …,
  Step2 = Table.SelectRows(Step1, …)
in
  Step2
```

You therefore copy *Step2* from the second query to the first query, as shown in the following example:

```
let
  Step1 = …,
  Step2 = …,
  Step3 = …
  Step2 = Table.SelectRows(Step1, …)
in
  Step3
```

Of course, this code is wrong. A simple copy and paste of the line will not suffice. Here are the three errors you typically need to address:

1. *Step2* is already defined in the original expression, and you receive the following error:

   ```
   The variable named 'Step2' is already defined in this scope
   ```

2. The first argument of *Table.SelectRows* was originally *Step1*, but you should now apply this transformation on *Step3*.

3. After the *in* keyword, you originally returned *Step3* as the value of this expression, but you should now return the value in the last identifier.

Here is the corrected expression:

```
let
  Step1 = …,
  Step2 = …,
  Step3 = …
  Step4 = Table.SelectRows(Step3, …)
in
  Step4
```

In bold you can see the changes needed to modify the expression. First, you need to rename the second *Step2* identifier to *Step4*. Then you need to modify the argument in *Table.SelectRows* to reflect the last step before *Table.SelectRows*, which is *Step3*. Finally, you must update the identifier after the *in* keyword to reflect the correct last step, which is *Step4*.

Whenever you copy lines of code from one query to another, you need to adjust the code and "rewire" the new transformation steps.

In some cases, you might want to copy many lines of codes from one query to another. In such cases, you may find it challenging to modify all the lines together—especially if you have many duplicate identifiers in the combined expression. To resolve this situation, you can apply a nested *let* expression, as shown in this example, which returns the same value as the preceding one:

```
let
  Step1 = …,
  Step2 = …,
  Step3 = …
  Step4 =
   let
     Step2 = Table.SelectRows(Step3, …)
   in
     Step2
in
  Step4
```

Note that the scope in the nested *let* expression contains all the identifiers in the external scope except *Step2*, which is locally redefined in the scope of the nested *let* expression and will not be perceived as a duplicate identifier. When M evaluates Step4, the outer Step2 is not overwritten by the value that was returned by the inner Step2. As explained earlier, the two Step2 identifiers have different scopes.

Finally, here is an example in which an external identifier is used in a nested *let* expression and then is redefined in the inner scope of the nested *let*.

```
let
  A = 1,
  B =
    let
      A = A + 1
    in
      A
in
  B
```

This expression returns the number *2*. The *A* identifier is defined twice. First, *A* is defined in the context of the upper *let* expression and receives the value of *1*. Then, inside the nested *let*, a new *A* identifier is defined with an expression that uses the external *A* identifier and increments it by one.

However, the inner *A* identifier is different from the external *A* identifier and cannot be accessed in the external *let* expression. Look at what happens when the same expression is used but this time you return the *A* identifier in the last *in* expression:

```
let
  A = 1,
  B =
    let
      A = A + 1
    in
      A
in
  A
```

This code returns the number *1* instead of *2*—even though *A* was incremented in the inner *let* expression. In the external scope, *A* is still 1. You can read the expression again, this time with the right scope in mind, as the M engine evaluates the expressions:

```
let
  A_external_scope = 1,
  B =
   let
     A_internal_scope = A_external_Scope + 1
   in
     A_internal_scope
in
  A_external_scope
```

> **Tip** Scope can be a confusing topic, but the bottom line is that you can avoid getting unexpected results by ensuring that you always use unique identifiers.

Now that you better understand *let* expressions, it's time to review the different types in M.

Types, Operators, and Built-in Functions in M

In M, a value is data that is produced by evaluating an expression. In this section, you will learn about the main kinds of values in the M language. Each kind of value is associated with a specific syntax, a set of values that are of that kind, a set of operators, functions that you can perform on that kind of values, and an inherent type definition.

Let's look at the different language elements that are type specific by looking at numeric values in M. Numbers can be represented as literals such as *0, 100, -12.5,* or *2.5e-7*. These values can be manipulated by a family of built-in M functions that start with the prefix *Number* followed by a dot and the function name. For example, *Number.Abs* is a built-in function that accepts a number as its argument and returns its absolute value. Numbers in M have built-in operators, such as =, <, >, <=, >=, +, and -. You will learn more details in this section.

M enables you to declare types in arguments or in returned values of custom functions and test whether a specific value is of a specific type. For example, the following expression typed in the formula bar will return *TRUE,* as illustrated in Figure 9-5.

```
= 1000 is number
```

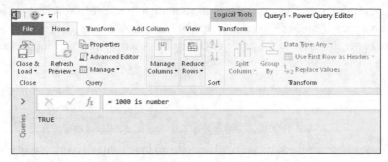

FIGURE 9-5 The expression *1000 is number* in the formula bar returns the value *TRUE*.

Note M is case sensitive. The uppercased Boolean values *TRUE* and *FALSE*, as demonstrated in Figure 9-5, are used for display purposes only. In M expressions, you should use the lowercased version (*true* or *false*); otherwise, you will receive an error. If you use *TRUE* in an M formula, you get this error:

```
Expression.Error: The name 'TRUE' wasn't recognized. Make sure it's spelled
correctly.
```

Types are also defined in built-in functions. For example, the *Number.Abs* function is declared as follows:

```
Number.Abs(number as nullable number) as nullable number
```

This line, called the *function declaration*, explains that *Number.Abs* accepts a single argument, which can be either a number or *null*. The returned value of this function is a number or *null*. Knowing this syntax allows you to understand that you can run *Number.Abs* on a number, like this:

```
= Number.Abs(-1000)
```

which results in that number being returned:

```
1000
```

You can also run the function on *null*, like this:

```
= Number.Abs(null)
```

which results in a *null* value:

```
null
```

However, if you run this function on other types, you will receive an error. For example, applying the function on the text value "*hello*", like this:

```
= Number.Abs("hello")
```

results in an error:

```
Expression.Error: We cannot convert the value "hello" to type Number.
```

For the sake of simplicity, in this chapter, we will refer to the built-in functions of a specific type as *Type.X*. For example, there are many *Number.X* functions, such as *Number.Abs*, as you will see in the next section. Now that you better understand the prevalent uses of types in M, the following sections go over the main types, their operators, and built-in functions.

Basic M Types

Understanding the types in M, as well as the ways you can operate on their values, is very useful when you want to transform a column, add a custom column, or apply a filter with complex logical expressions. While the user interface of the Power Query Editor enables you to achieve many transformations, the knowledge of M types, their operators, and built-in functions will help you achieve greater data-wrangling capabilities on columns.

In this section you will see examples of simple formulas that are used outside the context of data preparation. When you understand how these types can be operated, you will be able to easily apply their operators or built-in functions inside the formula bar to refine column-based transformations.

For example, imagine that you have a *Number.X* function that you cannot find in the user interface—say, *Number.Sqrt*, which will help you transform the numbers in Column1 to their square root values. You can select the numeric column in the Power Query Editor and apply any of the numeric transformations. Here is the formula after you select Scientific, followed by Absolute Value:

```
= Table.TransformColumns(Source,{{"Column1", Number.Abs, type number}})
```

Now you can change the *Number.Abs* to your *Number.X* function (in our example *Number.Sqrt*) to transform the numeric values in each cell of *Column1*:

```
= Table.TransformColumns(Source,{{"Column1", Number.Sqrt, type number}})
```

If the *Number.X* function requires more than one argument, you can use *each* followed by the function name and underscore (_) to represent the numeric value, and then you can add the other arguments. Here, for example, you raise the numbers in *Column1* by the power of 3:

```
= Table.TransformColumns(Source,{{"Column1", each Number.Power(_,3), type number}})
```

The following sections review the main basic types in M: *number, time, date, duration, text, null,* and *logical*.

The Number Type

In M, a number value is used for numeric and arithmetic operations. The following are examples of number: 1, −3.14, and 2.0e5. You can even use the hexadecimal format. For example: *0xff* returns the number *255*.

A number in M is represented with the precision of at least a 64-bit number, and numbers can range from approximately 5.0 × 10^324 to 1.7 × 10^308, with a precision of 15 or 16 digits.

The following special values are also considered to be number values:

- Positive infinity: +#*infinity*

- Negative infinity: -#*infinity*

  Infinities are produced by operations such as dividing a nonzero number by zero. For example, 1.0 / 0.0 yields positive infinity, and –1.0 / 0.0 yields negative infinity.

- Not-a-number, often abbreviated NaN: #*nan*

  A NaN value can be produced by invalid floating-point operations, such as dividing zero by zero.

You can compare two numbers by applying the logical operators >, >=, <, <=, =, and <>. Basic arithmetic operations can be done using +, -, *, and /.

M provides a rich set of built-in *Number.X* functions. Constant functions, such as *Number.PI*, which returns the value of Pi, enable you to use special numbers in your transformations. Information functions, such as *Number.IsEven*, return *true* or *false* if the number matches certain criteria. Conversion functions, such as *Number.From,* can convert values to numbers. For example, the following function will convert the text *"6"* to *6*:

```
= Number.From("6")
```

Many of the operations and trigonometry *Number.X* functions, such as *Number.Power* and *Number.Sin*, are also available in the Power Query Editor, on the Transform and Add Column tabs. To review the main *Number.X* functions go to https://msdn.microsoft.com/query-bi/m/number-functions.

The Time Type

In M, a time value is represented as the number of 100-nanosecond ticks since midnight. The maximum number of ticks since midnight corresponds to 23:59:59.9999999 hours. Time values may be constructed using the *#time* expression, whose syntax is *#time(hour, minute, second)*. For example, *2:53 PM* can be written in the formula bar as follows:

```
= #time(14, 53, 0)
```

which provides the following output:

```
2:53:00 PM
```

Time supports the logical operators =, <>, >=, >, <, and <= and can be used as a left or right operand of the +, -, and & operators with values of time and duration. For example, adding a duration of 7 minutes to the time 2:53 p.m. can be expressed as follows:

```
= #time(14,53,00) + #duration(0,0,7,0)
```

which provides the following output:

```
3:00:00 PM
```

Time.X functions enable you to extract the time elements from a time value or calculate the start or end of an hour. For example, applying *Time.Hour* on a time value, as shown here:

```
= Time.Hour(#time(14, 53, 0))
```

returns the hour as a number:

```
14
```

To learn more about the time functions, you can explore the relevant transformation in the Power Query Editor on the Transform and Add Column tabs. The reference for the time functions is provided at https://msdn.microsoft.com/query-bi/m/time-functions.

The Date Type

A date value is represented as the number of days since epoch (January 1, 0001 Common Era on the Gregorian calendar). The maximum number of days since epoch is 3,652,058, corresponding to December 31, 9999. Date values can be constructed with the *#date* expression, using this syntax: *#date(year, month, day)*. For example, April 2, 2018, can be written in the formula bar as follows:

```
= #date(2018, 4, 2)
```

which provides the following output (in U.S. locale):

```
4/2/2018
```

The date type supports the logical operators =, <>, >=, >, <, and <= and can be used as a left or right operand of the +, -, and & operators with duration values.

In Chapter 2, "Basic Data Preparation Challenges," you learned how to extract date values and apply date-related calculations in the Power Query Editor. For each transformation step, you can find the equivalent *Date.X* function. There are plenty of *Date.X* functions in M. For example, the function *Date.AddDays* receives a date as the first argument and the number of days to add as the second argument. In the following expression, you add 5 days to April 2, 2018:

```
= Date.AddDays(#date(2018, 4, 2), 5)
```

which results in output corresponding to April 7, 2018 (in U.S. locale):

```
4/7/2018
```

For a full list of *Date.X* built-in functions, see https://msdn.microsoft.com/query-bi/m/ date-functions. Like Date and Time values, M supports also DateTime and DateTimeZone values. Their types are datetime and datetimezone, and they can be auto-generated in the Power Query Editor when you apply relevant transformations on the Transform tab or on the Add Column tab. There are many *DataTime.X* and *DateTimeZone.X* functions, including *DateTime.LocalNow*, which allows you to calculate the current time and date, calculate the elapsed time of transactions, or apply relative time filters.

The Duration Type

A duration value stores a numeric representation of the distance between two points on a timeline, measured in 100-nanosecond ticks. The magnitude of a duration can be either positive or negative, with positive values denoting progress forward in time and negative values denoting progress backward in time. The minimum and maximum values that can be stored in a duration are 10,675,199 days 2 hours 48 minutes and 5.4775808 seconds backward or forward in time.

Duration values are constructed using the *#duration* expression. For example, a duration of 5 days and 10 minutes can be represented as follows:

```
#duration(5, 0, 10, 0)
```

and provides the following output:

```
5.00:10:00
```

The most common use of duration values is to apply them on binary operators such as + and - in conjunction with date, time, datetime, and datetimezone values. For example, you can add the duration of 5 days to April 2, 2018:

```
= #date(2018, 4, 2) + #duration(5, 0, 0, 0)
```

which results in output corresponding to April 7, 2018:

```
4/7/2018
```

Subtracting two date values or two time values results in a duration value. For example, the expression:

```
= #date(2018, 08, 28) - #date(2018, 01, 01)
```

results in the duration:

```
239.00:00:00
```

You can apply built-in *Duration.X* functions on duration values to extract the days, hours, minutes, or seconds component of duration, or you can use *Duration.TotalX* functions, such as *Duration.TotalSeconds* to compute how many seconds have elapsed in a certain duration. For example, the following expression computes the total number of seconds in 5 days:

```
= Duration.TotalSeconds(#duration(5, 0, 0, 0))
```

and provides the following output:

```
432000
```

For a full list of *Duration.X* built-in functions, see https://msdn.microsoft.com/query-bi/m/duration-functions.

The Text Type

Text values can contain arbitrary Unicode characters. You can concatenate two text values, by using the & operator, as demonstrated in Exercise 9-1.

M provides a wide variety of *Text.X* functions that can be applied on text values. For example, you can convert a number to text by applying the *Text.From* function. The following example concatenates between a text and a number by first converting the number to text:

```
= "Testing, Testing " & Text.From(123)
```

and it provides the following output:

```
Testing, Testing 123
```

Unlike with complex data types in M, you cannot use an operator such as *[]* or *{}* to access a certain character in the text. To access the first character, you can use the function *Text.At* with the text as the first argument and a zero-base index as the second argument. For example, the following function:

```
= Text.At("ABCD", 0)
```

provides the following output:

```
A
```

And this function:

```
= Text.At("ABCD", 1)
```

provides the following output:

```
B
```

For a full list of the text functions, see https://msdn.microsoft.com/query-bi/m/text-functions.

The Null Type

A null value is used to represent the absence of a value. You can apply logical or arithmetic operators on null, and the returned result will also be null. For example, in the following expressions, if A is null, then the results will be null:

```
= A < 5
= A >= 5
= A + 1
= A * 5
```

A special case for null is when you apply the equal (=) and not-equal (<>) operators on a null value. In the following expressions, the result is either *true* or *false* when *A* is null:

```
= A = null
```

produces the following output in the Preview pane:

TRUE

```
= A <> 5
```

produces the following output in the Preview pane:

FALSE

```
= A <> null
```

produces the following output in the Preview pane:

FALSE

```
= A is null
```

produces the following output in the Preview pane:

TRUE

Note that null is both a type and a value. So you can use either the operator *is* or the equal sign to test whether a certain value is a null.

The Logical Type

A logical value is used for Boolean operations and has the value *true* or *false*. The following operators are defined for logical values:

- *A > B*   (*A* greater than *B*)
- *A >= B*   (*A* greater than or equal to *B*)
- *A < B*   (*A* less than *B*)
- *A <= B*   (*A* less than or equal to *B*)
- *A = B*   (*A* equal to *B*)
- *A <> B*   (*A* not equal to *B*)
- *A or B*   (*A* or *B*)
- *A and B*   (*A* and *B*)
- *not A*   (Not *A*)

You can check whether a certain value is logical by using *is logical*. For example, if *A* contains the value *false*, the following expression will return *true*:

```
= A is logical
```

In the Preview pane, you see the result displayed as *TRUE*.

The logical operators are commonly used in *if* expressions, which are described later in this chapter.

Complex Types

It's time to formally introduce you to the complex types in M—lists, records, and tables—and the relationships between them. While the basic types can define a single, or atomic, value, the complex types include a structured format, which enables them to contain multiple basic types or even other complex types.

When you import data to Power Query, you typically work with tables. But a table can contain nested records, lists, and tables (when you work with unstructured data such as JSON or XML files). It can be converted into a list (when you drill down to a column), and can even be transformed into a list of records. Let's start with the simplest of the three types, the list type.

The List Type

A list value contains a sequence of values that can be enumerated. A list can contain any kind of values, including lists, records, tables, or any combination of different types. Lists can be constructed in an M expression by using an initialization syntax, in which curly brackets encapsulate comma-separated values. Here, for example, is a list that includes numbers, logical elements, and text:

```
= {1, 3, true, false, "Hello World"}
```

The following expression, as shown in Figure 9-6, is an example of the initialization of the list expression of the numbers 1, 2, and 3:

```
= {1, 2, 3}
```

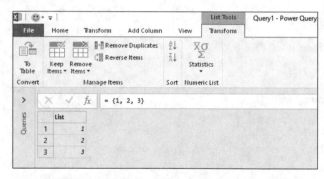

FIGURE 9-6 You can initialize a list in the formula bar using {}.

You can initialize the preceding list by using the following expression:

```
= {1:3}
```

If you want to create a list of incremental numbers from 1 to 100, you can apply the following initialization expression:

```
= {1:100}
```

Using such an expression is a very useful technique for creating iteration flows in Power Query, as discussed later in this chapter.

To create a list of incremental numbers between 1 and *N*, where *N* is provided by another query (for example, based on another data source), you can apply the following expression:

```
= {1:N}
```

You can achieve the same result by using the *List.Numbers* function:

```
= List.Numbers(1, N)
```

You can use the two dots operator (..) to define a numeric range in a list. For example, the following expression returns a list of the numbers *1, 4, 5, 6, 7, 8, 9, 10, 15*:

```
= { 1, 4..10, 15 }
```

The number of elements in a list can be determined by using the *List.Count* function:

```
= List.Count( { 1..10} )
```

which returns the following:

```
10
```

You can also define an empty list in M by using the curly brackets, without any elements in between. Applying *List.Count* on an empty list, like this:

```
= List.Count( {} )
```

returns zero.

List Operators

To concatenate two lists, you can use the concatenate (&) operator. Here is an example that returns the list *{1, 2, 3, 4, 5}*:

```
= {1, 2} & {3, 4, 5}
```

To determine whether two lists are equal, you can use the equal (=) and not-equal (<>) operators. The following expression entered in the formula bar returns *TRUE* in the Preview pane:

```
= {1, 2} = {1, 2}
```

The following expression entered in the formula bar returns *TRUE* in the Preview pane:

```
= {2, 1} <> {1, 2}
```

Two lists with the same elements and different order will not be equal.

To access an element in a list by its location, you can apply a zero-based index inside curly brackets. For example,

```
= {"A", "B", "C"}{0}
```

returns the following:

A

```
= {"A", "B", "C"}{2}
```

returns the following:

C

When you try to access an out-of-bounds location in a list you get an expression error. For example, here is an attempt to access the fourth element (index 3) in a list of three elements, *A*, *B*, and *C*:

```
= {"A", "B", "C"}{3}
```

which returns the following error:

```
Expression.Error: There weren't enough elements in the enumeration to complete the
operation.
```

You can also access the first or last elements in a list by using the built-in functions *List.First* and *List.Last*:

```
= List.First({"A", "B", "C"})
```

returns the following:

A

```
= List.Last({"A", "B", "C"})
```

returns the following:

C

List.X Functions

Knowing the common built-in M functions for lists can be very handy when you want to apply certain operations on a column, based on its contents. For example, you might want to be able to detect the average value in a numeric column and then apply a filter on it. To start working on the values in a column in M, you can right-click the header of the column and then select Drill Down; the result will be a list. From here you can apply one of the built-in functions. In Figure 9-6, you can see the transformation steps that are available on the Transform tab of the List Tools. You will find that M provides many more functions than the ones shown on the tab.

M includes a rich library of built-in functions for lists. The following are some of the most commonly used functions and their categories:

- **Information functions:** *List.Count*, which was already described, falls under this category, and so does *List.IsEmpty*, which returns *true* if the list is empty and *false* otherwise.

- **Selection functions:** These functions return a selected element in a list or sub list. For example, *List.Select* can be used to filter elements in the list followed by certain criteria. *List.FirstN* and *List.LastN* return a sub list of the first or last *N* items from the original list.

- **Transformation functions:** These functions manipulate a list. Some of the most commonly used of these functions are *List.Transform*, which manipulates the elements by a given function, and *List.Combine*, which acts like the concatenate (&) operator. *List.Accumulate*, which was mentioned in stage five of the maturity stages in learning M, is also under this function category and is explained later in this chapter.

- **Membership functions:** These functions apply logical operations on the elements in the list and return *true* or *false* if certain conditions are met. For example, *List.Contains* returns *true* if a certain value is found in the list.

- **Set operations:** These functions apply set operations on two or more lists. You can find the shared elements in two lists by using *List.Intersect*, or you can append lists and remove duplicates by using *List.Union*. A very useful function that is used in Chapter 10, "From Pitfalls to Robust Queries," is *List.Difference*, which returns all the elements in the list that are not available in the second list. You will use it on column names in order to be able to refer to other column names besides the ones that are mentioned.

- **Ordering functions:** In addition to *List.Sort*, which can be used on numbers or any type in which you can define an order function, you can also extract elements by their intrinsic value order rather than just by their order in the list. For example, *List.Min* and *List.Max* retrieve the lowest or highest values, and *List.MinN* and *List.MaxN* retrieve the *n*th lowest or highest values.

- **Arithmetic functions:** In this category are functions that can perform average, addition, and other numeric operations. For example, *List.Average* and *List.StandardDeviation* can work on numbers, datetime, and duration elements in lists of the same type. *List.Sum* can work on numbers and duration values to return the total sum of the values in the list.

- **Generator functions:** In this category are functions that generate lists. There are some very basic functions in this category, such as *List.Numbers*, described earlier in this section, and *List.Dates*, which returns a list of consecutive dates from start date, number of dates, and duration between dates. In this category, you can also find the *List.Generate* advanced function, which can create a list from an initial state and is described in the last section of this chapter.

To learn more about list functions, see https://msdn.microsoft.com/query-bi/m/list-functions.

The Record Type

In Power Query you work with record values in two common scenarios: when loading unstructured data, such as JSON files, and when you manipulate data in table rows. A record is a set of key/value pairs. The keys (also referred as field names) are unique text values, and the values (also referred as field values) can be any type of values, basic or complex.

To initiate a new record, you can use the opening and closing bracket operators, and in between you use comma-separated pairs with the syntax *key=value*. For example, the following formula represents a record with these pairs of field names and values: *ID=123*, *Name="Alice"* and *City="Wonderland"*:

```
= [ID=123, Name="Alice", City="Wonderland"]
```

You can view a record in the Power Query Editor as shown in Figure 9-7.

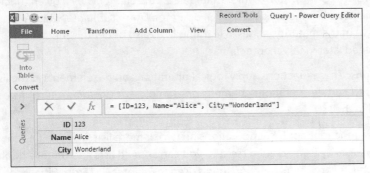

FIGURE 9-7 You can initialize a record in the formula bar of the Power Query Editor using *[]*.

When you work with tables, you can drill down to a record view by selecting or finding a specific row by using the curly brackets. Imagine that you have a table of employees (defined by the identifier *Employees*). The fourth row in the *Employees* table contains the information about Alice, whose ID is 123 and city is *Wonderland*. To access the fourth row, you can use 3 as the zero-based index in the following expression:

```
= Employees{3}
```

If you are not sure in which row to find Alice, you can search for the row whose employee name is Alice or whose ID is 123. Here are the relevant expressions, both of which return the same record (as shown in the Preview pane in Figure 9-7):

```
= Employees{[Name="Alice"]}
= Employees{[ID=123]}
```

> **Note** Retrieving a specific row as a record from a table, as demonstrated in the preceding expressions, fails if the associated column contains multiple values. For example, if you have two employees with the name *Alice* or two rows with ID *123*, you get the following error:
>
> ```
> Expression.Error: The key matched more than one row in the table.
> ```

When you know how to create, access, or find a specific record, you will probably want to access a certain field in that record. To do this, you can wrap the field name in brackets. For example, in the preceding record, you can access *Alice* by applying the following formula:

```
= [ID=123, Name="Alice", City="Wonderland"][Name]
```

Here is an example of a typical M expression that is auto-generated by Power Query when you apply a filter on a specific column. To be more specific, for the Wonderland narrative, you filter the rows in the Employees table to find Alice. Notice that the expression references the column name with a bracket:

```
= Table.SelectRows(Employees, each ([Name] = "Alice"))
```

This code is not directly referencing a column in a table but, rather, a field in a record. Each row in the Employees table is represented as a record when *Table.SelectRows* is invoked. The term *each* is a shortcut for a function, which enables you to write cleaner functions. In this case the function receives a record as its argument and returns true if the employee name is Alice. You will learn more about the *each* expression later in this chapter.

Record Operators

To merge two records or return a record with an updated value in the field of a record, you can use the & operator. Here is an example for a merge that returns the record *[ID=123, Name="Alice", City="Wonderland"]*:

```
= [ID=123, Name="Alice"] & [City="Wonderland"]
```

Returning a new record with a modified value in an existing field of a given record is one of the most common operations. You can use the & operator to do it. The following expression changes Alice's ID from *123* to *456*:

```
= [ID=123, Name="Alice"] & [ID=456]
```

Modifying a record that resulted from a Drill Down from a table row cannot affect the actual row, but a new copy of it. To change values in a table, you need to use one of the *Table.X* functions described in the next section. Note that M doesn't allow you to mutate existing value—no matter which type it is; once a value has been evaluated, you can only mutate its copy in a new expression. For example, in the following expression, you might think that you can mutate the ID of Alice from *123* to *456*, but the expression will return an error, as shown in Figure 9-8:

```
let
    Source = [ID=123, Name="Alice", City="Wonderland"],
    Source[ID]=456
in
    Custom1
```

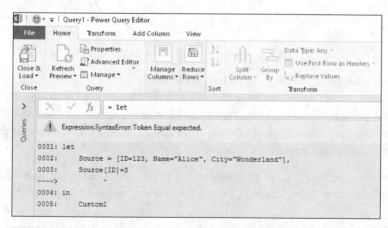

FIGURE 9-8 You cannot mutate a record by accessing its field.

To modify Alice's ID to *456*, you can use the following expression:

```
let
  Source = [ID=123, Name="Alice", City="Wonderland"],
  Result = Source & [ID=456]
in
  Result
```

To check whether two records are equal, you can use the equal (=) and not-equal (<>) operators. The following expression entered in the formula bar returns *TRUE* in the preview pane:

```
= [ID=123, Name="Alice"] = [Name="Alice", ID=123]
```

The order of the fields in the record is not important.

Record.X Functions

In Figure 9-7, you may have noticed that the Power Query Editor offers only a single record transformation command in the ribbon—the Into Table command, which is equivalent to the *Record.ToTable* function. While the ribbon doesn't offer other commands, you can find a few useful built-in *Record.X* functions in M.

Record.FieldCount returns the number of fields in the record. *Record.HasFields* returns *true* if there are fields and *false* if the record is empty. Note that an empty record can be represented by the opening bracket, followed by a closing one:

```
[]
```

You can add a key/value field pairs by using *Record.AddField* and update the value of a field in a record by returning a new record that combines two records with *Record.Combine,* as follows:

```
= Record.Combine( { [ID=123, Name="Alice"], [ID=456] } )
```

To learn more about *Record.X* functions, go to https://msdn.microsoft.com/en-us/query-bi/m/record-functions.

The Table Type

A table value is the most common type you are likely to see and work with in Power Query. When you connect to a data source using Power Query, you typically land on the Power Query Editor with a table. Most of the transformations that you create using the ribbon commands are translated into *Table.X* built-in functions. Tables are very prevalent in Power Query, and having a good understanding of their built-in functions will enable you to tackle new data preparation challenges.

As described in the preceding sections, you can access a column in a table by using the column name wrapped in brackets. For example, the following expression returns Column1 (as a list) of the MyTable table:

```
= MyTable[Column1]
```

You can access the first row of MyTable by using the following expression:

```
= MyTable{0}
```

You can access the value in the *X*th row and in Column*Y* of MyTable by using either one of these expressions:

```
= MyTable{X-1}[ColumnY]
= MyTable[ColumnY]{X-1}
```

The first expression accesses the *X*th record (e.g. 4th record, which is in row number 3, since the index is zero-based) and then retrieves its Column*Y* field value. The second expression accesses the list of all the values in the Column*Y* column and then retrieves the *X*th element of that list.

To initialize a table, you can apply the *#table* expression, as illustrated in Figure 9-9, as in this example:

```
= #table({"ID", "Name", "City"}, {{123, "Alice", "Wonderland"}, {234, "Bob",
"Wonderland"}})
```

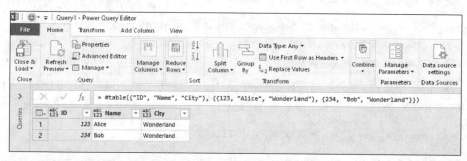

FIGURE 9-9 You can initialize a table in M using the *#table* expression. It is a useful syntax to start small tables that don't require external datasets.

There are many built-in table functions in M. The most common ones are well represented in the Power Query ribbons. You can learn about them at https://msdn.microsoft.com/en-us/query-bi/m/table-functions.

Let's review a short sample of table functions and look at the scenarios in which you would normally use them:

- *Table.RowCount*, *Table.ColumnCount*, and *Table.IsEmpty* are useful functions for verifying the size and width of a table or handling edge cases of empty tables. You will find these functions very handy in conjunction with *if* expressions, which are described in the next section.

- *Table.FirstValue* returns the value in the cell of the first column and first row.

- *Table.Profile* is a hidden gem, a very useful data exploration function that returns a new table with the statistical attributes of your numerical columns (*Min*, *Max*, *Average*, *Standard Deviation*, *Count*, *Null Count*, and *Distinct Count*).

- *Table.ColumnNames* returns the table's column names as a list. This is a very useful function, and it is used in Chapter 10 to dynamically refer to columns and avoid refresh failures when columns change.

- *Table.FromColumns*, *Table.FromList*, *Table.FromRecords*, and *Table.FromRows* are advanced functions that you use to create new tables from complex data structures, such as a list of nested lists or a list of nested records.

- *Table.ToColumns*, *Table.ToList*, *Table.ToRecords*, and *Table.ToRows* convert tables into complex data structures.

Conditions and *If* Expressions

You need to know how to use conditions and *if* expressions in M to achieve complex data preparation challenges. Your first encounter with the use of conditions is likely to be when you apply filters on specific columns in the Power Query Editor. Whenever you think that the user interface is not flexible enough to meet your filtering logic, it is a good time to try your luck at changing the conditions in the formula bar.

In the earlier section of this chapter on basic types, you learned about the logical operators: =, <>, <, <=, >=, >, *and*, *or*, and *not*. You can create logical expressions by applying these logical operators on supported types of values and encapsulating them in parentheses to build more complex expressions.

Here, for example, you can see a basic condition that was created in the Power Query Editor to filter rows if *Alice* is in the Name column:

```
= Table.SelectRows(Employees, each ([Name] = "Alice"))
```

And here, you can see a basic condition to filter rows if *Bob* is not in the Name column:

```
= Table.SelectRows(Employees, each ([Name] <> "Bob"))
= Table.SelectRows(Employees, each not ([Name] = "Bob"))
```

The second expression demonstrates the use of the operator *not*, instead of the not-equal sign (<>) to reach the same results.

In this expression, the logical expression that returns *true* or *false* is highlighted in bold. It is relatively easy to manipulate it in order to create complex conditions. Here, for example, is how you can filter the rows if *Alice* is found in the Name column and her ID is either *123* or *456*:

```
= Table.SelectRows(Employees, each ([Name] = "Alice" and ([ID]=123 or [ID]=456)))
```

Note that a new pair of parentheses is used in this expression to wrap up the condition *[ID]=123 or [ID]=456*. Without the inner parentheses, as demonstrated in the next expression, you will keep other employees with ID *456* in the end results.

```
= Table.SelectRows(Employees, each ([Name] = "Alice" and [ID]=123 or [ID]=456))
```

In that sense, writing logical conditions in M is not different from other computer languages.

Another scenario that might drive you to modify M expressions and improve your logical expressions is when you use conditional columns. For example, in Exercise 5-4 in Chapter 5, "Preserving Context," you applied conditional columns to provide additional context if certain values existed in other columns. When you find that the Conditional Column dialog box is not flexible enough for advanced logic, you will probably find yourself manipulating the logic in the formula bar to meet your needs.

Soon after you begin using conditional columns, you will discover the *if* expressions, which are created by Power Query when you apply conditional columns. Once you get used to their syntax, you will feel comfortable writing more complex logic directly inside the formula box of the Custom Column dialog box.

if-then-else

The syntax of the *if* expression is as follows:

```
= if (condition) then A else B
```

As a best practice, to make your code readable, you can break the expression into separate lines, and write it as follows:

```
= if (condition) then
  A
else
  B
```

You can nest additional *if* statements, as demonstrated in the following expression:

```
= if (condition_1) then
  A
else if (condition_2) then
  B
else
  C
```

If you are an Excel power user, you may find the M syntax too different from Excel. So, here are the preceding expressions written as Excel formulas:

```
IF(condition, A, B)
IF(condition_1, A, IF(condition_2, B, C))
```

An *if* Expression Inside a *let* Expression

A common error in using *if* expressions can happen when you try writing *if* expressions in the same manner you use to write conditions in other programming languages. For example, in the following scenario that handles edge cases, you have a table in Query1 and you would like to return *null* if Query1 is empty; otherwise, you would like to return the first row of Query1 (as a record). In this code, there is a typical mistake that you might make:

```
let
  if (Table.IsEmpty(Query1) then
      Result = null
  else
      Result = Query1{0}
in
  Result
```

This expression will not work. Inside a *let* expression, you should always use an identifier followed by the equal sign and only then write the expression. Here is the correct code:

```
let
  Result =
    if (Table.IsEmpty(Query1) then
        null
    else
        Query1{0}
in
  Result
```

> **Tip** In the Advanced Editor inside let expressions you cannot start a line with an *if* expression. In such cases, *if* expressions must have identifiers and should appear after the equal sign.

You can use *if* expressions inside functions (which you'll learn more about in the next section) as demonstrated in the following expression:

```
(employeeName) =>
  if employeeName = "Alice" then
    "Wonderland"
  else
    "Real World"
```

When you apply transformations on columns, you can include *if* expressions in M expressions by modifying the code in the formula bar. Let's look at this with a common scenario. Imagine that you import a data source that contains a Country column with mismatching case values (some countries are lowercase, others are uppercase). You decide to apply the Capitalize Each Word transformation step in the Power Query Editor. Here is the resulting M expression:

```
= Table.TransformColumns(Source,{{"Country", Text.Proper, type text}})
```

Now you discover that some countries incorrectly had their case changed (for example, *US* and *UK* were turned into *Us* and *Uk*). To resolve this issue, you can modify the preceding expression by using an *if* statement:

```
= Table.TransformColumns(Source,{{"Country", each if _ = "US" or _ = "UK" then _ else
Text.Proper(_), type text}})
```

> **Note** Basic Power Query users will probably perform unnecessary steps to resolve the country capitalization challenge. For example, you can duplicate the query. Then, you can keep US and UK rows in the first query and remove them from the second query. Next, you can capitalize the countries in the second query and then append back the two queries, as you have learned in Chapter 3, "Combining Data from Multiple Sources."
>
> Another option for awkwardly solving this problem is to duplicate the Country column. Then you can capitalize the original column. Then create a conditional column with the Country values from the original column, unless the duplicated column contains US or UK values. In that case, you will copy the values from the duplicated column to maintain US and UK in the new column. Finally, you would delete the original and the duplicated column and rename the conditional column *Country*. As you can now see, lightweight manipulations in M, as shown in the preceding expression, can save you a lot of time and unnecessary steps, and as a result can even improve the performance of your queries.

In the preceding example, you created a custom function, using the *each* expression to refine the transformation step and avoid capitalizing the words of certain country names. In the next section, you will better understand this syntax and learn about custom functions.

Custom Functions

As you progress in M's learning maturity stages, a crucial milestone that will enable you to resolve complex data challenges is the mastery of custom functions. While you can create complex custom functions in the Power Query user interface by converting an existing query into a function using the Create Function shortcut menu option in the Queries pane, being able to write freestyle custom functions in M using the Advanced Editor is a useful skill. For example, in Chapter 7 you created a custom function that performs a sequence of transformations to unpivot summarized tables. You could not have been able to create such a function without freestyle modifications in the Advanced Editor.

In M, taking aside the Create Function user interface, you can create a custom function by using the blank query, or by embedding a custom function inside an existing M expression in the Advanced Editor. Here is an example of a simple function that increments a number by one:

```
(X) => X + 1
```

> **Note** The X+1 result is a copy of the number because in M all values are immutable.

You can perform multiple steps inside a function by using a *let* expression. In this artificial example, when you invoke this function with the input of *X*, you return *X+2* by following two incremental steps:

```
(X) =>
let
  Step1 = X + 1,
  Step2 = Step1 + 1
in
  Step2
```

Often, when you write such expressions in the Advanced Editor, you may find out that Power Query modified the expression and wrapped your code in a *let* or *in* expression. The following expression, altered by Power Query, is equivalent to the preceding one:

```
let
  Source =
  (X) =>
   let
     Step1 = X + 1,
     Step2 = Step1 + 1
   in
     Step2
in
  Source
```

You can create a function that receives multiple arguments. Here is an example of a function that adds two numbers:

```
(X, Y) => X + Y
```

When you create a custom function, you can explicitly define the types of the arguments and the return type. In this example, for instance, *as number* declares that *number* is the type of the returned value of the function.

```
(X as number, Y as number) as number => X + Y
```

Of course, custom functions can accept different types of arguments. In this example, text and a number are received as arguments, and the returned result is concatenated text:

```
(X as text, Y as number) as text => X & Text.From(Y)
```

Functions can be defined with optional arguments. In the following expression, you declare *Y* as an optional argument. When the function will be invoked without the optional argument, *Y* receives a null value:

```
(X, optional Y) => if (Y = null) then X else X + Y
```

Note that the following implementation returns null, instead of *X*, if *Y* is not called as the argument, because *X + null* results in a null:

```
(X, optional Y) => X + Y
```

Finally, you can declare a function that receives no arguments. Such functions can be used in advanced scenarios, such as in *List.Generate*, which is explained in the last section of this chapter. Here, for example, is a function that accepts no argument and returns zero:

```
() => 0
```

Invoking Functions

Functions can be defined inside the scope of a *let* expression or as a separate query. You can invoke them as built-in functions by calling the function name, followed by an opening parenthesis, the argument values, and the closing parenthesis. In this example, the custom function *func*, which is defined in the first line inside the *let* expression, is invoked in the third line:

```
let
  func = (X) => X+1,
  Number1 = 1000,
  Result = func(Number1)
in
  Result
```

Functions can be passed as arguments of other functions. When a single-argument custom function is passed as an argument of another function, you can invoke it as an argument by calling the function name without the parentheses and the argument. You can see how in the next example.

In the following expression, you can see a query that loads a table of prices from a PricesTable query and multiplies the Price column by 0.98 (2% discount) if the price is greater than 10:

```
let
  FnGetPriceAfterDiscount =
    (price) =>
      if price > 10 then
        price * 0.98
      else
        price,
  Source = PricesTable,
  DiscountedPrices = Table.TransformColumns(
    Source,
    {{"Price", FnGetPriceAfterDiscount, type number}}
  )
in
  DiscountedPrices
```

In this expression, the custom function *FnGetPriceAfterDiscount* is invoked inside *Table.TransformColumns*. Because the custom function requires a single number argument, you could call it inside *Table.TransformColumns* without the need to use parentheses or explicitly referring to the number as an argument. For example, the following function:

```
= Table.TransformColumns(Source,{{"Price", FnGetPriceAfterDiscount, type number}})
```

is equivalent to the following syntax:

```
= Table.TransformColumns(Source,{{"Price",each FnGetPriceAfterDiscount(_), type number}})
```

The *each* Expression

The *each* expression in Power Query was designed to allow you to define simple functions in a user-friendly manner.

For example, the following expression receives a number and increments it by one:

```
(X) => X + 1
```

The same function can be written as follows:

```
(_) => _ + 1
```

This expression uses the underscore as the argument name. To simplify the code, here is a shortcut version:

```
each _ + 1
```

There are cases in which you can even avoid using the underscore in *each* expressions if your argument has fields (for example, a table or record). Look at this common expression, which is used when you filter values in column:

```
Table.SelectRows( Source, each [Price] > 5 )
```

The function's longer syntax is as follows:

```
Table.SelectRows( Source, (_)=> _[ Price] > 5 )
```

The first simplification of the preceding expression can be written using an *each*:

```
Table.SelectRows( Source, each _[ Price] > 5 )
```

But because you are referring to a field using brackets, you can avoid using the underscore. Therefore, you see the following expression in the formula bar:

```
Table.SelectRows( Source, each [Price] > 5 )
```

This expression is more readable than the others. It is useful to remember that it is just a shortcut to a regular function. So, in the future, you will be able to rewrite it and extend it to meet your data challenges.

Advanced Topics

To fully understand M as a programming language, a single chapter—or even a book—cannot completely describe the language in detail. There are many advanced elements in this language that are not covered in this book. Yet, in this final section of this chapter, you will briefly get to taste a portion of these advanced topics that may be useful for you, especially if you decide in the future to master M as a programmer.

Error Handling

Power Query provides built-in functionality that enables you to review and troubleshoot errors through the user interface. You can also replace error values or remove them altogether. In addition to using the existing user interfaces, in M, you can programmatically handle error cases as part of your transformation logic.

In M, an error is an indication that the evaluation of an expression could not produce a value. When an expression results in an error, your query returns an *Expression.Error* record. Normally when you don't apply explicit error handlers, your queries abort, prompting error messages. To "catch" the errors without causing a query to fail, you can apply a *try/otherwise* expression. Here is an example:

```
let
  Result = try Source[Column1] otherwise null
in
  Result
```

In this expression, *try/otherwise* is used to try to drill down to Column1 in the Source table. But when Column1 is not available in the source table, you can return *null* instead of causing the query to abort with an error. You can also write the same expression without the *otherwise* part:

```
let
  Result = try Source[Column1]
in
  Result
```

This expression returns an error record when Column1 is missing. The returned error record, which is shown in Figure 9-10, can be handled in the Power Query Editor, as any other transformation step.

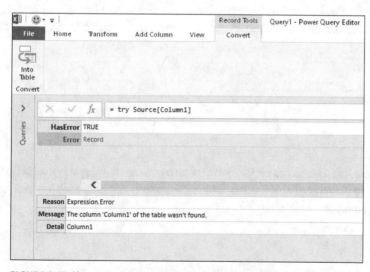

FIGURE 9-10 You can use a *try* expression to return an error record when the expression fails.

When the *try* expression succeeds, the result includes a record in which *HasError* is *false* and the Value field contains the result of the successful expression. The following formula demonstrates how errors can be programmatically handled without the use of the *otherwise* keyword:

```
let
  Attempt = try Source[Column1],
  Result =
  if Attempt[HasError] then
    null
```

```
        else
            Attempt[Value]
in
    Result
```

This expression returns null if Column1 doesn't exist in the Source table, and is equivalent to the *try/otherwise* expression:

```
let
    Result = try Source[Column1] otherwise null
in
    Result
```

M allows you to throw a customized error instead of the built-in error. The following example shows how to overwrite the *Message* value of the error record:

```
= try Source[Column1] otherwise error "Column1 is missing from AdventureWorks database"
```

To learn more about error handling, visit https://msdn.microsoft.com/en-us/query-bi/m/errors.

Lazy and Eager Evaluations

Inside a *let* expression, M does not evaluate the expressions in sequential order but takes a lazy approach. Each identifier is evaluated only if needed. In the following expression, for example, Step2 is not evaluated:

```
let
    Step1 = 1,
    Step2 = 10000000,
    Step3 = Step1 + 1
in
    Step3
```

In addition to *let* expressions, *list* and *record* expressions are also evaluated using lazy evaluation. All other expressions are evaluated using eager evaluation, which means they are evaluated immediately when they are encountered during the evaluation process.

Loops

If you have a software programming background, you may have been wondering why M is missing built-in loops. The answer is not simple. M was designed to perform sequences of transformations, and the iteration is already built in into the data structure. For example, to replace a value in a column, you don't need to write code that will iterate over each of the rows in the table. M does the iteration for you when you apply any of its table built-in functions.

Nevertheless, there are some special cases in which you might need to create explicit logic and iterate over a sequence to aggregate data. One of the most common scenarios is when you import data from websites and need to use a page number or an offset to import a small portion of the data. To be able to paginate over the entire dataset, you would need to loop over a range of numbers.

To perform the pagination, you can start with a custom function that imports a certain page by its number. For example, say that a custom function *FnLoadPageByNumber* that you have built can get paged search results from a website. Then you can create a list of numbers, as in this example:

```
= {1..10}
```

Next, you can convert the list into a table, as shown in Figure 9-6, by selecting To Table in the List Tools, Transform tab. Now after you rename Column1 *PageNumber*, transform the type of PageNumber column to Text, and then from the Add Column tab, you can select Invoke Custom Function and invoke the *FnLoadPageByNumber* function on the PageNumber column. Finally, you can expand the new column, and all of the pages' table objects will be appended together.

Recursion

Another way to repeat a sequence of transformation steps is by using recursion. Recursion in programming languages enables you to resolve complex computation tasks by using a divide-and-conquer approach. A classic example is Fibonacci numbers.

A Fibonacci sequence is characterized by the fact that every number, except 0 and 1, is the sum of the two preceding numbers in the sequence. So, because 0+1=1, 1 will be the next number, then because 1+1=2, 2 will be the next number, then 3 (1+2=3), then 5 (2+3=5), then 8 (3+5=8), then 13 (5+8=13), and so forth.

In M, you can implement a recursion by using the @ sign to re-invoke the main function inside the function and avoid the inner scope limitations. Here is the implementation of the Fibonacci recursion in M:

```
let
  Fibonacci =
    (n)=>
      if (n = 0) then
        0
      else if (n = 1) then
        1
      else
        @Fibonacci(n-1) + @Fibonacci(n-2)
in
  Fibonacci
```

The use of recursion in M is not recommended, however. The execution of recursion is taxing and will consume a lot of memory in any programming language, because it requires the operating system's memory stack to hold all the inner states of the recursion. As a result, when you run recursion on large datasets, or in the case of a large number to compute the Fibonacci number, you will quickly reach a memory stack overflow.

List.Generate

List.Generate enables you to implement endless types of iterations, including nested loops. This function generates a list of values from an initial state and a set of functions. Here is the function declaration of *List.Generate*:

```
List.Generate(initial as function, condition as function, next as function, optional
selector as nullable function) as list
```

Let's look at the inner workings of this function by using a simple example that returns the Fibonacci sequence below 100 (that is, {1, 2, 3, 5, 8, 13, 21, 34, 55, 89}) when used in the formula bar:

```
= List.Generate(
   ()=>[Previous = 0, Current = 1],
   each [Previous] + [Current] < 100,
   each [
      Current = [Previous] + [Current],
      Previous = [Current]
   ],
   each [Previous] + [Current]
)
```

In this example, *List.Generate* starts with an initial function that receives no input and returns a record of *Previous* and *Current* numbers. *Previous* is set to *0*, and *Current* is set to *1*. *List.Generate*'s second argument, the condition function *each [Previous] + [Current] < 100*, makes sure that the list is being generated as long as the condition is *true*. When *Previous* and *Current* reach a number above or equal to 100, the generation of the list ends.

The third argument is the next function, which defines the next state and advances the values in *Current* and *Previous* fields of the record. So, in the initial state, *Previous* was *0* and *Current* was *1*. In the next phase, *Current* advances to *[Previous] + [Current]*, which is 1 *(0+1=1)*, and *Previous* is assigned as *Current*, which is *1*. In the next step, *Current* is assigned as 2 *(1+1=2)*, and *Previous* is assigned as *1*. Next, *Current* is assigned as 3 *(2+1=3)*, and *Previous* as *2*, and so forth.

The fourth argument assigns the element for the output list during each iteration, which results in the Fibonacci sequence when the iterations end.

List.Generate enables you to resolve advanced challenges and work around the lack of loops. Nevertheless, you should always try first to use the built-in table functions to implement iteration logic because *List.Generate*, with its lazy evaluation, may be slower and consume more memory. Still, on small datasets, you should feel comfortable in using it. To see more examples of using *List.Generate*, such as nested loops, cursor-based pagination, and matrix multiplication, go to https://datachant.com/tag/list-generate/.

List.Accumulate

The *List.Accumulate* function accumulates a result from an input list. Starting from the initial value seed, this function applies an accumulator function and returns the final aggregated result. You can use this function to iterate over elements in a list and gradually aggregate the results into a desired output.

Here is the declaration of the function:

```
List.Accumulate(list as list, seed as any, accumulator as function) as any
```

Let's look at the different arguments of the function in a simple expression that goes over a list of incremental numbers and sums them up by using *List.Accumulate*:

```
= List.Accumulate({1, 2, 3, 4}, 0, (state, current) => state + current)
```

The result of this expression is 10. Let's look at this, step by step. The function starts with the input list *{1, 2, 3, 4}* and *0* as the initial state (the seed argument). In the first step, the accumulator function receives the value *0* as the initial *state* (which was defined as the second argument of *List.Accumulate*), and the value *1* as *current* (since the first element in the list is 1), and sums them. The result, value 1, is assigned to the new *state*.

In the second step, the accumulator function receives the value 1 as the *state* and the value 2 as *current* (since the second element in the list is 2), and sums them up. The value 3 (1+2=3) is assigned to the new *state*.

In the third step, the accumulator function receives the value 3 as the *state* and the value 3 as *current* (since the third element in the list is 3), and sums them up. The value 6 (3+3=6) is assigned to the new *state*.

In the fourth and final step, the accumulator function receives the value 6 as the *state* and the value 4 as *current* (since the last element in the list is 4), and sums them up. The value 10 (4+6=10) is assigned as the final output. The iterations end after the accumulator function runs on the last element in the list. The last result of the accumulator function is always the output of *List.Accumulate*.

The following is a *List.Accumulate* implementation of the Fibonacci sequence that returns the Fibonacci number *89*. Unlike with *List.Generate*, with *List.Accumulate* you cannot define a dynamic break condition. The function iterates over all the elements in the list. You initialize the list to numbers starting from *0* to *9*, but the actual values of the list don't take part in the calculation:

```
let
  Fibonacci =
    List.Accumulate(
      {0..9},
      [PreviousNum = 0, CurrentNum = 1],
      (state, current) =>
        [
          PreviousNum = state[CurrentNum],
          CurrentNum = state[CurrentNum] + state[PreviousNum]
        ]
    ),
  Result = Fibonacci[CurrentNum]
in
  Result
```

In this example, you can see that the seed argument is defined as a record of two numeric fields, *PreviousNum* and *CurrentNum*. The accumulator returns an updated version of this record by passing the *CurrentNum* value to *PreviousNum* and summing up *CurrentNum* and *PreviousNum* in the new value of *CurrentNum*.

In Chapter 11, "Basic Text Analytics," you will apply the *List.Accumulate* function to perform iterative text replacements on the same column. To learn about additional implementations of *List.Accumulate* go to https://datachant.com/2016/06/02/power-query-list-accumulate-unleashed/.

Summary

Learning M is your gateway to becoming a master data-wrangler, but with the game-changing user experience of the Power Query editor, you are not required to achieve master level in M to accomplish many of the real-life data challenges you will face. In this chapter you have learned the core principles of the M language. From here, you should feel more comfortable manipulating the expressions in the formula bar and the Advanced Editor when the time comes.

You have learned in this chapter about the six maturity stages in learning M. Identifying where you are currently will help you define your next goals in this journey and which areas you can focus on to move to the next stage. You have explored the different building blocks of the M language, including the *let* expression and the different types, operators, and built-in functions, including numbers, time, date, duration, text, logical, list, record, and table.

Applying conditions and writing *if* expressions in the formula bar, in the Custom Column dialog box and in the Advanced Editor can help you extend the logic of your queries beyond the capabilities provided by the built-in user interface. You have learned how to write a sequence of logical expressions by using the *and*, *or*, and *not* operators, as well as parentheses. You have also learned how and where you can write *if*, *then*, and *else* expressions in your code.

You have learned how to invoke built-in functions and how to extend their use with custom functions. Finally, in this chapter you have been introduced to error handling, recursion, and advanced list functions that can allow you to implement loops and iterate over data to achieve complex scenarios.

You are encouraged to return to this chapter as you advance your knowledge in M and face tougher challenges. In Chapter 10 you will learn how lightweight modifications of the M expression can become very handy in achieving robust and scalable queries.

CHAPTER 10

From Pitfalls to Robust Queries

Data is a precious thing and will last longer than the systems themselves.
—Tim Berners-Lee

IN THIS CHAPTER, YOU WILL

- Learn the main factors in creating weak queries and common pitfalls that lead to refresh failures and incorrect data

- Learn how awareness, best practices, and M modifications can help you prevent the pitfalls

- Learn how to avoid refresh failures due to the automatic detection and change of column types

- Learn how to avoid dangerous filtering that can lead to partial data in your reports

- Learn when reordering the position of columns is effective and how to reorder a subset of columns

- Learn how to remove and select columns and avoid future refresh errors

- Rename columns by their location in the table or by specific values

- Learn the dangers of splitting a column into columns instead of rows

- Improve the M formula when you merge multiple columns

The user experience of the Power Query Editor in Excel and Power BI is extremely rewarding, as it can turn your mundane yet crucial data preparation tasks into an automated-refresh flow. Unfortunately, as you progress on your journey to master data wrangling, you will face some common mistakes that many people make in the Power Query Editor. These mistakes can lead to the creation of vulnerable queries that will fail to refresh when the data changes. Even worse, these mistakes can lead to incorrect data in your reports. In this chapter, you will learn about these common pitfalls and how to build robust queries to avoid them.

The techniques in this chapter will help you create robust queries and think a step ahead in the never-ending battle to maintain a reporting system that will last longer than the data.

See Also I discuss the 10 pitfalls on my blog, at https://datachant.com/tag/pitfalls/. While you can explore all of the pitfalls in more details in my blog, this chapter encapsulates the main points and provides new examples, exercises, and solution sample files. The tenth pitfall, which focuses on the removal of duplicates, has already been discussed in Chapter 2, "Basic Data Preparation Challenges."

The Causes and Effects of the Pitfalls

The Power Query Editor operates on two core principles:

- It provides an easy-to-use user interface that translates your steps into programmatic transformation instructions.

- It loads a snapshot or a preview of the data to enable you to build the transformation logic.

While these principles are crucial to your success in resolving many data preparations challenges, they are also the culprits for key mistakes you may unintentionally make, which can lead to refresh failures or unexpected situations of missing or incorrect data, as illustrated in Figure 10-1.

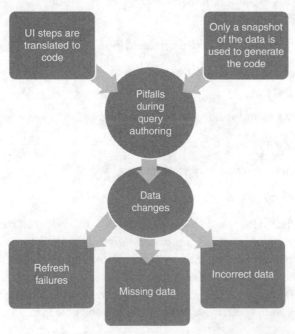

FIGURE 10-1 Several factors during the query authoring lead to refresh failures and data inconsistencies when the data changes.

Each step that you perform using the Power Query Editor user interface is added in Applied Steps, with an auto-generated formula line that plays a role in the bigger sequence of the transformation steps. As you build the transformation steps in the Power Query Editor, Power Query needs to make constant "decisions" about how to translate your UI selections into code. For example, the Unpivot Columns step described in Chapter 6, "Unpivoting Tables," is generated as an M expression to reference the unselected columns in your table instead of the selected ones. As another example of a translation decision, when you import a worksheet in an Excel file, Power Query "decides" in the M expression to reference the worksheet by name and not by its position in the workbook.

To be clear, the translation decisions that the Power Query Editor make are not random. They were designed by the Power Query team to help you create the necessary queries to reach your goals. But, while these translations might make sense during the creation of a query, they may fail you in the future. When you create a query, some of the decisions the Power Query Editor makes to generate the code rely on a preview of your data. When the data changes in a future refresh, some of the queries may no longer be robust enough to endure the changes.

In a typical case, when your data changes, a refresh error occurs, and it is an easy task for you to fix the query. But often, refresh failures keep returning, as your data may zigzag between multiple formats. Fixing the query to resist certain changes in your data today may not be able to handle other changes tomorrow.

The most common scenario for refresh failures originates in column name changes in your source tables. Most of the pitfalls in this chapter are related to incorrect handling of column names, which leads to refresh errors. You may think at this stage that it's not a big deal: Modifying your queries to reference the new column names is an easy task, and it can take only few minutes of your time to do so. You are right. It's easy to edit a query and adapt to the column changes.

But by now you have become very proficient with the Power Query Editor, and your queries may be quite complex. So, when your queries fail due to nonexistent column names, you may end up spending precious time fixing multiple steps that reference these column names. Do you think it makes sense to be locked in to a never-ending task of fixing the queries whenever a column name is missing in your data source? By now, your reports may be so important that hundreds of people in your organization could be dependent on them. A failure to refresh a report may hit you at an inconvenient time.

Finally, some of the pitfalls may not lead to refresh errors when the data changes. Instead, queries may simply ignore a portion of the data, which will lead to incorrect calculations, skewed charts, and incorrect KPIs in your report. Detecting these failures is not easy after the fact; avoiding them altogether is easier and is the focus of this chapter.

Before you look more closely at the pitfalls and how to avoid them, let's examine several common principles that you should be aware of first. These principles help minimize the pitfalls and are divided into three themes: awareness, best practices, and M modifications.

Awareness

To increase your awareness and reduce the chances of refresh failures or incorrect results in your reports, make sure you follow these recommendations after each transformation step you make in the Power Query Editor:

- Review the transformed results in the Preview pane. Make sure the data looks right. Scroll down to review more rows. Scroll right to review all columns. If you find anything odd, determine whether your step was created correctly or if it is time to consider an alternative transformation step.

- Always keep the formula bar open, and tell your colleagues to do so as well. (By default, the formula bar is hidden.) To enable the formula bar, go to the View tab and select the formula bar check box. Enabling the formula bar is fundamental to avoiding the pitfalls.

- Review the code in the formula bar. You don't need to understand M to effectively review the code. Pay close attention to the hardcoded elements in a formula, such as column names and values—especially if you provided these hardcoded elements in a dialog box or through a selection of a UI control in the relevant step. For example, if you delete Column1 in your query, you may see in the formula bar that the column was actually named Column1 with a trailing space. There is a good chance that this column name will be fixed in the future by the owner of the data source, and your step will fail. Frequent inspection of the formula bar will increase your awareness of such situations and allow you to prevent future failures.

Best Practices

The pitfalls described in this chapter can often be avoided by adhering to several best practices:

- Maintain a data contract with the colleagues who own the external data source. Communicate often and share the assumptions on your data. Work together to build change controls that help you stay prepared for planned changes. Make sure colleagues are aware of your reports, and engage with them so that they feel that they are part of your reporting project and share in the success of the project.

- Keep unrefreshed revisions of your report to track breaking changes. Your refreshed report today may fail or show unexpected results. By maintaining the old revisions of the report, you can compare the reports to identify the root causes for failures.

- As you will learn in this chapter, some pitfalls can be entirely avoided by making the right choices (for example, column removal) or by avoiding performing some unnecessary transformations (for example, changed type, column reordering).

M Modifications

There are a number of modifications you can perform at the formula level to create robust queries. While avoiding each pitfall may involve its own unique M modifications, the most common modification that you will rely on is based on the function *Table.ColumnNames*. This function allows you to modify a reference to a hardcoded column name into a dynamic reference that will not fail. You already encountered such a scenario in Exercise 3-4 in Chapter 3, "Combining Data from Multiple Sources." In that example, you appended multiple worksheets into a single table and promoted the contextual year data, 2015, as a column name for the first column. Then you renamed the column from 2015 to *Release Year*. The function *Table.ColumnNames* allowed you to rename the first column instead of renaming the 2015 column, which strengthened the query and helped you avoid a potential future refresh failure.

In this chapter, you will see various M modifications that include the *Table.ColumnNames* function to avoid the pitfalls. You will learn many other M modifications that will help you create robust queries and minimize the failures as the data changes.

Pitfall 1: Ignoring the Formula Bar

Early on in this book, as you followed along with the exercises, you many times needed to rely on information in the formula bar to better understand the transformation at hand or lightly modify the formula to achieve your goals. In Chapter 9, "Introduction to the Power Query M Formula Language," you learned the main principles of the M language, and by now you have formed some solid preferences about how much you like to use M. While many power users are eager to harness M to achieve their goals, others see M as a strange programming language that is not easy to understand.

If you are in the first group of users, the first pitfall will be easy to avoid. But if you belong to the second group, and M seems too alien for you to master, you will find this message very comforting: You do not need to learn M to resolve 90% of the data challenges you will face. Lightweight manipulations of the M formula will suffice to achieve most, if not all, of your goals. But if you use the Power Query Editor to create reports that have an impact on your organization, you will find the formula bar a strategic ally for your success.

Turn on the formula bar. Review it often. Learn how to identify the static elements, such as column names and values. These static values will be encapsulated in brackets or double quotes. See if these values make sense, and adhere to the best practices listed earlier in this chapter to prevent most of the pitfalls.

In case you jumped straight to this chapter and missed all the preceding chapters, here is how you turn on the formula bar: In the Power Query Editor, on the View tab, select the Formula Bar check box, as shown in Figure 10-2.

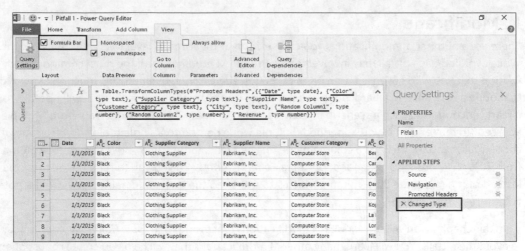

FIGURE 10-2 By enabling the formula bar, you can see how steps like the Changed Type refer to column names.

Exercise 10-1: Using the Formula Bar to Detect Static References to Column Names

This quick exercise demonstrates how to detect static column names in the formula bar and sets the stage for dealing with the second pitfall. You will use the sample workbook C10E01.xlsx, which can be downloaded from https://aka.ms/DataPwrBIPivot/downloads. This sample workbook summarizes the revenues from orders of the fictional company Wide World Importers.

1. Download the workbook C10E01.xslx and save it in the folder *C:\Data\C10*.

2. Open a blank new workbook or a new Power BI report.

   In Excel: On the Data tab, select Get Data, From File, From Workbook.

   In Power BI Desktop: On the Home tab, select Get Data, and in the Get Data dialog box, select File and then select Excel.

3. Select the file C10E01.xlsx and select Import.

4. In the Navigator dialog box, select Sheet1 and click Edit.

5. If the formula bar is not visible, go to the View tab and select the Formula Bar check box.

6. Notice that the last step in Applied Steps is Changed Type, and the following formula appears in the formula bar (refer to Figure 10-2):

   ```
   = Table.TransformColumnTypes(#"Promoted Headers",{{"Date", type date}, {"Color",
   type text}, {"Supplier Category", type text}, {"Supplier Name", type text},
   {"Customer Category", type text}, {"City", type text}, {"Random Column1", type
   number}, {"Random Column2", type number}, {"Revenue", type number}})
   ```

   Without focusing on the actual meaning of the step, you can see that there are many values here in double quotes. These values are the kind of things you should look for in the formula bar as you create your own queries if you want to avoid many of the pitfalls. In many cases these double-quoted values represent column names or values that you entered in dialog boxes.

In this case, you can see that there are two columns, named Random Column1 and Random Column2. Let's assume that, for the sake of this exercise, these columns contain meaning-less random numbers, and they are not needed in your report. In real-life scenarios, you will encounter column names that may have some arbitrary or temporary context to them. While you may keep them in your report or want to remove them, you can see in the Changed Type step that your code is already hardcoded with a reference to these columns. If these columns are not important, there is a good chance that you will no longer find them in the source table in the future, as the owner of the external data source may choose to remove them.

The following steps demonstrate the refresh error at this stage.

7. Close the Power Query Editor and load your query to your Excel worksheet or Power BI report.

8. In this step, let's pretend you are a different user now, and the owner of the data source. Open the workbook C10E01.xlsx and remove Random Column1 and Random Column2 from the worksheet. Save the workbook. You can go back to your previous role to discover the impact of this step.

9. Go back to your report and refresh it. You see the obvious refresh error:

```
Expression.Error: The column 'Random Column1' of the table wasn't found.
```

It is important to note that you have not explicitly specified the random columns in your report. Instead, the Power Query Editor "decided" to reference these columns. You will learn more about this in Pitfall 2, but for now, let's just look at how you can tackle this scenario through the three main principles mentioned earlier: awareness, best practices, and M modifications.

By having the formula bar open and looking for the double-quoted values in step 6, you dis-covered the risk of having your formula hardcoded with unimportant column names. You can now approach the data owners and bring their awareness to the existence of such columns. You can then define a data contract that allows you to be notified if they intend in the future to remove or rename these columns, and if these columns have any hidden business value, you may want to include them in your reports.

10. Finally, by modifying the M formula, you can remove the references to the random columns by removing the following part from the formula:

```
{"Random Column1", type number}, {"Random Column2", type number},
```

Here is the robust revision of the formula, which ignores the random columns:

```
= Table.TransformColumnTypes(#"Promoted Headers",{{"Date", type date}, {"Color",
type text}, {"Supplier Category", type text}, {"Supplier Name", type text},
{"Customer Category", type text}, {"City", type text}, {"Revenue", type number}})
```

There are still many columns in this formula that may be removed or renamed in the future. Do you really need to reference all the column names in this line? This is the topic of the second pitfall.

Pitfall 2: Changed Types

In Exercise 10-1, you encountered the most common pitfall in the Power Query Editor and the number-one factor for refresh failures due to column name changes: the Changed Type step. In the Applied Steps pane in Figure 10-2, the last step, Changed Type, was automatically added when you loaded the worksheet to the Power Query Editor.

To avoid the second pitfall, check the Applied Steps pane for Changed Type steps that you didn't explicitly create. The main scenario in which Changed Type is prone to refresh errors is when you load text files and spreadsheets to the Power Query Editor or when you promote the first row as headers. Any minor changes to column names or column removal on the data source will lead to refresh errors.

The simplest and most common solution to avoid this pitfall is to delete the Changed Type step in Applied Steps, as shown in Figure 10-3.

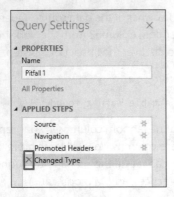

FIGURE 10-3 Delete the Changed Type step to avoid the second pitfall.

To clarify, you *do* need correct column types for some columns in your tables. Without the definition of types in some columns, you will not be able to perform arithmetic operations such as Sum and Average or apply time intelligence on these columns in Excel PivotTables or Power BI visualizations. This is why the Power Query Editor was designed to implicitly detect the types of all the columns in the table and change them for you. Without this automatic step, if you forget to explicitly change the type, you will not be able to calculate the sum of a numeric column when used in the Values pane of PivotTables or Power BI visuals.

Instead of allowing the automatic Changed Type step, delete it, and change the types manually—and consider doing it as late in the process as possible. Here are the reasons why.

> **Tip** "The better the later" is a useful motto for changing types in Power Query. It is a good practice to change the column types in the Power Query Editor rather than rely on the automatic Changed Type—and the later in the process you explicitly change the types, the better.

If you perform type changes as the latest necessary step, you gain the following advantages:

- **Performance/refresh time:** Type changes (for example, transforming text into datetime values) require some computation effort of the M engine. If you intend to significantly narrow down the number of rows by applying filters throughout the transformation sequence, you can decrease the refresh time of the query by manually applying the change type after the last filter step.

- **Error handling:** Changing column types may lead to cell-based errors for values that cannot be converted to the new type. When these errors appear earlier in the chain of transformation steps, it is sometimes more difficult to troubleshoot the issue.

> **See Also** For an example of an error that is difficult to detect due to an early Changed Type step, read the article https://datachant.com/2017/01/11/10-common-mistakes-powerbi-powerquery-pitfall-2/.

- **Persistence:** Early changes of types may not be persistent in some scenarios. For example, when you append multiple workbooks from a folder, the type changes made on the sample query level do not propagate to the appended results.

By now, you may be wondering if it is possible to configure the Power Query Editor to stop the auto-detection and change of types so you can avoid manually deleting the steps, as shown in Figure 10-3. The answer is yes. But you need to configure it for each workbook or Power BI file, and you cannot set it for all your future reports.

To configure the Power Query Editor to stop the auto-detection and change of types, launch the Query Options dialog box in Excel (on the Data tab, Get Data, Query Options), or the Options dialog box in Power BI Desktop (on the File tab, Option and Settings, Options). Go to Current Workbook in the Query Options dialog box in Excel or the Current File in the Options dialog box in Power BI Desktop and deselect the box Automatically Detect Column Types and Headers for Unstructured Sources, as shown in Figure 10-4.

Unfortunately, there is no such a check box under Global, Data Load, so you need to repeat the process of deselecting this box for each new report.

Finally, after you delete or prevent the creation of the default Changed Type step, you should explicitly change the types for the numeric and date/time columns that are needed for your analysis, or modify the original Changed Type step as explained in step 10 in Exercise 10-1. Note that in the formula that was described in Exercise 10-1 step 10, you have several text columns that are better removed from the Changed Type step to prevent future refresh failures if these columns are renamed. These columns are marked in bold in the next formula:

```
= Table.TransformColumnTypes(#"Promoted Headers",{{"Date", type date}, {"Color",
type text}, {"Supplier Category", type text}, {"Supplier Name", type text},
{"Customer Category", type text}, {"City", type text}, {"Revenue", type number}})
```

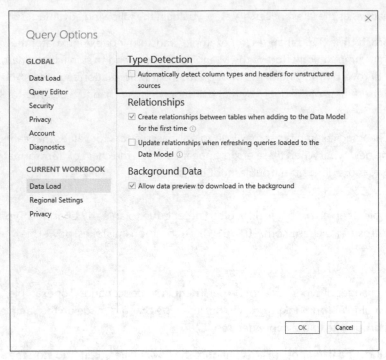

FIGURE 10-4 Disable the automatic detection and change of types.

To improve your query, you can either delete the Changed Type step in Applied Steps and manually change the types of Date and Revenue columns, or modify the M formula as follows:

```
= Table.TransformColumnTypes(#"Promoted Headers",{{"Date", type date},
{"Revenue", type number}})
```

> **Tip** If you work with tables that contain too many columns to perform an explicit type conversion and are looking for an automatic way to detect column types without referencing all column names, you will find the M expression in the following article very useful: http://datachant.com/2018/05/14/automatic-detection-of-column-types-in-powerquery.

Pitfall 3: Dangerous Filtering

The third pitfall is one of the most dangerous pitfalls. It is almost invisible; you can easily miss it when you create the query, and you may ignore its impact when it is refreshed. The third pitfall may create a bias in your reports, and when you will detect it, it may be too late: Your biased report may lead to badly informed business decisions. It all starts with the filter control in the Power Query Editor and its derived filtering step. It is such a trivial and common step that most of our queries include it.

Exercise 10-2, Part 1: Filtering Out Black Products

Before we really examine the risk of the third pitfall, let's look at a basic scenario that demonstrates the filtering error and how to avoid it. You will use the same sample data as in Exercise 10-1. As the chief analyst of Wide World Importers, you have been asked to analyze the impact on business if you stop importing products whose color is black. You decide to filter all the black products in your queries.

1. Open a blank new workbook or a new Power BI report.

   In Excel: On the Data tab, select Get Data, From File, From Workbook.

   In Power BI Desktop: On the Home tab, select Get Data, and in the Get Data dialog box, select File and then select Excel.

2. Select the file C10E01.xlsx and select Import.

3. In the Navigator dialog box, select Sheet1 and click Edit.

4. Delete the Changed Type step in Applied Steps.

5. Ensure that the formula bar is visible.

6. Change the type of the Date column to *Date* and the type of the Revenue column to *Decimal Number.*

   (At this point, following steps 4–6 you have successfully passed Pitfalls 1 and 2.)

7. Because the data contains many more colors than Black and Blue, filter out all the black products by clicking the filter control of the Color column and deselecting Black, as shown in Figure 10-5.

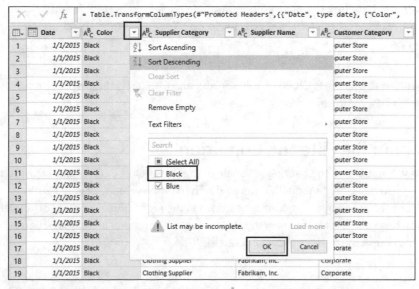

FIGURE 10-5 Deselecting the value Black leads to dangerous results.

Following this filtering step, you may expect to have as output products of all colors except Black.

8. Inspect the resulting code in the formula bar and especially notice the following code:

```
= Table.SelectRows(#"Changed Type", each ([Color] = "Blue"))
```

Fortunately, because you're aware of the first pitfall, you now inspect the formula bar more often, and you have learned to pay close attention to double-quoted values. So, the problem is obvious to you, and you easily spot it at this stage. Deselecting Black led the Power Query Editor to incorrectly assume that you selected Blue. As a result, only the blue products are filtered. If you use the output of this query without checking the formula bar, you may end up having only blue products in your analysis instead of having all the non-black products.

Fixing the formula at this stage is easy. You need to change the equal sign before Blue (= *"Blue"*) to a not-equal sign before Black (<> *"Black"*), as shown here:

```
= Table.SelectRows(#"Changed Type", each ([Color] <> "Black"))
```

You can also fix the incorrect condition without making this M modification by following steps 9 and 10.

9. Delete the Filtered Rows step from Applied Steps and select the filter control of the Color column. You will now apply the filter again in a better way.

10. In the Filter pane, select Text Filters and then select Does Not Equal. When the Filter Rows dialog box opens, enter *Black* next to Does Not Equal, and click OK to close the dialog box.

> **Tip** If you are not comfortable with M conditions, as explained in step 8, you can use the Text Filters dialog box to define the filtering condition, as explained in steps 9 and 10, and avoid the third pitfall altogether. It is always better to use Text Filters than selecting the values in the text pane.

You can download the solution files C10E02 - Solution.xlsx and C10E02 - Solution.pbix from https://aka.ms/DataPwrBIPivot/downloads.

The Logic Behind the Filtering Condition

At this stage, you may stop trusting the filtering rationale of the Power Query Editor and might start being concerned that you have unintentionally entered the third pitfall in many of your existing queries. How often have you used the filter control as shown in the preceding example? Fortunately, in most cases, when you deselect specific values in the Filter pane, the condition is created as you expect it to be, and you do not make the mistake shown in Exercise 10-2.

Here are the two rules that the Power Query Editor follows to auto-generate the filter condition when you select values in the Filter pane:

- When you try to filter values in the Filter pane, and the number of unselected values in the Filter pane is equal to the number of selected values, the Power Query Editor generates a positive condition, using the equal sign on the selected values.

- When the number of selected values in the Filter pane is higher than the number of unselected values, the Power Query Editor always favors the negative condition, using the not-equal sign on the items that are not selected.

Let's look at these rules on a simple column with the values 1 to 6:

1. Open a new Excel file or Power BI report and launch the Power Query Editor with a blank query.

2. In the formula bar, enter the following line:

   ```
   = {1..6}
   ```

3. In List Tools, on the Transform tab, click To Table and click OK to close the To Table dialog box.

4. Select the filter control of Column1. The Filter pane opens.

5. Deselect value 1 and close the Filter pane. Notice that 1 has been correctly filtered out from the table. Also notice that the formula bar includes the following line:

   ```
   = Table.SelectRows(#"Converted to Table", each ([Column1] <> 1))
   ```

6. Click the Filter pane again, and this time deselect both values 1 and 2. The results are as you expect. Notice the following line in the formula bar:

   ```
   = Table.SelectRows(#"Converted to Table", each ([Column1] <> 1 and [Column1] <> 2))
   ```

7. Click the Filter pane again. This time deselect values 1, 2, and 3. The results look good. Only the values 4, 5, and 6 are shown in the Preview pane. But the formula bar contains the positive condition (positive in this context is a condition that uses the equal sign on the values you didn't deselect in the Filter pane):

   ```
   = Table.SelectRows(#"Converted to Table", each ([Column1] = 4 or [Column1] = 5 or
   [Column1] = 6))
   ```

   However, the correct condition is the negative condition (negative condition in this context is a condition that uses the not-equal sign on the values you deselected in the Filter pane), which should look like this:

   ```
   = Table.SelectRows(#"Converted to Table", each ([Column1] <> 1 and [Column1] <> 2
   and [Column1] <> 3))
   ```

Why is the positive condition dangerous when you deselected the values 1, 2, and 3? Imagine that in the future you also have the values 7, 8, 9, and 10 in your data, and not just 1 to 6. In step 7 you wanted to filter out values 1, 2, and 3 and keep all the rest. When you refresh the report in the future, values 7, 8, 9, and 10 will be filtered out from your report if you use the positive condition.

This example is simple, but it gives you a taste of what can happen when you work with large datasets and encounter the third pitfall: Only a subset of the values will be loaded to the pane. In Exercise 10-2, for example, you had more than two colors in the dataset, but only the black and blue values were loaded in the Filter pane. Deselecting the Black value led to an equal number of selected and not selected values, which then led to the positive condition.

One of the most dangerous and common factors that will lead you to the third pitfall is using the search box in the Filter pane. You usually use the search box when you have a long list of values in the Filter pane, and you want to zoom in on the desired values instead of scrolling down to the results. Deselecting values from the found values will *always* lead to a positive condition, and may get you in trouble.

Exercise 10-2, Part 2: Searching Values in the Filter Pane

You will use the sample workbook C10E01.xlsx, which you used in Exercise 10-1 and 10-2 part 1. The workbook can be downloaded from https://aka.ms/DataPwrBIPivot/downloads.

1. If you skipped the former exercises in this chapter, download the workbook C10E01.xslx and save it in the folder *C:\Data\C10*.

2. Open a blank new workbook or a new Power BI report.

   In Excel: On the Data tab, select Get Data, From File, From Workbook.

   In Power BI Desktop: On the Home tab, select Get Data, and in the Get Data dialog box, select File and then select Excel.

3. Select the file C10E01.xlsx and select Import.

4. In the Navigator dialog box, select Sheet1 and click Edit.

5. To avoid the second pitfall, delete the Changed Type step in Applied Steps and change the type of the Date column to *Date* and the type of the Revenue column to *Decimal Number*.

   Imagine that you want to filter out all rows whose city is *Baldwin City*.

6. Select the filter control of City column. The Filter pane opens. Since the list of cities that starts with the letter *A* is long, and you would need to scroll down to find the cities that start with the letter *B*, you may prefer using the search box in the Filter pane. Let's zoom in to all the cities that start with *Ba* to find the value Baldwin City.

   Enter the prefix *Ba* in the search box. The results include multiple cities in the pane, and luckily *Baldwin City* is the first result, so you can easily deselect it. Unfortunately, when you look at the formula bar you can see that the resulting expression has an incorrect positive condition:

   ```
   = Table.SelectRows(#"Changed Type", each ([City] = "Baraboo" or [City] = "Bayou
   Cane" or [City] = "Bazemore" or [City] = "Beaver Bay" or [City] = "Bombay Beach" or
   [City] = "Greenback" or [City] = "Wilkes-Barre"))
   ```

As a result, you will fall prey to the third pitfall, as your report will include all the cities that contains the substring *Ba* except for *Baldwin City*, and all the other cities (and there are many of them that don't start with *Ba*) will be filtered out.

7. To fix this issue, you would need to fix the formula:

```
= Table.SelectRows(#"Changed Type", each ([City] <> "Baldwin City"))
```

As you can see, the steps you made in this exercise are common, so you may experience the third pitfall quite often. The best defenses are to use the Text Filters dialog box instead of the search box in the Filter pane. But if you insist on using the search box, keep verifying the contents of the formula bar, and correct your formulas when needed.

Pitfall 4: Reordering Columns

The fourth pitfall happens when you reorder the position of columns in the Power Query Editor. In many cases, you don't really care about the exact order of your columns but would like to apply a specific order on a small subset of the columns. For example, you might want to flip between two columns or move a newly added custom column from the right end of the table to a certain position.

When you perform the reordering step, a *Table.ReorderColumns* function is generated with a reference to all the column names in your table. By referencing all columns, you weaken your query and increase the chance of refresh failures in the future, when columns are renamed or removed from the source data.

In many cases, the reordering step may be removed from Applied Steps altogether. For example, when you create a custom column that applies some calculations on another column in the table, you might want to place the new column next to its source column to verify the correctness of the code. In such cases, after you have confirmed that your code is correct, it is recommended that you delete the reorder step to reduce the chance of refresh failures.

In some cases the reordering of a table is important. If you want to control the order of the fields that will be shown in a PivotTable in Excel, or if you need to load a query to a worksheet, you can control the order of the columns. There are also some advanced scenarios that require a certain order of columns in your query. For example, in Exercise 4-4 in Chapter 4, "Combining Mismatched Tables," you relied on the reordering step to move a calculated column to the beginning of the table to transpose it and then use it as headers.

If your reorder step is crucial, try to apply it after you keep only the columns that are really needed in your report. (You'll learn more about the selection of columns when we get to the fifth pitfall.) It would not make sense to load a table with hundreds of columns, reorder them, and then keep the columns you need. Keeping only the dozen or so columns you need and reordering them will ensure that you create a much more robust query. In Exercise 10-3, you will learn how to reorder a subset of columns without referencing the complete column names, which will further improve the robustness of your query.

Exercise 10-3, Part 1: Reordering a Subset of Columns

You start this exercise with the Wide World Importers revenue dataset from Exercise 10-1 and perform a basic reordering of the columns City and Revenue.

1. Open a blank new workbook or a new Power BI report.

   In Excel: On the Data tab, select Get Data, From File, From Workbook.

   In Power BI Desktop: On the Home tab, select Get Data, and in the Get Data dialog box, select File and then select Excel.

2. Select the file C10E01.xlsx and select Import.

3. In the Navigator dialog box, select Sheet1 and click Edit.

4. Delete the Changed Type step from the Applied Steps pane.

5. Move the City column to be the second column and Revenue to be the third column, as shown in Figure 10-6.

Before:

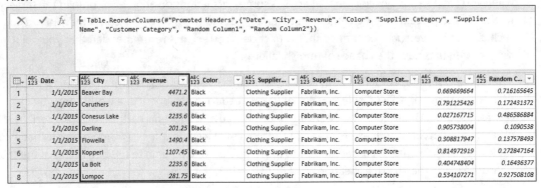

After:

FIGURE 10-6 Reordering the City and Revenue columns in the Power Query Editor.

6. Inspect the formula bar, which contains the following line:

   ```
   = Table.ReorderColumns(#"Promoted Headers",{"Date", "City", "Revenue", "Color",
   "Supplier Category", "Supplier Name", "Customer Category", "Random Column1",
   "Random Column2"})
   ```

   Obviously, this function will fail to refresh if column names such as Random Column1 and Random Column2 change in the source table. Can you rewrite this formula to refer to the list of column names above for the reordering step, but somehow only mention *"City"* and *"Revenue"* in the code? Yes, you can.

7. Remove this part from the preceding formula:

```
{"Date", "City", "Revenue", "Color", "Supplier Category", "Supplier Name",
"Customer Category", "Random Column1", "Random Column2"}
```

Replace it with the following code, which returns the same list of column names:

```
List.InsertRange(List.Difference(Table.ColumnNames(#"Promoted Headers"),
{"City", "Revenue"}), 1, {"City", "Revenue"})
```

The final formula is as follows:

```
= Table.ReorderColumns(#"Promoted Headers",List.InsertRange(List.Difference(
Table.ColumnNames(#"Promoted Headers"), {"City", "Revenue"}), 1, {"City", "Revenue"}))
```

Let's look at how, with a combination of *List.InsertRange*, *List.Difference*, and *Table.ColumnNames*, you achieved your goal and generated the same list of column names by referencing only *City* and *Revenue*.

List.InsertRange receives a list as an input and inserts another list in a certain zero-based offset. So, if you have a list A, to add *City* and *Revenue* as the second and third items in list A, you can write the following formula:

```
List.InsertRange(A, 1, {"City", "Revenue"}
```

As you can see at the preceding *Table.ReorderColumns* formula, *List.InsertRange* is used as explained above. Now, if list A can contain all the column names except City and Revenue, you will be able to apply *List.InsertRange* on A and get the desired order. This is where *List.Difference* has a role. This function accepts a list as its first argument and another list as its second, and it returns a new list with all the items in the first list that are not in the second list (the left-anti join of the two lists). So, if you apply *List.Difference* on a list and use a subset of the list as the second argument, you get as a result a new list that contains all the items from the original list except for all the items in the subset.

Therefore, if B is the list of column names, then the following function will return all the column names except City and Revenue:

```
A = List.Difference(B, {"City", "Revenue"})
```

Now when you use *Table.ColumnNames* in the following formula, instead of *B*, you can build all the pieces for the full expression:

```
B = Table.ColumnNames(#"Promoted Headers")
```

Finally, when you combine all the elements together, you reach the final formula (provided here in multiline format for better readability):

```
= Table.ReorderColumns(
    #"Promoted Headers",
    List.InsertRange(
        List.Difference(
            Table.ColumnNames(#"Promoted Headers"),
            {"City", "Revenue"}
        ),
        1,
        {"City", "Revenue"}
    )
)
```

Exercise 10-3, Part 2: The Custom Function *FnReorderSubsetOfColumns*

The technique you have been exploring in part 1 would be useful in many reports, and you might want to reuse it. You can simplify your experience by using a custom function that implements the logic you used in step 7. To see how to do this, continue the exercise with the following steps:

8. Create a blank query and paste the following code into the Advanced Editor:

```
(tbl as table, reorderedColumns as list, offset as number) as table =>
    Table.ReorderColumns(
        tbl,
        List.InsertRange(
            List.Difference(
                Table.ColumnNames(tbl),
                reorderedColumns
            ),
            offset,
            reorderedColumns
        )
    )
```

9. Rename the custom function *FnReorderSubsetOfColumns*.

10. Remove the Reordered Columns step in Applied Steps and click the fx button in the formula bar to create a new step. Then apply the following formula in the formula bar:

```
= FnReorderSubsetOfColumns(#"Promoted Headers", {"City", "Revenue"}, 1)
```

The results are the same as you obtained after step 5. You can see that invoking the function *FnReorderSubsetOfColumns* is easy. The function receives the table, the subset of the reordered column names as a list, and the zero-based index; it then performs the reordering in a robust manner, without referencing any other column names.

> **See Also** There are other ways to implement Table.ReorderColumns and avoid refresh errors. You can use a third argument to ignore missing fields or add null values for missing fields. While these techniques prevent refresh failures, they may give you unexpected results. Read more at https://datachant.com/2017/01/18/power-bi-pitfall-4/.

You can download the solution files C10E03 - Solution.xlsx and C10E03 - Solution.pbix from https://aka.ms/DataPwrBIPivot/downloads.

Pitfall 5: Removing and Selecting Columns

The fifth pitfall is related to a very common operation in the Power Query Editor: removing columns. While the removal of unnecessary columns is a crucial part of building efficient reports (fewer columns means a smaller memory footprint and smaller file size), each time you delete a column, you weaken your query and expose it to the possibility of future refresh failures.

Each time you remove a column in the Power Query Editor, you take the risk that a future refresh may fail when the removed column is missing in the external data source. Do you have a good data contract with the owner of the source table? Consider that, for the same reasons you decide to remove certain columns, the owner of the source table might bi the same in the future, and determine that these columns are unimportant.

To reduce the risk of refresh failures, you can follow a simple best practice: Focus on the columns you want to keep rather than on the ones you need to remove. The Power Query Editor enables you to remove or keep columns. While it is a more direct user experience to press the Delete button on the selected columns you wish to remove, it is recommended in many cases that you select the columns you wish to keep. Exercise 10-4 demonstrates this process on Random Column1 and Random Column2 in the Wide World Importers dataset from Exercise 10-1.

Exercise 10-4: Handling the Random Columns in the Wide World Importers Table

1. Open a blank new workbook or a new Power BI report.

    In Excel: On the Data tab, select Get Data, From File, From Workbook.

    In Power BI Desktop: On the Home tab, select Get Data, and in the Get Data dialog box, select File and then select Excel.

2. Select the file C10E01.xlsx and select Import.

3. In the Navigator dialog box, select Sheet1 and click Edit.

4. Delete the Changed Type step in Applied Steps.

5. Remove the two random columns from Exercise 10-1 by selecting Random Column1 and Random Column2 and pressing Delete.

6. Notice that the formula bar includes the following line:

    ```
    = Table.RemoveColumns(#"Promoted Headers",{"Random Column1", "Random Column2"})
    ```

    Now, if the source table will no longer include one of these columns, the refresh will fail. In the next step you will remove the random columns in a different way, and improve the robustness of the query.

7. Remove the last step in Applied Steps, and then select Choose Columns on the Home tab and deselect Random Column1 and Random Column2. Close the dialog box and notice the following line in the formula bar:

```
= Table.SelectColumns(#"Promoted Headers",{"Date", "Color", "Supplier Category",
"Supplier Name", "Customer Category", "City", "Revenue"})
```

Ignoring the Missing Column

In some situations, the number of columns you need to keep may be too high, and the risk of removing a few columns may be lower than the problems associated with specifying large number of columns.

Often, it doesn't matter if you remove or select columns. You will eventually deal with external data sources that are likely to change. To help prevent refresh errors, there is an optional argument that you can use in *Table.RemoveColumns* and *Table.SelectColumns* that allows you to ignore errors instead of failing to refresh. The third argument is *MissingField.Ignore* or *MissingField.UseNull*.

MissingField.Ignore ignores the missing column, while *MissingField.UseNull* keeps the column name on errors but fills it with nulls. *MissingField.UseNull* is more practical than its sibling *MissingField.Ignore* in conjunction with *Table.SelectColumns,* as it enables you to ensure that your selected column names will be included in the end results. However, both options may expose you to errors that are difficult to detect. Thus, a refresh failure may be preferable to the unexpected results that you may incur with these arguments.

Selecting or Removing Columns Based on Their Position

In many scenarios, removing or selecting columns based on their position is more certain than referencing them by name. Using the function *Table.ColumnNames* to get the list of all column names and *List.Range* to retrieve a subset of the columns enables you to select any subset of columns based on their position.

Each one of the following formulas removes the first column in a table:

```
= Table.RemoveColumns(Source, List.First(Table.ColumnNames(Source)))
= Table.RemoveColumns(Source, Table.ColumnNames(Source){0})
```

Using *List.FirstN*, this formula removes the first two columns in the table:

```
= Table.RemoveColumns(Source, List.FirstN(Table.ColumnNames(Source), 2))
```

This formula removes the last column in the table:

```
= Table.RemoveColumns(Source, List.Last(Table.ColumnNames(Source), 1))
```

And this formula keeps the second and third column names in the table:

```
= Table.SelectColumns(Source, List.Range(Table.ColumnNames(Source), 1, 2))
```

List.Range receives a list as the first argument, a zero-based offset, and the count of items to return. You can apply the code *List.Range(Table.ColumnNames(Source), 1, 2)* to return the two column names in the Source table in offset 1, which is the second position in the list.

You can also select individual columns. The following formula is equivalent to the one above:

```
= Table.SelectColumns(Source, {Table.ColumnNames(Source){0}, Table.ColumnNames(Source){1}})
```

This code is practical when you need to select nonadjacent columns. In the case of the Wide World Importers table, this formula removes the random columns, assuming that they are always the seventh and eighth columns (offsets 6 and 7):

```
= Table.RemoveColumns(#"Promoted Headers", {Table.ColumnNames(#"Promoted Headers"){6}, Table.ColumnNames(#"Promoted Headers"){7}})
```

Selecting or Removing Columns Based on Their Names

There are countless possibilities for selecting or removing columns in M. The following two examples involve removing the random columns in a generic way. The following formula applies *List.Select* on the column names to remove columns that contain the substring *Random*:

```
= Table.RemoveColumns(#"Promoted Headers", List.Select(Table.ColumnNames(
#"Promoted Headers"), each Text.Contains(_, "Random")))
```

And here are the same results, using *Table.SelectColumns* and the negative logic (that is, you can select all the columns that don't contain *"Random"*):

```
= Table.SelectColumns(#"Promoted Headers", List.Select(Table.ColumnNames(
#"Promoted Headers"), each not Text.Contains(_, "Random")))
```

You can download the solution files C10E04 - Solution.xlsx and C10E04 - Solution.pbix from https://aka.ms/DataPwrBIPivot/downloads.

Pitfall 6: Renaming Columns

Renaming columns is another common data preparation step. It is common to rename columns quite often to improve the user experience and expose report consumers to user-friendly names. But each time you rename a column in the Power Query Editor, you expose the query to higher chances of refresh failures in the future. Following the techniques described in the section "Pitfall 5: Removing and Selecting Columns," earlier in this chapter, you can increase the robustness of the query by modifying the formula and avoiding referencing the current column names.

Let's look at this issue on the Wide World Importers dataset and examine the different ways to rename columns. For the sake of this example, assume that you expect that all the column names that start with the prefix *Random Column* will in the future be renamed in the source table. Say that in your analysis, you were asked to rename these columns *Factor 1*, *Factor 2*, and so forth, as shown in Figure 10-7.

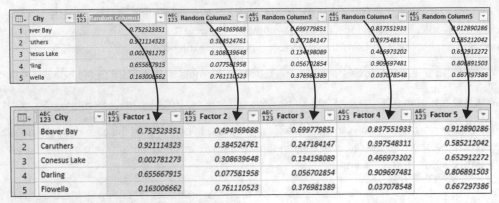

FIGURE 10-7 A column renaming challenge is to rename the *Random* columns without referencing their names.

Exercise 10-5: Renaming the *Random* Columns in the Wide World Importers Table

For this exercise, you should use the sample workbook C10E05.xlsx, which can be downloaded from https://aka.ms/DataPwrBIPivot/downloads. The sample workbook summarizes the fictional revenues of Wide World Importers.

1. Download the workbook C10E05.xslx and save it in the folder *C:\Data\C10*.

2. Open a blank new workbook or a new Power BI report.

   In Excel: On the Data tab, select Get Data, From File, From Workbook.

   In Power BI Desktop: On the Home tab, select Get Data, and in the Get Data dialog box, select File and then select Excel.

3. Select the file C10E05.xlsx and select Import.

4. In the Navigator dialog box, select Sheet1 and click Edit.

5. Delete the Changed Type step from the Applied Steps pane. You can see in the Preview pane of the Power Query Editor that you now have seven *Random* columns. In this exercise, you will learn multiple ways to rename these columns.

   Manually rename the columns Random Column1 and Random Column2 to *Factor 1* and *Factor 2*, respectively. The formula bar now includes the following line:

   ```
   = Table.RenameColumns(#"Promoted Headers",{{"Random Column1", "Factor 1"},
   {"Random Column2", "Factor 2"}})
   ```

   When the source table no longer includes one of these columns, the refresh will fail.

   Imagine that the data owner of the source table notifies you that he plans in the future to rename these columns, but he guarantees that the columns will always be positioned in the same order in the table. Under this assumption, you can reference these columns by their position. Here, for example, is how you can rename the first two random columns:

```
= Table.RenameColumns(#"Promoted Headers",{{Table.ColumnNames(#"Promoted Headers"){6},
"Factor 1"}, {Table.ColumnNames(#"Promoted Headers"){7}, "Factor 2"}})
```

The Custom Function *FnRenameColumnsByIndices*

To rename the columns based on their position in the table, you can write a custom function that enables you to rename a large subset of column names without the need to separately write each pair of old and new column names. In this section you will learn how to create such a function.

For example, once the function is ready, and named *FnRenameColumnsByIndices*, you can invoke it to rename the random columns in step 5 to *Factor 1* and *Factor 2*:

```
= FnRenameColumnsByIndices(#"Promoted Headers", {"Factor 1", "Factor 2"}, {6, 7})
```

The custom function approach is scalable, allowing you to rename a large number of columns at once and even import the old and new column names from an external list. The function also enables you to use a range of indices. For example, to rename all columns starting from the fourth column and ending at the tenth column to Factor 1, Factor 2,...Factor 7, without using the custom function, you could apply smart transformations.

Let's start with an ineffective method. You could write a lot of code that specifies each pair of old and new column names, as follows:

```
= Table.RenameColumns(
    #"Promoted Headers",
        {
            {Table.ColumnNames(#"Promoted Headers"){6}, "Factor 1"},
            {Table.ColumnNames(#"Promoted Headers"){7}, "Factor 2"},
            {Table.ColumnNames(#"Promoted Headers"){8}, "Factor 3"},
            {Table.ColumnNames(#"Promoted Headers"){9}, "Factor 4"},
            {Table.ColumnNames(#"Promoted Headers"){10}, "Factor 5"},
            {Table.ColumnNames(#"Promoted Headers"){11}, "Factor 6"},
            {Table.ColumnNames(#"Promoted Headers"){12}, "Factor 7"}
        }
)
```

To avoid this complication, you can create smart renaming as follows:

```
= FnRenameColumnsByIndices(
    #"Promoted Headers",
    List.Transform(
        {1..7},
        each "Factor " & Text.From(_)
    ),
    {6..12}
)
```

In this formula, the second argument is a dynamic list that is created using *List.Transform*. Its first argument is a list of indices from 1 to 7. Its output is a transformed list of text concatenating the prefix *Factor* and the relevant index. The third argument of *FnRenameColumnsByIndices* is a list between 6 and 12 for the indices of the columns to rename.

Now, let's review the function *FnRenameColumnsByIndices*:

```
(Source as table, ColumnNamesNew as list, Indices as list) =>
let
    ColumnNamesOld = List.Transform( Indices, each Table.ColumnNames(Source){_} ),
    ZippedList = List.Zip( { ColumnNamesOld, ColumnNamesNew } ),
    #"Renamed Columns" = Table.RenameColumns( Source, ZippedList )
in
    #"Renamed Columns"
```

Let's look at this custom function, step by step. The arguments are *Source* for the table to rename, *ColumnNamesNew* for the list of new column names, and *Indices* for the list of indices in the source table. The first line inside the *let* expression receives the indices and returns the relevant column names in the Source table:

```
ColumnNamesOld = List.Transform(Indices, each Table.ColumnNames(Source){_}),
```

The next line uses *List.Zip* to create a list of nested lists. Each nested list contains two members—the old and new column names from the same index of the different lists:

```
ZippedList = List.Zip( { ColumnNamesOld, ColumnNamesNew } ),
```

For example, this *List.Zip* formula:

```
List.Zip({"a","b","c"}, {"A", "B", "C"}}
```

returns the following list of nested lists:

```
{{"a", "A"}, {"b", "B"}, {"c", "C"}}
```

The latter format is the required format for the second argument of *Table.RenameColumns*—a list of nested lists, which are pairs of old and new column names, and is used in the third line inside the *let* expression:

```
#"Renamed Columns" = Table.RenameColumns(Source, ZippedList)
```

The *Table.TransformColumnNames* Function

There is yet another way to rename the columns. Recall that in Chapter 4, you used the function *Table.TransformColumnNames* to rename all columns. You applied it to replace underscores with spaces or capitalize the headers. This function can also be used in this scenario to replace the column names using a generic rule:

```
= Table.TransformColumnNames(#"Promoted Headers", each Text.Replace(_, "Random Column",
"Factor "))
```

The advantage of this method is that it successfully renames the columns, even if the random columns will be reordered in the source table. Still, you need to be careful about the renaming logic you use to avoid renaming columns that you were not supposed to rename.

> **Tip** In most cases, a simple rename, as you have always done, will suffice. Don't overthink it.

You can download the solution files C10E05 - Solution.xlsx and C10E05 - Solution.pbix from https://aka.ms/DataPwrBIPivot/downloads.

Pitfall 7: Splitting a Column into Columns

The seventh pitfall can be as dangerous as the filtering pitfall (Pitfall 4), as it may lead to missed data. It can happen when you apply Split Column By Delimiter into columns on delimiter-separated values with a varying range of values.

Split Column By Delimiter is typically used to achieve two types of operations:

- The basic operation enables you to split a column into multiple columns. It is often used to split date and time columns into separate date and time columns or to divide client names into first and last names. The Split Column By Delimiter dialog box enables you by default to split a column into columns.

- The advanced operation of Split Column By Delimiter enables you to split multiple comma or other delimiter-separated values into rows. This operation is extremely useful. It allows you to create a new table that associates each split value with its entity. As shown in Figure 10-8, you can create a reference table to the source table that pairs between product codes and colors to find out how many products you have by colors.

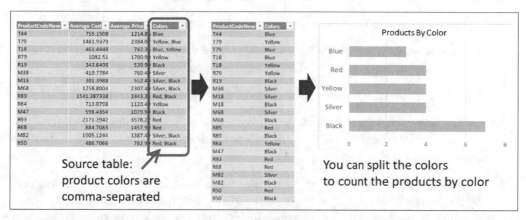

FIGURE 10-8 Split the comma-separated AdventureWorks Colors column to find how many products are released by color.

In Exercise 2-8 in Chapter 2, you worked with the AdventureWorks product table and split the Colors column to find the associations between products and colors in order to determine how many products are released by color. Recall that you split the Colors column into rows to solve that challenge. The next exercise will show you what can happen when you split a column into columns instead of into rows.

The seventh pitfall, as you will see in Exercise 10-6, happens when you split delimited-separated values and ignore the advanced (and relatively hidden) option to split the column into rows. If you don't select that option, you end up with the default option of splitting the column into columns, which exposes your queries to missing crucial information when new data is loaded to your report.

Exercise 10-6: Making an Incorrect Split

In this exercise you will repeat Exercise 2-8, but this time, you will see what happens when you use the incorrect split option, Split into Columns. This exercise demonstrates the risks and shows you how easy it is to fall prey to this pitfall.

You will use the sample workbook C10E06.xlsx, which can be downloaded from https://aka.ms/ DataPwrBIPivot/downloads. The sample workbook summarizes the AdventureWorks product codes (a new variation of codes) by average cost, average price, and comma-separated colors. As the head of data science in AdventureWorks, you would like to create a report that shows how many products you have for each color (refer to Figure 10-8).

1. Download the workbook C10E06.xslx and save it in the folder *C:\Data\C10*.

2. Open a blank new workbook or a new Power BI report.

   In Excel: On the Data tab, select Get Data, From File, From Workbook.

   In Power BI Desktop: On the Home tab, select Get Data, and in the Get Data dialog box, select File and then select Excel.

3. Select the file C10E06.xlsx and select Import.

4. In the Navigator dialog box, select Products and click Edit.

5. Delete the Changed Type step from the Applied Steps pane.

6. In the Queries pane, right-click Products and select Reference. Your goal is to create a new table with a mapping between the product codes and the colors.

7. Rename the new query *Products and Colors* and keep the new query selected.

8. On the Home tab, select Choose Columns, and in the dialog box that opens, select ProductCodeNew and Colors. Click OK to close the dialog box, and all the unselected columns are removed from your Products and Colors query.

9. Select the Colors column, and on the Transform tab, select Split Column and then select By Delimiter. In the Split Column by Delimiter dialog box that opens, notice that the comma delimiter is selected by default and the option Each Occurrence of the Delimiter is selected, as shown in Figure 10-9. Unfortunately, by default, when you close the dialog box, the split is made into columns rather than rows. To split by rows, you need to expand the Advanced Options section and switch the Split Into option from Columns to Rows, as you did in Exercise 2-8.

   At this stage, keep the default split by columns option, so you can learn the implications of going through the default experience. Click OK to close the dialog box.

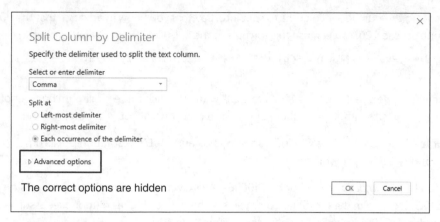

FIGURE 10-9 The Split Column by Delimiter dialog box hides the Split into Rows option under Advanced Options.

10. Notice in the Power Query Editor that the Colors column has been split into Colors.1 and Colors.2. In Applied Steps, select the Split Column By Delimiter step and review the line in the formula bar:

```
= Table.SplitColumn(Products_Table, "Colors", Splitter.SplitTextByDelimiter(",",
QuoteStyle.Csv), {"Colors.1", "Colors.2"})
```

This formula instructs the M engine to split Colors into two columns—only two. You will put it to the test soon.

11. Because your goal is to map between product codes and colors, you need to use the Unpivot transformation to have a table of code and color pairs, so select the ProductCodeNew column.

12. On the Transform tab, expand the Unpivot Columns drop-down and select Unpivot Other Columns. Colors.1 and Colors.2 are transformed into Attribute and Value columns. The latter includes the colors, now paired correctly to their corresponding product codes. At this stage, notice that some colors start with a space character. To fix this, you can apply a Trim step on the Value column or go to Applied Steps and in Split Column By Delimiter, click the settings icon and change the delimiter to Custom, and then enter a comma and a space (,). Here is the corrected formula for the Split Column By Delimiter step:

```
= Table.SplitColumn(Products_Table, "Colors", Splitter.SplitTextByDelimiter(", ",
QuoteStyle.Csv), {"Colors.1", "Colors.2"})
```

13. Remove the Attribute column and load the queries to your report to start the analysis. If you like, build a bar chart by using a PivotChart like the one shown in Figure 10-8.

14. To test what happens when a certain product code has more than two colors, save your report and open C10E06.xslx.

15. In cell D3, add two more colors to the existing two and change the Colors value from Yellow, Blue to Yellow, Blue, Black, Red. Save the workbook C10E06.xslx and close it. Go back to your exercise report and refresh it. The new colors are not included in the report.

To solve this problem, you should follow Exercise 2-4 and split the Colors column into rows. However, if for some reason you must split the column into columns and not into rows, you can scale up your solution by increasing the number of columns to split into. Say that you know in advance that the number of colors cannot exceed 20. You can use this formula at the Split Column By Delimiter step:

```
= Table.SplitColumn(Products_Table, "Colors", Splitter.SplitTextByDelimiter(", ",
QuoteStyle.Csv), 20)
```

Replacing the hardcoded part, {"Colors.1", "Colors.2"}, with 20, which is the maximum number of columns you expect, will strengthen your query and ensure that you will not miss data.

You can download the solution files C10E06 - Solution.xlsx and C10E06 - Solution.pbix from https://aka.ms/DataPwrBIPivot/downloads.

Make sure you also download the workbook C10E06-v2.xlsx, which contains the second version of the workbook C10E06.xlsx, with the modified color values. The queries in the solution files assume that you have the workbook C10E06-v2.xlsx in the folder *C:\Data\C10*.

Pitfall 8: Merging Columns

In the preceding section, "Splitting a Column into Columns," you learned how to avoid the seventh pitfall by splitting columns into rows instead of into columns. You also saw that if you simply must split a comma-separated column into columns, you can switch the second argument and call for the number of columns to generate. In this section, you will learn how to improve the query when you handle the reverse transformation: merging columns.

When you merge multiple columns into a single column, the generated formula first transforms all the numeric columns into text and then combines all the columns together. The following code is auto generated (and indented and formatted here with multiple lines for better readability) when you merge three columns in the Source table, the first of which are numeric (Numeric Column1 and Numeric Column 2) and the third of which is textual (Textual Column3):

```
#"Merged Columns" = Table.CombineColumns(
    Table.TransformColumnTypes(
        Source, {
            {"Numeric Column1", type text},
            {"Numeric Column2", type text}
        },
        "en-US"
    ),
    {"Numeric Column1", "Numeric Column2", "Textual Column3"},
    Combiner.CombineTextByDelimiter(":", QuoteStyle.None),
    "Merged"
)
```

In this formula, you can see that *Table.TransformColumnTypes* enforces the type conversion of all the numeric columns, and then merges the relevant columns. This formula exposes the query to unnecessary refresh failures. You can modify the code and scale it to merge a given list of columns, without referencing any hard-coded column names.

Say that you have the column names to merge in the ColumnsToMerge list. Here is the modified formula you can use instead of the preceding one:

```
#"Merged Columns" = Table.CombineColumns(
    Table.TransformColumnTypes(
        Source,
        List.Transform(
            ColumnsToMerge,
            each {_, type text}
        ),
        "en-US"
    ),
    ColumnsToMerge,
    Combiner.CombineTextByDelimiter(":", QuoteStyle.None),
    "Merged")
```

The main change between the two formulas is that this part of the code:

```
{
    {"Numeric Column1", type text},
    {"Numeric Column2", type text}
}
```

is replaced with a *List.Transform* function that generates the same code, but without referencing the column names:

```
List.Transform(
    ColumnsToMerge,
    each {_, type text}
)
```

This code iterates over each column name in ColumnsToMerge and transforms it into a list of column names and a text type: *{_, type text}*.

While you may not commonly need such a function, this example is an important demonstration of the use of list functions to write scalable and robust versions of your auto-generated formulas.

More Pitfalls and Techniques for Robust Queries

I mentioned earlier that I talk about 10 pitfalls in my blog series at DataChant, and you can see that this chapter does not cover the ninth and tenth pitfalls. This section mentions them briefly, and for more information, you can visit my blog.

The ninth pitfall has to do with expanding table columns. Expand Table Columns is a common transformation that you apply when you combine multiple files from a folder, merge between two tables, or work with unstructured datasets such as JSON.

When you expand table columns, you are required to select the columns to expand. As a result, the Power Query Editor auto-generates a formula with hardcoded column names, and new column names can be missed. To learn more about the Expand Table Columns transformation and how to avoid missing new columns, go to https://datachant.com/2017/02/07/power-bi-pitfall-9/.

The tenth pitfall focuses on the removal of duplicates, and it is covered earlier in this book, in Exercise 2-7, Chapter 2.

Summary

In this chapter you have improved your data-wrangling skills by focusing on long-term thinking. It looks at how you can make your queries last longer, without needing to constantly edit them as the data changes. You have learned about the most common pitfalls that lead to refresh failures and incorrect data—as well as three important themes for avoiding them: awareness, best practices, and M modifications. Having the formula bar active and reviewing it frequently can help you detect unexpected hardcoded double-quoted values, or incorrect conditions.

In this chapter you have also learned some best practices that can reduce failures. Having a formal or informal data contract with your colleagues who own the data sources can help you build the correct assumptions on the data and make good decisions about resolving your data preparation challenges.

You have also learned how to apply lightweight modifications to M formulas to strengthen your queries. To conclude this chapter, Table 10-1 lists the main pitfalls, their impacts, and how to avoid them.

TABLE 10-1 The Main Pitfalls, Their Impacts, and How to Avoid Them

Pitfall Number and Main Feature	Impact	How to Avoid the Pitfall
Pitfall 1: Ignoring the formula bar	Lack of awareness of the potential failures of the auto-generated M code	Activate the formula bar and keep reviewing its code. Look for double-quoted values to verify that they are consistent with your user interface selections.
Pitfall 2: Changed types	High probability for future refresh errors	Delete the Changed Type step. Turn off automatic detection of types in the Query Options dialog box for each workbook or Power BI report. Change the types manually on numeric/date/time columns. The later you change the types, the better.
Pitfall 3: Dangerous filtering	High probability for incorrect data	Avoid using the values in the Filter pane. Use the Filter Rows dialog box instead or audit the formula bar to ensure that your filtering logic was created as expected.
Pitfall 4: Reordering columns	High probability for future refresh errors	Avoid reordering columns if possible. Use M function to reorder only a subset of the columns.
Pitfall 5: Removing and selecting columns	Medium probability for future refresh errors	If you have a small number of columns to keep, use Choose Columns instead of Remove Columns. In many cases the columns you choose to keep are more likely to stay in your source data. Use M to remove or select columns by their position in the table.
Pitfall 6: Renaming columns	Medium probability for future refresh errors	Use the function *Table.TransformColumnNames* in M to rename columns by their values, or use *Table.ColumnNames* with zero-based indices to rename by position.
Pitfall 7: Splitting a column into columns	High probability for missing data	Avoid using Split into Columns. Use the advanced option and Split into Rows instead. If Split into Columns is required, use the maximum number of columns as the second argument.
Pitfall 8: Merging columns	Medium probability for refresh errors	All the columns will be referenced in the code. Modify the M code if needed to merge a large number of columns or if the list of column names to merge is dynamic.
Pitfall 9: Expanding table column	Medium probability for missing data	See https://datachant.com/2017/02/07/power-bi-pitfall-9/.
Pitfall 10: Merging duplicates	High probability for refresh errors and failures to create relationship between lookup and fact tables	See Chapter 2, Exercise 2-7, in the section "When a Relationship Fails," and make sure you lowercase/uppercase and trim the values before you remove duplicates in the column that is in the relationship in lookup tables.

CHAPTER 11

Basic Text Analytics

Words empty as the wind are best left unsaid.

—Homer

IN THIS CHAPTER, YOU WILL

- Learn how to search for keywords in textual columns and apply this technique as a simple topic detection method

- Learn how to load an external list of keywords and apply them dynamically in the search

- Use a Cartesian product or a custom function to search for keywords

- Use *Table.Buffer* and *List.Buffer* to improve the performance of keyword detection reports

- Learn several methods to split words, ignore common words, and count word occurrences in your analysis

- Learn how to prepare your textual data and load it in a Word Cloud custom visual in Power BI

This chapter shows how to use Power Query to gain fundamental insights into textual feeds. Many tables in your reports may already contain abundant textual columns that are barren, untapped, and devoid of meaning. As a paraphrase to Homer's saying that empty words are best left unsaid, you may find many words in your reports that are "empty as the wind." These textual columns are most likely ignored in your report or used only to provide some context when you drill down to specific rows. But you can learn much more from these textual columns. In Chapters 12, "Advanced Text Analytics: Extracting Meaning," and 13, "Social Network Analytics," you will learn very useful methods for leveraging textual columns and tap into new insights as you unravel these hidden treasure troves.

The techniques in this chapter are extremely useful in analyzing tables with textual input, such as client feedback in surveys, operational comments, or social network feeds. You will learn how to apply common transformations to extract meaning from words. You will start the journey with basic techniques to detect keywords and gradually improve your toolset to solve common text-related analytical challenges, whose implementations in Power Query are more complex. The text analytics journey will continue in the Chapter 12 with advanced text analytics on Azure, including text translation, sentiment analysis, and detection of key phrases—all with no help from data scientists or software developers.

Searching for Keywords in Textual Columns

The first text analytics challenge in this chapter is very common: finding specific keywords in textual feeds. While this task may seem trivial, it becomes challenging when there are many keywords to search for or when you want to dynamically load the keywords from an external source without further modification to your queries. In Exercise 11-1 you will learn how to detect a small set of predefined keywords.

Exercise 11-1: Basic Detection of Keywords

In this exercise, you will search for keywords in messages that Microsoft Press posts on its official Facebook page (https://www.facebook.com/microsoftpress). When you detect the keywords, you will be able to find out which topics are promoted the most by the Microsoft Press social team.

To analyze the Microsoft Press Facebook posts, you need to download the source workbook C11E01.xlsx from https://aka.ms/DataPwrBIPivot/downloads and save it in *C:\Data\C11*.

You can open the file and review its table, which includes columns for the following: Facebook messages (Message column), the date the post was published (Date column), the post's unique identifier (Post ID column), and the URL to the actual post on Facebook (URL column).

You can select Refresh All on the Data tab to update the workbook with the latest Facebook posts, but make sure you follow the exercises in this chapter on the original workbook, without refreshing it.

> **See Also** In Chapter 13 you will learn how to import the actual Facebook posts with Power Query. The focus of the current chapter is text analytics. Therefore, you start this exercise with the dataset stored in the Excel file C11E01.xslx. If you cannot wait, you can review the query in the solution file that imports the posts directly from Facebook.

Imagine that you are a data analyst working on the Microsoft Press social media team. Your first assignment is to estimate which of the following book topics are promoted the most on Facebook:

- Microsoft Excel
- Visual Studio
- Azure
- Windows

Can you detect these four keywords in the Message column of your dataset? This exercise walks through the steps to do so.

1. Open a blank new workbook or a new Power BI Desktop report.

   In Excel: Open a new Excel workbook and on the Data tab, select Get Data, From File, From Workbook.

   In Power BI Desktop: Open a new report and select Get Data, Excel, Connect.

2. Select the file C11E01.xslx from *C:\Data\C11* and select Import.

3. In the Navigator dialog box, select Sheet1 and click Edit.

4. When the Power Query Editor opens, notice that Microsoft Press Facebook posts are stored in the Message column, as shown in Figure 11-1.

FIGURE 11-1 A preview of Microsoft Press Facebook posts in the Power Query Editor shows the status updates in the Message column. Your challenge in this exercise is searching for keywords in this column.

Because Power Query is case sensitive in searches, in the following steps you will duplicate the Message column and work on the duplicate copy, where all the text is lowercased. You will keep the original messages intact for cases in which you should include the original text in your report to maintain the specific uppercased characters in the messages.

5. Select the Message column. On the Add Column tab, select Duplicate Column.

6. Select the new column Message - Copy, and on the Transform tab, select Format and then select Lowercase.

7. Rename the Message - Copy column *Lowercased*.

Next, you will create a Topic column and populate it with one of the detected topics: Microsoft Excel, Visual Studio, Azure, or Windows.

8. On the Add Column tab, select Conditional Column. The Add Conditional Column dialog box opens.

9. As shown in Figure 11-2, create a new column that returns one of the four topics if they are found in the Lowercased column. To do so, follow these steps:

    a. Enter *Topic* in the New Column Name box.

    b. Set Column Name to Lowercased.

    c. Set Operator to Contains.

    d. Enter *microsoft excel* in the Value box.

    e. Enter *Microsoft Excel* in the Output box.

> **Note** In step 9d you use a lowercase version for the topic (microsoft excel) because the search is case sensitive. In step 9e you use the capitalized version for reporting purposes.

10. While you are still in the Add Conditional Column dialog box, select Add Rule. A new condition row is added in the dialog box. Repeat step 9, with the following exceptions: In step 9d, enter the keyword *visual studio* in the Value box, and in step 9e enter *Visual Studio* in the Output box.

11. Select Add Rule. Repeat step 9 with the following exceptions: In step 9d, enter the keyword *azure* in the Value box, and in step 9e enter *Azure* in the Output box.

12. Repeat step 9 with the following exceptions: In step 9d, enter the keyword *windows* in the Value box, and in step 9e enter *Windows* in the Output box.

13. Enter *Other* in the Otherwise box. Verify that you have configured the dialog box as shown in Figure 11-2, and click OK to close the dialog box.

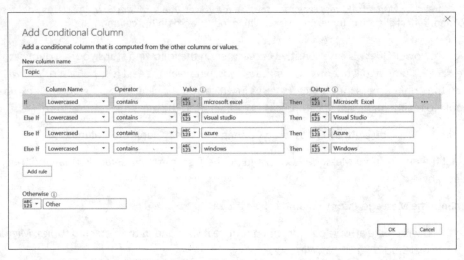

FIGURE 11-2 The Add Conditional Column dialog box has conditions to detect the topics Microsoft Excel, Visual Studio, Azure, and Windows.

The Preview pane includes the new Topic column. Obviously, this method is not very effective at detecting all the book topics in Microsoft Press Facebook posts. Many rows are classified as Other. Some posts promote other books on topics such as Office 365 or SQL Server. Other posts promote general sales discounts. Consider the following message: *"visit www.microsoftpressstore.com today—and discover deals, new books, and special promotions!"*

To keep things simple, you can assume that this approach met your objectives, and you can now filter out the rows with Other in the Topic column.

14. Click the filter control in the Topic column header, deselect Other in the Filter pane, and click OK.

15. Finally, remove the Lowercased column, rename the query *Microsoft Press Posts*, and load your report.

You can review the solution files C11E01 - Solution.xlsx or C11E11 - Solution.pbix, which are available at https://aka.ms/DataPwrBIPivot/downloads.

Now that you have accomplished your goal, let's review the main caveats of the method you used in this exercise:

- Caveat #1: Topic detection is limited to a short list of keywords.

  If you have a massive number of keywords, it would not be practical to manually add many keywords in the Add Conditional Column dialog box. You should find an alternative way to approach this challenge in a scalable way.

- Caveat #2: Topic detection is limited to a static list of keywords.

  In this method, you had to type the keywords in the dialog box. Alternatively, you could edit the underlying M formula, but the result would be the same. The keywords are hardcoded in the formula. If you are required to load the list of keywords from an external source, and you don't know in advance which keywords should be detected, this method will not be effective. You need to find a method that will allow you to dynamically load a list of keywords from an external source (and ensure that the performance of this operation doesn't slow you down).

- Caveat #3: Topic detection is limited to one keyword per message.

  Some Facebook posts may contain multiple keywords. For example, consider the following post:

  "New book! Programming for the Internet of Things: Using Windows 10 IoT Core and Azure IoT Suite".

  In this post you missed the *Windows* keyword because the logic prioritized the *Azure* keyword in the Add Conditional Column dialog box and its derived M formula. In some cases, you would do better to allocate multiple keywords to the same message to ensure that the message will be counted for each keyword.

- Caveat #4: Words that are contained as substrings of longer words may be falsely detected.

  Because you applied the Contains operator, you may detect keywords that are substrings in longer words. For example, consider the keyword *Excel*. What will be the impact on these two fake messages?

  *"This SQL Server book is **excel**lent."*

  *"Read this C# book to **excel** in software development"*.

In both examples, you miss the real topic of the book. To avoid false detection of topics, you need to split the messages into words and match the keywords with the split words. You will learn more about this challenge later in this chapter.

Next we address the first three caveats and introduce a great method to compare multiple datasets: using a Cartesian product.

Using a Cartesian Product to Detect Keywords

In this exercise you will learn an effective method to detect large number of keywords. In the previous exercise you used a conditional column to detect four keywords (refer to Figure 11-2). Would you consider using the same approach to search for a large set of keywords? Adding a long list of keywords manually would be time-consuming and quite challenging if you needed to periodically detect different keywords.

To scale up the solution used in Exercise 11-1 and detect a large number of topics from a dynamic list of keywords, you can apply a Cartesian product between Microsoft Press posts and the list of keywords. When you use the Cartesian product, a temporary larger table is created, as shown in Figure 11-3. The table consists of all the combinations between Facebook posts and keywords.

> **Note**   In set theory, a Cartesian product can be applied on multiple sets to produce a set of all the combinations of members from the different sets—one from each set. In Power Query, you can apply a Cartesian product on any two tables (and even on the same table) by adding to the first table a custom column with a reference to the second table. Then, by expanding the new column, you can reach the Cartesian product, as shown in Figure 11-3.

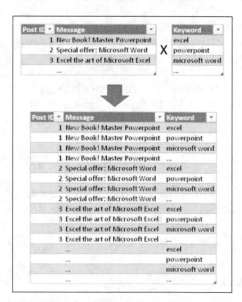

FIGURE 11-3 Here you apply a Cartesian product between messages and keywords.

In Figure 11-3, you can see three messages in the top-left table. To the right is another table with keywords. The Cartesian product creates a new table with all the combinations of message/keyword pairs, as shown at the bottom of Figure 11-3. This technique can help you explore all the combinations and then apply further computations on each pair. In this case, the computations will include searching for the keyword in the message and then filtering the matching rows.

> **Note** There are many applications of a Cartesian product that can help you gain new insights about your data. By mapping all the combinations between multiple datasets or entities, you can apply what-if calculations, basket analysis, and computations of methods from graph theory (such as finding the shortest path).

If you are not sure yet how to apply a Cartesian product or why doing so is useful in achieving a large-scale keyword search, follow along with the next exercise to find answers to your questions.

Exercise 11-2: Implementing a Cartesian Product

As the chief analyst on the Microsoft Press social team (you've been promoted since Exercise 11-1—congratulations!), your next challenge is to analyze Microsoft Press Facebook posts by topic, as demonstrated in Figure 11-4. To detect the topics, you can apply a Cartesian product between the Facebook posts and a large set of keywords, as shown in the slicer in Figure 11-4.

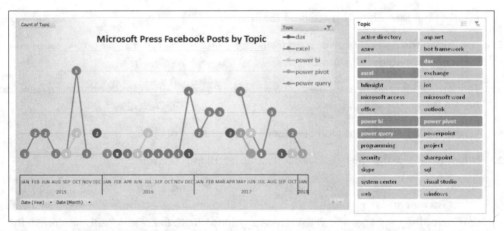

FIGURE 11-4 The workbook C11E02 - Solution.xslx can be used to analyze Microsoft Press Facebook posts by topic. (This workbook is available for download from https://aka.ms/DataPwrBIPivot/downloads.)

Part 1: Initial Preparations

In this exercise, you will use the same data source from Exercise 11-1, which included Microsoft Press Facebook posts. To start the exercise, you will perform some initial preparations.

1. Download the workbook C11E01.xslx from https://aka.ms/DataPwrBIPivot/downloads and save it to *C:\Data\C11*.

2. Open a blank new workbook or a new Power BI Desktop report.

   In Excel: Open a new Excel workbook and on the Data tab, select Get Data, From File, From Workbook.

   In Power BI Desktop: Open a new report and Select Get Data, Excel, Connect.

3. Select the file C11E01.xlsx from *C:\Data\C11* and select Import.

4. In the Navigator dialog box, select Sheet1 and click Edit.

5. Rename the query *Microsoft Press Posts*.

   Next, you will create a reference to the Microsoft Press Posts query to build a new table of posts and their topic, where the same Post ID can have multiple rows.

6. In the Queries pane, right-click the Microsoft Press Posts query and select Reference.

7. Rename the new query *Post Topics*.

8. While Post Topics is selected in the Queries pane, select Choose Columns on the Home tab.

9. In the Choose Columns dialog box, select Post ID and Message and click OK.

10. Select the *Message* column. On the Add Column tab, click Duplicate Column.

11. Select the *Message - Copy* column. On the Transform tab, click Format and then select Lowercase.

12. Rename the Message - Copy column *Lowercased*.

13. Download the text file Keywords.txt from https://aka.ms/DataPwrBIPivot/downloads and save it in your local folder, *C:\Data\C11*.

14. To load your keywords as a new query, while the Power Query Editor is open, click New Source on the Home tab and import Keywords.txt by selecting File, Text/CSV.

15. When the Keywords.txt dialog box opens with a preview of the file, click OK.

16. When the Keywords query is loaded, rename its column *Keyword*.

17. To lowercase all the keywords, select the Keyword column, and then, on the Transform tab, select Format and then select Lowercase. This step ensures that you are working on a lowercase version of the messages and will not miss anything due to the case-sensitive nature of the filtering that you will apply in the next section.

Part 2: The Cartesian Product

Now that you have completed the initial preparations in steps 1–17, you are ready for the Cartesian product. By using a custom column, you will be able to create all combinations of Facebook posts and topics and then apply a filter to match between posts and topics. Continue the exercise with the following steps:

18. In the Queries pane, select the Post Topics query.

19. On the Add Column tab, select Custom Column. When the Custom Column dialog box opens, make the following changes:

    a. Enter *Cartesian* in the New Column Name box.

    b. Set the following formula under Custom Column Formula:
       ```
       = Keywords
       ```

    c. Click OK to close the dialog box.

20. The Cartesian column is added, with the Keywords table in each row. At this stage, each Keywords table is represented as a *[Table]* object in the Power Query Editor. It's time to expand it.

21. Click the expand icon in the Cartesian header name. (Alternatively, select the Cartesian column, and then select Expand on the Transform tab.) In the Expand pane, keep the Keyword column checked and deselect Use Original Column Name As Prefix. Then click OK.

    You can now see in the Preview pane that the Cartesian product was successfully implemented. It is time to learn why the Cartesian product is so helpful. With all the combinations of messages and keywords, you can apply a filter to keep only the matching rows. You can use the Add Conditional Column transformation step, which is followed by a filter on the new conditional column.

22. On the Add Column tab, select Conditional Column. The Add Conditional Column dialog box opens. Make the following changes to set it as shown in Figure 11-5:

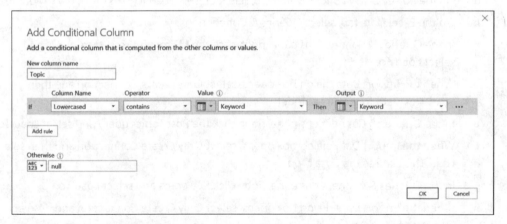

FIGURE 11-5 The Add Conditional Column dialog box can handle the matching between each Microsoft Press Facebook post and a keyword value in the Cartesian product.

    a. Enter *Topic* in the New Column Name box.

    b. Set Column Name to Lowercased.

    c. Set Operator to Contains.

    d. In the Value drop-down, choose Select a Column and then select Keyword.

    e. In the Output drop-down, choose Select a Column and then select Keyword.

    f. Enter *null* in the Otherwise box.

    g. Click OK to close the dialog box.

The Topic column is now added. It contains many null values for all the combinations of posts that don't contain the given keywords. It's time to filter out all the rows that contain null values.

23. Click the filter icon on the Topic column and select Remove Empty in the Filter pane.

24. Remove the columns Message, Lowercased, and Keyword.

Let's review what you have achieved so far. By using a Cartesian product, you were able to map posts to specific topics from a dynamic list. Two tables will be needed in your report. The first table is Microsoft Press Posts, with many columns including Post ID and Message. The second table is Post Topics, with the columns Post ID and Topic.

Part 3: Relationships

In this section, you will move from data preparation to modeling so that you can perform analysis of posts by topic. While data modeling is not the focus of this book, the steps are included here in case you are new to Power Pivot in Excel or modeling in Power BI Desktop. In the following steps you will create the relationship between the posts and topics that would allow you to create a variety of visuals and PivotTables that are fed from the two tables.

25. If you use Excel, follow these steps to load Microsoft Press Posts and Post Topics queries into the Data Model:

   a. On the Power Query Editor's Home tab, select Close & Load to load the query to your report.

   b. On the Excel Data tab, select Queries & Connections.

   c. In the Queries & Connections pane, right-click the Microsoft Press Posts query and select Load To.

   d. When the Import Data dialog box opens, select Only Create Connection and then select Load This Data to the Data Model.

   e. In the Queries & Connections pane, right-click the Post Topics query and select Load To.

   f. When the Import Data dialog box opens, select Only Create Connection and then select Load This Data to the Data Model.

   g. In the Queries & Connections pane, right-click Keywords and select Load To.

   h. When the Import Data dialog box opens, select Only Create Connection and deselect Load This Data to the Data Model.

   i. On the Data tab, select Manage Data Model. When the Power Pivot window opens, on the Home tab, select Diagram View.

If you use Power BI Desktop, follow these steps to unload Keywords from the report:

   a. In the Queries pane of the Power Query Editor, right-click the Keywords query and deselect Enable Load.

   b. On the Home tab, select Close & Apply.

   c. Select the Relationships icon in the left pane of Power BI Desktop.

26. To create the relationship between the two tables, as shown in Figure 11-6, drag and drop the Post ID field from the Microsoft Press Posts table to Post ID in the Post Topics table.

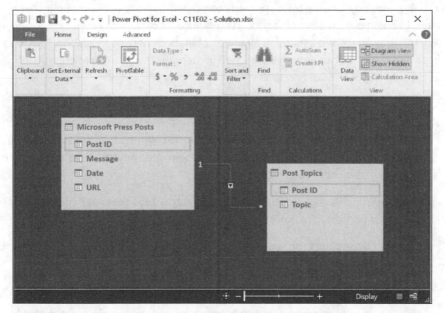

FIGURE 11-6 Create a relationship between Post ID in Microsoft Press Posts and Post ID in Post Topics.

You are ready to start the analysis (refer to Figure 11-4). Download the solution workbook C11E02 - Solution.xlsx or Power BI report C11E02 - Solution.pbix from https://aka.ms/DataPwrBIPivot/downloads and see how these connected tables in the Data Model can be used in a PivotChart and a slicer to determine how many Facebook posts are published by topic over time.

Save your report. An important performance improvement step needs to happen soon, but before we start looking at performance considerations, let's see what you have achieved so far. Of the first three caveats that were listed at the end of Exercise 11-1, the Cartesian product method addresses them as follows:

- You were able to load a **larger list** of keywords, without applying each one of them manually in the Add Conditional Column dialog box. Caveat #1 was addressed.

- You were able to **dynamically** load the list of keywords from an external file, without knowing in advance which keywords would be used. Caveat #2 was addressed, but your solution can be improved in terms of performance, so keep the Power Query Editor open so we can discuss the performance improvement in the next section.

- You were able to associate **multiple topics to single posts** in cases where a single message contains two or more keywords. Caveat #3 was addressed.

Part 4: Performance Improvement

Consider for a moment the performance of your solution. When you refresh the report, notice that the query loads relatively quickly. The Cartesian product combined with the filtering of matching rows is implemented in an efficient method that doesn't require a lot of memory consumption. When you created the Cartesian product and expanded all the combinations between Facebook posts and keywords, the expanded table was not entirely consumed in memory. Instead, the M engine performed the transformations on small portions of two tables.

This is an important and powerful capability of Power Query: Whenever possible, multiple transformation steps are applied on a small portion of the data and Power Query iterates over the dataset, chunk by chunk, until the entire dataset is transformed. This approach ensures that the M engine will not load the entire dataset in memory unless it is required. As a result, the Cartesian product doesn't leave a significant memory footprint.

Nevertheless, you can still significantly improve the performance of the Cartesian product by following these steps in your workbook or Power BI report from Exercise 11-2:

1. In the Power Query Editor, select the Post Topics query and select Added Custom in the Applied Steps pane. You get the following formula in the formula bar:

```
= Table.AddColumn(#"Renamed Columns", "Cartesian", each Keywords),
```

In this step, the M engine accesses the keywords for each row. Surprisingly, the way that M implements this step along with the expand step that follows leads to redundant loads of the keywords from the external text file.

To fix this step and enforce the M engine to load the Keywords table from the external text file only once, you can use the M function *Table.Buffer* on Keywords. By doing so, you explicitly instruct the M engine to store the entire Keywords table in memory and ensure that the M engine will not access the text file multiple times.

> **Tip** While *Table.Buffer* is extremely helpful in improving the load time in this exercise, you should not apply it every time you merge between two tables. For example, when you combine tables using Merge Queries or Append Queries, *Table.Buffer* is not helpful. However, it can help when you use custom columns whose computation requires access to a second data source.

Why is *Table.Buffer* useful when you load external sources in formulas of custom columns? Custom columns are designed to handle row-level calculations, without considering any efficiencies between each calculated cell. Moreover, by default, the M engine is designed to reduce the memory footprint, which results in the unload of the Keywords table while the custom column is being computed. *Table.Buffer* is used as a cue for the M engine to stop using its low memory consumption approach in this special case, which led to excessive I/O operations to load the Excel Keywords file.

2. To add *Table.Buffer*, select the Advanced Editor and add this row after the *let* line:

```
KeywordsBuffer = Table.Buffer(Keywords),
```

3. Next, change this line from this:

```
#"Added Custom" = Table.AddColumn(#"Renamed Columns", "Cartesian", each Keywords),
```

to the following:

```
#"Added Custom" = Table.AddColumn(#"Renamed Columns", "Cartesian", each
KeywordsBuffer),
```

When you load the query now, you may not notice the improvement in load time, as the dataset is relatively small. To compare the load time of the Post Topics query before and after the use of *Table.Buffer*, you can download the workbook C11E02 - Refresh Comparison.xlsx from https://aka.ms/DataPwrBIPivot/downloads.

In the C11E02 - Refresh Comparison.xlsx workbook, you can measure how quickly the query is loading with *Table.Buffer*. As shown in Figure 11-7, you can compare the load time of the Post Topics query (without *Table.Buffer*) and the Post Topics - Faster query (with *Table.Buffer*) and witness the improvement in load time in the second query.

4. To perform the comparison, open the workbook, select Queries & Connections on the Data tab, and then select Refresh All. Notice that Post Topics - Faster loads faster than Post Topics.

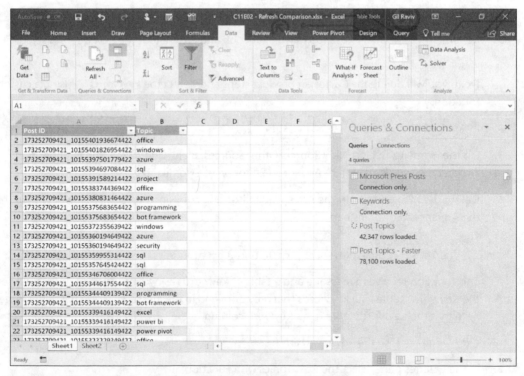

FIGURE 11-7 The Post Topics - Faster query loads faster using *Table.Buffer*.

> **Tip** To measure the improvement in refresh time, it is recommended that you test the query on datasets that are large enough. To artificially increase your dataset, you can multiply your table by using the M function *Table.Repeat*. In the C11E02 - Refresh Comparison.xlsx workbook, you can multiply Microsoft Press Posts 100 times by using the following function as the last step of the query:
>
> ```
> = Table.Repeat(#"Changed Type", 100)
> ```

In the next exercise you will learn an alternative method for detecting keywords: using a custom function.

Exercise 11-3: Detecting Keywords by Using a Custom Function

If you felt that the Cartesian product method is unintuitive and that there is probably another more direct approach to detect the list of keywords, you are right. There is another method. In this section you will learn how to apply a custom function instead of a Cartesian product. While this technique is more intuitive, you will see that it has a much slower load time than the Cartesian product solution. However, if you apply *Table.Buffer* to it, this method turns out to be the faster of the two methods.

1. Open the workbook C11E02 - Refresh Comparison.xlsx and open the Power Query Editor.

2. Right-click Post Topics in the Queries pane and select Duplicate.

3. Rename the new query *Post Topics with Function* and ensure that the new query is selected in the Queries pane.

    Next, you will delete the Cartesian product steps and detect the keywords by using a custom function.

4. In Applied Steps, delete the last five steps.

5. On the Home tab, select New Source, Other Sources, Blank Query. Rename the new query *FnDetectKeywords* and select Advanced Editor on the Home tab.

6. Delete the M expression in the Advanced Editor, and copy and paste the following function to the Advanced Editor instead:

    ```
    (Message, Keywords)=>
        Table.SelectRows(Keywords, each Text.Contains(Message, [Keyword]))
    ```

    This function receives a message and a table of keywords as two inputs and returns a subset of the Keywords table with keywords that are contained in the message. Note that it is assumed here that the Keywords table has a Keyword column.

    Click Done to close the Advanced Editor.

7. In the Queries pane select the Post Topics with Function query.

8. On the Add Column tab, select Custom Column. Enter *Keywords* in the New Column Name box and enter the following formula in the Custom Column Formula box:

```
= FnDetectKeywords([Lowercased], Keywords)
```

The new custom column will detect the keywords in each cell of the Lowercased column.

> **Note** As you found out in Exercise 11-2, adding a custom column can be time-consuming; in that example, the M engine kept reloading the keywords from their data source. To deal with this, you will apply *Table.Buffer* on *Keywords* at the end of this exercise.

9. Click OK to close the Custom Column dialog box, and then expand the Keywords column. (Don't use Keywords as a prefix for the new column name.)

10. You can see that the new Keyword column includes the detected topics. In rows without matching keywords, you see *null* values.

11. Click the filter control in the Keyword column header and select Remove Empty.

12. Remove the columns Message and Lowercased and rename the column Keyword to *Topic*.

13. To load the query to the report and compare the performance of the three queries in the workbook, select Refresh All on the Data tab while the Workbooks & Connections pane is open.

    Notice that the new query is the slowest. It is a bit slower than the Post Topics query where the Cartesian product was used without *Table.Buffer*. It's time to learn how *Table.Buffer* can improve the performance of this query.

14. Open the Power Query Editor and right-click Post Topics with Function in the Queries pane. Select Duplicate and rename the new query *Post Topics - Fastest*.

15. With Post Topics - Fastest selected, select Advanced Editor on the Home tab.

16. In the Advanced Editor, add this row after the *let* line:

```
KeywordsBuffer = Table.Buffer(Keywords),
```

17. Replace *Keywords* with *KeywordsBuffer* in this line:

```
#"Added Custom" = Table.AddColumn(#"Renamed Columns", "Keywords", each
FnDetectKeywords([Lowercased], Keywords)),
```

    Your modified line should look like this:

```
#"Added Custom" = Table.AddColumn(#"Renamed Columns", "Keywords", each
FnDetectKeywords([Lowercased], KeywordsBuffer)),
```

18. Load the query to the report and compare the time it takes to load the four queries in the workbook by selecting Refresh All on the Data tab.

As shown in Figure 11-8, the query Book Reviews - Fastest is faster than its Cartesian product sibling Book Reviews - Faster, which you created earlier. However, if you forget to apply the *Table.Buffer* improvement, the function technique is the slowest method, as shown for the Post Topics with Function query in Figure 11-8.

Why is the Book Reviews - Fastest query faster than the Cartesian product method when *Table.Buffer* is applied and slower without it? You can see that the reference to Keywords is implemented inside the function in step 6. The M engine, which was designed by default to minimize memory consumption, thinks that the Keywords data can be released after the function is executed to free unused memory. Thus, the Keywords table may keep reloading for each calculation of the cells in the new column. In the Cartesian product method, the Keywords table is referenced in the scope of the main query. As a result, the M engine does not load the Keywords table as often as it loads it when using the custom function.

When you apply *Table.Buffer*, the M engine "understands" that it needs to keep the Keywords table in memory. The Cartesian product method therefore becomes slower (even when *Table.Buffer* is used in the Cartesian product query). The Cartesian product method becomes slower because it is more expensive in terms of memory consumption and transformation steps. The engine needs to duplicate each row in the book reviews table by the number of rows in the Keywords table and then apply the relevant filter. These are extra steps that don't occur with the custom function in the Book Reviews - Fastest query, and they have a performance toll.

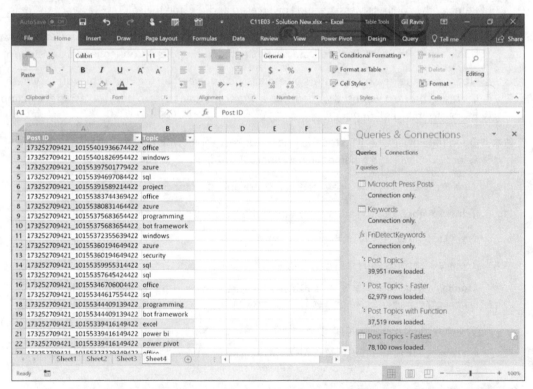

FIGURE 11-8 The Book Reviews - Fastest query using the custom function with *Table.Buffer* loads the fastest.

You can review the solution in the workbook C11E03 - Solution.xlsx, which is available from https://aka.ms/DataPwrBIPivot/downloads.

Which Method to Use: Static Search, Cartesian Product, or Custom Function?

In Exercises 11-1, 11-2, and 11-3 you have learned three methods to detect keywords. The first method involves applying a static short list of keywords as conditions in the Add Conditional Column dialog box. The second technique is to apply a Cartesian product to dynamically load a long list of keywords; you found out that the use of *Table.Buffer* can improve the load time of this query. Finally, the third technique involves using a custom function; you learned that this technique is the slowest, but it can become the fastest if *Table.Buffer* is applied.

In real-life challenges, you will most often use the first technique on short lists. For dynamic or long lists, if writing custom M functions is not your favorite practice, you can use the Cartesian product. If you feel comfortable with M, you can apply the custom function technique—but don't forget to use *Table.Buffer*.

> **Tip** The techniques to detect keywords in textual columns are also very effective for filtering text by keywords in the text. Recall that you created the Topic column in the preceding exercises, and then you filtered out empty values. Such techniques can be useful for filtering purposes.

Word Splits

Recall from Exercise 11-2 the fourth caveat: Words that are contained as substrings of longer words may be falsely detected. In this section, you will learn how to split textual columns into words to improve the detection of keywords. Word splits can also help you count word occurrences and visualize your data in word clouds.

To improve your keyword detection and gain new insights into your textual columns, you will learn in this section how to split textual columns into words and display the results in Excel PivotTables and Pivot Charts and in Power BI word clouds.

Exercise 11-4: Naïve Splitting of Words

In this exercise you will load Microsoft Press Facebook posts and split the messages into words. You will then learn how to ignore common words such as *the*, *and*, *in*, and *on*.

Part 1: Splitting Words with Spaces

In this section, you will start with the naïve approach to our challenge, and split words by spaces, and later on, you will move toward an improved solution in the proceeding sections.

1. Download the workbook C11E01.xslx from https://aka.ms/DataPwrBIPivot/downloads and save it to *C:\Data\C11*.

2. Open a blank new workbook or a new Power BI Desktop report.

In Excel: Open a new Excel workbook and on the Data tab, select Get Data, From File, From Workbook.

In Power BI Desktop: Open a new report and Select Get Data, Excel, Connect.

3. Select the file C11E01.xslx from *C:\Data\C11* and select Import.

4. In the Navigator dialog box, select Sheet1 and click Edit.

5. Rename the query *Microsoft Press Posts*.

    To create a reference to the Microsoft Press Posts query to build a new table of post IDs and words, in the Queries pane, right-click the Microsoft Press Posts query and select Reference.

6. Rename the new query *All Words*.

7. With All Words selected in the Queries pane, choose Select Columns on the Home tab. When the Choose Columns dialog box opens, select Post ID and Message and then click OK.

8. Right-click the Message column, select Split Column, and then select By Delimiter. Alternatively, on the Home tab, select Split Columns and then select By Delimiter.

    The Split Column By Delimiter dialog box opens. As you learned in Chapter 10, "From Pitfalls to Robust Queries," splitting the textual column into columns (which is the default option) does not scale well—especially since you have many words in the Message column.

9. Follow these steps in the Split Column By Delimiter dialog box to split the Message column into rows:

    a. Set Delimiter to Space.

    b. Expand Advanced Options.

    c. Select Rows.

    d. Click OK to close the dialog box.

10. Rename the new column *Word*.

A naïve user might think that this transformation solves the challenge, but many words contain trailing punctuation marks, which will lead to multiple variations of the same word. For example, you can find many instances of the word "excel" with a trailing comma, exclamation point, or colon. To effectively resolve this issue, you need to separate the words from their punctuation.

Part 2: Splitting Words from Punctuation

In this section, you will take a smarter approach to splitting words and will extend the split to any punctuation that is detected in the messages. Continue Exercise 11-4 with the following steps:

11. Create a blank query, name it *Punctuations*, and in the formula bar of the Power Query Editor, enter the following formula:

```
= {" ", "~", ",", ".", "?", "!", "(", ")", "[", "]", "{", "}", "@", "#", "$", "%",
"^", "&", "*", "-", "+", "=", ":", ";", "|", "<", ">", "/", """, "'", "\", """",
"#(tab)", "#(cr)", "#(lf)"}
```

This expression creates a list of punctuation marks as well as special characters to detect tabs, carriage returns, and line feed characters.

12. In the Queries pane, select the All Words query.

13. In the Applied Steps pane, select the step Split Column By Delimiter and examine the formula bar. As shown in Figure 11-9, the M expression is quite complex.

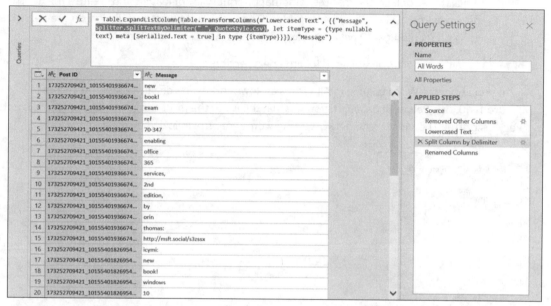

FIGURE 11-9 The step Split Column by Delimiter doesn't handle punctuation marks. To resolve this, you need to modify the formula.

In the formula bar, notice that there is a two-step formula that splits the Message column into List objects and then expands it. You really don't need to understand it entirely but can just focus on the important part, which is highlighted in Figure 11-9:

```
Splitter.SplitTextByDelimiter(" ", QuoteStyle.Csv)
```

Change the highlighted section to the following:

```
Splitter.SplitTextByAnyDelimiter(Punctuations, QuoteStyle.Csv)
```

Following this modification, you can apply the split on any delimiter defined in the Punctuations list. Isn't it cool?

> **Tip** If you need to split a column by multiple delimiters, you can use Split Column By Delimiter in the user interface to split by a single delimiter and then modify the M formula. Change *Splitter.SplitTextByDelimiter* to *Splitter.SplitTextBy**Any**Delimiter* and provide a list of textual values instead of a single delimiter. This technique can be used when you split a column into columns or into rows.

Thanks to the split by any of the punctuation marks, you now have many more rows with blank values. Next, you will filter them out.

14. Select the last step in Applied Steps and click the filter control of the Word column header. In the Filter pane, select Remove Empty.

15. Close the Power Query Editor and load the queries Microsoft Press Posts and All Words into the Data Model. Ensure that the Punctuations query is not loaded and create a relationship between Post ID fields in the two tables. (This is similar to what you did in Exercise 11-2 when you connected Post ID between Microsoft Press Posts and Post Topics.)

16. Save the report. You will need it in the next section.

If you apply the Word column in All Words as Rows and Values of a PivotTable, as shown in Figure 11-10, or a Power BI bar chart, you see that the list of the most commonly found words is not very insightful. The most commonly occurring words are *http*, followed by *the* and *and*.

Row Labels	Count of Word
http	601
the	475
and	465
msft	430
to	427
microsoft	379
on	313
it	288
of	269
for	266
Grand Total	**3913**

FIGURE 11-10 The most commonly occurring words in Microsoft Press posts are *http*, followed by *the* and *and*. This is not very surprising or insightful when you think of it.

Why is *http* the most commonly occurring word? Because the messages in Microsoft Press posts include many URLs, which start with the prefix *http://*. Wouldn't it be nice if you could avoid splitting such phrases and treat them as single words?

Part 3: Splitting Words by Spaces and Trimming Off Punctuation

In this section you will handle the punctuations differently. Instead of splitting the message by any of the punctuation marks, as you did in the preceding section, you will split the messages only by space, tab, carriage return, and line feed. Then, if you find punctuation marks at the beginning or the end of the words, you will trim them.

1. If you didn't save the workbook or report from Exercise 11-4 , follow steps 1–16 again.

2. Launch the Power Query Editor. In the Queries pane, right-click the All Words query and select Duplicate.

3. Rename to new query *All Words - Trim Punctuations*.

4. While the new query is selected, in Applied Steps, select Split Column by Delimiter.

5. In the formula bar, delete *Punctuations* in the following code section:

```
Splitter.SplitTextByAnyDelimiter(Punctuations, QuoteStyle.Csv)
```

Instead of *Punctuations*, enter the list *{" ", "#(tab)", "#(cr)", "#(lf)"}*, as follows:

```
Splitter.SplitTextByAnyDelimiter({" ", "#(tab)", "#(cr)", "#(lf)"}, QuoteStyle.Csv)
```

The messages are now split by spaces, tabs, carriage returns and new lines, so you can look for leading and trailing punctuation in the split values and trim them.

6. With the Split Column by Delimiter step still selected in the Applied Steps pane, select the Message column in the Preview pane, and on the Transform tab, select Format and then select Trim.

7. In the Insert Step dialog box, select Insert to add the new step. The trim step by default removes white spaces from the beginning and end of the text. But you can modify it to also trim the punctuation.

Notice the following formula in the formula bar:

```
= Table.TransformColumns(#"Split Column by Delimiter ",{{"Message", Text.Trim,
type text}})
```

Change *Text.Trim* to *each Text.Trim(_, Punctuations)*, as shown in this formula:

```
= Table.TransformColumns(#"Split Column by Delimiter ",{{"Message",
each Text.Trim(_, Punctuations), type text}})
```

Instead of using the default *Text.Trim*, you can explicitly define a new function that will call *Text.Trim* with other arguments. The term *each* creates the necessary function. Recall from Chapter 9, "Introduction to the Power Query M Formula Language," that the *each* keyword is used to create simple functions. The second argument in *Text.Trim* defines the list of characters or strings to trim. In this case you use the Punctuation list that was defined in the preceding exercise as that argument.

> **Note** To be more efficient here, because you already used the space, tab, carriage return and new line characters in the Split step, you can create a duplicate Punctuations list and remove these characters from the new list. Then you can use the new list as the second argument in *Text.Trim*.

Now, if you create a PivotTable from All Words - Trim Punctuations, you find, as shown in Figure 11-11, that *http* is no longer detected.

Option 2 = Split by Space, Trim by Punctuations	
Row Labels ⏷	Count of Word
and	461
for	260
microsoft	370
new	248
of	263
on	276
the	463
to	400
windows	238
with	239
Grand Total	**3218**

FIGURE 11-11 The list of the most commonly occurring words in Microsoft Press posts now does not include *http*.

You can now save the report. You will need it in the next exercise. You can review the solution files C11E04 - Solution.xlsx or C11E04 - Solution.pbix, which are available at https://aka.ms/DataPwrBIPivot/downloads.

Exercise 11-5: Filtering Out Stop Words

In Exercise 11-4, you learned how to split messages into words but ended up with a trivial outcome. It is not surprising that the most commonly occurring words are conjunctions, prepositions, and adjectives, as shown in Figure 11-11. Wouldn't it be useful if you could filter out those common words and have your report focus on the more important nouns, verbs, and adjectives in your messages?

To filter out the common words—or, as we will refer to them in this section, *stop words* (a term that is commonly used by computer science practitioners)—you can create a list of words in a separate text file, load them into the query, and filter them out. In this exercise you will learn how to do it.

1. Open your solution from Exercise 11-4, or open the downloaded workbook C11E04 - Solution. xlsx or Power BI report C11E04 - Solution.pbix.

2. Launch the Power Query Editor, and in the Queries pane, right-click the All Words - Trim Punctuations query and select Reference.

3. When a new query is created, name it *No Stop Words*.

4. Load the file Stop Words.txt from https://aka.ms/DataPwrBIPivot/downloads and save it in *C:\Data\C11*.

5. Import the file Stop Words.txt by selecting the New Source, File and Text/CSV option on the Home tab of the Power Query Editor.

6. Ensure that the new query will be named Stop Words and rename its column *Stop Word*. Notice in the Preview pane that all the stop words in the dataset are already lowercased. As a good practice, you should explicitly lowercase them now and avoid cases in the future when uppercase characters will be imported, and will be ignored as stop words due to the case sensitive logic that assumes all stop words are lowercase.

Select the Stop Word column and, on the Transform tab, select Format and then select Lowercase.

Next, you will filter out the stop words. In the query No Stop Words, the Word column already contains all the lowercased words in the messages. You will merge between the words and the stop words by using a left anti merge, which will filter out all the words in No Stop Words that appear in Stop Words.

7. Follow these steps to filter out the stop words:

    a. Select the No Stop Words query in the Queries pane.

    b. On the Home tab, select Merge Queries.

    c. When the Merge dialog box opens, in the No Stop Words table, click the Word column header and ensure that the Word column is now highlighted.

    d. In the drop-down menu below the No Stop Words table, select Stop Words.

    e. In the Stop Words table, click the Stop Word column header and ensure that it is highlighted.

    f. Set Join Kind to Left Anti (Rows Only In First), as shown in Figure 11-12, and click OK to close the dialog box.

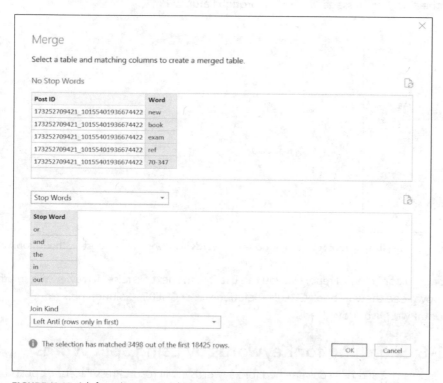

FIGURE 11-12 A left anti merge can be used to filter out stop words.

Following the merge step, the Stop Words column is added with the Table objects. If you click on the space of any of the Stop Words cells (not on the *Table* link, which drills down to a single step), you see that all tables contain null values. The null values are shown because of the Left Anti operation, which returns no rows from the second table of the merge. There is nothing to extract from the Stop Words query.

8. Remove the Stop Words column and load the report. Ensure that the Stop Words query is not loaded and that No Stop Words is loaded to the Data Model.

When you are finished with the preceding steps, you can apply the Word column in the No Stop Words table to a PivotTable and count word occurrences (refer to Figure 11-13). Some interesting insights may be revealed when the Stop Words are filtered out.

Here are two examples of such insights when you review the top 10 topics:

- One of the most common words is *2016*, which reflects the large number of major releases by Microsoft during 2016 (Office 2016, Excel 2016, Windows Server 2016, and so forth).

- Another common word is *50*, which is mentioned in many messages that promote books with a 50% discount. Did you know that on Saturdays you may get 50% discounts on Microsoft Press books? Based on the second most commonly occurring word, you can drill down to the data and find the common message "Save 50% through Saturday!"

No Stop Words

Row Labels	Count of Word
2016	147
50	169
book	155
ebook	128
exam	157
microsoft	370
new	248
saturday	134
save	221
windows	238
Grand Total	**1967**

FIGURE 11-13 The PivotTable lists the most commonly occurring words in Microsoft Press posts without stop words.

Save your workbook or Power BI report so you can use it in the next exercise. To review the solution of this exercise, download the workbook C11E05 - Solution.xlsx or C11E05 - Solution.pbix from https://aka.ms/DataPwrBIPivot/downloads.

Exercise 11-6: Searching for Keywords by Using Split Words

Recall that in Exercises 11-2 and 11-3 you searched for keywords in Microsoft Press Facebook posts by using the *contains* M operator. One of the caveats of using *contains* is that it could lead to false detection of words when the keyword is a substring of another word. For example, the keyword *excel* can be a substring of the word *excellent*. In this exercise, you will use the split words technique that was used in Exercise 11-5 to improve the accuracy of the keyword search.

Part 1: Using a Merge Queries Inner Join to Match Between Columns

You start this exercise with a very useful technique to filter a table by multiple values, using Merge Queries.

1. Open your workbook or Power BI report from Exercise 11-5 or download the workbook C11E05 - Solution.xlsx or C11E05 - Solution.pbix from https://aka.ms/DataPwrBIPivot/downloads and open it.

2. Launch the Power Query Editor. Select New Source on the Home tab and import Keywords.txt by selecting File, Text/CSV. (If you downloaded this file in Exercise 11-2, it should already be in *C:\Data\C11\Keywords.txt*.)

3. When the Keywords.txt dialog box opens, with a preview of the file, click OK to close the dialog box.

4. When the Keywords query is loaded, rename its column *Keyword*.

5. To lowercase all the keywords, select the Keyword column and then, on the Transform tab, select Format, Lowercase.

    Next, you will create a new query, Post Topics, from the No Stop Words query, which already includes the post IDs and their associated words.

6. In the Queries pane, right-click the No Stop Words query and select Reference. Rename the new query *Post Topics*.

7. To filter all the words that appear in Keywords, follow these steps:

    a. Select the Post Topics query in the Queries pane.

    b. On the Home tab, select Merge Queries.

    c. When the Merge dialog box opens, in the Post Topics table, click the Word column header and ensure that the Word column is now highlighted.

    d. In the drop-down below the Post Topics table, select the Keywords table.

    e. In the Keywords table, click the Keyword column header and ensure that it is highlighted.

    f. Set Inner (Only Matching Rows) as Join Kind and click OK to close the dialog box.

8. Rename the column Word to *Topic*.

9. To avoid situations in which the same keyword is mentioned multiple times in the same post, you can select the columns Post ID and Topic and then, on the Home tab, select Remove Rows and then select Remove Duplicates. Now each topic can be mentioned only once per post ID.

At this stage, you could finish the exercise. But here is a new challenge: Did you notice that some of your keywords in the Keywords.txt file include two-word keywords such as *power query*, *power bi*, and *power pivot*? Because you started this exercise with the split words, you will not able to detect those two-word keywords. Your messages are already split. In the next section you will learn how to resolve this situation.

Save your workbook or Power BI report. You will use it to detect the multi-word keywords in the next portion of this exercise.

Part 2: Detecting Multi-Word Keywords

To detect keywords such as *power query* and *power bi* in Microsoft Press posts in this exercise, you need to temporarily replace the separating space with another character, such as underscore, but only when you detect the two-word keywords in the Message column. Then you can apply the split by spaces, which will not affect the two-word keywords anymore. Once the messages are split into words, you will be able to transform the two-word keywords back to their space-separated form.

Figure 11-14 summarizes the solution at a high level. You will use a conversion table with Source and Destination columns, with the two-word keywords with space-separated values in Source and underscore-separated values in Destination. After the conversion table is built, you will replace all Source keywords with Destination keywords (step 1 in Figure 11-14), apply the split on the messages (step 2), and replace each underscore with a space (step 3).

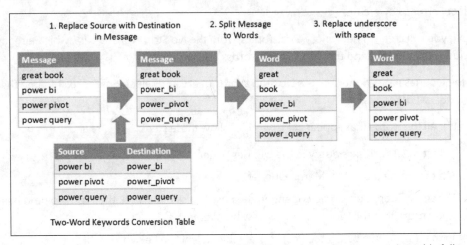

FIGURE 11-14 You can detect two-word keywords in split words by using a conversion table following this transformation sequence.

As shown in Figure 11-14, you start this solution by creating a conversion table. You can build this table as a reference from the Keywords query. Continue this exercise by following these steps:

10. With the Power Query Editor open, select the Keywords query in the Queries pane and then select Reference. Rename the new query *Conversion Table*.

11. To keep only the keywords that contain space in the Conversion Table query, follow these steps while the table is selected:

a. On the Transform tab, select Format and then select Trim. Even though the Keywords text file doesn't include leading or trailing spaces, it is a good practice to trim it before the next step.

b. Click on the filter control in the Keyword column header. In the Filter pane, select Text Filters, Contains.

c. When the Filter Rows dialog box opens, enter Space in the text box which is located to the right of the Contains drop-down menu and click OK to close the dialog box. You should now see in the Preview pane nine rows with two-word keywords.

12. Rename the column Keyword to *Source*.

13. To duplicate the Source column to a Destination column with the same values separated by underscores instead of spaces, follow these steps:

a. Select the Source column. On the Add Column tab, select Duplicate column.

b. Rename the column *Destination*.

c. With the Destination column selected, select Replace Values on the Home tab.

d. When the Replace Values dialog box opens, set the space ( ) character as Value to Find and set the underscore (_) as Replace With. Then click OK to close the dialog box.

The Conversion Table query is ready (refer to Figure 11-14), and it's time to learn how to use it. In the next steps, you will need to replace each Source value with its corresponding Destination value in each Message value before the Split step. Replacing a single value is easy in the Power Query Editor, but in this case, you have a sequence of Source/Destination pairs that you need to replace.

Unfortunately, the Power Query Editor doesn't have a user interface button to apply multiple replacements of strings. Moreover, the M function *Table.ReplaceValue* doesn't have a corresponding sibling *Table.ReplaceValues*. Instead, you can use an advanced technique that involves using the *List.Accumulate* function to perform the multiple text replacements of Source to Destination values.

Recall that *List.Accumulate*, which is examined in Chapter 9, receives a list as an input, an initial object, and an accumulator function. The accumulator function should have a state object and a current object (which is a member in the input list in the current iteration). It returns the state object after its transformation. Finally, *List.Accumulate* returns the accumulated result after the accumulator function has iterated over the list. Before you proceed, now is a good time to go back and review *List.Accumulate* in Chapter 9 to ensure that you understand the M expressions you are about to use. Even if you are not comfortable with M, you can still follow along, as you don't need to fully understand the explanations of the expressions.

Before you implement *List.Accumulate*, let's look at how you can convert the Conversion Table query into a list of Source/Destination pairs, which can be used as an input of *List.Accumulate*. Figure 11-15 illustrates how such a list can be created using the function *Table.ToRecords*, which was designed to return a list of records (one record per row in the original table).

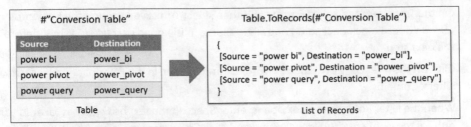

Source	Destination
power bi	power_bi
power pivot	power_pivot
power query	power_query

Table

```
{
[Source = "power bi", Destination = "power_bi"],
[Source = "power pivot", Destination = "power_pivot"],
[Source = "power query", Destination = "power_query"]
}
```

List of Records

FIGURE 11-15 The M function *Table.ToRecords* can transform the conversion table into a list of records.

Now that you know how to build the list of records, you're ready to learn which function can be used to implement the accumulation step for *List.Accumulate*. Basically, the function should receive the Facebook Post message and replace the current Source text with the corresponding Destination text. For example, *power bi* will be replaced with *power_bi*, which will allow you to avoid splitting the keyword *power bi* into two words later on.

Here is the accumulator function:

```
(message, conversionRecord) =>
    Text.Replace(
        message,
        conversionRecord[Source],
        conversionRecord[Destination]
    )
```

The purpose of this function is to use *Text.Replace* on the Facebook post message (the first argument) and replace *Source* (the second argument) with *Destination* (the third argument).

14. You now have all the pieces for the entire *List.Accumulate* formula:

```
List.Accumulate(
    Table.ToRecords(#"Conversion Table"),
    [Message],
    (message, conversionRecord) =>
        Text.Replace(
            message,
            conversionRecord[Source],
            conversionRecord[Destination]
        )
)
```

When this formula is used in a custom column, it goes over each row and modifies the value in the Message column by looking at all the Source keywords in Message and replacing them one by one with their corresponding Destination keywords.

The *List.Accumulate* formula in step 14 will be used inside the custom column function. It will run for each row in the Microsoft Press posts. For each row, it will iterate over the list of Source/Destination keyword pairs in the conversion table. The initial state (the second argument of *List.Accumulate*) is the value in Message column. The accumulator function (the third argument of *List.Accumulate*) contains the state and current arguments (named *message* and *conversionRecord*). The state argument contains the value in the current cell in the Message column. The current argument of the accumulator function is the current record of the Source/Destination pair. The accumulator function will replace in the message the current Source keyword with its Destination counterpart. In the next iteration of *List.Accumulate*, the next Source/Destination pair will be evaluated.

In the following steps, you will use the *List.Accumulate* expression to replace spaces with underscores for the keywords in the messages, and this will happen before the Split step.

15. With the Power Query Editor open, in the Queries pane select the All Words - Trim Punctuations query. This query performs the word split. In Applied Steps, select the step Lowercased Text, which is one step before Split Column By Delimiter.

16. With Lowercased Text selected in Applied Steps, select Custom Column on the Add Column tab. When the Insert Step dialog box opens, select Insert.

17. Make the following changes in the Custom Column dialog box that opens:

    a. Enter *Modified Message* in the New Column Name box.

    b. Copy and paste the *List.Accumulate* formula from step 14 to the Custom Column Formula box, and click OK to close the dialog box.

The new Modified Message column now contains the Facebook posts with the replaced values. To test that *List.Accumulate* worked, you can add a temporary step that filters the Message column if it contains *power query* and *power pivot*. When you do this, you find a row in the Preview pane that has the following text in the Message column:

```
"microsoft office 2016 step by step …
· solve business intelligence problems with power pivot and power query …"
```

If you look at the Modified Message column, you see that the message has changed to the following:

```
"microsoft office 2016 step by step …
· solve business intelligence problems with power_pivot and power_query …"
```

18. If you added the temporary filter, remove it now by deleting the Filter Rows1 step after the Added Custom step in Applied Steps.

19. Select the Added Custom column in Applied Steps, and delete the Message column. When the Insert Step dialog box opens again, select Insert.

20. Rename the Modified Message column to *Message*. When the Insert Step dialog box opens again, select Insert.

Now all the two-word keywords contain the underscore as a separator. They are protected from being split in the next transformation step that was already created in Applied Steps.

21. To move forward in the transformation steps and recover back the space character, in the Queries pane, select No Stop Words query, and in Applied Steps, select its last step. This is where you should fix the words and replace the underscore with the space character.

22. To remove underscores, you have two options. The first option is relatively easy: If you can assume that there are no important words with underscores, you can apply Replace Value on the Word column and replace the underscores with spaces.

The second option is more effective when your data contains words with underscores (not the keywords). To remove underscores from the underscored keywords only, follow these steps:

a. With the No Stop Words query selected, select Custom Column on the Add Column tab.

b. When the Custom Column dialog box opens, enter *Modified Word* in the New Column Name box.

c. Copy and paste the following code to the Custom Column Formula box:

```
List.Accumulate(
    Table.ToRecords(#"Conversion Table"),
    [Word],
    (word, conversionRecord) =>
        if word = conversionRecord[Destination] then
            conversionRecord[Source]
        else
            word
)
```

Click OK to close the Custom Column dialog box.

The formula above is a bit simpler than the *List.Accumulate* formula in step 14. It will be used inside the custom column function, so it will run for each row in the Microsoft Press posts. Like the *List.Accumulate* formula in step 14, it iterates over the list of records of Source/Destination keyword pairs. Its initial state (the second argument of *List.Accumulate*) is the value in the Word column. The accumulator function (the third argument of *List.Accumulate*) contains the state and current arguments (named *word* and *conversionRecord*). The state argument contains the value in the current cell in the Word column. The current argument of the accumulator function is the current record of the Source/Destination pair. The accumulator function compares between the current word and the word in the Destination column (the underscore-separated keyword). If they match, the value in Source is returned because you would like to revert the keyword back from Destination to Source. If the current word does not match Destination, you keep the original word. In the next iteration of *List.Accumulate*, the next Source/Destination pair is evaluated.

23. To test the formula, filter the Word column by *power_bi*, and you see that the new Modified Word column contains *power bi*. After you confirm that the preceding step was done properly, remove the filter step.

24. Remove the Word column and rename Modified Word to *Word*.

25. In the Queries pane, select the Post Topics query and click the filter control of the Topic column as a temporary step. You should now see in the Filter pane that all the two-word keywords have been found.

Finally, before you load the Post Topics query into your report, you can improve the load time by using *Table.Buffer* or *List.Buffer*. Recall that in steps 14 and 22, you added a custom column that accessed the conversion table. You learned in Exercises 11-2 and 11-3 that the M engine may access external sources multiple times when it references external queries inside a custom column. In the next steps, you will include *List.Buffer* to reduce load time and also to "fix" this issue.

26. With the All Words - Trim Punctuations query selected, select Advanced Editor on the Home tab.

    Insert the following new line before the line that starts with #*"Added Custom"*:

    ```
    BufferedList = List.Buffer(Table.ToRecords(#"Conversion Table")),
    ```

    In #*"Added Custom"* step, replace *Table.ToRecords(#"Conversion Table")* in the first argument of *List.Accumulate* with *BufferedList*. Here is the entire #*"Added Custom"* step after the modification:

    ```
    #"Added Custom" = Table.AddColumn(#"Lowercased Text", "Modified Message",
        each List.Accumulate(
            BufferedList,
            [Message],
            (message, conversionRecord) =>
                Text.Replace(
                    message,
                    conversionRecord[Source],
                    conversionRecord[Destination]
                )
        )
    ),
    ```

27. Click Done to close Advanced Editor.

28. With the No Stop Words query selected, select Advanced Editor on the Home tab.

    Insert the following new line before the line that starts with #*"Added Custom"*:

    ```
    BufferedList = List.Buffer(Table.ToRecords(#"Conversion Table")),
    ```

    In #*"Added Custom"* step, replace *Table.ToRecords(#"Conversion Table")* in the first argument of *List.Accumulate* with *BufferedList*. Here is the entire #*"Added Custom"* step after the modification:

    ```
    #"Added Custom" = Table.AddColumn(#"Removed Columns", "Modified Word",
        each List.Accumulate(
            BufferedList,
            [Word],
            (word, conversionRecord) =>
                if word = conversionRecord[Destination] then
                    conversionRecord[Source]
                else
                    word
        )
    ),
    ```

Now you can load the Post Topics query and build new visualizations that show which topics are published the most on the Microsoft Press Facebook page, as shown in Figure 11-16.

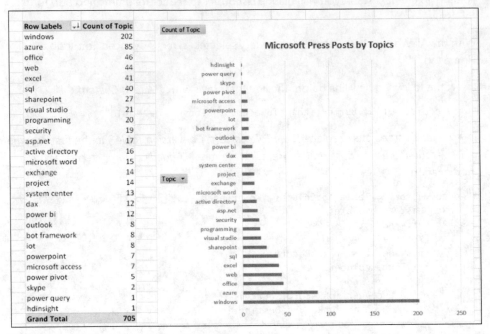

FIGURE 11-16 The solution workbook shows the number of Facebook posts by topic, in this case in a PivotTable and PivotChart in Excel.

You can review the solution files C11E06 - Solution.xlsx or C11E06 - Solution.pbix, which are available at https://aka.ms/DataPwrBIPivot/downloads.

Exercise 11-7: Creating Word Clouds in Power BI

As a finale for this chapter, it's time to see how Power BI can help you visualize textual columns in a word cloud. In the preceding section, you learned how to split and count words, as well as how to ignore stop words in a report. It turns out that for small datasets, you can load all the messages to a word cloud in Power BI without needing to split it into words.

This exercise walks through the customization of a word cloud custom visual and shows how to ignore stop words without the need to split the words. Following the steps below, you can create a word cloud like the one in Figure 11-17.

1. Open Power BI Desktop.

2. On the Home tab, in the Custom Visuals section, select From Marketplace.

3. When the Power BI Custom Visuals dialog box opens, type *Word Cloud* in the search box and click the search icon.

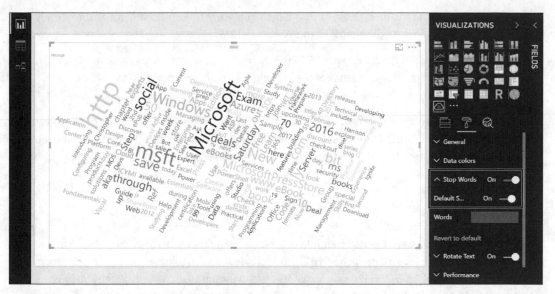

FIGURE 11-17 You can use a word cloud in Power BI to visualize words in messages. The Stop Words options breaks the messages into single words in the visualization level.

4. The Word Cloud custom visual appears in the search results. Select Add. When the visual is loaded into your Visualizations pane, click OK in the notification dialog box.

5. Open a blank new workbook or a new Power BI Desktop report.

   In Excel: Open a new Excel workbook and on the Data tab, select Get Data, From File, From Workbook.

   In Power BI Desktop: Open a new report and select Get Data, Excel, Connect.

6. Select the file C11E01.xslx from *C:\Data\C11* and select Import.

7. In the Navigator dialog box, select Facebook Posts and click Load.

8. Select the Word Cloud visual in the Visualizations pane. Drag and drop the Message field to Category. The Word Cloud visual is loaded.

9. Select the Word Cloud visual on the report canvas. In the Visualizations pane, select the Format icon. Turn on Stop Words and turn on Default Stop Words. You now see that Power BI removes the stop words quite effectively. To add to the list of stop words, you can type the relevant words in the Stop Words text box.

   If you try to load a large number of messages into the Word Cloud visual, the interaction of your report may slow down. To improve the performance of the report, you can use the Power Query Editor to split the words, as you learned to do in Exercises 11-4 and 11-5 and then feed the split words column into the Word Cloud visual. Another important reason to perform this type of split is to show the most common words in other visuals, such as a bar chart. These visuals don't include a built-in stop words implementation and will not automatically split large messages into single words, as the Word Cloud visual does.

You can review the Power BI report C11E07 - Solutions.pbix from https://aka.ms/DataPwrBIPivot/downloads, which combines several of the techniques you have learned in this chapter and provides analysis of the Microsoft Press Facebook posts by words and topics over time.

This report combines the main solutions you have learned in this chapter. With the powerful interaction between the visuals that are available in Power BI and the techniques in this chapter, you can now get a better view of the true essence of textual feeds.

Summary

In this chapter, you have learned multiple techniques to gain insights into textual feeds. Whereas you can use direct text manipulation to clean textual data such as dates, codes, or addresses, other techniques described in this chapter are better for analyzing text. In the chapter you have used a dataset of Microsoft Press Facebook posts to search for keywords and detect topics from text.

By using conditional columns in the Power Query Editor, you have learned how to detect limited numbers of keywords. The Cartesian product is a very effective method for dynamically detecting large numbers of keywords from an external list, and you have also learned how to create a custom function to search for keywords. To improve your reports' performance, you learned about the *Table.Buffer* and *List.Buffer functions* which reduce excessive calls to external data sources when you're using custom columns.

In this chapter, you have also learned how to split words and ignore stop words. You have learned useful techniques for filtering a table by keywords in an external source by using Merge Queries. To ignore stop words, you applied Merge Queries with an anti left join. This technique is handy for filtering out rows from an external list. To match between the split words and a list of keywords, you applied Merge Queries with an inner join, which is very useful for filtering your data from an external list of keywords.

In this chapter, you have also learned how to detect keywords with multiple words through temporary manipulation of messages by using *List.Accumulate* and a conversion table. Finally, in this chapter you have learned how to load textual feeds into Word Cloud visuals in Power BI.

You are just at the beginning of your text analytics journey. In Chapter 12 you will learn how to harness the power of artificial intelligence and learn how to perform advanced text analytics tasks on Azure, such as implementing text translation, sentiment analysis, and detection of phrases—with no help from data scientists or software developers.

CHAPTER 12

Advanced Text Analytics: Extracting Meaning

Everything in this world has a hidden meaning.

—*Nikos Kazantzakis*

IN THIS CHAPTER, YOU WILL

- Learn how to deploy Microsoft Azure Cognitive Services to harness the power of artificial intelligence in your analysis of textual feeds

- Learn how to translate messages in Excel and Power BI by using the Microsoft Translator Text API

- Detect sentiment in messages by using the Cognitive Services Text Analytics API

- Learn how to group messages into batches to reduce API calls

- Extract phrases from messages by using the Microsoft Text Analytics API

- Handle multilingual feeds, and extend your Text Analytics queries to detect languages

In Chapter 11, "Basic Text Analytics," you learned the fundamental steps to gain insights into textual feeds. You learned how to detect keywords in textual columns and learned how to split and count words to extract more meaning from the data. In this chapter, you will take a significant step further and learn how to translate text, apply sentiment analysis, extract key phrases, and harness the power of Microsoft's cloud-based Cognitive Services to do the magic. Using the Power Query Web connector and a few M functions, you will be able to truly extract meaning from text—without the help of data scientists or software developers.

Microsoft Azure Cognitive Services

Accomplishing a computer-based language translation or sentiment analysis task does not require that you master a lifetime of studies and practice in artificial intelligence or computer science. Not very long ago, if you wanted to implement such methods and apply them in your reports, you needed large teams of software developers and data scientists. Until very recently, due to the computational and implementation complexities, very few organizations or businesses had reporting solutions that could utilize the power of artificial intelligence to extract meaning from textual feeds.

Fortunately, in this new era, artificial intelligence has become a commodity. You can now utilize cloud-based services to understand language and extract meaning. Microsoft's Azure-based Cognitive Services allows you to integrate artificial intelligence in your business workflows. It offers services in five human cognition domains: vision, speech, language, knowledge, and search. With simple interfaces (web APIs), you can integrate some of these services into your reports in order to analyze your textual feeds.

> **See Also** Azure Cognitive Services is available at https://azure.microsoft.com/en-us/services/cognitive-services/.

In this chapter, you will learn how to create Excel and Power BI queries that can process textual feeds for language translation, sentiment analysis, and detection of key phrases. You will use two web APIs that are part of the language services in Azure Cognitive Services: the Text Analytics API and the Translator Text API, as shown in Figure 12-1.

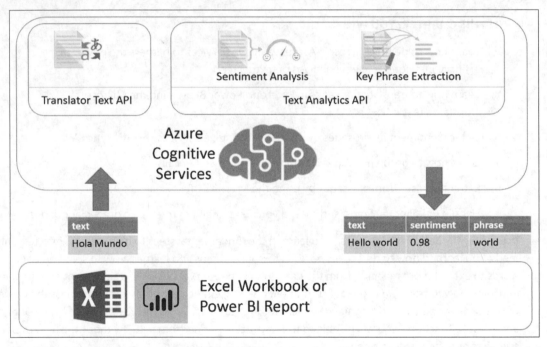

FIGURE 12-1 In this flow diagram of the Excel/Power BI solution, there is no server-side development. The magic is done by Azure Cognitive Services in a black box.

Typically, in advanced implementations of text analytics, you would have a complex architecture diagram, with a variety of components that specialize in specific elements in a complex set of tasks. Luckily, Microsoft has implemented all the complex stuff on Azure Cognitive Services. You can treat it as a magical black box. After you pass text to that black box, it returns the text translated to your desired language, a sentiment score or a list of extracted key phrases. Therefore, your architecture is quite basic: a single Excel workbook or Power BI report, in which all the data preparation and data movement is done by the Power Query engine, with the black box doing its magic to return the text enriched with meaning.

Figure 12-2 illustrates the three main steps in this solution: You implement a report that loads a textual column from an external data source, then it feeds the text to the Azure Cognitive Services Translator Text API or Text Analytics API, and finally the results return from Azure Cognitive Services to the report. It is important to note that these three steps are conducted in a single refresh operation. When you complete the query, each time you refresh the report, the three steps reoccur, providing the desired results.

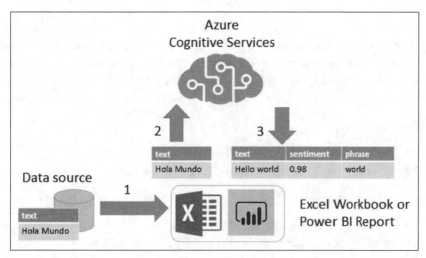

FIGURE 12-2 A single refresh takes three steps, from external data source to cognitive results.

Azure Cognitive Services is an example of Software as a Service (SaaS). This means you are not required to write any server-side code or worry about the availability of external servers or computers to do the job. All you need is to connect to your dataset, prepare it, upload to Azure Cognitive Services, and get the response and load it to your report—all in a single report and with a lot of help from Power Query. The interface between the report and Cognitive Services uses HTTP *POST* requests to upload the text to the services. This is all done with simple M functions that you will learn about later in the chapter.

To start using the Translator Text and Text Analytics APIs, you need to obtain two API keys, as described in the next section.

API Keys and Resources Deployment on Azure

Azure Cognitive Services is built as a cloud-based service that is simple to use via web APIs. Cognitive Services requires an account and a subscription on Azure, so you must deploy a relevant resource on Azure and obtain API keys that will enable you to call the service via web calls. This section explains how to deploy the services on the Azure portal and obtain these APIs.

> **Note** Cognitive Services is available for free without a time limit if you need to run a monthly report on small datasets. If this is the first time you have used Cognitive Services, you can try it for free.

Deploying the Translator Text API

Follow these steps to deploy the Microsoft Translator Text API on Azure and begin using it in your Excel workbook or Power BI report:

> **Note** Because Microsoft is constantly adding new features, the following instructions may not be fully accurate by the time you read this chapter. If that is the case, follow the instructions at www.microsoft.com/en-us/translator/trial.aspx#get-started.

1. Sign in to Azure:

   a. If you don't have an account, sign up at https://azure.microsoft.com.

   b. If you already have an account, sign in to https://portal.azure.com.

2. To subscribe to the Translator Text API, while signed in to Azure, go to https://portal.azure.com/#create/Microsoft.CognitiveServicesTextTranslation.

3. Follow these steps to create a resource on Azure for the Translator Text API:

   a. In the Name box, enter *Translation-Resource*.

   b. Select your Azure subscription.

   c. Select the pricing tier. You can use the free tier for textual feeds that are below 2 million characters. Read more about pricing at https://azure.microsoft.com/en-us/pricing/details/cognitive-services/translator-text-api/.

   d. Select a new resource group or select an existing one. Resource groups help you combine and manage multiple resources on Azure. If this is your first time using Azure, you can create a new resource group, and name it *Translation-Res-Group*.

   e. Read the notice and confirm that you have read it.

   f. Select Pin to Dashboard.

   g. Click Create.

4. Click Dashboard in the left pane of the Azure portal and select the Translation-Resource tile. In the Translation-Resource page that opens, click Keys in the left pane, under Resource Management.

5. As shown in Figure 12-3, you can now obtain a copy of KEY 1 or KEY 2 (which you will use later in this chapter, in Exercise 12-1). You do not need to save the key as an interim step outside the report. You can at any time log in to the Azure portal and repeat step 4 to access this page.

Note Ensure that the keys are not shared with anyone outside your team. You will learn about the security aspects of API keys in Power Query later in this chapter.

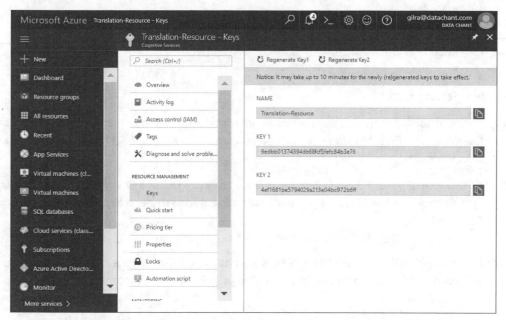

FIGURE 12-3 You can copy one of the keys in the Keys view of the Translator Text API resource page.

Now that you know how to deploy a Translator Text API resource on Azure and obtain its API key, you can do the same thing with the Text Analytics API, which is needed for sentiment analysis and extraction of key phrases.

Deploying the Text Analytics API

In this section you will learn how to deploy the Text Analytics resource on Azure and obtain the API key. Following these steps will enable you to apply sentiment analysis and key phrase extraction in your Excel workbook or Power BI report:

1. Sign in to Azure:

   a. If you don't have an account, sign up at https://azure.microsoft.com.

   b. If you already have an account, sign in to https://portal.azure.com.

2. To subscribe to the Text Analytics API, while signed in to Azure, go to https://portal.azure.com/#create/Microsoft.CognitiveServicesTextAnalytics.

3. Follow these steps to create a resource on Azure for the Text Analytics API:

   a. In the Name box, enter *Text-Analytics-Resource*.

   b. Select your Azure subscription.

c. Select the location for the resource.

   d. Select the pricing tier. You can use the free tier for textual feeds that are below 5,000 messages and 5,000 characters each. Read more about the pricing of Text Analytics at https://azure.microsoft.com/en-us/pricing/details/cognitive-services/text-analytics/.

   e. Set a new resource group or select an existing one. If this is the first time you are using Azure, you can create a new resource group and name it *Text-Analytics-Res-Group*.

   f. Read the notice and confirm that you have read it.

   g. Select Pin to Dashboard.

   h. Select Create.

4. Click Dashboard in the left pane of the Azure portal and select the *Text-Analytics-Resource* tile. When the *Text-Analytics-Resource* page opens, click Keys in the left pane, under Resource Management.

5. As shown in Figure 12-3, you can now obtain a copy of KEY 1 or KEY 2 (which you will use later in the chapter as the API for sentiment analysis in Exercise 12-2 and key phrase extraction in Exercise 12-4).

Note   As noted earlier, ensure that the keys are not shared with anyone outside your team. You will learn about the security aspects of API keys in Power Query later in this chapter.

Pros and Cons of Cognitive Services via Power Query

The techniques you will learn in this chapter to translate text, run sentiment analysis, and detect key phrases will be extremely useful. However, before you consider these implementations, you should be aware of the pros and cons of following this self-service approach.

As you will learn in this chapter, the integration between Excel and Cognitive Services requires a moderate knowledge of Power Query. However, you can easily follow this chapter's exercises, and then use what you have learned as a template in Excel or Power BI to address any textual feeds you may want to analyze.

The entire solution doesn't require any advanced data science, machine learning, or software development skills. Any Excel user who follows the steps in this chapter can implement Cognitive Services and immediately gain new insights. This means information workers can easily tap into textual feeds in their own analysis tools and can gain immeasurable business value.

Before you apply the techniques in this chapter, you should be aware of the caveats described in the following sections.

Excessive API Calls

Cognitive Services is a paid service. It is important you understand the limitations of Power Query when you use this service, or you will end up consuming excessive API calls and may be surprised with unplanned requirements to upgrade the pricing tier. To avoid excessive API calls, make sure you consider the following.

Small datasets: When using the Power Query Editor to build a query, work on small datasets. You can temporarily use the transformation step Keep Top Rows before calling Cognitive Services to reduce the dataset temporarily.

Data preview download in background: By default, perhaps without your awareness, Power Query loads data in the background to allow a seamless user experience when you select any transformation steps in the Power Query Editor Applied Steps pane or move between queries. This design enables you to quickly see the transformed data in the Preview pane. When working with paid or rate-limited web APIs such as Cognitive Services, you will quickly reach your API limits. To avoid the triggering of unnecessary and unplanned API calls, you can turn off the background data preview on a per-report basis.

In the Power Query Editor, on the File tab, select Options and Settings and then select Query Options. Select Data Load under Current Workbook in Excel, or Current File in Power BI Desktop and disable Allow Data Preview to Download in the Background (see Figure 12-4). Disabling this feature is required in each workbook or Power BI report in which you integrate with Cognitive Services. If this feature is not disabled, Power Query will keep loading data previews in the background and will spend unnecessary API calls to Cognitive Services.

FIGURE 12-4 In the Query Options dialog box, don't allow data preview to download in the background.

Even after you turn off this option, be aware that each time you open the Power Query Editor and navigate to certain queries, a series of API calls to Cognitive Services will be triggered to provide you the latest results in the Preview pane.

Lack of incremental refresh: While in Power BI Premium you can implement an incremental refresh, which will prevent excessive API calls. Excel and Power BI (not Premium) don't have such a mechanism for incremental refresh. Each time a report is refreshed, the query loads the entire dataset, and it does not store any interim results from the previous refresh. As a result, if you often need to refresh a report that integrates with Cognitive Services, you will send large portions of the same dataset again and again—which is not an efficient way to keep the rate of API calls low.

To solve this limitation, you can implement the queries that are described in this chapter on multiple Excel files. Each file will load only an increment of the data to Cognitive Services, based on a predefined period, and it will store the results in a worksheet. Then, using the Folder connector, as described in Chapter 3, "Combining Data from Multiple Sources," you can append all the increments into a single report, thus using only the necessary amount of API calls.

Privacy and Security

Ensure that your corporate policies allow you to use Cognitive Services. While Azure is probably the most secure cloud platform, your company may prohibit you from using it on confidential datasets. If you are not sure if you can use Cognitive Services, contact your IT department for guidance.

If you need to share a report with other report authors outside your team, remember to remove the API keys before you send the report to them. You will later learn more about it in this chapter.

Unsupported Scheduled Refresh

The techniques in this chapter can be refreshed only using Excel or Power BI Desktop. If you try to apply a scheduled refresh on a dataset on the Power BI service, you will end up getting refresh errors. While you can develop a custom connector that can support scheduled refresh through the On-premises Data Gateway, this approach requires advanced development skills, which are beyond our scope in this book.

> **Tip** Given the limitations just discussed, it is recommended that you apply the techniques in this chapter in ad hoc analysis scenarios, on small datasets, or as proofs of concept for larger implementations outside Excel and Power BI.

Text Translation

Translating your textual data in Excel or Power BI using Power Query can be a very useful way to automate gaining insights about multilingual data. In this section, you will learn how to use Power Query to automate the translation of textual columns by interfacing with the Cognitive Services Translator Text API. You may be used to the routine of manually copying and pasting text from your datasets to your favorite web translator to try to decipher multilingual data. The technique that you will learn in this section will enable you to automate this process to gain visibility into untapped textual feeds, as illustrated in Figure 12-5.

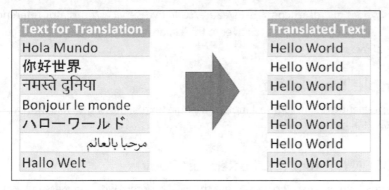

FIGURE 12-5 You can automate the translation of bulk messages in Excel or Power BI.

The Translator Text API Reference

While the Translator Text API reference is rich, with a wide variety of capabilities, this chapter focuses on the most basic method for translating a single message. This method is the *Translate* call of version 3.0 of the API (currently the latest version). For the full list of the API calls, see https://docs.microsoft.com/en-us/azure/cognitive-services/translator/reference/v3-0-reference.

The *Translate* call translates a string from one language to another. The request is passed as a web request with the request URI *https://api.cognitive.microsofttranslator.com/translate*, followed by the API version number as a value of the *api-version* parameter and a two-digit language code as a value of the *to* parameter for the target language you want to translate to. Here is an example for a request URI that translates text to English, using the current 3.0 API version:

```
https://api.cognitive.microsofttranslator.com/translate?api-version=3.0&to=en
```

If you wish to translate the text to a specific language, you can find which languages are supported at https://docs.microsoft.com/en-us/azure/cognitive-services/translator/languages and apply the two-digit code as a value for the *to* parameter. For example, the following URI translates *Hola Mundo* to Dutch:

```
https://api.cognitive.microsofttranslator.com/translate?api-version=3.0&to=nl
```

To get the translation result, you need to be authorized by the service, and you get authorized by passing the API key in the call. In Exercise 12-1 you will learn how to pass the API key in the header *Ocp-Apim-Subscription-Key*. You will also pass the relevant text that you wish to translate. In version 3.0 of the API, the text should be sent in a JSON format in the body of the request:

```
[
    {"Text":"Hola Mundo"}
]
```

Inside this JSON array, you can pass up to 25 textual messages of 1,000 characters each (including spaces) and up to a total of 5,000 characters (including spaces) for the entire block of messages. To break long messages into small pieces that the API can accept, you can use the *BreakSentence* API call, which is explained at https://docs.microsoft.com/en-us/azure/cognitive-services/translator/reference/v3-0-break-sentence. We have many techniques to cover in this chapter, so in Exercise 12-1 we focus on passing only a single textual message.

Exercise 12-1: Simple Translation

In this exercise you will implement the simple translation of a single textual message, *Hola Mundo*, by using Translator Text API version 3.0.

Part 1: Building the JSON Content for the Request Body

In the first part of the exercise, you will learn how to create the JSON content with the message you wish to translate, as needed in the request body of the Translate API call.

1. Open a blank Excel workbook or a new Power BI Report:

    In Excel: On the Data tab, in the Get & Transform Data section, select From Other Sources and then select Blank Query.

    In Power BI Desktop: Expand the Get Data drop-down and select Blank Query.

2. In the formula bar, enter the following formula to make a record of the text for translation:

    ```
    = [Text = "Hola Mundo"]
    ```

    This M formula, when translated to JSON, will be converted to the following format:

    ```
    {"Text" = "Hola Mundo"}
    ```

    Convert the record into JSON by wrapping what's in the formula bar with the *Json.FromValue* function:

    ```
    = Json.FromValue([Text = "Hola Mundo"])
    ```

3. In the Preview pane you now see a CSV icon. Right-click that icon and select Text. You can now see that the first row in the new table contains the desired format:

    ```
    {"Text" = "Hola Mundo"}
    ```

4. It's time to create the entire JSON block, including the wrapping brackets. In Applied Steps, select the Source step. Now, in the formula bar, modify the formula by wrapping the record in curly brackets, as follows:

    ```
    = Json.FromValue( { [Text = "Hola Mundo"] } )
    ```

    By adding the curly brackets, you have entered the M record into a list. Now select the last step in Applied Steps, Imported Text, to see how the modification will impact the JSON format. The first row in the table will have exactly the same format that you need for the JSON content:

    ```
    [{"Text":"Hola Mundo"}]
    ```

5. Now that you know how to craft the JSON content with the translated text, delete Query1. You will soon use the last *Json.FromValue* as the request body of another M expression.

Tip M and JSON have opposite definitions for records and lists. In M, brackets are used to define a record. In JSON, brackets define a list. In M, curly brackets are used to define a list, and in JSON they are used to define a record. This knowledge will help you craft the relevant JSON formats in M as you work on many web APIs.

Part 2: Building the API Key Parameter

It's time to create a parameter for the API key, which will serve you later inside the API call. Continue Exercise 12-1 with the following steps:

6. Log in to the Azure portal and repeat steps 4–5 from the section, "Deploying the Translator Text API," and copy one of the two API keys of the Translator Text API.

7. To create a parameter for the Translator Text API key that you copied in step 6, follow these steps:

   a. On the Home tab of the Power Query Editor, expand the Manage Parameters drop-down and select New Parameter.

   b. When the Parameters dialog box opens, in the Name box, enter *APIKey*; then, in the Current Value box, paste the API key from step 6, as demonstrated in Figure 12-6. Then click OK to close the dialog box.

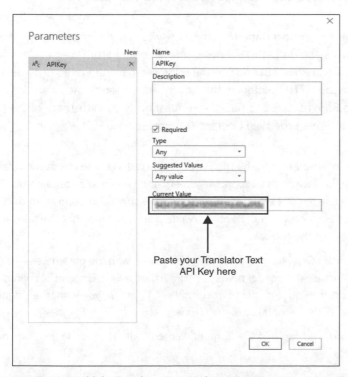

FIGURE 12-6 Add the Translator Text API key as a parameter.

Part 3: Creating the Web Request

In this portion of the exercise, you will create the main web request call and retrieve the translated message from the response. Follow these steps to continue Exercise 12-1:

8. Create a new blank query and rename the query *Translated Message*.

9. With the Translated Message query selected in the Queries pane, select Advanced Editor on the Home tab, and enter the following M expression:

```
let
    Source = Web.Contents(
        "https://api.cognitive.microsofttranslator.com/" &
        "translate?api-version=3.0&to=en",
        [
            Headers = [
                #"Ocp-Apim-Subscription-Key" = APIKey,
                #"Content-Type" = "application/json"
            ],
            Content = Json.FromValue({[Text = "Hola Mundo"]})
        ]
    )
in
    Source
```

Let's look closely at this expression. The main function that is used here is *Web.Contents*, which can also be created when you select the Web connector through Get Data.

> **Note**   Typically, when you want to import data from the web, you are not required to write the M expression from scratch, as you do in this exercise. You can select From Web in Get Data in Excel, or Web in Get Data in Power BI and use the From Web dialog box to provide the URL. You can even provide the HTTP headers in the Advanced section of the From Web dialog box. However, when you are required to pass the request body, as in the case of the Translator Text API, you need to create the *Web.Contents* M expression.

Web.Contents contains two main elements: the URL, which is passed as the first argument, and the *Options* argument, which is passed as a second argument and is used as a container for all the other elements you can use to craft a web request, such as *Headers* and *Content*. In the M expression, you can see that *Headers* is a record of key/value pairs. Each includes the relevant HTTP header that is required for the API call.

The *Headers* record includes the *Ocp-Apim-Subscription-Key* header with the parameter *APIKey* that you created in step 7. Because the header name contains a dash, which is a special character in M, you must wrap it as a double-quoted identifier, using #"...". *Content-Type* is another required header, and it is represented as the second key in the *Headers* record.

Following the *Headers* record, you can find the *Content* element, with the *Json.Value* that you created in step 4.

Note that you can also create *Web.Contents* by using more options, including *RelativePath* and *Query*, and you can move more elements from the URL into the *Options* argument. Here is the relevant M expression, with the new elements in bold. You can see in this new expression that the URL contains only the domain name:

```
let
    Source = Web.Contents(
        "https://api.cognitive.microsofttranslator.com",
        [
            RelativePath = "translate",
            Query = [
                #"api-version" = "3.0",
                to = "en"
            ],
            Headers = [
                #"Ocp-Apim-Subscription-Key" = APIKey,
                #"Content-Type" = "application/json"
            ],
            Content = Json.FromValue({[Text = "Hola Mundo"]})
        ]
    )
in
    Source
```

> **Tip** There are several advantages to using *RelativePath* and *Query* in *Web.Contents*. The *RelativePath* field in many cases improves the chances that your advanced queries will support schedule refresh on the Power BI service. The use of *Query* enables the M engine to automatically apply URI encoding on the query values and avoid unexpected handling of the text by the service.

10. Copy and paste the new expression and click Done to close the Advanced Editor.

11. When a notification bar appears in the Preview pane, select Edit Credentials. The Web Access dialog box opens. Ensure that Anonymous is selected, and click Connect.

12. In the Preview pane, look for the JSON icon with the text *api.cognitive.microsofttranslator.com*. Right-click this icon and select JSON. The JSON response includes a list with a single record.

13. Because you passed only a single message, select the record by clicking the hyperlink.

    In the Preview pane you now see a record of *detectedLanguages* and a list of *Translations*. If you click on the white space of the *detectedLanguages* cell, you can see the result record, with *language=es* and *score=1*. This means the service identified the source language as Spanish, with 100% certainty. Because your focus is to get the translated text in English, you can ignore this record and drill down to the translated text.

14. Click the *List* hyperlink in the *translations* field.

15. In the Preview pane, which now shows a list with a single record, click the *Record* hyperlink. You now see a new record with *text* and *to* fields. The translated text is located as the value of *text*.

16.   Right-click the cell with the value *Hello World* and select Drill Down from the shortcut menu.

17.   Load the Translated Message query into your workbook or Power BI report, and save it.

You can download the solution files C12E01 - Solution.xlsx and C12E01 - Solution.pbix from https://aka.ms/DataPwrBIPivot/downloads.

Sharing the Report Without the API Key

If you need to share the workbook or Power BI report that you created in Exercise 12-1 with others, you should note that the API key is stored in a non-secure manner. Any user who can open this report in Excel or Power BI Desktop will be able to get the API key. Chapter 8, "Addressing Collaboration Challenges," covers several methods of sharing workbooks and Power BI reports with others. Obfuscating the API key before you share the report is a minimal change you should make to avoid exposing the API key to others.

Follow these steps to remove the API key before you share the workbook or report:

1.   Open the workbook you prepared in Exercise 12-1 and launch the Power Query Editor. (If you didn't save the workbook, you can download C12E01 - Solution.xlsx or C12E01 - Solution.pbix from https://aka.ms/DataPwrBIPivot/downloads.)

2.   Select the APIKey parameter.

3.   Replace the API key in the Current Value box with the following text:

"paste your key here"

4.   When you share the report, instruct your colleagues to follow steps 1 and 2 and replace the text *"paste your key here"* with their API key. Then they can refresh the report.

In Power BI Desktop, you can now go one step further and improve the user experience by creating a Power BI template, as discussed in Chapter 8. When you create a template, users can enter their keys before they load the report. You will see how to implement this after the next exercise. But before you do, you will learn how to handle multiple API calls.

Exercise 12-2: Translating Multiple Messages

In this exercise, you will convert the Translate query into a function so that you can reuse it on multiple messages. Recall that while the Translator Text API allows you to send 25 messages in a single API call, this approach is not sufficient for sending massive numbers of messages. In this exercise you will learn how to send large numbers of messages, but to keep the implementation simple, you will still send only one message per API call.

1.   Open your saved workbook or Power BI report from Exercise 12-1. If you didn't save the report, download one of the solution files C12E01 - Solution.xlsx or C12E01 - Solution.pbix from https://aka.ms/DataPwrBIPivot/downloads and open it.

2.   Launch the Power Query Editor.

3.   Follow these steps to create query parameters that will be used later instead of the hardcoded URL parameters *text* and *to* that were used in Exercise 12-1:

Handling the *text* parameter in the request body:

a. On the Home tab, expand the Manage Parameters drop-down and select New Parameter.

b. When the Parameters dialog box opens, in the Name box, enter *InputText*; and then, in the Current Value box, enter *Hola Mundo*. Then click OK.

Handling the *to* parameter:

c. Repeat step 3a, and then, in the Name box, enter *TranslateToLanguage*.

d. In the Current Value box, enter *en*. Then click OK.

4. In the Queries pane, select the Translated Message query and then select Advanced Editor.

Next, you will modify the M formula and replace the hardcoded values with the new parameters from step 3. Here is part of the expression you will find in the Advanced Editor. In bold are the hardcoded values *"en"* and *"Hola Mundo"* that need to be replaced (Note that the expression here is indented differently, to make the formula more readable)

```
= Json.Document(
    Web.Contents(
        "https://api.cognitive.microsofttranslator.com", [
            RelativePath = "translate",
            Query = [
                #"api-version" = "3.0",
                to = "en"
            ],
            Headers = [
                #"Ocp-Apim-Subscription-Key" = APIKey,
                #"Content-Type" = "application/json"
            ],
            Content = Json.FromValue({[Text = "Hola Mundo"]})
        ]
    )
)
```

5. Replace the text *"Hola Mundo"* with *InputText* and the text *"en"* with *TranslateToLanguage*. Here is the modified formula:

```
= Json.Document(
    Web.Contents(
        "https://api.cognitive.microsofttranslator.com", [
            RelativePath = "translate",
            Query = [
                #"api-version" = "3.0",
                to = TranslateToLanguage
            ],
            Headers = [
                #"Ocp-Apim-Subscription-Key" = APIKey,
                #"Content-Type" = "application/json"
            ],
            Content = Json.FromValue({[Text = InputText]})
        ]
    )
)
```

6. Select the last step in Applied Steps and ensure in the Preview pane that you still get the translated *Hello World* text. This will help you verify that the changes you have made are correct.

7. You are now ready to convert the Translated Message query into a custom function.

    a. In the Queries pane, right-click the Translated Message query and select Create Function.

    b. When the Create Function dialog box opens, in the Function Name box, enter *FnTranslate*, and then click OK to close the dialog box.

8. Load a table with multiple messages, as shown in Figure 12-5, and translate them to English by following these steps:

    a. While the Power Query Editor is still open, download the workbook C12E02.xlsx from https://aka.ms/DataPwrBIPivot/downloads and save it in *C:\Data\C12*.

    b. On the Power Query Editor Home tab, select New Source, File, Excel.

    c. When the Import Data dialog box opens, navigate to *C:\Data\C12* and select C12E02.xlsx.

    d. When the Navigator dialog box opens, select the table TextForTranslation and click OK.

9. In the Power Query Editor, rename the new query *Translated Messages*.

10. While the Translated Messages query is selected in the Queries pane, select Invoke Custom Function on the Add Column tab.

11. When the Invoke Custom Function dialog box opens, set Function Query to *FnTranslate*.

12. Notice that the Text for Translation column was incorrectly populated as APIKey. Unfortunately, you cannot assign parameters as function arguments via the Invoke Custom Function dialog box. For now, keep Text for Translation as APIKey, and you can fix it shortly.

13. Select Column Name in the InputText drop-down. Notice that Text for Translation is populated in the drop-down menu to the right.

14. At the bottom of the Invoke Custom Function dialog box, enter *en* in the text box below TranslateToLanguage. Click OK to close the dialog box.

15. Rename the FnTranslate column *Translated Text*.

16. In the formula bar, you will see the formula

    ```
    = Table.AddColumn(#"Changed Type", "FnTranslate", each FnTranslate(
    [Text for Translation], [Text for Translation], "en"))
    ```

    Change it to the following formula by replacing the first instance of *[Text for Translation]* with the *APIKey* parameter, as shown here:

    ```
    = Table.AddColumn(#"Changed Type", "FnTranslate", each FnTranslate(APIKey,
    [Text for Translation], "en"))
    ```

Depending on your privacy settings in the Query Options dialog box, you will most likely encounter the following notification warning in the Preview pane of the Power Query Editor:

`Information is required about data privacy.`

17. Click Continue. The Privacy Levels dialog box opens. Here you can set the privacy levels of your data sources. To ensure that you don't upload confidential data to untrusted sources, you can set the privacy levels for the file C12E02.xlsx and Cognitive Services as shown in Figure 12-7:

   a. Select *c:* in the first drop-down menu and set the privacy level to Organizational.

   b. Set the privacy level of https://api.cognitive.microsofttranslator.com as Organizational.

   c. Click Save.

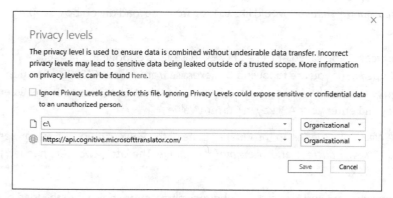

FIGURE 12-7 Set privacy levels to allow Power Query to pass the messages for translation.

> **Tip**   If you accidentally set the privacy levels for your data sources to different levels, such as Public and Organizational, the query will not work. In such cases, whenever you wish to clear the privacy levels, you can select Data Source Settings on the Power Query Editor Home tab and clear the permissions of the two data sources.

You can now see the translated text in the Preview pane of the Power Query Editor. All your messages were translated to English. Hello World! You can now close and load the query. If you use Power BI Desktop, save your report. In the next section you will learn how to share it without exposing the API key.

Sharing a Report Without an API Key: The User-Friendly Way

If you followed Exercise 12-2 in Power BI Desktop, in this section you learn how to export your report into a Power BI template, which you can share with other report authors without the API key. If you didn't follow Exercise 12-2, you can start from the solution file C12E02 - Solution.pbix, which is available for download from https://aka.ms/DataPwrBIPivot/downloads.

Note If you are only interested in the solution in Excel, you can skip to the end of this section and download the solution workbook for Excel, which incorporates the techniques you learned in Chapter 8 and loads the API key from the worksheet. You can then instruct others to provide their API key in the relevant cell. In addition, this solution resolves the firewall errors explained in Chapter 8.

You can improve your solution in the Power BI report by creating a template to ensure that your API key is not shared with others while maintaining a user-friendly experience for those who will get the report. Recall that in Chapter 8 you already learned how to create a Power BI template (.pbit file). We describe it again in this section because the current report is a special case: It has two parameters, *InputText* and *TranslateToLangauge*, that you would like to hide from the load dialog box, keeping only *APIKey* as the sole parameter.

1. Open the Power BI report you saved at the end of Exercise 12-2, or download C12E02 - Solution.pbix and open it. (If you are following this exercise from a fresh C12E02 - Solution. pbix, you will need to update the APIKey. On the Home tab, select Edit Queries. In the Queries pane, select APIKey and enter your API key in Current Value.)

   On the Home tab select Edit Queries. In the Queries pane of the Power Query Editor, you see three parameters: APIKey, *InputText*, and *TranslateToLanguage*. The latter two were needed for the custom function in Exercise 12-2.

2. To avoid having the *InputText* and *TranslateToLanguage* parameters show up in the load dialog box when the template will be opened, convert them into queries:

   a. In the Queries pane, right-click InputText and select Convert to Query.
   b. Right-click TranslateToLanguage and select Convert to Query.

3. On the Home tab, select Close & Apply. Back in the Power BI main window, on the File tab, select Export and then select Power BI Template.

4. In the Export a Template dialog box, write brief instructions for your colleagues and click OK.

5. Select a name for the template and save it.

You can download the solution files C12E02 - Solution.pbit from https://aka.ms/DataPwrBIPivot/ downloads. An alternative solution using Excel is provided in C12E02 - Solution.xlsx.

If you share your report with other report authors, Figure 12-8 illustrates the user experience they will have when they open the solution template in Power BI or the solution workbook in Excel.

Tip To revoke an API key, you can go to the Keys view of your Translator Text Resource on the Azure portal and select Regenerate Key1 or Regenerate Key2.

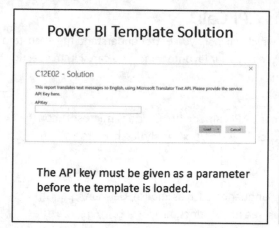

Power BI Template Solution

C12E02 - Solution   ×

This report translates text messages to English, using Microsoft Translator Text API. Please provide the service
API Key here.

APIKey

[   ]

                                        Load ▼ Cancel

The API key must be given as a parameter
before the template is loaded.

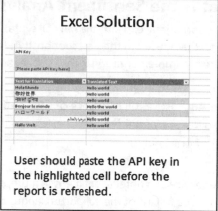

Excel Solution

API Key

[Please paste API key here]

Text for Translation	▼	Translated Text	▼
Hola Mundo		Hello world
你好世界		Hello world
세계 여보		Hello world
Bonjour le monde		Hello the world
ハローワールド		Hello world
مرحبا بالعالم		Hello world
Hallo Welt		Hello world

User should paste the API key in
the highlighted cell before the
report is refreshed.

FIGURE 12-8 You can share your text translated Power BI report (using a template) and Excel workbook (using a named range), without revealing the API key.

Sentiment Analysis

A fundamental element in the success of any business or organization is a repetitive process of feedback collection, analysis, and improvement. You may already receive feedback from your clients in many formats, but the textual format is the most challenging one. How can you quantify qualitative data such as textual user feedback? How can you determine the overall user sentiment about a specific product or brand? Can you measure it over time? Wouldn't you want to have an automated way to extract sentiment scores from your textual feeds?

In this section you will learn how to process textual feeds and gain a sentiment score for each message. You will learn how to use Power Query to automate the sentiment analysis workload by interfacing with the Cognitive Services Text Analytics API. As shown in Figure 12-9, in the end result, each message will receive a score between 0 to 1, where 0 implies that a message contains a negative sentiment, and 1 implies that it contains a positive sentiment.

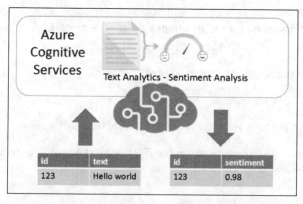

FIGURE 12-9 You can use the Sentiment Analysis API to upload text messages and return a sentiment score between 0 (negative sentiment) and 1 (positive sentiment).

What Is the Sentiment Analysis API Call?

This section briefly explains the API call syntax, which will help you better understand the M custom function that is used in the next section. If APIs are not your favorite thing, you can skip this section and move to the implementation in the next section.

> **See Also** For a full reference of the Sentiment API call, see https://docs.microsoft.com/en-us/azure/cognitive-services/text-analytics/how-tos/text-analytics-how-to-sentiment-analysis.

The service can detect sentiment in multiple languages, such as English, German, Spanish, and French. For a full list of the supported languages, see https://docs.microsoft.com/en-us/azure/cognitive-services/text-analytics/text-analytics-supported-languages.

The request is passed as a web *POST* request, with the following request URI, which is also referred to as *Endpoint*:

```
https://[location].api.cognitive.microsoft.com/text/analytics/v2.0/sentiment
```

To find the specific *[location]* value that is required for your *Endpoint*, you can access your Text Analytics resource on the Azure portal and find it in the Overview pane, under Endpoint. For example, if your location is *West US*, this is your *Endpoint*:

```
https://westus.api.cognitive.microsoft.com/text/analytics/v2.0/sentiment
```

Preparing Your Data

Before you send your textual feed to the Sentiment Analysis service, you should be aware of some recommendations and restrictions:

1. Along with each message, you should indicate a unique identifier and the language of the message.

2. It is recommended to limit the messages to one or two sentences per message rather than sending a large block of text. Each message should be under 5,000 characters. The Sentiment Analysis service is more accurate when you provide small chunks of text to work on.

3. You can send up to 1,000 separate messages in a single API call.

4. The service accepts up to 100 requests per minute.

5. Each request can contain up to a maximum of 1 MB as the total size of the messages.

6. The content must be in JSON format. (Don't worry about the JSON format. Power Query can easily convert a table into JSON format for you.)

Here is an example of JSON-formatted content that can be sent in the body of the API request call:

```
{
    "documents": [
        {
            "language": "en",
            "id": "1",
            "text": "We love this trail and make the trip every year."
        },
        {
            "language": "en",
            "id": "2",
            "text": "Poorly marked trails! I thought we were goners. Worst hike ever."
        },
        {
            "language": "en",
            "id": "3",
            "text": "This is my favorite trail. It has beautiful views."
        }
    ]
}
```

The Sentiment Analysis API service returns the results in the JSON format, as follows:

```
{
    "documents": [
        {
            "score": 0.87631344795227051,
            "id": "1"
        },
        {
            "score":  0.05087512731552124,
            "id": "2"
        },
        {
            "score": 0.97651207447052,
            "id": "3"
        }
    ],
    "errors": []
}
```

Don't worry: Parsing JSON in Power Query is simple and intuitive.

Exercise 12-3: Implementing the *FnGetSentiment* Sentiment Analysis Custom Function

In this exercise you will learn how to create a custom function in Power Query to prepare your messages for the API request call and process the sentiment score in the response.

The *FnGetSentiment* Custom Function

Before you begin the exercise, take a look at the following function, which is the custom function you will learn to create. This custom function will enable you to run sentiment analysis on an input table or, even better, to run it over a large dataset of messages by reusing it on subsets of 1,000 messages each:

```
(Source) =>
let
    #"Removed Other Columns" = Table.SelectColumns(Source, {"id", "text"}),
    #"Added Custom" = Table.AddColumn(#"Removed Other Columns", "language", each "en"),
    JSONRequest = Json.FromValue([documents = #"Added Custom"]),
    JSONResponse = Json.Document(
        Web.Contents(
            "https://westus.api.cognitive.microsoft.com/text/analytics/v2.0/sentiment", [
                Headers = [
                    #"Ocp-Apim-Subscription-Key" = TextAnalyticsAPIKey
                ],
                Content =  JSONRequest
            ]
        )
    ),
    documents  = JSONResponse[documents],
    #"Converted to Table" = Table.FromList(
      documents, Splitter.SplitByNothing(), null, null, ExtraValues.Error
    ),
    SentimentScores = Table.ExpandRecordColumn(
        #"Converted to Table", "Column1", {"score", "id"}, {"score", "id"}
    )
in
    SentimentScores
```

> **Tip** This custom function was created by following the next steps. While it is easy to copy and paste custom functions that were created by others and then reuse them, you should know that many complex functions can be created step-by-step using the user interface for most of the logic. You can consider this exercise an opportunity to practice creating advanced custom functions, with a little help from the Power Query Editor's user interface, which will accelerate your ability to write simple building blocks of M code that eventually achieve complex scenarios.

Part 1: Loading the Data

For this exercise you will use the Microsoft Press Facebook posts dataset from Chapter 11 (see https://www.facebook.com/microsoftpress).

> **Note** You will run this exercise on a small dataset of 10 posts only. Otherwise, you might be charged for using a high volume of transactions by the Text Analytics service, or you might reach your maximum limit on the free tier. Take another look at the section "Pros and Cons of Cognitive Services via Power Query" at the beginning of this chapter.

To analyze the Microsoft Press Facebook posts, you need to download the source workbook C11E01. xlsx from https://aka.ms/DataPwrBIPivot/downloads and save it in *C:\Data\C11*.

1. Open a blank workbook or a new Power BI Desktop report and import the workbook C11E01.xslx from *C:\Data\C11* to the Power Query Editor.

2. In the Navigator dialog box, select Sheet1 and click Edit.

3. When the Power Query Editor opens, rename the query *Posts*.

   Notice that Microsoft Press Facebook posts are stored in the Message column and that the unique identifier is in the Post ID column. The table contains far more than 10 rows, and you need to keep only the top 10 rows.

4. On the Home tab, select Keep Rows and then select Keep Top Rows. When the Keep Top Rows dialog box opens, set Number of Rows to 10 and click OK. **Don't skip this step.** The original dataset is much larger than 10 rows.

> **Tip** Using the Keep Top Rows step in your queries is very practical in scenarios beyond this exercise. It can help you limit the dataset that is loaded to the Preview pane and can speed up your development time. When you finish the main development effort, you can remove this step and verify that your queries are working.

Part 2: Preparing the Messages

In the next sequence of steps, you will learn how to prepare the messages before you send them to the Sentiment Analysis service. To continue Exercise 12-3, follow these steps:

5. In the Queries pane, right-click the Posts query and select Reference.

6. Rename the new query *GetSentiment*.

7. With the GetSentiment query selected, rename the Message column to *text* and Post ID to *id*.

8. Perform the following data validations:

   a. Ensure that your text column doesn't contain empty values. You can use the filter control to test it. If you find empty or null values, you should remove blanks.

   b. Ensure that there are no duplicate values in the id column. If there are, you can remove them by using Remove Duplicates under Remove Rows on the Home tab.

   Steps 7 and 8 are crucial steps. If you do not rename these columns as text and id, or if you send empty values in text or duplicate values in id, the Sentiment Analysis API service will refuse to process the messages.

> **Tip** In the future, when you run this method on your own data, if you don't have unique identifiers for your messages, you can create an index column in the Add Column tab as your id column.

9. On the Home tab, select Choose Columns, and in the Choose Columns dialog box that opens, select text and id. Then, click OK.

    It's time to add the language column. This is not a mandatory requirement, so if you have mixed languages, you can skip the next step.

    For simplicity in this exercise, assume that all the messages are in English. You will therefore use the code *en*. In the last section of this chapter you will learn which country codes you can use and how to dynamically apply the language code when you have mixed languages in your text column.

10. On the Add Column tab, select Custom Column. When the Custom Column dialog box opens, in the New Column Name box, enter *language*; then, in the Custom Column Formula box, enter *"en"*. Then click OK.

    As shown in Figure 12-10, you can now see in the Preview pane of the Power Query Editor the three columns that are needed in the API call in JSON format.

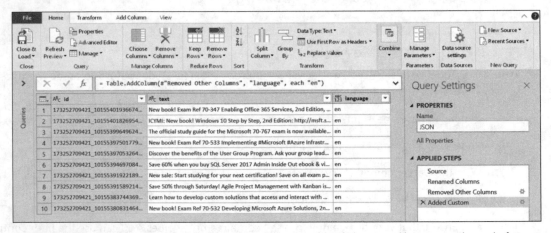

FIGURE 12-10 To run the sentiment analysis, you should have a table of id, text, and language columns before you convert them to JSON and upload them to Cognitive Services.

Part 3: Converting the Table to JSON Format

In these steps, you will have Power Query convert your table to JSON format. To continue Exercise 12-3, follow these steps:

11. To convert the table to JSON format, you will need to adhere to the API requirements and include the following element in the JSON body:

    {documents = ...}

Recall from Exercise 12-1 that JSON records are defined by curly brackets and can be created in M by using *Json.FromValue* on an M record. To create a record for *documents*, you can wrap *documents* with brackets and assign the table of messages as the value of *documents*. To do it, select the fx control next to the formula bar. A new step, Custom1, is added as the last step of the query in the Applied Steps pane. It has the following formula:

```
= #"Added Custom"
```

Change the formula to the following:

```
= [documents = #"Added Custom"]
```

12. To convert the record into a JSON file, modify the preceding formula in the formula bar by wrapping it with the function *Json.FromValue*. Here is the modified formula:

```
= Json.FromValue([documents = #"Added Custom"])
```

In the Preview pane of the Power Query Editor, you can now see the JSON icon that represents the JSON binary content you just created. Next, you will see how to send away the JSON content.

Part 4: Setting Up the API Key

In the next steps, you will create a parameter for the API Key. To continue Exercise 12-3, follow these steps:

13. Go to the Azure portal and open the Text Analytics resource. Copy Key1 or Key2 from the Keys view.

14. On the Home tab, expand the Manage Parameters drop-down and select New Parameter. In the Parameters dialog box that opens, make the following changes:

   a. In the Name box, enter *TextAnalyticsAPIKey*.

   b. In the Current Value box, paste the API key that you retrieved in step 13.

   c. Click OK to close the Parameters dialog box.

Part 5: Sending the Web Request

Now it's time to send the web request with the JSON-formatted textual messages to the API service. To continue Exercise 12-3, follow these steps:

15. In the Power Query Editor, select the GetSentiment query in the Queries pane and select the fx button near the formula bar. The Custom2 step is created, and it has the following formula:

```
= Custom1
```

16. In the formula bar, replace the M formula with the following formula:

```
= Web.Contents(
    "https://westus.api.cognitive.microsoft.com/text/analytics/v2.0/sentiment", [
        Headers = [
            #"Ocp-Apim-Subscription-Key" = TextAnalyticsAPIKey
        ],
        Content = Custom1
    ]
)
```

Note If your Text Analytics resource was configured in a different location than U.S. West, replace *westus* in the preceding formula with your location. You can find the location name in the Overview pane of the Text Analytics resource in the Azure portal.

Let's examine the code that you pasted into the Power Query Editor.

The preceding formula passes the Sentiment Analysis endpoint (the URL address) as the first argument. The second argument is a record with the fields *Headers* and *Content*. In *Headers* you passed the API key via *Ocp-Apim-Subscription-Key*, as you have done in the preceding exercises. The *Content* attribute is set to the JSON content from the Custom1 step.

17. When a notification bar appears in the Preview pane, select Edit Credentials. The Web Access dialog box opens. Ensure that Anonymous is selected and click Connect.

18. If you see the following notification (which you may or may not, depending on your privacy settings):

```
Information is required about data privacy.
```

click Continue and in the Privacy Levels dialog box that opens, set the privacy levels of your data sources to Organizational (similarly to step 17 in Exercise 12-2).

19. If you encounter the following error, set the workbook or Power BI report to ignore privacy levels:

```
Formula.Firewall: Query 'Query1' (step 'Invoked Custom Function') references other
queries or steps, so it may not directly access a data source. Please rebuild this
data combination.
```

Follow these steps to do so:

   a. In the Power Query Editor, on the File tab, select Options and Settings. Then select Query Options in Excel or Options in Power BI.

   b. Under Current Workbook in Excel or Current File in Power BI, go to Privacy.

   c. Select the Ignore the Privacy Levels option and click OK.

   d. Select Refresh Preview in the Power Query Editor.

Note Ignoring privacy levels may be a necessity when working in this scenario. While there are some advanced ways to rebuild a query in a way that may prevent the preceding error, it is beyond the scope of this book to describe these techniques, and the effort required to perform these modifications may not be cost-effective.

Part 6: Handling the Response

You should now see an icon in the Preview pane such as *[location].cognitive.microsoft.com* (where *[location]* represents your Text Analytics resource location, such as *westus*). This icon represents the content that was returned by the API. Its format is JSON, but as you will see in the next steps, in the Power Query Editor it is easy to handle the JSON format. To continue Exercise 12-3, follow these steps:

20. Double-click the icon in the Preview pane.

    A record is shown in the Preview pane, with the documents and errors fields and with *List* objects as values. This is the point when you can track down whether any specific errors were returned by the Sentiment Analysis API, and drill down to errors by clicking the errors List hyperlink. For the scope of this exercise, assume that there are no errors. Later in this exercise, you will learn how to avoid common errors.

21. Select the *List* object of the documents field. The record is converted into a list of 10 record objects.

22. In List Tools, on the Transform tab, select To Table. When the To Table dialog box opens, keep the default selections and click OK.

23. Expand the Column1 column as illustrated in Figure 12-11. In the Expand pane, ensure that score and id are selected and deselect Use Original Column Name As Prefix. Then click OK.

    You now have the sentiment scores and their associated messages identifiers.

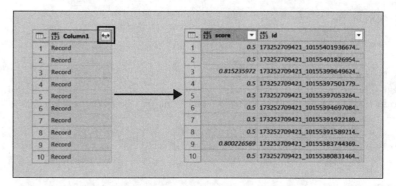

FIGURE 12-11 Converting JSON to a table is very intuitive in the Power Query Editor. The Sentiment Analysis score column is transformed into a table with the associated id.

Part 7: Creating a Custom Function

In this section you will create a custom function from the GetSentiment query. To continue Exercise 12-3, follow these steps:

24. In the Queries pane, right-click GetSentiment and select Duplicate. A new query is created. Rename it *FnGetSentiment*.

25. In the Queries pane, select FnGetSentiment. On the Home tab, select Advanced Editor.

26. In the Advanced Editor for FnGetSentiment, notice the following expression (the expression below was lightly modified to fit the format of the book, but the expression returns the same result):

```
let
    Source = Posts,
    #"Renamed Columns" = Table.RenameColumns(
        Source,{{"Post ID", "id"}, {"Message", "text"}}
    ),
    #"Removed Duplicates" = Table.Distinct(#"Renamed Columns", {"id"}),
    #"Filtered Rows" = Table.SelectRows(
        #"Removed Duplicates", each [text] <> null and [text] <> ""
    ),
    #"Removed Other Columns" = Table.SelectColumns(
        #"Filtered Rows",{"id", "text"}
    ),
    #"Added Custom" = Table.AddColumn(
        #"Removed Other Columns", "language", each "en"
    ),
    Custom1 = Json.FromValue([documents = #"Added Custom"]),
    Custom2 = Json.Document(
        Web.Contents(
            "https://westus.api.cognitive.microsoft.com/" &
                "text/analytics/v2.0/sentiment", [
                Headers = [
                    #"Ocp-Apim-Subscription-Key" = TextAnalyticsAPIKey
                ],
                Content = Custom1
            ]
        )
    ),
    documents = Custom2[documents],
    #"Converted to Table" = Table.FromList(
        documents, Splitter.SplitByNothing(), null, null, ExtraValues.Error
    ),
    #"Expanded Column1" = Table.ExpandRecordColumn(
        #"Converted to Table", "Column1", {"score", "id"}, {"score", "id"}
    )
in
    #"Expanded Column1"
```

27. To convert the code to a custom function, remove the first two lines after *let*. These lines are specific to the current dataset and will not serve you in a function. The custom function should work well on any table with a textual feed and unique identifiers. You can therefore remove the reference to *Posts* and the rename of the columns. The rename will take place outside the function, when you use the function on other datasets.

28. Remove the next two lines as well. *Table.Distinct* and *Table.SelectRows* were used for verification purposes to ensure that the data doesn't include duplicate identifiers or empty text values, which will result in errors.

Now, with the first four rows after *let* removed, the first line of your code after *let* should look as follows:

```
# "Removed Other Columns" = Table.SelectColumns(#"Filtered Rows",{"id", "text"}),
```

29. Replace #*"Filtered Rows"* with *Source* and add the function header *(Source)=>* before *let*. For cosmetic purposes, you can also replace the following step names:

    a. Replace the two instances of #*"Expanded Column1"* (above and below the *in* line) with *SentimentScores*.

    b. Replace the two instances of *Custom1* with *JSONRequest*.

    c. Replace two instances of *Custom2* with *JSONResponse*.

Here is the final function (with light modifications to fit the format of the book):

```
(Source) =>
let
    #"Removed Other Columns" = Table.SelectColumns(Source, {"id", "text"}),
    #"Added Custom" = Table.AddColumn(#"Removed Other Columns", "language", each "en"),
    JSONRequest = Json.FromValue([documents = #"Added Custom"]),
    JSONResponse = Json.Document(
        Web.Contents(
            "https://westus.api.cognitive.microsoft.com" &
                "/text/analytics/v2.0/sentiment", [
                Headers = [
                    #"Ocp-Apim-Subscription-Key" = TextAnalyticsAPIKey
                ],
                Content = JSONRequest
            ]
        )
    ),
    documents = JSONResponse[documents],
    #"Converted to Table" = Table.FromList(
        documents, Splitter.SplitByNothing(), null, null, ExtraValues.Error),
    SentimentScores = Table.ExpandRecordColumn(
        #"Converted to Table", "Column1", {"score", "id"}, {"score", "id"})
in
    SentimentScores
```

Are you ready to use it?

Part 8: Invoking *FnGetSentiment*

In the next sequence of steps, you will learn how to invoke the custom function and extract its sentiment scores. To continue Exercise 12-3, follow these steps:

30. To invoke the custom function, create a new reference query from the Posts query and rename it *Sentiment Scores*.

31. In the new query, rename the columns from Message to *text* and Post ID to *id*. Next, invoke the custom function by using a custom step (which you do by selecting the fx button near the formula bar) and pasting this formula:

```
= FnGetSentiment(#"Renamed Columns").
```

32. Before you load the query Sentiment Scores to your report, make sure you change the type of the score column to *Decimal Number*. Rename score to *Sentiment Score* and id to *Post ID*.

33. With Sentiment Score query selected in the Queries pane, select Merge Queries on the Home tab and follow these steps to merge Sentiment Scores and Posts, as shown in Figure 12-12:

    a. The Merge dialog box opens. Select the Post ID column on the Sentiment Scores table.

    b. Select Posts as the second query.

    c. Select the Post ID column on the Posts table.

    d. Set Join Kind to Right Outer (All from Second, Matching from First) and click OK.

FIGURE 12-12 Merge posts with sentiment scores.

Having a right outer join will ensure that you will not lose any posts in your data when the service omits certain erroneous textual messages from its response. (More details on such potential errors are described in the next section.)

34. After the merge, expand the new Posts column. In the Expand pane, select all the columns from the Posts table except for Post ID, which is already available in the merged table. You can now load the Sentiment Scores to your report and unload the Posts table. Save the report. You will need it in the next exercise.

You can download the solution files C12E03 - Solution.xlsx and C12E03 - Solution.pbix from https://aka.ms/DataPwrBIPivot/downloads.

Avoiding Errors

To avoid getting errors from the Text Analytics Sentiment API calls, follow these steps before you run *FnGetSentiment* on your datasets:

1. Ensure that your unique identifier column is named id.

2. Ensure that your message column is named text.

3. Remove empty values and nulls from the text column. There is no point in sending empty values. If you send empty values along with non-empty ones, the service will remove the empty messages from the documents list of the results (which you expanded in step 23 of Exercise 12-3 part 6) and will include an error in the errors list. Sending empty values is a waste of a transaction call.

4. Remove duplicates from the id column, as shown in step 8 of Exercise 12-3 part 8. Keeping duplicate identifiers will result in a general error for the entire API call. All messages will not be processed. This is the error you will receive with duplicate values in the id column:

```
DataSource.Error: Web.Contents failed to get contents from 'https://westus.api.
cognitive.microsoft.com/text/analytics/v2.0/sentiment' (400): Bad Request
```

5. Ensure that your messages are not longer than 5,000 characters. Longer messages will lead to the following error in the errors list (which can be expanded in step 20 of Exercise 12-3 part 6):

```
A document within the request was too large to be processed. Limit document size
to: 5120 characters.
```

To trim down long messages to 5,000 characters, follow these steps:

a. Select the text column.

b. On the Home tab, select Split Column. Then select By Number of Characters.

c. When the Split Column by Number of Characters dialog box opens, in the Number of Characters box, enter *5000*.

d. In the Split drop-down, select Once, As Far Left As Possible.

6. Don't pass more than 1,000 rows of messages per API call. Beyond 1,000 messages, you will receive a *Bad Request* error for the entire call. While you can easily apply the Keep Top Rows method to limit the number of messages, in the next section you will learn how to split large datasets into groups of 1,000 rows each and run Sentiment Analysis on these groups.

Exercise 12-4: Running Sentiment Analysis on Large Datasets

Because the Sentiment Analysis API can process only 1,000 messages per transaction, in this exercise you will learn how to run the custom function *FnGetSentiment* on multiple subsets of your data. The technique will come in handy in many other scenarios where you would need to split large datasets into groups of smaller datasets and apply a custom function on the subsets.

You can start this exercise where you left off in Exercise 12-3, or you can open the Excel workbook C12E04.xlsx or the Power BI report C12E04.pbix, which are available to download from https://aka.ms/DataPwrBIPivot/downloads.

> **Note** To minimize the number of API calls, you will run on a small dataset of 100 messages and will group them into 10 blocks of 10 messages. When you implement this solution on your own data, you will apply it on large datasets and will group the data into blocks of 1,000 messages.

1. If you didn't save your work after completing Exercise 12-3, you can take a shortcut and open the Excel workbook C12E04.xlsx or the Power BI report C12E04.pbix and launch the Power Query Editor.

2. In the Queries pane, select the *TextAnalyticsAPIKey* parameter; then in the Preview pane, paste your own Sentiment Analysis API key in the Current Value box.

3. Select the Posts query, and in Applied Steps, select the settings control on the Kept First Rows step. When the Keep First Rows dialog box opens, change the number of rows from 10 to 100 and click OK.

4. In the Queries pane, right-click the Posts query and select Reference. Rename the new query *Scored Posts*.

5. Rename the Post ID column *id* and the Message column *text*.

6. Remove empty values from the text column and remove duplicate values from the id column.

7. On the Add Column tab, select Index Column.

8. Select the Index column. On the Transform tab, select Standard and then select Integer-Divide. When the Integer-Divide dialog box opens, set Value to 10 and click OK.

    You can now see that the first 10 rows received 0 as the index. The second 10 messages received 1 as the index, and so forth.

> **Note** In the future, when working on large datasets beyond 1,000 messages, in step 8, you should set Value to 1,000 rather than to 10, which is used here only for learning purposes.

9. With the Index column selected, select Group By on the Transform tab. The Group By dialog box opens. Follow these steps to set the Group By dialog box as shown in Figure 12-13:

   a. In the New Column Name box, enter *Subset*.

   b. In the Operation drop-down, select All Rows.

   c. Click OK to close the Group By dialog box.

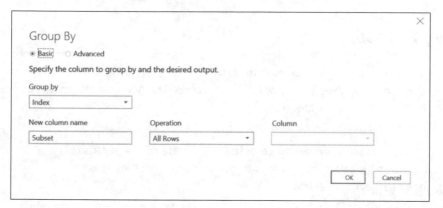

FIGURE 12-13 Group By enables you to divide and conquer the Sentiment Analysis 1,000-message limit.

10. You can now see in the Preview pane a new table with Index and Subset columns. A total of 10 rows hold the subsets in table objects.

11. On the Add Column tab, select Invoke Custom Function.

12. When the Invoke Custom Function dialog box opens, select FnGetSentiment as the Function Query.

13. Ensure that Subset is selected in the Source drop-down menu and click OK.

14. If needed, follow steps 17–19 from Exercise 12-3 part 5 to edit the credentials and set the privacy levels.

15. Remove the Index and Subset columns.

16. Expand the FnGetSentiment column. In the Expand pane, ensure that score and id are selected, and deselect Use Original Column Name As Prefix. Then click OK.

17. Follow steps 32–34 in Exercise 12-3 to rename the columns and merge them with the Posts query.

Tip If you use Power BI Desktop, you can keep the Scored Posts query with the Sentiment Score and Post ID columns without the merge. Loading them to the report will create an automatic one-to-one relationship between Posts and Sentiment Score and will allow you to associate between the posts and their corresponding sentiment scores.

You can now load the Scored Posts query into your report and start analyzing posts based on their sentiment scores.

You can review the solutions for Exercise 12-4 in C12E04 - Solution.xlsx and C12E04 - Solution.pbix, which are available to download from https://aka.ms/DataPwrBIPivot/downloads.

Save your report. Next, you will learn how to extract key phrases from your messages.

Extracting Key Phrases

The Azure Text Analytics API enables you to reuse the techniques in Exercises 12-3 and 12-4 to analyze your messages and return key phrases instead of sentiment scores. The API syntax is similar, and we can therefore skip the introductory steps in this section.

> **See Also** To learn more about the reference of the Key Phrase API, see https://docs.microsoft.com/en-us/azure/cognitive-services/text-analytics/how-tos/text-analytics-how-to-keyword-extraction.

In this section you will learn how to modify the *FnGetSentiment* query function to extract key phrases.

In Chapter 11 you learned how to split words and analyze the number of word occurrences or topics. Having an easy way to apply artificial intelligence to magically extract key phrases from textual feeds takes you one step further in extracting real essence and meaning from your textual data.

Exercise 12-5: Converting Sentiment Logic to Key Phrases

To follow this exercise, you can start with your solution from Exercise 12-4 or take a shortcut and start from the Excel workbook C12E04 - Solution.xlsx or the Power BI report C12E04 - Solution.pbix, which are available to download from https://aka.ms/DataPwrBIPivot/downloads.

1. Open C12E04 - Solution.xlsx or C12E04 - Solution.pbix and launch the Power Query Editor.

2. In the Queries pane, right-click the FnGetSentiment query and select Duplicate.

3. Rename the new query *FnGetKeyPhrases* and select Advanced Editor.

4. In the Advanced Editor, replace *sentiment* in the following URL:

   ```
   https://...api.cognitive.microsoft.com/text/analytics/v2.0/sentiment
   ```

   with *KeyPhrases*, as shown here:

   ```
   https://westus.api.cognitive.microsoft.com/text/analytics/v2.0/KeyPhrases
   ```

5. Replace *score* twice in the following line:

   ```
   SentimentScores = Table.ExpandRecordColumn(#"Converted to Table", "Column1",
   {"score", "id"}, {"score", "id"})
   ```

with *keyPhrases*, so that you end up with the following modified line:

```
SentimentScores = Table.ExpandRecordColumn(#"Converted to Table", "Column1",
{"keyPhrases", "id"}, {"keyPhrases", "id"})
```

> **Note** The M engine is case sensitive. Make sure that *keyPhrases* starts with a lowercase k.

6. Replace the identifier *SentimentScores* with *KeyPhrases* in the line shown in step 5 and also in in the last line of the function.

The modified *FnGetKeyPhrases* custom function is provided here. Open the Advanced Editor and confirm that you have ended up with the same expression as shown here:

```
(Source) =>
let
    #"Removed Other Columns" = Table.SelectColumns(Source, {"id", "text"}),
    #"Added Custom" = Table.AddColumn(#"Removed Other Columns", "language",
each "en"),
    JSONRequest = Json.FromValue([documents = #"Added Custom"]),
    JSONResponse = Json.Document(
        Web.Contents(
            "https://westus.api.cognitive.microsoft.com" &
                "/text/analytics/v2.0/KeyPhrases", [
                Headers = [
                    #"Ocp-Apim-Subscription-Key" = TextAnalyticsAPIKey
                ],
                Content = JSONRequest
            ]
        )
    ),
    documents = JSONResponse[documents],
    #"Converted to Table" = Table.FromList(
        documents, Splitter.SplitByNothing(), null, null, ExtraValues.Error),
    KeyPhrases = Table.ExpandRecordColumn(
        #"Converted to Table", "Column1", {"keyPhrases", "id"},
{"keyPhrases", "id"})
in
    KeyPhrases
```

7. In the Queries pane, right-click Scored Posts and select Duplicate.

8. Rename the duplicated query *Key Phrases*. While Key Phrases is selected, delete all the steps after Group Rows in Applied Steps. You are now ready to apply the new custom function on the grouped table in the following steps.

9. On the Add Column tab, select Invoke Custom Function.

10. When the Invoke Custom Function dialog box opens, set Function Query to *FnGetKeyPhrases*.

11. Set Source to Subset and click OK.

12. Remove the columns Index and Subset.

13. Expand the FnGetKeyPhrases column. In the Expand pane, ensure that keyPhrases and id are selected, and deselect Use Original Column Name As Prefix. Then click OK

14. Ensure that your credentials and privacy levels are correct (as you have done following steps 17–19 in Exercise 12-3 part 5).

15. Expand the results.

16. In the Preview pane ensure that you now have the keyPhrases column with *List* objects and the id column. Expand the keyPhrases column to new rows to extract the key phrases from the List objects. Each row will include the combination of a key phrase and its identifier.

17. If you use Power BI Desktop, load the Key Phrases table into a Word Cloud visual, as shown in Figure 12-14. (For a refresher on how to load a Word Cloud custom visual, refer to Exercise 11-7 in Chapter 11.)

Tip To show multi-word phrases in the word cloud, you can turn off Word-Breaking under the General section of the Format view and turn off Stop Words. In addition, make sure the Key Phrases table is connected to Scored Posts through the shared Post ID column. Then edit the relationship to be a bidirectional relationship by setting Both as Cross Filter Direction in the Edit Relationship dialog box.

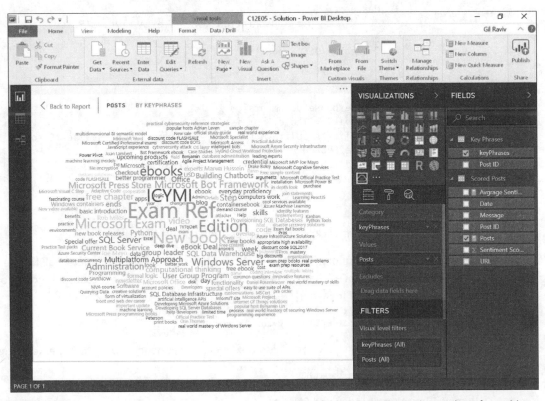

FIGURE 12-14 Use the Word Cloud visual in Power BI to show the extracted key phrases by number of repetitions.

The solution file C12E05 - Solution.pbix is available to download from https://aka.ms/ DataPwrBIPivot/downloads. Make sure this report will be set to ignore privacy levels, as explained in Exercise 12-4, to ensure that it will be refreshed after you provide the API key.

Multi-Language Support

At the time this book went to press, both the Sentiment Analysis and Key Phrase API calls support a limited range of languages. To view the full list of the supported languages, see https://docs.microsoft. com/en-us/azure/cognitive-services/text-analytics/text-analytics-supported-languages.

If your language is not supported, you can consider applying the Translate Text API that you used in the first part of this chapter and translating your messages to one of the supported languages.

Replacing the Language Code

If your entire dataset consists of messages of a single supported language, you can replace the code with your supported language code by following these steps:

1. Find your language code in the supported languages page https://docs.microsoft.com/en-us/ azure/cognitive-services/text-analytics/text-analytics-supported-languages.

2. Open the Advanced Editor to edit your custom functions *FnGetSentiment* and *FnGetKeyPhrases*.

3. Replace *en* with your language code in the following line:

```
#"Added Custom" = Table.AddColumn(#"Removed Other Columns", "language", each "en"),
```

4. If you end up working with datasets with mixed languages, adding the *language* custom column with a single value will lead to false analysis of sentiment and missed key phrases. To resolve this challenge, you can remove the #"Added Custom" line from your code.

To do so, take a look of the following three steps:

```
#"Removed Other Columns" = Table.SelectColumns(Source, {"id", "text"}),
#"Added Custom" = Table.AddColumn(#"Removed Other Columns", "language", each "en"),
JSONRequest = Json.FromValue([documents = #"Added Custom"]),
```

Remove the #"*Added Custom*" step, and don't forget to "rewire" the next line with the preceding one. Replace #"Added Custom" with #"Removed Other Columns" as shown in bold in the following two lines:

```
#"Removed Other Columns" = Table.SelectColumns(Source, {"id", "text"}),
JSONRequest = Json.FromValue([documents = #"Removed Other Columns"]),
```

Dynamic Detection of Languages

If you have mixed languages in your textual feeds, and if the technique in step 4 in the preceding section is not working well, you can use the Language Detection API call in Text Analytics to dynamically detect the languages of individual messages, filter the messages that have supported languages, and send them to the Sentiment Analysis or Key Phrases API service.

The Language Detection API is described at https://docs.microsoft.com/en-us/azure/cognitive-services/text-analytics/how-tos/text-analytics-how-to-language-detection.

Exercise 12-6: Converting Sentiment Logic to Language Detection

The Language Detection API has a similar syntax to the Sentiment Analysis and Key Phrases API calls. You can follow the same steps as in Exercise 12-5 to change the original *FnGetSentiment* function to the new custom function *FnDetectLangauges*, shown here:

```
(Source) =>
let
    #"Removed Other Columns" = Table.SelectColumns(Source, {"id", "text"}),
    JSONRequest = Json.FromValue([documents = #"Removed Other Columns"]),
    JSONResponse = Json.Document(
        Web.Contents(
            "https://westus.api.cognitive.microsoft.com" &
                "/text/analytics/v2.0/languages", [
                Headers = [
                    #"Ocp-Apim-Subscription-Key" = TextAnalyticsAPIKey
                ],
                Content = JSONRequest
            ]
        )
    ),
    documents = JSONResponse[documents],
    #"Converted to Table" = Table.FromList(
        documents, Splitter.SplitByNothing(), null, null, ExtraValues.Error),
    DetectedLanguages = Table.ExpandRecordColumn(
        #"Converted to Table", "Column1", {"detectedLanguages", "id"},
{"detectedLanguages", "id"})
in
    DetectedLanguages
```

Because the three Text Analytics APIs are similar, we do not go over the details in this exercise for running language detection. Instead, you can jump straight to the solution files C12E06 - Solution.xlsx and C12E06 - Solution.pbix, which are available for download from https://aka.ms/DataPwrBIPivot/downloads. These files apply language detection on the multi-lingual "Hello World" messages from Exercise 12-1 and return their detected languages.

Congratulations! You can complete the proceeding steps to combine all the tools you have learned in this chapter to perform advanced text analytics of sentiment analysis and detection of key phrases on multi-lingual textual feeds.

1. Detect the language on each message by using the Detect Languages API (which can apply to blocks of 1,000 messages each).

2. Create a list of supported languages.

3. Using the techniques described in Chapter 11, split your messages into to intermediary queries:

   a. First, a query with all messages of the supported languages, including their detected languages.

   b. Second, a query with all unsupported languages.

4. Run Translation to English (or another supported language) on the second query and append the results with the first query.

5. Run Sentiment Analysis and Key Phrase Detection on the appended results.

Summary

In this chapter, you have learned how to translate text, find sentiment scores, extract key phrases, and detect languages in Excel and Power BI, with a little help from Cognitive Services on Azure. When you put these techniques into practice on real-life data, you will be able to harness the power of artificial intelligence to extract new meaning from your textual feeds.

Before you apply these techniques on real datasets, review the section "Pros and Cons of Cognitive Services via Power Query" at the beginning of this chapter and follow the tips to reduce the number of excessive API calls. Make sure your API key will not be shared with others and remember that this solution will most likely not be refreshed via the scheduled refresh on the Power BI service (unless Microsoft supports it by the time you read this chapter). You will still be able to refresh the report via Power BI Desktop and Excel.

The powers of sentiment analysis and the detection of key phrases can be increased tenfold when you combine them with your current datasets and correlate them with your existing numeric attributes and measures. By doing so, you can gain new insights into human behaviors and opinions and learn more about how they affect your company performance.

Chapter 13, "Social Network Analytics," delivers on the promise from Chapter 11 and explores another aspect of human behaviors—the social ones—and looks at how to tap into data from Facebook and analyze it in Excel and Power BI.

Social Network Analytics

Facebook is uniquely positioned to answer questions that people have, like, what sushi restaurants have my friends gone to in New York lately and liked?...These are queries you could potentially do with Facebook that you couldn't do with anything else...

—*Marc Zuckerberg*

IN THIS CHAPTER, YOU WILL

- Learn how to connect to Facebook in Excel and Power BI to load a wide range of endpoints and edges

- Import the Facebook pages you like and find out when you liked them

- Learn who in your Facebook network is using Power BI and connected to Facebook via Excel and Power BI

- Learn how to traverse the social graph

- Analyze any Facebook page and measure the engagement levels through comments and shares

- Analyze multiple Facebook pages, using custom functions

There are abundant data sources you can connect to by using the Get Data menus of Excel and Power BI. Each one of these data sources can lead you to interminable possibilities for insight. From flat files to data lakes, from organizational repositories to online web services—with your new Power Query data-wrangling skills, the sky is the limit.

As we are getting closer to the end of this book, it's time for you to learn how to use a rich resource of public information to practice your new skills. Working with real and varied datasets can lead to new learning opportunities. Exploring unknown public data that is different from your usual organizational data can allow you to discover new techniques as you are introduced to new data challenges that may be beyond your current expertise.

For these reasons, this chapter focuses on the analysis of social networks, particularly Facebook. Power Query includes a Facebook connector, which can allow you to connect to your profile or any public page you want to analyze. The data is available for everyone, and it can allow you to practice with data preparation of unstructured datasets, handle a varied set of tables, and tackle uncleaned data from rich and heterogenous datasets.

Beyond the learning potential, if you are an analyst of social media, you will find this chapter very useful for tapping into user engagement levels and identifying social behavior trends. If you are not a social media analyst, no worries: In this chapter you will try out some great tools for learning about your company's brands and competitors or for creating great demos to show your colleagues.

Getting Started with the Facebook Connector

This section introduces you to basic experience with the Facebook connector and shows you how to connect to your profile on Facebook.

Facebook provides rich sets of APIs for developers to interface with the social network, gain insights, and engage users. The primary API, the Facebook Graph API, allows applications to use the Facebook social graph (see https://developers.facebook.com/docs/graph-api/). Like the social network itself, the social graph allows applications to traverse nodes and edges in the network, reading and writing data on behalf of users, pages, or groups and with alignment with the permissions that were provided by the users or the administrators of pages and groups. While some of the endpoints in the social graph are protected from the prying eyes of applications, many data points are open to everyone.

To connect to Facebook data via an app, you are required to log in to your Facebook account and give the app permission to read and/or write data on your behalf. In the next exercise you will follow simple steps to connect to your Facebook profile using the Facebook connector in Power Query, which is one of the many Facebook apps in existence.

Exercise 13-1: Finding the Pages You Liked

In this exercise, you will import the Facebook pages that you have liked, and find the dates when you liked them. Then you will learn how to extract the profile and image URLs from the Facebook ID of each of those pages. To start the exercise, you need a Facebook account, so create one if you don't already have one.

 Note If you don't have a Facebook account, you cannot follow this exercise. Please sign up on Facebook to proceed.

1. Connect to Facebook using either Excel or Power BI Desktop (see Figure 13-1):

   In Excel: Open a blank workbook. On the Data tab, select Get Data, From Online Services, From Facebook.

   In Power BI Desktop: Open a blank report. On the Home tab, select Get Data. When the Get Data dialog box opens, select Online Services; then scroll down, select Facebook, and select Connect. You can also enter Facebook in the search box and then select Facebook and click Connect.

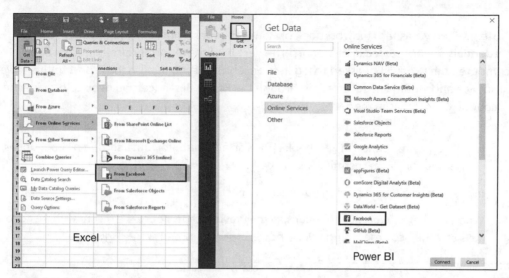

FIGURE 13-1 To connect to Facebook in Excel and Power BI select Get Data on the Data tab of Excel or the Home tab of Power BI Desktop.

2. If this is your first time connecting to Facebook and you see the warning dialog box about potential changes that may occur to the API, select the box Don't Warn Me Again for This Connector, and click Continue.

3. The Facebook dialog box opens. Here is where you can select the Facebook entity you want to import. By default, *me* is the proposed entity. This is a shortcut to your own Facebook profile. You can set different Facebook object names in this box. For example, *microsoftpress* is the object name for Microsoft Press Facebook page. For now, keep the default *me* and click OK.

> **Tip** The Facebook dialog box includes the Connection drop-down menu, which allows you to import specific edges in the graph, such as friends, posts, or likes. Due to constant Facebook API changes, not all of these edges are useful. For example, although you can use the combination of *me* and *likes*, as described in this exercise, trying to import likes on other Facebook object names will lead to empty data.

4. The Facebook Access dialog box opens. If this is the first time you are connecting to Facebook using Excel or Power BI, follow these steps:

   a. Select Sign In, and if asked to provide your Facebook credentials, do so.

   b. In the Facebook dialog box that opens, look at the type of permissions the Microsoft Power BI app will receive: your public profile, friend list, timeline posts, status updates, personal description, likes, and email address. Edit the permissions if you like, and click Continue.

Note When you share the workbook or Power BI report with colleagues, your Facebook credentials are not stored in the report. The next time the report is refreshed from a new computer, the user will be asked to log in to Facebook. If you publish the report to the Power BI service and would like to refresh it through the Power BI service, you need to provide the Facebook credentials in the dataset settings.

    c. If you own a page or a Facebook app as an administrator and a second prompt opens, asking for further permissions, click OK.

5. In the Facebook Access dialog box, click Connect.

6. When the Power Query Editor opens, in the Preview pane, notice the record with the following keys and their corresponding values: *name*, *connections*, and *id* (see Figure 13-2).

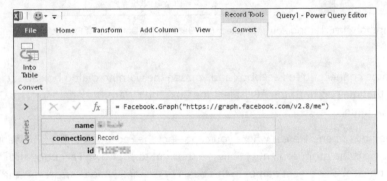

FIGURE 13-2 The Facebook Graph API results are initially shown as a record in the Power Query Editor. You can navigate through the graph by clicking the Record hyperlink.

While this record doesn't reveal a lot of valuable insight yet, we need to discuss a few important elements that are available for you in this step. In the formula bar, you will notice the following line:

```
= Facebook.Graph("https://graph.facebook.com/v2.8/me")
```

The M function *Facebook.Graph* receives a single argument, the URL. To learn how you can manipulate this URL, you need to learn a few basic Graph API principles. (There are many other interesting things you could learn about the Graph API, but they are beyond the scope of this chapter.)

The first part in the URL that is important is the API version (version 2.8 in this case). In many cases, Facebook provides new content when new versions of the APIs are released. You can try to modify the version number in the URL to reach these new elements. It is also important to note than an API version is limited in time. To learn when your version will expire, go to the Facebook official Graph API Changelog page: https://developers.facebook.com/docs/graph-api/changelog.

> **Tip** If you plan to publish refreshable reports using the Facebook connector, you should take a careful look at the Changelog page. The version used in this chapter, version 2.8, will stop being available on April 18, 2019. To ensure that your reports will keep refreshing after that date, you can update the formula bar with the latest version and test to make sure the modified query works as expected.

The second important part in the URL is the Graph API endpoint—in this case, *me*. This endpoint returns your user information. It is also where you can create more sophisticated Graph API calls, apply parameters to refine your calls, and extract specific datasets. You will see a few common examples later in this chapter, in Exercise 13-2.

7. In the Preview pane, find the *Record* hyperlink of the connections field and click it.

   The Preview pane includes the following keys and their corresponding *Table* objects: *books*, *feeds*, *friends*, *games*, *likes*, *movies*, *permissions*, *posts*, and *television*. Each of these entities is called an *edge* in the Facebook Graph API. Selecting the hyperlink of any of these *Table* objects allows you to drill down to the relevant edges and load the relevant data.

   The Facebook Graph API has more edges than the ones you see in the Preview pane in step 7. For a full list, go to https://developers.facebook.com/docs/graph-api/reference/v3.1/user. Recall from step 4b that you granted specific permissions for the Power BI app to access your profile. By design, not all the permissions are requested by the app. As a result, you will not be able to read all the edges that are available on Facebook. The following steps demonstrate this limitation.

8. Delete the last step in Applied Steps and edit the formula in formula bar by adding */family* at the of the URL, as shown here:

   ```
   = Facebook.Graph("https://graph.facebook.com/v2.8/me/family")
   ```

   Now after you press Enter, the Preview pane shows an empty result. The reason is that the Power BI app didn't request the *user_relationship* permissions. As a result, the family edge is empty.

9. Modify the formula bar so the formula is back to its initial state:

   ```
   = Facebook.Graph("https://graph.facebook.com/v2.8/me")
   ```

   Repeat step 7 to drill down to the *Table* object of the connections field.

10. To drill down to the Facebook pages you have liked, select the *Table* hyperlink next to *likes*, as shown in Figure 13-3. The Preview pane will now show Facebook pages that you have liked, including the *id* column (the Facebook ID) and the *created_time* column (which can tell you when you liked a page) for each of the pages.

    The created_time column can be used to extract date, time and hour, which can be very useful as separate columns.

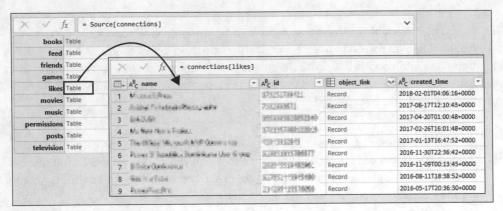

FIGURE 13-3 You can drill down to the Facebook pages you have liked in the Power Query Editor by clicking the Table hyperlink next to likes.

11. To add a new Date column from the created_time column, first change its type to Date/Time/Timezone, and while the column is selected, go to the Add Column tab and select the Date drop-down menu. Then select Date Only to add the new Date column.

12. Now that you have the new Date column, change the type of the created_time column to *Time*. You can now extract the hour portion from Time. Select the created_time column and then, on the Add Column tab, select Time, Hour, Hour. The new Hour column will show the hour of the day, and it will allow you to create charts that show the most active hours of the day when you most commonly like new Facebook pages. (You can see this analysis in the Power BI template file that is provided as a solution for this exercise at the end of the exercise.)

13. Remove the object_link column and rename the first three columns *Facebook Page*, *ID*, and *Time*.

Tip The Facebook object ID that is now stored in the ID column is very useful. It is a unique identifier that you can use to create relationships between tables and create custom columns that enrich your reports with additional information. For example, you can add a custom Page URL column in the Power Query Editor by using this formula:

```
= "https://www.facebook.com/" & [ID]
```

14. If you use Power BI, follow the preceding tip to add the Page URL column. Also add the URL of the page's picture by following these steps:

    a. On the Add Column tab, select Add Column. The Custom Column dialog box opens.

    b. In the New Column Name box, enter *Picture*.

c. In the Custom Column Formula box, enter the following formula, and click OK to close the dialog box:

```
= "https://graph.facebook.com/" & [ID] & "/picture?type=large"
```

> **Tip** In Power BI Desktop, you can categorize a URL column as Web Image or Web URL, and you can use visualizations such as a slicer, table, or matrix to show the actual images and use hyperlinks in your report.

15. Rename the query *Facebook Pages I Like* and load the query to your workbook or Power BI report. You can now use a PivotChart in Excel or a line chart in Power BI to see how many pages you have liked over time. The data in this report is equivalent to the data you can see when you go to https://www.facebook.com/me/likes.

You can download the solution files C13E01 - Solution.xlsx and C13E01 - Solution.pbit from https://aka.ms/DataPwrBIPivot/downloads.

Analyzing Your Friends

In this section you will briefly explore one of the most sought-after scenarios for analysis on Facebook: the ability to analyze your friends. In the first exercise you will learn how to import your friends and their friends and build the queries that will enable you to visualize social graphs. In the second exercise you will learn how to import the pages that your friends like.

In the Facebook Graph API, you can use the *friends* edge to traverse the social graph. Unfortunately, for you as an analyst (and fortunately for any user who seeks privacy), a Facebook app can only traverse the Facebook graph starting from you through friends who have approved the app, and then traversing to their friends who have also approved the app. In Exercise 13-2 you will explore this scenario.

Exercise 13-2: Finding Your Power BI Friends and Their Friends

Follow the steps in this exercise to use the Facebook connector to extract your Facebook friends and their friends and build cool visuals as demonstrated in Figure 13-4 (also available in the Power BI solution file that is described at the end of this exercise).

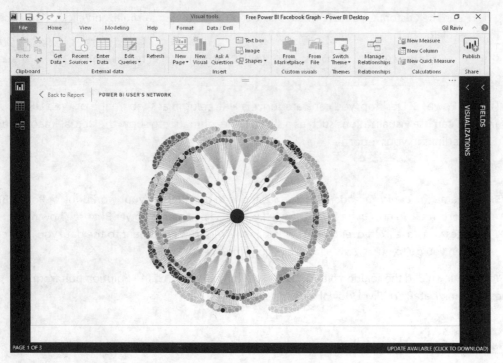

FIGURE 13-4 As shown in this screenshot of C13E02 - Solution.pbit, you can build a social graph of Power BI and Excel users who have used the Facebook connector.

As you will see soon, only your friends who have imported Facebook data via Power Query (in Excel or Power BI) will be visible.

1. Open a blank new workbook or a new Power BI Report.

   In Excel: On the Data tab, select Get Data, From Online Services, From Facebook.

   In Power BI Desktop: On the Home tab, select Get Data. When the Get Data dialog box opens, select Online Services; then scroll down, select Facebook, and select Connect. You can also enter Facebook in the search box and then select Facebook and click Connect.

2. In the Facebook dialog box, keep *me* in the first text box, in the Connection drop-down select Friends, and click OK. When you see a dialog box that provides a preview of the data, click Edit. You can now see a list of friends in the Preview pane.

Note In the Power Query Editor, if you see an empty table in the Preview pane, you will not be able to continue this exercise; you must first connect in Facebook with users who have used the Facebook connector in Excel or Power BI. The following steps assume that you have such friends on Facebook. If you don't, ask your friends to follow one of the exercises in this chapter, and you will see them in the Preview pane.

3. To determine the friends of your friends who are using the Facebook connector, expand the object_link column. The object_link column shows a record of elements that the Facebook connector allows you to extract. The connections column contains all the Graph API edges that you can import from the user interface.

    In the Expand pane, deselect all the columns except for connections. Make sure the Use Original Column Name As Prefix check box is not selected, and click OK.

4. Expand the connections column. In the Expand pane, deselect all the columns except for friends. Make sure the Use Original Column Name As Prefix check box is not selected, and click OK.

5. Expand the friends column. In the Expand pane, deselect all the columns except for *name* and *id*. Make sure the Use Original Column Name As Prefix check box is not selected, and click OK.

    You now have two new columns in the Preview pane: name.1 and id.1. For each of your friends in the name column, you may now have multiple rows, each with a unique user id (in the id.1 column) to represent your friend's friends. Because of the restriction that only app users can be shown via the *friends* edge, the two new columns include only friends of friends who use the Facebook connector. You can also see first-degree friends in the name.1 column.

    Why do you see first-degree friends in the column that should only show you second-degree friends? The answer is simple: For every first-degree friend who shares mutual friends with you, you will see these mutual friends in the name.1 column.

    From here you have two interesting scenarios to follow. First, you can add a new column that will mark the mutual friends in the name.1 column. This step will allow you to analyze how many mutual friends each of your friends has, and then drill down to those mutual friends. Second, when you want to build the social graph, you can filter out rows with mutual friends. These rows are redundant—you already have other rows in the table where the mutual friend from column name.1 are located in the name column of those other rows.

6. To identify mutual friends, on the Add Column tab, select Custom Column. In the Custom Column dialog box, follow these steps:

    a. Enter *IsMutual* in the New Column Name box.

    b. Enter the following formula in the Custom Column Formula box, and click OK to close the dialog box:

        ```
        List.Contains(#"Expanded friends"[name], [name.1])
        ```

    Notice that the new column, IsMutual, contains TRUE or FALSE values in the Preview pane. To remove the redundant rows in your social graph report, you can apply a filter to keep only rows with false values in IsMutual.

    Let's briefly explain the formula in the Custom Column dialog box. The function *List.Contains* returns true when the item in the second argument is found in the list in the first argument. In Chapter 9, "Introduction to the Power Query M Formula Language," you learned that columns can be represented as lists when you refer to the column name inside brackets following the table name. In this case, the table in #"*Expanded friends*" returns its name column as a list using #"*Expanded friends*"*[name]. The second argument in List.Contains is [name.1] which* represents the second-degree friend name we look for in the list.

Even though you cannot further traverse the graph beyond your second-degree friends, it allows you to build social graphs in Power BI such as the one illustrated in Figure 13-4.

You can download the solution file C13E02 - Solution.pbit (which is illustrated in Figure 13-4) or the query in C13E02 - Solution.xlsx. Both files are available at https://aka.ms/DataPwrBIPivot/downloads.

> **Tip**   There are more efficient ways to traverse the social graph by using advanced API calls. For example, when copied as a single line, the following M function calls for your 100 friends and the first 50 friends of each of your friends:
>
> ```
> =Facebook.Graph("https://graph.facebook.com/v3.0/me?fields=friends.limit(100)
> {name,id,friends.limit(50){name,id}}")
> ```

Exercise 13-3: Find the Pages Your Friends Liked

This exercise is a spin-off of Exercise 13-2. Instead of importing your friends' friends, you will import your friends' liked pages. Following the limitations in the preceding exercise, you can only import a limited subset of your friends—only those who have imported Facebook data via Power Query will be visible. But you will be able to learn which pages they like and what their common interests are as reflected by their liked pages, as illustrated in Figure 13-5.

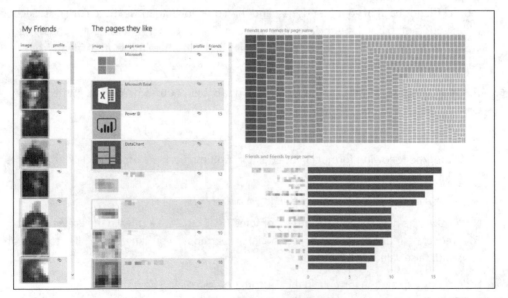

FIGURE 13-5   You can enrich your report with Facebook profile pictures and hyperlinks. Review the solution file C13E03 - Solution.pbit.

1. Open a blank new workbook or a new Power BI Report.

   In Excel: On the Data tab, select Get Data, From Online Services, From Facebook.

   In Power BI Desktop: On the Home tab, select Get Data. When the Get Data dialog box opens, select Online Services; then scroll down, select Facebook, and select Connect. You can also enter *Facebook* in the search box and then select Facebook and click Connect.

2. In the Facebook dialog box, keep *me* in the first text box, select Friends in the Connection drop-down, and click OK. When you see a dialog box that provides a preview of the data, click Edit.

3. To determine what pages your friends like, expand the object_link column. In the Expand pane, deselect all the columns except for connections. Make sure the Use Original Column Name As Prefix check box is not selected, and click OK. Now expand the connections column. In the Expand pane, deselect all the columns except for likes. Make sure the Use Original Column Name As Prefix check box is not selected, and click OK.

4. Rename the query *Base*, and in the Queries pane, right-click the Base query and select Reference in the shortcut menu.

5. Rename the new query *Friends*, and while the Friends query is selected, remove the likes column.

6. In the Queries pane, right-click the Base query and select Reference in the shortcut menu. Rename the new query *Pages*, and while the Pages query is selected, remove the name and id columns.

7. While the Pages query is selected, expand the likes column. In the Expand pane, deselect all the columns except for name and id. Make sure the Use Original Column Name As Prefix check box is not selected, and click OK.

8. To avoid having multiple pages, select the id column, and on the Home tab, select Remove Rows, Remove Duplicates.

   Next, as some of your friends may not have any liked pages, you need to remove the empty row.

9. Select the filter control of the id column and select Remove Empty.

   It's time to create a new table that will map your friends and their liked pages.

10. In the Queries pane, right-click the Base query and select Reference in the shortcut menu. Rename the new query *Friends and Pages*, and while the Friends and Pages query is selected, remove the name column and rename the id column *friend id*.

11. While the Friends and Pages query is selected, expand the likes column. In the Expand pane, deselect all the columns except for id. Make sure the Use Original Column Name As Prefix check box is not selected, and click OK.

12. Rename the id column *page id*.

   You can now enrich the Pages and Friends queries with the profile and image URLs, as you learned in Exercise 13-1.

Here is the formula for the profile URL:

```
"https://www.facebook.com/" & [id]
```

Here is the formula for the picture URL:

```
"https://graph.facebook.com/" & [id] & "/picture?type=large"
```

13. Load the queries to your Excel workbook or Power BI report, and follow these steps:

   a. Unload the base query (as you learned in Chapter 3, Exercise 3-1).

   b. In PowerPivot in Excel or the Relationships view in Power BI Desktop, create the relationship between the id column in Friends and the friend id column in Friends and Pages. Then, create a relationship between the id column in Pages and the page id column in Friends and Pages.

You can download the solution file C13E03 - Solution.pbit (which is illustrated in Figure 13-5) or the queries in C13E03 - Solution.xlsx. Both files are available at https://aka.ms/DataPwrBIPivot/downloads.

> **Tip** There are more efficient ways to traverse the social graph in this exercise by using advanced API calls. For example, the following M function calls for up to 100 of your friends (who used Facebook connector in Power Query) and up to 50 of their liked pages (When used as single line expression):
>
> ```
> =Facebook.Graph("https://graph.facebook.com/v3.0/me?fields=friends.limit(100){name,id,likes.limit(50){name,id}}")
> ```

Analyzing Facebook Pages

One of the most common business use cases for using the Facebook connector in Excel and Power BI is to analyze user engagement in Facebook pages. In the next exercises you will learn how to read the public posts from any Facebook page and analyze the number of comments and shares for each of the imported posts.

You will start with a basic exercise to extract posts and comments, which will enable you to extract additional meaning from posts and user comments and use the text analytics techniques from Chapter 11 and Chapter 12 on any Facebook page. Later in this section, you will learn how to efficiently extract comments and count the number of comments and shares to analyze users' engagement. These tools, together with the text analytics method you have mastered, can be handy in analyzing the public opinions and brand sentiment of your company's or competitors' products, as illustrated in Figure 13-6.

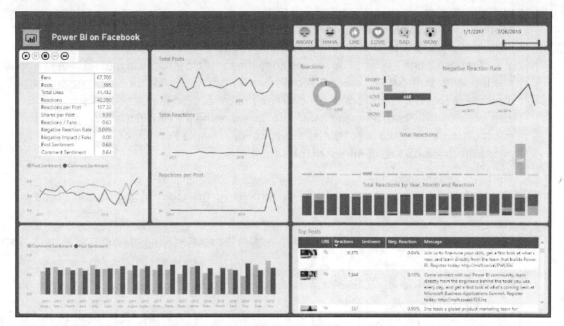

FIGURE 13-6 You can analyze any Facebook page using Power Query and apply Text Analytics (learned in Chapter 12) to get sentiment from posts and comments.

Exercise 13-4: Extracting Posts and Comments from Facebook Pages—The Basic Way

In Chapter 11, "Basic Text Analytics," you analyzed the posts of the Microsoft Press Facebook page. In this exercise you will learn the basic steps to import posts and comments from any Facebook page. As you will learn, these steps are inefficient in analyzing all pages and may be too slow to load pages with a high number of comments.

1. Open a blank new workbook or a new Power BI Report.

   In Excel: On the Data tab, select Get Data, From Online Services, From Facebook.

   In Power BI Desktop: On the Home tab, select Get Data. When the Get Data dialog box opens, select Online Services; then scroll down, select Facebook, and select Connect. You can also enter *Facebook* in the search box, select Facebook, and click Connect.

2. The Facebook dialog box opens. Enter *microsoftpress* in the first text box, select *Posts* in the Connection drop-down menu, and click OK to close the dialog box. In the next preview dialog box, select Edit to launch the Power Query Editor.

Note You can repeat this exercise on any other Facebook page. In step 2, replace *micro-softpress* in the first text box with the Facebook page name. To find the page name, open the Facebook page in your browser and copy the root folder name in the URL. For example, the URL of the official Power BI Facebook page is https://www.facebook.com/microsoftbi. To analyze that page, you would need to enter *microsoftbi* in the text box of step 2. You can also edit the Facebook page name later by changing the URL in the *Facebook.Graph* function in the formula bar of the source step. For example: *Facebook.Graph("https://graph.facebook.com/v2.8/**microsoftbi**/posts")*.

In the Preview pane, you see the following columns: message, created_time, id, object_link, and story.

3. To extract Date, Time, and Hour columns from the created_time column, repeat steps 11 and 12 of Exercise 13-1.

4. To get user-friendly column names, rename the message, created_time, id, and story columns *Message*, *Time*, *ID*, and *Story*.

In steps 6–14, you will learn the basic steps for extracting Facebook comments. Although these steps are trivial to follow in the user interface, you will find that they lead to slow load and excessive API calls to Facebook, especially for active Facebook pages like Microsoft Press. In Exercise 13-5 you will learn how to improve these queries. For now, let's follow the basic yet slower steps. You should be warned that due to the excessive calls made by Power Query to the Facebook Graph API in this method, you may get the following Facebook error at some point:

```
Facebook: (#17) User request limit reached
```

When you get this error, you need to stop working on the report and wait a few hours. Facebook implements a throttling mechanism to block excessive API calls made by users. Fortunately, once you follow step 5, you will prevent the errors.

Tip When working with slow queries, during the development of the queries it is recommended that you reduce the number of rows as a temporary step to minimize the load time of the query. To do so, use the Keep Top Rows dialog box. When you finish the development, you can remove this step and load the entire dataset.

5. On the Home tab, select Keep Rows, Keep Top Rows. Enter *100* in the Number of Rows text box of the Keep Top Rows dialog box, and click OK. Now when you have only 100 rows, you can proceed with the exercise and prevent slow load and *User request limit reached* errors as you develop the query. Remember that later you will need to undo this step when you complete the data preparations phase.

6. Expand the object_link column. In the Expand pane, deselect all the columns except for connections; make sure the Use Original Column Name As Prefix check box is not selected, and click OK.

7. The object_link column changes to the connections column. Expand it, and in the Expand pane, ensure that the comments field is selected. Make sure the Use Original Column Name As Prefix check box is not selected, and click OK.

   You now have the new comments column instead of the original connections column. In each row you see the *Table* objects, which contain the table of comments that each post received.

> **Note** In step 7, you can see in the Expand pane that the *likes* field is also available. If you expand it, Power Query will return empty table objects. The Facebook connector cannot load the number of likes each post has received. To read the number of likes, you would need to develop your own Custom Connector or use advanced M queries, which are not covered in this book.

   As a best practice, remove any duplicate values in the ID column. Later in this exercise, you will need to create a relationship between Posts and Comments, assuming that the ID column in Posts contains unique values. Without the next step, the load will fail.

8. Select the ID column, and on the Home tab, select Remove Rows, Remove Duplicates.

9. Rename the query *Posts - Base*.

10. In the Queries pane, right-click the Posts - Base query and select Reference. Rename the new query *Posts*.

11. Select Posts in the Queries pane, and remove the comments column.

12. In the Queries pane, right-click the Posts - Base query and select Reference. Rename the new query *Comments*.

13. While Comments is selected in the Queries pane, select the Choose Columns on Home tab. In the Choose Columns dialog box, select the columns ID and comments, and click OK.

14. Still in the Comments query, expand the comments column and, in the Expand pane, deselect all fields except *message* and *id*. Make sure the Use Original Column Name As Prefix check box is not selected (as seen in Figure 13-7), and click OK.

15. Rename the id.1 column *Comment ID*, and rename the message column *Comment*.

   You may see that in the Comment and Comment ID columns you have empty values. This means that some of the posts have no user comments. You can filter out these rows.

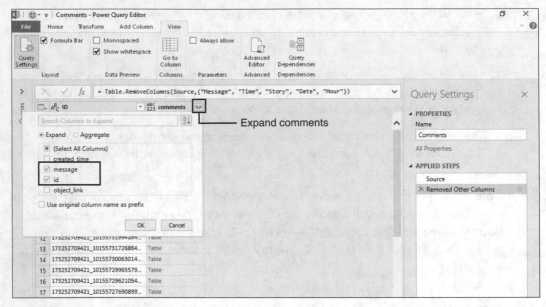

FIGURE 13-7 Expand the comments column and select the *message* and *id* fields to extract comments from each post.

16. Select the filter control of the Comment column and select Remove Empty to filter out rows with no comments.

You can now enrich the Posts and Comments query and include their URL.

17. Select the Posts query and follow these steps:

    a. On the Add Column tab, select Custom Column. The Custom Column dialog box opens.

    b. In the New Column Name box, enter *Profile*.

    c. In the Custom Column Formula box, enter the following formula:

        `"https://www.facebook.com/" & [ID]`

    d. Click OK to close the dialog box.

18. Select the Comments query and follow steps 17a–17d with one exception in the formula bar: Use Comment ID instead of ID:

    `"https://www.facebook.com/" & [Comment ID]`

19. Before you load your queries, you can remove the Kept First Rows step in the Applied Steps of Posts - Base query. Recall that you kept only 100 rows in step 5 to avoid getting errors and slow load in the Preview pane during the development of the report.

20. You can now load the queries to your Excel workbook or Power BI report, following these steps:

    a. Unload the Posts - Base query (as learned in Chapter 3, Exercise 3-1).

    b. In Power Pivot in Excel or the Relationships view in Power BI Desktop, create the relationship between the ID column in Posts and the ID column in Comments.

21. Save your report; you will use it in the next section and learn how to limit your report by time and improve load time.

Download the solution files C13E04 - Solution.xlsx and C13E04 - Solution.pbix from https://aka.ms/ DataPwrBIPivot/downloads.

Short Detour: Filtering Results by Time

In Exercise 13-4, you learned that the loading time of Facebook data can be long, especially if you analyze an active Facebook page with a large number of posts and comments. To limit your report to a specific period and decrease the load time, you can tune your query and use the parameters *since* and *until* in the *Facebook.Graph* URL. Let's demonstrate it on the solution file from Exercise 13-4.

1. Open your saved work from Exercise 13-4 or one of the solution files C13E04 - Solution.xlsx or C13E04 - Solution.pbix from https://aka.ms/DataPwrBIPivot/downloads.

2. Launch the Power Query editor.

3. In the Queries pane, select the Posts - Base query.

4. In Applied Steps, select Source. You will see the following formula:

```
= Facebook.Graph("https://graph.facebook.com/v2.8/microsoftpress/posts")
```

5. To filter the results and show only posts since the year 2017, add the URL parameter *since=2017-01-01* following a question mark, as shown in this formula (when copied as a single line expression):

```
= Facebook.Graph("https://graph.facebook.com/v2.8/microsoftpress/
posts?since=2017-01-01")
```

To filter the results and show only posts that occurred in 2017, add the URL parameter *until=2017-12-31* shown in the following formula (when copied as a single line expression):

```
= Facebook.Graph("https://graph.facebook.com/v2.8/microsoftpress/
posts?since=2017-01-01&until=2017-12-31")
```

6. In the Preview pane you can now see the filtered posts from 2017.

Exercise 13-5: Analyzing User Engagement by Counting Comments and Shares

In this exercise you will analyze the engagement levels to any Facebook page and learn a better method of extracting comments. In Exercise 13-4 you imported the posts and comments of a given Facebook page. The next step is to count how many comments, and shares each post received. Currently, following recent Facebook API changes, and due to a limitation of the Facebook Connector, you cannot load the number of likes each post receives. As a workaround, in this exercise we will focus on the count of comments and shares as engagement metrics. For example, the number of shares for each post, as illustrated in Figure 13-8, can be summed up over time to reflect audience engagement.

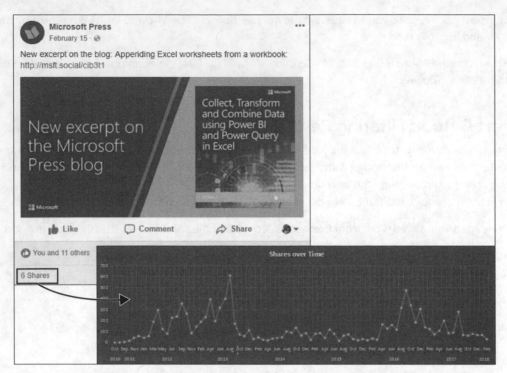

FIGURE 13-8 The Facebook connector enables you to measure user engagement by extracting the number of shares for each post.

> **Note** There are advanced techniques for extracting the count of likes and the total reactions (Wow, Sad, Angry, Haha, and Love) from posts of public pages, but they are beyond the scope of this book, as they require advanced Graph API knowledge and extensive development effort in M.

1. Open your saved work from Exercise 13-4 or one of the solution files C13E04 - Solution.xlsx or C13E04 - Solution.pbix from https://aka.ms/DataPwrBIPivot/downloads.

2. Launch the Power Query editor.

3. In the Queries pane, select the Posts - Base query.

4. In Applied Steps, select Source. You will see the following formula:

   `= Facebook.Graph("https://graph.facebook.com/v2.8/microsoftpress/posts")`

5. Add a question mark followed by this parameter in the URL in the *Facebook.Graph* function:

   `fields=message,created_time,comments,story,shares`

The modified M formula should look as follows (copy it as a single line expression):

```
= Facebook.Graph("https://graph.facebook.com/v2.8/microsoftpress/
posts?fields=message,created_time,comments,story,shares")
```

While we are changing the Facebook Graph URL, let's also change the version from v2.8 to v3.0 or the latest version currently available by Facebook. The modified M formula should look as follows (as a single line expression):

```
= Facebook.Graph("https://graph.facebook.com/v3.0/microsoftpress/
posts?fields=message,created_time,comments,story,shares")
```

> **Tip** You can modify the URL to try the latest version of the Facebook Graph API or to get additional data points. For example, by adding the *shares* field to the URL, you will be able to get new information that is not provided by Power Query Editor through the default user interface.

This URL imports the posts with the explicit fields that are mentioned in the *fields* parameter. When you use this technique, you must specify all the fields you need to have in the report—in this case, message, created_time, comments, and story. Specifying the likes column here will not help because you would get empty results.

6. Because you explicitly imported the fields in step 5, there is no need to expand them from the object_link column, so in Applied Steps, delete the steps Expanded object_link and Expanded connections. If you have the Kept First Rows step, you can delete it as well.

7. In the Queries pane, select the Posts query.

8. Remove the object_link column.

9. Expand the shares column, and in the Expand pane, keep *count* checked, select the Use Original Column Name As Prefix check box, and click OK.

10. When the shares column is transformed to shares.count, rename it *Shares Count* and change its type to Whole Number.

   Now when you have the number of shares per post in Shares Count, it is time to address the number of comments. There are several ways to count comments per post. If you are familiar with PowerPivot in Excel or Modeling in Power BI, you can create a simple DAX measure to count the rows in the Comments table. If you prefer to count the number of rows in Power Query, follow the next steps.

11. While the Posts query is still selected, select the Source step in Applied Steps.

12. See that the comments column includes either a Table object or a null value in each cell. You can create a custom column to count the number of rows in each table, or return zero when the value in comments is null, following these steps:

    a. On the Add Column tab, select Custom Column. Select Insert in the Insert Step dialog box. The Custom Column dialog box opens.

    b. Enter *Comments Count* in New Column Name.

    c. Enter the following formula in the Custom Column Formula:

```
if [comments] = null then 0 else Table.RowCount([comments])
```

    d. Click OK to close the Custom Column dialog box.

13. Change the type of Comments Count to Whole Number.

14. Save this workbook or report; you will use it in Exercise 13-6.

Now that you can count the number of shares and comments per post you can assess user engagement on any public Facebook page.

You can download the solution files C13E05 - Solution.xlsx and C13E05 - Solution.pbix from https://aka.ms/DataPwrBIPivot/downloads.

Exercise 13-6: Comparing Multiple Pages

In this exercise you will learn how to extend the analysis of a single Facebook page into a multi-page analysis. You will perform this exercise on two Facebook pages:

- The official Facebook page of Microsoft Excel: https://www.facebook.com/microsoftexcel

- The official Facebook page of Power BI: https://www.facebook.com/microsoftbi

You can start with your saved report from the end of Exercise 13-5. You can also start from one of the solution files, C13E05 - Solution.xlsx or C13E05 - Solution.pbix, both available from https://aka.ms/DataPwrBIPivot/downloads.

1. Open the solution file and launch the Power Query Editor.

Your first task is to create a table with the two Facebook object names. In this case, looking at the URLs of the official Facebook Pages of Excel and Power BI, you can see that the Facebook page names are *microsoftexcel* and *microsoftbi*.

2. Create a blank query, paste the following line into the formula bar, and press Enter:

```
= #table({"PageObjectName", "Page"}, {{"microsoftexcel", "Excel"}, {"microsoftbi",
"Power BI"}})
```

3. Rename the Query1 query *Pages*.

4. In the Queries pane, select Posts - Base. Your objective at this stage is to reuse its steps on each one of the pages.

5. Right-click the Posts - Base query and select Duplicate. Rename the duplicated query *LoadPosts*.

6. On the Home tab, select the Manage Parameters drop-down and then select New Parameter. When the Parameters dialog box opens, make the following changes:

    a. In the Name box, enter *PageName*.

    b. In the Current Value box, enter *microsoftpress*.

    c. Click OK to close the dialog box.

> **Note** In the Current Value box you use *microsoftpress* as a temporary value. Its purpose is to reduce the time to load the preview in step 8, as your Preview pane will already be loaded with the results of the Microsoft Press page, which are stored in Power Query cache. You will not use this value for long.

7. In the Queries pane, select the LoadPosts query, and in Applied Steps, select the Source step.

8. In the formula bar, replace *microsoftpress* with "*& PageName & *". This is the original formula:

```
= Facebook.Graph("https://graph.facebook.com/v2.8/microsoftpress/
posts?fields=message,created_time,comments,story,shares")
```

Here is the modified version:

```
= Facebook.Graph("https://graph.facebook.com/v2.8/"
& PageName & "/posts?fields=message,created_time,comments,story,shares")
```

9. To create a function from the LoadPosts query, in the Queries pane, right-click LoadPosts and select Create Function. In the Create Function dialog box that opens, enter *FnLoadPostsByPage* in the Function Name box, and click OK to close the dialog box.

    As shown in Figure 13-9, the LoadPosts query is now a sample query. Any changes you apply on LoadPosts will propagate to the *FnLoadPostsByPage* custom function. You do not need to modify any of the items under *FnLoadPostsByPage* folder.

10. Right-click the Pages query and select Reference. Rename the new query *Posts - All Pages*.

11. In the Queries pane, select the Posts - All Pages query. On the Add Column tab, select Invoke Custom Function.

12. When the Invoke Custom Function dialog box opens, in the Function Query drop-down, select FnLoadPostsByPage. Ensure that PageObjectName is selected in the PageName drop-down, and click OK to close the dialog box.

    A new column, FnLoadPostsByPage, is added next to the Page column, with *Table* objects. Each object represents the results from the Facebook Page in its row.

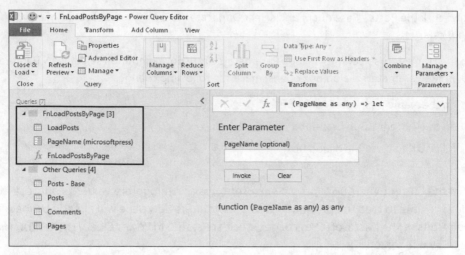

FIGURE 13-9 The *FnLoadPostsByPage* custom function is generated in step 9. You can now invoke this function on multiple Facebook pages. To edit the function, make the changes in the Load Posts query.

13. Expand the FnLoadPostsByPage column. In the Expand pane, ensure that all the columns are checked. Make sure the Use Original Column Name As Prefix check box is not selected and click OK.

Now, in the Posts - All Pages query, you have all the posts you need.

14. Unfortunately, you lost the column types in step 13, so change the type in Posts - All Pages by changing the Time column to *Time*, the Date column to *Date*, and the Hour column to *Whole Number*.

Recall that the queries Posts and Comments are still referencing Posts - Base, the original query that loaded the Microsoft Press posts. You need to modify them to reference the Posts - All Pages query.

15. In the Queries pane, select the Posts query. In Applied Steps, select the Source step. Modify the line in the formula bar to the following:

```
= #"Posts - All Pages"
```

16. In the Queries pane, select the Comments query, and in Applied Steps, select the Source step to modify the line in the formula bar to the formula shown in step 15.

Now both Posts and Comments start from the base query Posts - All Pages. It's safe to delete the Posts - Base query as you no longer need it.

17. To load the modified queries, follow these steps:

In Excel: On the Home tab of the Power Query Editor, select the Close & Load drop-down and then select Close & Load To. In the Import Data dialog box that opens, select Create Connection only to ensure that only Posts and Comments are loaded to the Data Model.

In Power BI Desktop: To ensure that LoadPosts and Posts - All Pages are not loaded to the report, right-click each of these queries in the Queries pane and deselect Enable Load for each of them.

18. Load the Pages query to the Data Model in Excel or to a Power BI report and create a relationship between the PageObjectName column in Pages and the PageObjectName column in Posts.

Now you can determine which Facebook page receives the most shares over the time and which product is most active on Facebook, as illustrated in Figure 13-10.

You can download the solution files C13E06 - Solution.xlsx and C13E06 - Solution.pbix from https://aka.ms/DataPwrBIPivot/downloads.

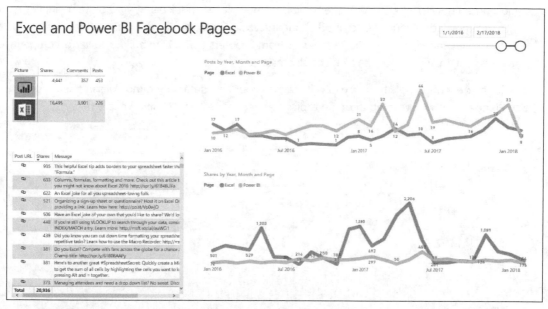

FIGURE 13-10 C13E06 - Solution.pbix provides a comparison between Excel and Power BI Facebook pages in Power BI.

To learn more about the analysis of Facebook data in Excel and Power BI and to learn how you can visualize the data, follow my blog at https://datachant.com/category/facebook-insights/.

Summary

In this chapter, you have explored the social graph and learned how to import data from Facebook to answer a variety of personal and business questions. You have also learned how to connect to Facebook in Excel and Power BI to load multiple endpoints (such as your profile and any Facebook page) and edges (such as page likes, friends, posts, and comments).

You have learned several practical techniques for using the Facebook connector and analyzing your profile and any public page. In Exercise 13-1 you imported the Facebook pages you like and learned how to sort the pages based on when you liked them.

In Exercise 13-2 you learned how to traverse the social graph and find first- and second-degree friends who have connected to Facebook via the Facebook connector. Although this technique is limited and cannot load your entire list of friends, it's a good tool for "spying" on your network to assess how many users in your network have adopted Power Query and Power BI. In Exercise 13-3, you examined the common pages that are liked by your friends (again, the limited list of friends who use Power Query's Facebook connector).

In Exercise 13-4 you learned a basic method for extracting posts and comments, and in Exercise 13-5 you learned how to improve the queries and import the number of shares per post. Finally, in Exercise 13-6 you learned how to extend the queries to import multiple Facebook pages via a custom function. Now, with the knowledge you have acquired about analyzing Facebook pages, posts, and comments, you can apply the advanced text analytics techniques from Chapters 11 and 12 to build a powerful competitive analysis tool on any brand with a Facebook presence.

In the next and final chapter, you will practice your new data-wrangling skills in a series of challenges that will wrap up the main topics covered in the book. I think you are ready.

CHAPTER 14

Final Project: Combining It All Together

To write it, it took three months; to conceive it three minutes; to collect the data in it all my life.

—*F. Scott Fitzgerald*

IN THIS CHAPTER, YOU WILL

- Act as the chief data officer of the fictitious company Wide World Importers

- Tackle challenging datasets and apply your skills to prepare the messy data for analysis

- Combine Unpivot and Pivot sequences in a complex real-life scenario, with multiple files of summarized data

- Use different Merge transformations to compare two tables

Congratulations. You have reached the final chapter. It is time to challenge your data-wrangling skills and test your capabilities with a final project.

You have come a long way. In the preceding chapters of this book, you have learned how to clean messy datasets, combine multiple tables, resolve mismatched column names, unpivot and pivot data, and tackle many other data challenges. It's time to put all that knowledge to the test and apply your new data-wrangling powers on a large-scale challenge.

Exercise 14-1: Saving the Day at Wide World Importers

Imagine that you are the new chief data officer at Wide World Importers. Last weekend, the company experienced a massive cyber-attack that was targeted at the company's data warehouse. A team of specialists is trying to assess the risks to the revenue data, and you have been asked to reconstruct a new summary report of the company's revenues from an old exported data, which was not affected by the cyber-attack. Your predecessor kept reports of the company's revenues in three Excel workbooks for the years 2015–2017. Each of the workbooks has 12 worksheets—one for each month of the year. In addition, 2018 revenues were recently exported in a new challenging format.

Can you import all the data from each of the 36 total worksheets and combine it with the data of 2018 to create a single table, similar to the one in Figure 14-1?

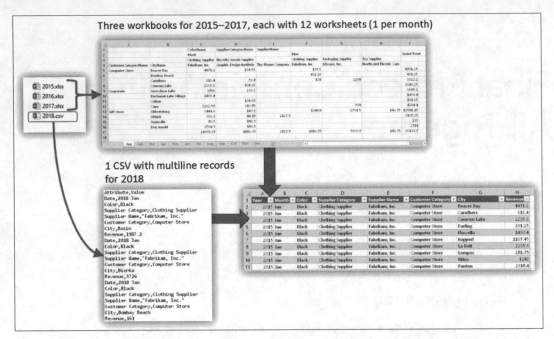

Three workbooks for 2015–2017, each with 12 worksheets (1 per month)

2015.xlsx
2016.xlsx
2017.xlsx
2018.csv

1 CSV with multiline records for 2018

FIGURE 14-1 Your challenge is to combine multiple tables of Wide World Importers from three workbooks for 2015–2017 revenues. Each with 12 worksheets (1 per month), and an additional CSV file with multiline records for 2018 revenues.

To start the exercise, download the zip file C14E01.zip and the result table in C14E01 - Goal.xlsx. Both files are available at https://aka.ms/DataPwrBIPivot/downloads. Extract the four files from the ZIP file into the folder *C:\Data\C14\C14E01*.

Review each of the workbooks 2015.xlsx, 2016.xlsx, and 2017.xlsx, as well as their worksheets. Each worksheet includes a 2×3 summarized table, with the customer categories and cities in the rows and product colors, supplier categories, and supplier names in the columns.

For 2018, the revenues data is stored in a comma-separated values (CSV) file with the columns Attribute and Value, as illustrated in the bottom left of Figure 14-1. Your goal is to combine all the data together to build a cohesive report for Wide World Importers revenues, as shown in C14E01 - Goal.xlsx.

Note You are encouraged to stop reading for now. Try to solve this challenge by yourself. Spend a couple hours trying it. If you need help, you can read the clues in the following section.

Clues

Not sure how to proceed? You can break down the challenge into subtasks:

1. Import the folder and keep the Excel workbooks.

2. Create a new column with the 36 rows of Table objects (comprised of the 36 worksheets from the three workbooks with the 12 worksheets of revenues for each month of the years 2015–2017).

3. For each worksheet, skip the first row and remove the Grand Total column and row.

4. Apply the function *FnUnpivotSummarizedTable* on each worksheet. (Refer to Chapter 7, "Advanced Unpivoting and Pivoting of Tables.")

5. Include the 2018.csv file after you follow the Pivot sequence covered in Chapter 7.

6. Append the 2018 revenues to the unpivoted data. Note that there are some mismatching column names. You can go back to Chapter 3, "Combining Data from Multiple Sources," to refresh your memory on column name normalization.

> **Note** You are encouraged to stop reading for now. Try to solve this challenge by yourself. Spend a few more hours trying it. If you need help, read Chapter 7 again. If you need further help, you can follow Exercise 14-1 step by step.

Part 1: Starting the Solution

To transform the pivoted data from the years 2015–2017 and append to it the multiline records of 2018, you can follow the steps in this exercise.

1. Download the zip file C14E01.zip from https://aka.ms/DataPwrBIPivot/downloads, and extract the four files into the folder *C:\Data\C14\C14E01*.

2. Open a blank workbook or Power BI report:

    In Excel: On the Data tab, select Get Data, From File, From Folder.

    In Power BI Desktop: Select Get Data, File, Folder.

3. Select the folder path *C:\Data\C14\C14E01* and click OK. In the next dialog box, click Edit. The Power Query Editor opens.

4. To filter out the file 2018.csv, which has a different format from the other files (you will handle it later), select the filter control on the Name column and select 2018.csv. Then click OK to close the Filter pane.

5. Rename the query from C14E01 to *Revenues*.

6. Click the Combine Files icon in the Content column header.

7. When the Combine Files dialog box opens, right-click Sample File Parameter1 and select Edit.

8. When Power Query Editor opens and Revenues is selected, remove the last three columns.

9. Remove the .xlsx extension from the *Source.Name* values to extract the year and rename the column *Year*. (There are multiple ways to remove the file extension. If you are not sure how to do it, revisit Chapter 3.)

10. Rename the column from Name to *Month*.

    In the Data column you have the Table objects, each with the summarized tables. Before you apply the unpivot sequence, you should remove the first row, which doesn't include any valuable data and will not work well if you apply the Unpivot sequence on it. You should also remove the Grand Totals at the last column and row. The following steps walk through how to accomplish these.

11. In the Add Column tab, select Custom Column. The Custom Column dialog box opens. Make the following changes:

    a. Enter *Skip First Row* in the New Column Name box.

    b. Set the following formula in the Custom Column Formula box and then click OK:

```
= Table.Skip([Data], 1)
```

    The new column returns the table object in the Data column after the first row is skipped.

    c. Remove the Data column.

12. On the Add Column tab, select Custom Column. The Custom Column dialog box opens. Make the following changes:

    a. Set New Column Name to No Grand Total Column.

    b. Set the following formula in Custom Column Formula and then click OK:

```
= Table.RemoveColumns(
    [Skip First Row], {
        List.Last(Table.ColumnNames([Skip First Row]))
    }
)
```

    This formula removes the last column. You use *Table.ColumnNames* to retrieve the column names of each table object in Data column and apply *List.Last* to get the last column name.

    c. Remove the Skip First Row column.

13. On the Add Column tab, select Custom Column. The Custom Column dialog box opens. Make the following changes:

    a. Set New Column Name to Summarized Table.

    b. Set the following formula in Custom Column Formula and then click OK:

```
= Table.RemoveLastN([No Grand Total Column], 1)
```

    c. Remove the No Grand Total Column column.

> **Note** An alternative way to clean the summarized tables, instead of following steps 11–13, is to use a single function. You can create a blank query with the following code:
>
> ```
> (inputTable) =>
> let
>     SkipFirstRow = Table.Skip(inputTable, 1),
>     NoGrandTotalColumn = Table.RemoveColumns(
>         SkipFirstRow, {
>             List.Last(Table.ColumnNames(SkipFirstRow))
>         }
>     ),
>     Result = Table.RemoveLastN(NoGrandTotalColumn, 1)
> in
>     Result
> ```
>
> Name the query *FnCleanSummarizedTable* and then invoke it in the Revenues query, by selecting Invoke Custom Column on the Add Column tab and applying it on the Data column.

Part 2: Invoking the Unpivot Function

In this portion of the Exercise 14-1 solution, you will apply the custom function *FnUnpivotSummarizedTable*. Recall that in Exercise 7-3 you created that function to unpivot summarized tables. At this point in Exercise 14-1, you are now ready to unpivot the summarized Wide World Importers table for the years 2015–2017. Follow these steps to continue Exercise 14-1:

14. Follow these steps to copy *FnUnpivotSummarizedTable* from Exercise 7-3:

    a. Save your current report and keep it open.

    b. Open the workbook C07E03 - Solution.xlsx from https://aka.ms/DataPwrBIPivot/downloads.

    c. On the Data tab, select Queries & Connections.

    d. In the Queries & Connections pane, right-click FnUnpivotSummarizedTable and select Copy.

    e. Go back to your current Exercise 14-1 workbook or report and launch the Power Query Editor.

    f. Right-click anywhere in the background space of the Queries pane and select Paste to copy the *FnUnpivotSummarizedTable* function.

15. In the Queries pane, select the Revenues query.

16. On the Add Column tab, select Custom Column. The Custom Column dialog box opens. Make the following changes:

    a. Enter *Unpivoted* in the New Column Name box.

    b. As shown in Figure 14-2, set the following formula in Custom Column Formula and then click OK:

```
= FnUnpivotSummarizedTable([Summarized Table], {"Customer Category", "City"},
{"Color", "Supplier Category", "Supplier Name"}, "Revenue")
```

FIGURE 14-2 To unpivot the summarized table, invoke the *FnUnpivotSummarizedTable* function by using the Custom Column dialog box.

    c. Remove the Summarized Table column.

17. Expand the Unpivoted column. In the Expand pane, deselect Use Original Column Name As Prefix and click OK.

You can see in the Preview pane that all the worksheets have been unpivoted correctly. It's time to handle the 2018 revenues.

Part 3: The Pivot Sequence on 2018 Revenues

Recall that in in step 4 of this exercise, you filtered out the file 2018.csv. This file contains comma-separated values of attribute/value pairs, and you can assume that each multi-line revenue record in 2018.csv file starts with the Date attribute. In this part of the exercise, you need to import it and apply the Pivot sequence that you learned in Chapter 7. Follow these steps to continue Exercise 14-1:

18. Import the file 2018.csv in the Power Query Editor by selecting New Source on the Home tab. Rename the new query *2018 Revenues*.

19. On the Transform tab, select Use First Row as Headers.

20. On the Add Column tab, select Index Column.

21. On the Add Column tab, select Conditional Column. When the Add Conditional Column dialog box opens, make the following changes:

    a. Enter *Row ID* in the New Column Name box.

    b. Set Column Name to Attribute.

    c. Keep equals as the operator.

    d. Enter *Date* in the Value box.

    e. Set Output to Select a Column and select the Index column.

    f. Enter *null* in the Otherwise box.

    g. Click OK.

22. Select the Row ID column, and on the Transform tab, select Fill, Down. Delete the Index column.

23. Select the Attribute column, and on the Transform tab, select Pivot Column. When the Pivot Column dialog box opens, make the following changes:

    a. Set Values Column to Value.

    b. Expand Advanced Options.

    c. Set Aggregate Value Function to Don't Aggregate.

    d. Click OK.

24. Remove the Row ID column.

You have now completed the Pivot sequence for 2018 revenues, and it's time to combine the results.

Part 4: Combining the 2018 and 2015–2017 Revenues

The steps you need to take in this portion of the exercise are discussed in Chapter 4, "Combining Mismatched Tables." You now have two tables with mismatching column names. Notice that the Revenues query includes the columns Year and Month, and the 2018 Revenues query includes the Date column. Follow these steps to continue Exercise 14-1:

25. Select the Revenues query. Select the first two columns, Year and Month, and select Merge Columns on the Transform tab.

26. When the Merge Columns dialog box opens, select Space as Delimiter, enter *Date* in the New Column Name box, and click OK.

27. On the Home tab, select Append Queries. When the Append dialog box opens, set Table to Append to 2018 Revenues and click OK.

> **Note** In step 16, you declared the column names to use for the unpivoted revenues of the years 2015–2017. If you used different names as Row fields or Column fields arguments in *FnUnpivotSummarizedTable*, you have additional mismatching column names at this stage. To fix this, use the same column names as in step 16 or rename 2018 Revenues to match the Revenues query before the append.

28. Change the type of the Revenue column to Currency or Decimal Number, and change the type of the Date column to Date.

29. Finally, load the Revenues query to your report, and disable the load for the 2018 Revenues query:

In Excel: On the Data tab, select Queries & Connections. Right-click 2018 Revenues and select Load To. In the Import Data dialog box that opens, select Only Create Connection and click OK.

In Power BI Desktop: In the Power Query Editor, right-click the 2018 Revenues query in the Queries pane and deselect Enable Load.

You can review the solution files C14E01 - Solution.xlsx and C14E01 - Solution.pbix, which are available at https://aka.ms/DataPwrBIPivot/downloads.

Exercise 14-2: Comparing Tables and Tracking the Hacker

Thanks to your success in Exercise 14-1, you were able to create the revenues report, which helped your company, Wide World Importers make informed decisions to keep the business running after the cyber-attack. According to the Cybersecurity team's investigation, the attackers tampered with the revenues values in the data warehouse.

Your task now is to compare the summarized revenues from Exercise 14-1 against the compromised data in C14E02 - Compromied.xlsx, which is available at https://aka.ms/DataPwrBIPivot/downloads, with the goal of identifying which records were tampered by the hacker and are compromised. Can you find the records that contain the modified revenues? Can you find the hacker's message in the data?

Try to resolve this challenge by creating a query that compares C14E01 - Solution.xlsx and C14E02 - Compromised.xlsx. While you may be able to find the differences in the tables by using PivotTables or DAX measures, focus on finding a solution using the Power Query Editor.

Clues

If you are not sure how to tackle this challenge, here are a few clues to help you get started:

1. The hacker made changes in the Revenue column. You can merge the two tables to find the mismatching revenues. Use all the columns except the Revenue column for the merge and then expand the Revenue column from the second table. Next, apply a filter on the two Revenue columns to find differences.

2. To find the new rows that the hacker added, you can apply Merge Columns with an anti right join between the summarized table from Exercise 14-1 and the compromised table. This way, only rows that exist in the compromised table will be detected during the expand step, which comes after the Merge.

Exercise 14-2: The Solution

To find the mismatching revenues, you need to merge the two tables using all the columns except for Revenue. If you can't figure this out on your own, you can follow the steps in this exercise.

1. Import the Revenues table from C14E01 - Solution.xlsx to the Power Query Editor in Excel or Power BI Desktop. Rename the query *Correct*.

2. Import the Revenues table from C14E02 - Compromised.xlsx to the Power Query Editor in Excel or Power BI Desktop.

3. In the Queries pane, select the Correct query. Then, on the Home tab, select the Merge Queries drop-down and then select Merge Queries as New.

4. When the Merge dialog box opens, make the following changes:

   a. In the Correct table, hold down the Ctrl key and select Date, Color, Supplier Category, Supplier Name, Custom Category, and City. Make sure to preserve the order of the columns.

   b. In the drop-down menu below the Correct table, select the Compromised query. In the Compromised table, hold down the Ctrl key and select Date, Color, Supplier Category, Supplier Name, Custom Category, and City. Make sure to preserve the order of the columns.

   c. In the Join Kind drop-down, select Inner (Only Matching Rows), as shown in Figure 14-3, and click OK to close the Merge dialog box.

5. Rename the new query *Compromised Rows* and expand the Compromised column. In the Expand pane, deselect all columns except for Revenue. Using the original column name as the prefix, rename the new column *Compromised.Revenue*.

To filter the mismatched revenue rows, you will need to apply a filter condition that is not available in the user interface. You can create a temporary filter condition through the user interface, and then modify it in the formula bar to meet your needs.

FIGURE 14-3 The Merge Dialog Box can be used to compare two tables and find mismatching values.

6. Click the filter control in the header of the Revenue column, and select Number Filters, Does Not Equal. Enter *12345* in the text box next to the Does Not Equal drop-down menu. In the formula bar, you see this expression:

```
= Table.SelectRows(#"Expanded Compromised", each [Revenue] <> 12345)
```

7. To filter rows in which Revenue values are not equal to Revenue.Compromised values, modify the formula as follows:

```
= Table.SelectRows(#"Expanded Compromised",
    each [Revenue] <> [Compromised.Revenue])
```

You should now see seven rows with different values in Revenue and Compromised.Revenue.

Detecting the Hacker's Footprints in the Compromised Table

In the next steps, you will apply a right anti merge to detect the rows in the compromised table that were added by the hacker and are not found in the original table. Follow these steps to continue Exercise 14-2:

8. In the Queries pane, select the Correct query. Then, on the Home tab, select the Merge Queries drop-down and then select Merge Queries as New.

9. When the Merge dialog box opens, make the following changes:

    a. In the Correct table, hold down the Ctrl key and select Date, Color, Supplier Category, Supplier Name, Custom Category, and City. Make sure to preservçe the order of the columns.

    b.   In the drop-down menu below the Correct table, select the Compromised query. In the *Compromised* table, hold down the Ctrl key and select Date, Color, Supplier Category, Supplier Name, Custom Category, and City. Make sure to preserve the order of the columns.

    c.   In the Join Kind drop-down, select Right Anti (Rows Only in Second), and click OK to close the Merge dialog box.

10. Rename the new query *Hacker's Instructions*.

11. Select the Compromised column and remove all the other columns.

12. Extract all fields in the Compromised column.

13. Find the Hacker's message.

14. Load the Hacker's Instructions query to your Excel workbook or Power BI Report.

You can review the solution files C14E02 - Solution.xlsx, and C14E02 - Solution.pbix, which are available at https://aka.ms/DataPwrBIPivot/downloads.

> **See Also** For advanced table comparison queries, see the following blog posts:
> - https://datachant.com/downloads/compare-tables-excel-power-bi/
> - https://datachant.com/2017/08/10/compare-tables-excel-power-bi-part-2/

Summary

Now that you have finished this final project, you are officially a powerful data wrangler. With the Power Query Editor at your disposal, you can now make a significant impact in your business—and beyond. In this project you have applied a combination of skills, including appending multiple workbooks and worksheets, applying advanced Unpivot and Pivot, using custom functions, and using Merge to compare datasets.

You are encouraged to use this book as a reference guide. Keep the solution samples for future use. You will find them useful in the future, when you tackle new problems. While your datasets may be completely different from the data in this book, you will gradually figure out how to reuse the techniques and extend the solutions to address your specific data challenges.

Learning Power Query is an ongoing process. To improve your data-wrangling capabilities, it is recommended that you keep exploring messy datasets in Power Query and challenge yourself to do more. Now is a good time to return to Chapter 9, "Introduction to the Power Query M Formula Language," and see which parts of the M reference or syntax you understand better now and when you can use M to extend your UI-based queries.

From the time you started the book to now, you have most likely discovered new features and capabilities of Power Query in Excel and Power BI, as well as new use cases in which Power Query can save hundreds of hours. It is a good time to see how you can unleash your new data-wrangling powers in products such as Microsoft Analysis Services, Microsoft Flows, and Power Apps, which now also include Power Query. Your journey has just started. Hope you enjoy the ride.

Index

Numerals and Symbols

F

DATACHANT

Your next stop in mastering **Power Query**

CHALLENGE YOURSELF
The author's new exercises that didn't get published in the book are offered for you to try out.

SOLVE EXERCISES
Find more solutions to the exercises in this book.

SHARE FEEDBACK
Get answers to the toughest exercises in the book and propose ideas for the next revision.

ENGAGE YOUR AUDIENCE
Get the best sample reports to impress your end users (and your boss).

Visit the author's blog at
datachant.com/next

Save 30% off the list price of DataChant reports with discount code **PQBOOK30**